DSM-III
CASE BOOK

FIRST EDITION

DSM-III

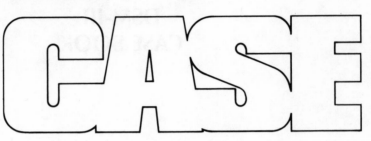

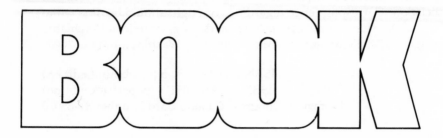

A Learning Companion to the Diagnostic and Statistical Manual of Mental Disorders (Third Edition)

Robert L. Spitzer, M.D.
Andrew E. Skodol, M.D.
Miriam Gibbon, M.S.W.
Janet B. W. Williams, M.S.W.

Biometrics Research,
New York State Psychiatric Institute

Department of Psychiatry,
Columbia University

American Psychiatric Association

ISBN 0-89042-050-5 (casebound edition)
ISBN 0-89042-051-3 (paperback edition)
Library of Congress Catalog Card Number 81-65970

FIRST PRINTING, 25,000, JUNE 1981
BOOK CLUB EDITION, 15,000, JULY 1981
SECOND PRINTING, 15,000, OCTOBER 1981

The Classical Cases contained in Chapter 6 are reprinted with permission as follows:
Emil Kraepelin, *Lectures on Clinical Psychiatry*, translated by Thomas P. Johnstone, Hafner Publishing Co., New York, 1968.

Eugen Bleuler, *Dementia Praecox*, translated by Joseph Zinkin, International Universities Press, Inc., New York, 1950.

Wilkins, R.H., Brody, I.A., "Alzheimer's Disease," *Archives of Neurology*, July 1969, 21:109-10, American Medical Association, Chicago, 1969.

Breuer, J., Freud S., *Studies in Hysteria*, translated by A.A. Brill, Beacon Press, Boston, 1937.

Freud, S., *Collected Papers, Volume III*, translated by Alix and James Strachey, Basic Books, Inc., New York, 1959.

Kasanin, J., "The Acute Schizoaffective Psychoses," *American Journal of Psychiatry*, 13:97-126, 1933, American Psychiatric Association, Washington, D.C., 1933.

Paul Hoch, Philip Polatin, "Pseudoneurotic Forms of Schizophrenia," *Psychiatric Quarterly*, 23:248-276, 1949, Human Sciences Press, New York, 1949.

Ayd, F.J., Blackwell, B., *Discoveries in Biological Psychiatry*, J. B. Lippincott Company, Philadelphia, 1970.

Hervey Cleckley, *The Mask of Sanity, Fifth Edition*, C.V. Mosby Company, St. Louis, 1976.

Table of Contents

Acknowledgments

We gratefully acknowledge the contributions of our colleagues listed below. Without their cases this book would not have been possible. Special thanks are due to Drs. Dennis Cantwell, Allen Frances, Richard Friedman, Rachel Gittelman, Joaquim Puig-Antich, and Lawrence Sharpe, who have either contributed or reviewed a considerable number of cases. Thanks are also due to Betty Appelbaum for her meticulous copy editing and to Maggie Bunce and Marie Junger, who typed seemingly endless revisions of the manuscript. Drs. Keith Brodie, John Talbott, Lew Robbins, and Robert Campbell served as an Ad Hoc Committee of the Board of Trustees and made many helpful suggestions in reviewing this book.

Hagop Akiskal, M.D.
Nancy Andreasen, M.D., Ph.D.
Robert L. Arnstein, M.D.
Lorian Baker, Ph.D.
Stephen Bauer, M.D.
Robert Benjamin, M.D.
Justin D. Call, M.D.
Dennis Cantwell, M.D.
Mark Chalem, M.D.
Paula J. Clayton, M.D.
Anthony Costello, M.D.
Robert L. Custer, M.D.
Carlo C. DiClemente, Ph.D.
Steven L. Dilts, M.D., Ph.D.
Jean Endicott, Ph.D.
Armando R. Favazza, M.D.
Leslie M. Forman, M.D.
Allen J. Frances, M.D.
Richard Friedman, M.D.
Abby J. Fyer, M.D.
Paul H. Gebhard, Ph.D.
Rachel Gittelman, Ph.D.
Yonkel Goldstein, Ph.D.
Donald W. Goodwin, M.D.
Richard Green, M.D.
John G. Gunderson, M.D.

Katherine Halmi, M.D.
Roger Harman, Ph.D.
Steven Hyler, M.D.
Helene A. Jackson, M.S.W.
Richard Jenkins, M.D.
Edwin E. Johnstone, M.D.
David Kahn, M.D.
Helen Kaplan, M.D., Ph.D.
Otto Kernberg, M.D.
Donald F. Klein, M.D.
Robert S. Lampke, M.D.
Jerome H. Liebowitz, M.D.
Thomas F. Liffick, M.D.
John Lion, M.D.
Z. J. Lipowski, M.D.
George J. McAfee, M.D.
Richard Markoff, M.D.
Gary J. May, M.D.
Heino F. L. Meyer-Bahlburg,
   Dr. rer. nat.
Theodore Millon, Ph.D.
Klaus Minde, M.D.
John Money, Ph.D.
J. Lawrence Moodie, M.D.
Roger Peele, M.D.
Judith A. Perry, M.D.

Ethel S. Person, M.D.
Gerald C. Peterson, M.D.
Harrison G. Pope, Jr., M.D.
Lloyd F. Price, M.D.
Joaquim Puig-Antich, M.D.
Judith L. Rapoport, M.D.
Douglas Roszell, M.D.
Graenum R. Schiff, M.D.
Phillip Schlobohm, M.D.
Benjamin Seltzer, M.D.
David Shaffer, M.D.
Arthur Shapiro, M.D.
Elaine Shapiro, Ph.D.
Lawrence Sharpe, M.D.
Michael Sheehy, M.D.
David A. Soskis, M.D.
Laurie Stevens, M.D.
Alan Stone, M.D.
Donn L. Tippett, M.D.
William M. Valverde, M.D.
Betsy P. Weiner, M.D.
Paul H. Wender, M.D.
Katherine Whipple, Ph.D.
Lorna Wing, M.D.
George Winokur, M.D.
Charlotte Zitrin, M.D.

Introduction

This collection of case vignettes grew out of our experience in teaching DSM-III. We have found that these relatively brief descriptions of real patients, edited to focus on information relevant to differential diagnosis, are the most effective (and painless) way for clinicians to get experience in applying the principles of DSM-III to a wide range of patients. We have chosen this method over that of providing case records or longer case summaries since our experience has been that with the use of longer cases, discussions of diagnosis often bog down in the swamp of details not relevant to the focused purpose of establishing a diagnosis. (Such nondiagnostic information, however, is obviously necessary in actual clinical records.) In addition, routine case summaries often inadvertently omit crucial diagnostic information, whereas these case vignettes, for the most part, have been prepared to ensure that all available information relevant to making a diagnosis has been included.

These case vignettes have been drawn from our own experience and from the practices of a large number of clinicians, among them many well-known experts in particular areas of diagnosis and treatment. The identities of the patients have been disguised by altering such details as age and occupation. Following Freud's example, we have provided pseudonyms for each subject in order to make the cases easier to refer to. These pseudonyms are listed in the index. We have also included a number of historical cases from the writings of such great nosologists as Emil Kraepelin, Eugen Bleuler, and Sigmund Freud himself. We have made no effort to disguise the identity of these historical patients; we have, however, taken the liberty of providing appropriate names for those who were nameless.

Each case vignette is followed by a discussion of our diagnosis according to the diagnostic criteria in the third edition of the American Psychiatric Association's *Diagnostic and Statistical Manual of Mental Disorders* (DSM-III). These discussions include important diagnostic considerations, such as the rationale for making each particular diagnosis, other disorders to be considered in formulating each diagnosis, and, in some cases, recognition of diagnostic uncertainty because of inadequate information or ambiguity in the clinical features or the classification itself. Each discussion concludes with the DSM-III diagnosis and its code number. To aid the reader we have noted in parentheses the page number of the diagnostic criteria in the DSM-III manual. Except in Chapter 3, Cases for Multiaxial Evaluation, we list only those axes on which a diagnosis has been made.

In preparing this book, we have asked several of our nosologically sophisticated colleagues to review many of the cases and discussions. In some, our colleagues took issue with our diagnostic assessments. In a few cases we were convinced by their arguments and modified our diagnoses and discussions. In other cases we have presented alternative approaches in addition to our own preferred diagnostic formulations. The reader may also find cases in which a convincing argument can be made for a diagnosis that we have not considered. Despite the increase in reliability made possible by the use of diagnostic criteria, some degree of ambiguity is inevitable when diagnoses are made of real patients. Therefore, we hope that the reader will seriously consider our formulations, but not regard them as infallible.

These case vignettes can be used for a variety of purposes. They should be of value to experienced clinicians, facilitating their learning the new concepts and terminology in DSM-III. All clinicians, regardless of their level of experience and training, may benefit from reading descriptions of cases that are examples of diagnostic categories rarely seen in most treatment settings. Teachers and students of abnormal psychology (e.g., psychology, psychiatry, social work, and psychiatric nursing) will find the vignettes useful as illustrations of various types of psychopathology. Similarly, other professionals, such as internists and attorneys, may find these case illustrations instructive. These cases should prove helpful to professionals studying for specialty examinations, such as the psychiatry boards: they can serve as a means of testing their knowledge of diagnosis. Research investigators can use them to assess the level of diagnostic expertise and the reliability with which members of their staff can make diagnostic assessments.

Although the discussions of the cases in this book do not include treatment considerations or references to alternative classification systems, the vignettes may serve as useful points of departure for discussions of such subjects. (We acknowledge that the kind of information included in these cases is a function of the diagnostic system used; alternative systems of classification are likely to require other kinds of information.) Finally, these cases provide a historical point of reference as illustrations of diagnostic concepts in the United States in 1980 and, by means of the historical cases, a comparison with diagnostic concepts of the past.

Ideally this book should provide several examples of virtually all the diagnostic categories in DSM-III. Obviously, a book of such scope could not be completed and made available within the first year after the publication of DSM-III—a time of great need for such a book. We therefore decided to publish this first edition with a smaller number of cases. Our plan is to publish a second edition within a year or two. To this end we are now collecting additional cases to illustrate categories not covered in this edition or to replace some of the cases and discussions presented here. We invite the reader to submit comments about the cases included here and new cases for possible inclusion in a second edition.

April 15, 1981

Robert L. Spitzer, M.D.
Andrew E. Skodol, M.D.
Miriam Gibbon, M.S.W.
Janet B. W. Williams, M.S.W.

Mental Disorders in Adults

Mental Disorders in Adults

The Radiologist

1 A 38-year-old radiologist is evaluated after returning from a 10-day stay at a famous out-of-state diagnostic center to which he had been referred by a local gastroenterologist after "he reached the end of the line with me." He reports that he underwent extensive physical and laboratory examinations there, including X-ray examinations of the entire gastrointestinal tract, esophagoscopy, gastroscopy, and colonoscopy. Although he was told that the results of the examinations were negative for significant physical disease, he appears resentful and disappointed rather than relieved at the findings. He was seen briefly for a "routine" evaluation by a psychiatrist at the diagnostic center, but had difficulty relating to the psychiatrist on more than a superficial level.

On further inquiry concerning the patient's physical symptoms, he describes occasional twinges of mild abdominal pain, sensations of "fullness," "bowel rumblings," and a "firm abdominal mass" that he can sometimes feel in his left lower quadrant. Over the last few months he has gradually become more aware of these sensations and convinced that they may be due to a carcinoma of the colon. He tests his stool for occult blood weekly and spends 15 to 20 minutes every 2–3 days carefully palpating his abdomen as he lies in bed at home. He has secretly performed several X-ray studies on himself in his own office after hours.

Although he is successful in his work, has an excellent attendance record, and is active in community life, the patient spends much of his limited leisure time at home alone in bed. His wife, an instructor at a local school of nursing, is angry and bitter about this behavior, which she describes as "robbing us of what we've worked so hard and postponed so much fun for." Although she and the patient share many values and genuinely love each other, his behavior causes a real strain on their marriage.

When the patient was 13 years old, a heart murmur was detected on a school physical exam. Since a younger brother had died in early childhood of congenital heart disease, the patient was removed from gym class until the murmur could be evaluated. The evaluation proved the murmur to be benign, but the patient began to worry that the evaluation might have "missed something" and considered his occasional sensations of "skipping a beat" as evidence that this was so. He kept his fears to himself, and they subsided over the next two years, but never entirely left him.

As a second-year medical student he was relieved to share some of his health concerns with his classmates, who also worried about having the diseases they were learning about in pathology. He realized, however, that he was much more preoccupied with and worried about his health than they were. Since graduating from medical school, he has repeatedly experienced a series of concerns, each following the same pattern: noticing a symptom, becoming increasingly preoccupied with what it might mean, and having a negative physical evaluation. At times he returns to an "old" concern, but is too embarrassed to pursue it with physicians he knows, as when he discovered a "suspicious" nevus only one week after he had persuaded a dermatologist to biopsy one that proved to be entirely benign.

The patient tells his story with a sincere, discouraged tone, brightened only by a note of genuine pleasure and enthusiasm as he provides a detailed account of the discovery of a genuine but clinically insignificant ureteral anomaly as the result of an intravenous pyelogram he had ordered himself. Near the end of the interview he explains that his coming in for evaluation now is largely at his own insistence, precipitated by an encounter with his nine-year-old son. The boy had accidentally walked in while he was palpating his own abdomen for "masses" and asked, "What do you think it is this time, Dad?" As he describes his shame and anger (mostly at himself) about this incident, his eyes fill with tears.

Discussion of The Radiologist

It is apparent that this doctor's symptoms are not due to any physical disorder. Preoccupation with physical symptoms without an organic basis can be seen in psychotic disorders, such as Schizophrenia or Major Depression with Psychotic Features, but there is no evidence of any psychotic features in this case. This suggests, therefore, a Somatoform Disorder — a mental disorder with physical symptoms suggesting physical disorder, but for which there is positive evidence, or a strong presumption, that the symptoms are linked to psychological factors.

A variety of physical symptoms without organic basis is seen in Somatization Disorder. In this case the symptoms are few, whereas in Somatization Disorder there is a large number of different symptoms that appear in many different organ systems. Furthermore, in Somatization Disorder the preoccupation is generally with the symptoms themselves. In this case the disturbance is preoccupation with the fear of having a serious disease resulting from the unrealistic interpretation of physical signs or sensations. The persistence of this irrational fear, despite medical reassurance, to the point that it interferes with social and/or occupational functioning indicates Hypochondriasis.

DSM-III Diagnosis:

Axis I: 300.70 Hypochondriasis (p. 251)

Sam Schaefer

2 A psychiatrist was asked by the court to evaluate a 21-year-old man arrested for robbery because his lawyer raised the issue of his competence to stand trial. During the course of a two-and-a-half-hour evaluation the patient acknowledged frequent run-ins with the law since about the age of 11 and incarceration in various institutions for criminal offenses, but was reluctant to provide details about them.

During the interview he appeared calm and in control, sat slouched in the chair, and had good eye contact. His affect showed a good range. Thought processes were logical, sequential, and spontaneous even when describing many difficulties with his thinking. He seemed guarded in answering most questions, and in fact hesitated quite frequently before answering, particularly questions about his psychiatric symptoms. He gave the impression of thoughtfully considering his answers before responding and seemed to be pretending a reluctance to talk about symptoms suggesting psychosis when, in fact, he apparently enjoyed elaborating the details of presumably psychotic experiences.

He claims to have precognition on occasion, knowing, for instance, what is going to be served for lunch in the jail; that people hear his thoughts, as if they were broadcast on the radio; and that he does not like narcotics because Jean Dixon doesn't like narcotics either, and she is in control of his thoughts. He states that he has seen a vision of General Lee in his cell, and that his current incarceration is a mission in which he is attempting to be an undercover agent for the police, although none of the local police realize this. He says that "Sam Schaefer" is his "case name." He feels that the Communists are taking over and are locking up those who would defend the country. Despite the overtly psychotic nature of these thoughts as described, the patient does not seem to be really engaged in these ideas; he seems to be simply reciting a list of what appears crazy rather than recounting actual experiences and beliefs.

He was asked about the processes and procedures of a trial, and stated that there was a jury, which he thought consisted of eight to ten friends. He also thought there was a judge present, who asked for money and made decisions about the procedure. He described the prosecuting attorney as someone who pointed out all your faults and tried to make the jury think that you were bad, and the defense attorney as someone who tried to point out your good points. He saw no particular reason why he could not cooperate with his attorney. When asked the date, he said that it was June 28, either 1970 or 1985. When asked his age, he replied 20, and gave his birthdate as 9-14-58. He then saw the inconsistency in the dates he gave for the year and said that this therefore must be 1978, since he was 20 and was born in 1958. When asked where he was, he said it was a Communist control center in Austin, Texas. He reported that he graduated from high school in 1976. When asked to do serial 7s, his responses were 88, 76. Asked to do additions, he responded: $4 + 6 = 10, 4 + 3 = 7, 4 + 8 = 14$. Asked to recall Presidents, he mentioned Ford and said that Agnew was President before him.

When asked the color of the red rug in the room, he said it was orange; his blue and white striped shirt he said was white on white. When presented with some questions from an aphasia screening test, he copied a square faithfully except for rounding the corners; a cross was copied as a capital "I." When shown a picture of a clock, he said he did not know what it was, but it looked familiar. A dinner fork was identified as a "pitchfork."

When asked whether he thought he was competent to stand trial, he replied yes, and said he did not think there was anything wrong with him mentally. When told that the examiner agreed with his assessment, he thought for several seconds and then, somewhat angered, protested that he probably couldn't cooperate with his attorney because he couldn't remember things very well, and therefore was incompetent to stand trial.

Discussion of Sam Schaefer

This gentleman is in trouble and apparently he has concluded that his best chance of avoiding prosecution is to prove that he is crazy and therefore not competent to stand trial. He goes about trying to prove this by claiming to have a variety of unrelated bizarre beliefs and by giving responses to questions that would suggest severe cognitive impairment. However, he presents the responses in a manner that is inconsistent with the disorganization of psychological functioning that would be expected if the symptoms were genuine. Furthermore, some of his responses to the questions testing cognitive functioning, although clearly wrong, indicate that he knows the correct response (e.g., rounding the corners of a square indicates appreciation that a square has four sides). If there is any doubt about his motivation, it is removed when he becomes angry with the examiner for agreeing that he is sane and competent to stand trial.

There is little question that in this case the "psychotic" symptoms are under voluntary control. The differential diagnosis is therefore between a Factitious Disorder and Malingering. Since the goal this fellow hopes to achieve is obviously recognizable in view of his circumstances (facing prosecution), and does not require an understanding of his individual psychology, what is involved is an act of malingering, which in DSM-III is given a V code for a condition not attributable to a mental disorder that is a focus of attention.

This clinical picture — the faking of symptoms suggesting a psychosis and giving responses that are near-misses — has been called the Ganser syndrome. DSM-III lists it as an example of a Factitious Disorder with Psychological Symptoms. However, some believe that this may have been a mistake and that, in most instances, as in this case, Ganser syndrome is an example of malingering, not of a Factitious Disorder.

From the history there is a strong suggestion of Antisocial Personality Disorder—a diagnosis that needs to be ruled out, but that will be of no help to this man in avoiding prosecution. Even if there were sufficient evidence to warrant a diagnosis of Antisocial Personality Disorder, it would be appropriate to note Malingering first. Lying is a common symptom of Antisocial Personality Disorder; but when it is elaborated to create the impression of a mental disorder, then it should be identified in its own right as the V code Malingering.

DSM-III Diagnosis:

Axis I: **V65.20 Malingering (p. 331)**
Axis II: **R/O Antisocial Personality Disorder**

Junior Executive

3 A 28-year-old junior executive was referred by a senior psychoanalyst for "supportive" treatment. She had obtained a master's degree in business administration and moved to California a year and a half earlier to begin work in a large firm. She complained of being "depressed" about everything: her job, her husband, and her prospects for the future.

She had had extensive psychotherapy previously. She had seen an "analyst" twice a week for three years while in college, and a "behaviorist" for a year and a half while in graduate school. Her complaints were of persistent feelings of depressed mood, inferiority, and pessimism, which she claims to have had since she was 16 or 17 years old. Although she did reasonably well in college, she consistently ruminated about those students who were "genuinely intelligent." She dated during college and graduate school, but claimed that she would never go after a guy she thought was "special," always feeling inferior and intimidated. Whenever she saw or met such a man, she acted stiff and aloof, or actually walked away as quickly as possible, only to berate herself afterward and then fantasize about him for many months. She claimed that her therapy had helped, although she still could not remember a time when she didn't feel somewhat depressed.

Just after graduation, she married the man she was going out with at the time. She thought of him as reasonably desirable, though not "special," and married him primarily because she felt she "needed a husband" for companionship. Shortly after their marriage, the couple started to bicker. She was very critical of his clothes, his job, and his parents; and he, in turn, found her rejecting, controlling, and moody. She began to feel that she had made a mistake in marrying him.

Recently she has also been having difficulties at work. She is assigned the most menial tasks at the firm and is never given an assignment of importance or responsibility. She admits that she frequently does a "slipshod" job of what is given her, never does more than is required, and never demonstrates any assertiveness or initiative to her supervisors. She views her boss as self-centered, unconcerned, and unfair, but nevertheless admires his success. She feels that she will never go very far in her profession because she does not have the right "connections" and neither does her husband, yet she dreams of money, status, and power.

Her social life with her husband involves several other couples. The man in these couples is usually a friend of her husband's. She is sure that the women find her uninteresting and unimpressive, and that the people who seem to like her are probably no better off than she.

Under the burden of her dissatisfaction with her marriage, her job, and her social life, feeling tired and uninterested in "life," she now enters treatment for the third time.

Discussion of Junior Executive

This woman's marriage and occupational functioning are severely affected by her chronically depressed mood, low self-esteem, and pessimism. Although she now complains also of loss of interest and energy, it is unlikely that this represents a significant change from her usual condition. Since her depression is not severe enough to meet the criteria for a major depressive episode, and the mood disturbance and associated symptoms have persisted for more than two years, the diagnosis of Dysthymic Disorder is made.

Many clinicians would regard her depressive symptoms as an expression of a Personality Disorder rather than an Affective Disorder. They would argue that it is impossible to separate her depressive symptoms from the characteristic and persistent way in which she relates to the world and to herself and that treatment should be focused on her characterological style as well as on the affective symptoms. However, in classifying Dysthymic Disorder under the broad rubric of Affective Disorders, DSM-III makes no assumption that the optimal treatment is necessarily biological or should be directed merely at symptom relief.

We would not quarrel with a clinician who wished to note, in addition, on Axis II, Atypical or Other (Masochistic) Personality Disorder, in order to emphasize the presence of many self-defeating personality features, such as the patient's lack of assertiveness and her tendency to be excessively critical of herself and others.

DSM-III Diagnosis:

Axis I: 300.40 Dysthymic Disorder (p. 222)

Joe College

4 A 19-year-old college freshman spends an afternoon drinking beer with fraternity brothers. After eight or ten glasses, he becomes argumentative with one of his larger companions and suggests that they step outside and fight. Normally a quiet, unaggressive person, he now speaks in a loud voice and challenges the larger man to fight with him, apparently for no good reason. When the fight does not develop, he becomes morose and spends long periods looking into his beer glass. He seems about to cry. After more beers, he begins telling long, indiscreet stories about former girl friends. His attention drifts when others talk. He tips over a beer glass, which he finds humorous, laughing loudly until the bartender gives him a warning look. He starts to get up and say something to the bartender, but trips and falls to the floor. His friends help him to the car. Back at the fraternity house, he falls into a deep sleep, awaking with a headache and a bad taste in his mouth. He is again the quiet, shy person his friends know him to be.

Discussion of Joe College

Although intoxication in the physiologic sense occurs in social drinking, maladaptive behavior is required for the mental-disorder diagnosis of a substance-induced intoxication. In this case there is evidence of impaired judgment (picking a fight and telling indiscreet stories) plus physiologic (incoordination and unsteady gait) and psychologic (labile mood and drifting attention) signs of intoxication. This is therefore Alcohol Intoxication, since obviously alcohol is the offending substance.

The diagnosis of Alcohol Idiosyncratic Intoxication is not made unless such marked behavioral changes occur after the ingestion of an extremely small amount of alcohol, an amount that would be insufficient to cause intoxication in most people. This fellow has apparently drunk enough to "do in" anyone.

DSM-III Diagnosis:

Axis I: 303.00 Alcohol Intoxication (p. 131)

Ashamed

5 A 27-year-old engineer requested consultation because of irresistible urges to exhibit his naked penis to female strangers.

The patient, an only child, had been reared in an orthodox Jewish environment. Sexuality was strongly condemned by both parents as being "dirty." His father, a schoolteacher, was authoritarian and punitive, but relatively uninvolved in the home. His mother, a housewife, was domineering, controlling, and intrusive. She was preoccupied with cleanliness and bathed the patient until he was ten years old. The patient remembers that he feared he might have an erection in his mother's presence during one of his baths; however, this did not occur. His mother was opposed to his meeting and dating girls during his adolescence. He was not allowed to bring girls home; according to her, the proper time to bring a woman home was when she was "your wife, and not before." Despite his mother's antisexual values, she frequently walked about the house partially disrobed in his presence. To his shame, he found himself sexually aroused by this stimulation, which occurred frequently throughout his development.

As an adolescent the patient was quiet, withdrawn, and studious; teachers described him as a "model child." He was friendly but not intimate with a few male classmates. Puberty occurred at 13, and his first ejaculation occurred at that age during sleep. Because of feelings of guilt, he resisted the temptation to masturbate, and between the ages of 13 and 18 orgasms occurred only with nocturnal emissions.

He did not begin to date women until he moved out of his parents' home, at age 25. During the next two years he dated from time to time, but was too inhibited to initiate sexual activity.

At age 18, for reasons unknown to himself, during the week before final exams, he first experienced an overwhelming desire to engage in the sexual activity for which he now sought consultation. He sought situations in which he was alone with a woman he did not know. As he would approach her, he became sexually excited. He would then walk up to her and display his erect penis. He found that her shock and fear further stimulated him, and usually he would then ejaculate. At other times he fantasized past encounters while masturbating.

He felt guilty and ashamed after exhibiting himself and vowed never to repeat it. Nevertheless, the desire often overwhelmed him, and the behavior recurred frequently, usually at periods of tension. He felt desperate, but was too ashamed to seek professional help. Once, when he was 24, he had almost been apprehended by a policeman, but managed to run away.

For the last three years the patient has managed to resist his exhibitionistic urges. Recently, however, he met a young woman, who has fallen in love with him and is willing to have sexual intercourse with him. Never having had intercourse before, he felt panic lest he fail in the attempt. He likes and respects his potential sexual partner, but also condemns her for being willing to engage in premarital relations. He has once again started to exhibit himself and fears that, unless he stops, he will eventually be arrested.

Discussion of Ashamed

One could discuss at great length the childhood experiences that may have contributed to the development of this disorder in this patient. Regarding the diagnosis, however, there can be little discussion. The repetitive exposing of his genitals to strangers for the purpose of achieving sexual excitement with no attempt at further sexual activity establishes the diagnosis of Exhibitionism.

Many clinicians would assume that there is also a coexisting personality disorder, but without more information about the patient's personality functioning, such a diagnosis cannot be made.

DSM-III Diagnosis:

Axis I: 302.40 Exhibitionism (p. 272)

Wealthy Widow

6 A wealthy 72-year-old widow was referred by her children, against her will, as they thought she was becoming "senile" since the death of her husband six months previously. After the initial bereavement, which was not severe, the patient had resumed an active social life and become a volunteer at local hospitals. The family encouraged this, but over the past three months had become concerned about her going to local bars with some of the hospital staff. The referral was precipitated by her announcing her engagement to a 25-year-old male nurse, to whom she planned to turn over her house and a large amount of money. The patient's three sons, by threat and intimidation, had made her accompany them to this psychiatric evaluation. While one of her sons was talking to the psychiatrist, the patient was heard accusing the other two of trying to commit her so they could get their hands on her money.

Initially in the interview the patient was extremely angry at her sons and the psychiatrist, insisting that they couldn't understand that for the first time in her life she was doing something for herself, not for her father, her husband, or her children. She then suddenly draped herself over the couch and asked the psychiatrist if she was attractive enough to capture a 25-year-old man. She proceeded to elaborate on her fiancé's physique and sexual abilities and described her life as exciting and fulfilling for the first time. She was overtalkative and repeatedly refused to allow the psychiatrist to interrupt her with questions. She said that she went out nightly with her fiancé to clubs and bars and that although she did not drink, she thoroughly enjoyed the atmosphere. They often went on to an after-hours place and ended up breakfasting, going to bed, and making love. After only three or four hours' sleep, she would get up, feeling refreshed, and go shopping. She was spending about $700 a week on herself and giving her fiancé about $500 a week, all of which she could easily afford.

The patient agreed that her behavior was unusual for someone of her age and social position, but stated she had always been conventional and now was the time to change, before it was too late. She refused to participate in formal testing, saying "I'm not going to do any stupid tests to see if I am sane." She had no obvious memory impairment and was correctly oriented in all areas. According to the family, she had no previous history of emotional disturbance.

Discussion of Wealthy Widow

As the story unfolds, many readers will wonder, as we did, whether this poor lady is suffering only from avaricious children rather than a mental disorder. It does seem, however, that her alternately irritable and expansive mood, pressure of speech, decreased need for sleep, and poor judgment (signing her house over to someone she has only recently met) represent more than a new start in life for someone who has been too "conventional." In fact, all of these features are quite characteristic of a manic syndrome and, in the absence of features suggesting Schizophrenia or an Organic Mental Disorder, justify a diagnosis of Bipolar Disorder, Manic, without Psychotic Features.

Bipolar Disorder first appearing at age 72 is certainly uncommon. One would want to be careful to rule out the possibility of a physical disorder, such as a brain tumor or degenerative central nervous system disorder, that might be causing an Organic Affective Syndrome. Since the workup to rule out a physical disorder has not yet been done, the qualifying term "(Provisional)" is added to this diagnosis.

DSM-III Diagnosis:

Axis I: 296.42 Bipolar Disorder, Manic, without Psychotic Features (p. 208) (Provisional)

The Sailor

7 Psychiatric consultation was requested by an emergency-room physician on an 18-year-old male who had been brought into the hospital by the police. The youth appeared exhausted and showed evidence of prolonged exposure to the sun. He identified the current date incorrectly, giving it as September 27 instead of October 1. It was difficult to get him to focus on specific questions, but with encouragement he supplied a number of facts. He recalled sailing with friends, apparently about September 25, on a weekend cruise off the Florida coast, when bad weather was encountered. He was unable to recall any subsequent events and did not know what had become of his companions or how he had gotten to the hospital. He had to be reminded several times that he was in a hospital, since he expressed uncertainty as to his whereabouts. Each time he was told, he seemed surprised.

There was no evidence of head injury or dehydration. Electrolytes and cranial nerve examination were unremarkable. Because of the patient's apparent exhaustion, he was permitted to sleep for six hours. Upon awakening, he was much more attentive, but was still unable to recall events after September 27, including how he had come to the hospital. There was no longer any doubt in his mind that he was in the hospital, however; and he was able to recall the contents of the previous interview and the fact that he had fallen asleep. He was able to remember that he was a student at a southern college, maintained a B average, had a small group of close friends, and reported a good relationship with his family. He denied any previous psychiatric history and did not abuse drugs or alcohol.

Because of the patient's apparently sound physical condition, a sodium amytal interview was performed. During this interview he related that neither he nor his companions were particularly experienced sailors capable of coping with the ferocity of the storm they had encountered. Although he had taken the precaution of securing himself to the boat with a life jacket and tie line, his companions had failed to do this and had been washed overboard in the heavy seas. He had completely lost control of the boat and felt he was saved only by virtue of good luck and his lifeline. He had been able to consume a small supply of food that was stowed away in the cabin over a three-day period. He never saw either of his sailing companions again. He had been picked up on October 1 by a Coast Guard cutter and brought to shore, and subsequently the police had brought him to the hospital.

Discussion of The Sailor

The differential diagnosis of acute memory loss begins with a consideration of an Organic Mental Disorder, such as Delirium, Dementia, or Amnestic Syndrome, which may be due to head trauma, cerebrovascular accidents, or drug use. The normal physical and neurological examination and the absence of a history of drug use rule out these possibilities in this patient. With the amytal interview it becomes clear that the amnestic period developed following a particularly traumatic and life-threatening experience. Amnesia (memory loss that is too extensive to be considered "forgetfulness") that is not due to an Organic Mental Disorder justifies the diagnosis Psychogenic Amnesia. In this case, the circumscribed nature of the amnesia and the perplexity and disorientation during the amnestic period, all following a traumatic event, are quite characteristic of the diagnosed disorder.

DSM-III Diagnosis:

Axis I: 300.12 Psychogenic Amnesia (p. 255)

The Singer

8 A 27-year-old singer was referred by a friend for evaluation. Eight months before, her boyfriend had been stabbed to death during a mugging from which she escaped unharmed. After a period of mourning she appeared to return to her usual self. She helped the police in their investigation and was generally considered an ideal witness.

Nevertheless, shortly after the recent arrest of a man accused of the murder, the patient began to have recurrent nightmares and vivid memories of the night of the crime. In the dreams she frequently saw blood and imagined herself being pursued by ominous, cloaked figures. During the day, especially when walking somewhere alone, she often drifted off in daydreams, so that she forgot where she was going. Her friends noted that she began to startle easily and seemed to be preoccupied. She left her change or groceries at the store, or when waited on could not remember what she had come to buy. She began to sleep restlessly, and her work suffered because of poor concentration. She gradually withdrew from her friends and began to avoid work. She felt considerable guilt about her boyfriend's murder, although exactly why was not clear.

Discussion of The Singer

Most people who have experienced a traumatic event that is generally outside of the range of human experience, such as witnessing a murder, repeatedly think about the event for some time. In this case, however, there is the development of a specific syndrome characterized by reexperiencing the trauma (recurrent nightmares and vivid memories of the murder), reduced involvement with the external world (drifting off in daydreams, withdrawal from friends), and other symptoms, such as exaggerated startle response, sleep disturbance, memory disturbance (could not remember what she came to the store to buy), trouble concentrating, and guilt. This is called Post-traumatic Stress Disorder.

Since the symptoms of the disorder began after a latency period of more than six months following the trauma, it is subtyped Delayed.

If the patient had experienced only mild and nonspecific anxiety symptoms, the diagnosis would be Adjustment Disorder with Anxious Mood.

DSM-III Diagnosis:

Axis I: 309.81 Post-traumatic Stress Disorder, Delayed (p. 238)

Perpetual Patient

9 In 1945, at the age of 18, the patient became apprehensive about leaving home to go to an out-of-state college for her freshman year. In September, one day while with her mother shopping for clothing for college, she began to have episodes in which she would stop walking and become stiff for a few moments without explanation, then proceed to talk and act appropriately. The next day she became more silent. Sometimes she made inappropriate remarks, but at other times she acted and talked quite normally. Silences, refusal to eat, and inappropriate comments such as "Daddy, kill me" precipitated a consultation, and then hospitalization, almost on the day that the patient was to have been admitted to college.

In the early days of hospitalization, the patient vaguely suggested that she might be having auditory hallucinations, and at times gave "confused" or silly answers that were out of keeping with her 121 IQ score on psychological testing. When by herself, she would write coherent letters and short stories that were regarded as publishable. Partly because of the "lack of progress" and the bizarreness of her behavior at times, she was diagnosed as having "Catatonic Dementia Praecox."

Early in her hospitalization the patient received individual psychotherapy four times a week. She continued to receive psychotherapy in and out of the institution, with a series of 9 therapists, for the next 20 years. From the beginning of her hospitalization, she was frequently negativistic, precipitated physical fights, mutilated herself in many minor ways, and self-induced vomiting. These behaviors contributed to her receiving a great deal of attention in a public institution with limited staff. She stated that she wanted to try every form of therapy there was, "even lobotomy"; and her wishes were carried out, except for the lobotomy. She received a dozen electroconvulsive treatments, four dozen insulin subcoma treatments, dance therapy, occupational therapy, recreational therapy, psychodrama (loved it), group psychotherapy, and art therapy, in addition to individual psychotherapy and lots of attention from ministers and priests.

After the first three stormy years of her hospitalization, the patient was transferred to the care of a woman psychiatrist, became much calmer, registered at a local university, and did well at her studies. Nevertheless, "hysterical" vomiting, violence, and negativistic acts would take place whenever discharge from the institution was mentioned. In two more years, working primarily with women therapists, she held a job and acted appropriately, and she eventually accepted discharge to a female psychotherapist as "recovered" at age 24.

One evening, after six uneventful years and satisfactory occupational functioning, the patient appeared at the hospital, distraught at being unable to reach her therapist by phone, and asked to be readmitted. She was admitted despite the difficulties in determining the genuineness of her behavior and of her statements about suicide and "confusion." A series of many forms of psychotherapies, including individual psychotherapy, commenced immediately, and lasted nearly a decade.

When the patient was 40, a change in the approach to her was initiated when it was decided that she had a "Hysterical Personality." For the next five years, a series of efforts to place her in the community was blocked by negativism, threats, minor self-mutilations, self-induced vomiting, occasional inappropriate comments, and other attention-getting behavior, none of which was "rewarded," however, with individual therapy, psychodrama, etc. Eventually, now in her mid-40s, she was discharged, despite complaints that she was not ready. When told that the discharge was being carried out, over her objections, the patient vomited; but the therapist stated that she would be discharged nevertheless. She pulled down her pants and defecated in the office, but was still discharged. For the next six years she continued to function outside the institution.

Discussion of Perpetual Patient

This woman was able to engage the attention of countless dedicated mental health professionals over many years. Her remarkable illness persisted despite a trial of nearly every known treatment. The pattern of her symptoms, from the start, does not correspond to any recognizable illness, and she seemed able to produce them at will (e.g., defecation in public when her discharge was imminent). Over the years her behavior seems to have been designed to achieve one goal: continuing to be treated as a psychiatric patient.

In the past such a case might have been called Hysteria because of the exaggerated, self-dramatizing nature of the symptoms. These histrionic features were also noted by the hospital personnel who took care of this patient. In DSM-III the voluntary production of psychological symptoms for the purpose of assuming the patient role (and not for an obviously understandable goal, as in Malingering) is called Factitious Disorder with Psychological Symptoms.

In addition to the factitious production of symptoms, this woman's long-term functioning is characterized by self-dramatization, incessant drawing of attention to herself, and irrational, angry outbursts. In her relationships with people she is vain, demanding, and dependent. On this basis we would add an Axis II diagnosis of Histrionic Personality Disorder.

DSM-III Diagnosis:

Axis I: 300.16 Factitious Disorder with Psychological Symptoms
            (p. 287)
Axis II: 301.50 Histrionic Personality Disorder (p. 315)

Superstitions

10 A 20-year-old junior at a Midwestern college complained to his internist that he was having difficulty studying because, over the last six months, he had become increasingly preoccupied with thoughts that he could not dispel. He now spent hours each night "rehashing" the day's events, especially interactions with friends and teachers, endlessly making "right" in his mind any and all regrets. He likened the process to playing a videotape of each event over and over again in his mind, asking himself if he had behaved properly and telling himself that he had done his best, or had said the right thing every step of the way. He would do this while sitting at his desk, supposedly studying; and it was not unusual for him to look at the clock after such a period of rumination and note that, to his surprise, two or three hours had elapsed. His declining grades worried him. He admitted, on further questioning, that he had a two-hour grooming ritual when getting ready to go out with friends. Here again, shaving, showering, combing his hair, and putting on his clothes all demanded "perfection." In addition, for several years he had been bothered by certain "superstitions" that, it turned out, dominated his daily life. These included avoiding certain buildings while walking on campus, always sitting in the third seat in the fifth row in his class-rooms, and lining up his books and pencils in a certain configuration on his desk before studying.

Discussion of Superstitions

Obsessions are recurrent ideas that are not experienced as volun-tarily produced, but rather as thoughts that invade consciousness and are experienced as senseless (ego-dystonic). Certainly this patient experiences his rumination about the day's events as not under voluntary control. It is less clear that he regards the *content* of these thoughts as senseless, although he clearly attempts to ignore or suppress them. This ambiguity about whether such thoughts repre-sent true obsessions or merely obsessional brooding could be of diagnostic importance in distinguishing Obsessive Compulsive Dis-order from Compulsive Personality Disorder or Generalized Anxiety Disorder, in which rumination is often present. In this case, however, there are also clear signs of compulsions — repetitive behavior per-formed according to certain rules or in a stereotyped fashion that serves no useful function, is not pleasurable in itself, and is generally experienced as senseless (the patient's grooming rituals and "super-stitions").

Compulsive Personality Disorder is frequently, but not invariably, associated with Obsessive Compulsive Disorder. However, in this case there is no evidence to justify that additional diagnosis.

DSM-III Diagnosis:

Axis I: 300.30 Obsessive Compulsive Disorder (p. 235)

Equal Rights

11 A 45-year-old man and his 33-year-old wife went to a family therapist for help with their four-year marriage. The husband complained that his wife was devoted to pursuing a career in architecture, whereas he, a successful businessman, wanted her to have children before they were too old. He insisted that if she really loved him she would be willing to go along with his desire and at least postpone her career plans. She felt that this was an unfair demand, that they were equally entitled to pursue their career interests. On the subject of children, she said she might eventually want one, but she could not currently see herself as a mother.

History revealed that the husband had had two manic episodes, both resulting in brief hospitalizations, five and ten years previously. Ever since the last episode he had been on lithium carbonate and had apparently been asymptomatic.

Discussion of Equal Rights

DSM-III does not include a classification of disturbed dyadic or family units. Therefore, it is necessary to make separate diagnoses for the husband and for the wife.

For the husband, the V code Marital Problem for a condition not attributable to a mental disorder that is a focus of attention or treatment is appropriate because there is no evidence that the current marital problem is due to his Bipolar Disorder. The husband's continuing treatment with lithium carbonate justifies the diagnosis of Bipolar Disorder, in Remission.The Marital Problem is listed first because it is the focus of this evaluation.

For the wife, all that can be said with the information available is that she also has a Marital Problem.

DSM-III Diagnosis:

Husband:
Axis I: **V61.10 Marital Problem (p. 333)**
          296.46 Bipolar Disorder, Manic, in Remission (p. 217)
Wife:
Axis I: **V61.10 Marital Problem (p. 333)**

Ulcers

12 A 42-year-old trial lawyer, married and the mother of two children, is referred for consultation by her gastroenterologist following her third hospitalization for duodenal ulcer disease. Her ulcer disease was first diagnosed four years ago, but an upper gastrointestinal (GI) series at that time showed evidence both of an active ulcer and of scarring secondary to previously healed ulcers. The gastroenterologist has requested the consultation for help in considering the possibility of surgery, prompted by the seriousness of the bleeding episode that precipitated the patient's last admission and by the fact that she seems to "ignore pain." His referral note indicates that he sees no clear connection between the bleeding episodes and the patient's highly stressful occupation.

The patient appears exactly on time for her appointment; she is neatly and conservatively dressed. She presents an organized, coherent account of her medical problem and denies any past or immediate family history of significant mental disorder. She appears genuinely worried by her recent hospitalization, frightened by the prospect of surgery, and doubtful that speaking to a psychiatrist will produce any meaningful help. As she points out, "Ulcers are supposed to be related to stress, and that just isn't true with me." She then produces a detailed, written outline of her professional life over the past five years side by side with a chronology of her ulcer attacks. Indeed, there seems to be no temporal relationship between her attacks and several dramatic and highly taxing court cases in which she has appeared.

During the second evaluation session, the patient discusses her background. She is the oldest of four children and the clear favorite of her father, also an attorney. He had, and communicated, a strong expectation that she would become a lawyer and that she would succeed in this field. The patient experiences herself as having fulfilled this expectation admirably, and displays a rare smile while describing several of her more dramatic courtroom triumphs. There is no evidence that she herself experiences these difficult cases as stressful; in fact, she seems to enjoy them.

She married a law-school classmate, who is also quite successful and who works noncompetitively in an unrelated legal field. Their marriage seems sound. As she begins to talk about her two sons, aged eight and four, the patient becomes noticeably more tense, and appears much more concerned and upset than usual while describing minor crises they have experienced with friends or in school. With great surprise, she discovers that the chronology of these crises corresponds clearly to five of her seven ulcer attacks, including all of those that resulted in hospitalization. She admits that despite being upset by her sons' problems, she finds it difficult to share her concerns about parenting with her husband or friends. At the end of the session she comments: "You'd have made a good lawyer. I'm glad I'm not arguing against you." She herself suggests that some further sessions may be in order.

Discussion of Ulcers

In the past, certain disorders, such as duodenal ulcer, were assumed to be caused by emotional factors and were classified as Psychophysiologic Disorders. In DSM-III the corresponding category is called Psychological Factors Affecting Physical Condition, but it is to be used only in cases in which a relationship between psychologically meaningful environmental stimuli and the initiation or exacerbation of a physical disorder can be demonstrated. This case attests to the fact that it is often difficult to demonstrate the role of psychological factors and that the precise nature of the psychologically meaningful stimuli frequently is not obvious.

The dramatic demonstration of the relationship between her children's minor crises and the exacerbations of this woman's ulcer justify the Axis I diagnosis of Psychological Factors Affecting Physical Condition. The presence of the duodenal ulcer is noted on Axis III.

DSM-III Diagnosis:

Axis I: **316.00 Psychological Factors Affecting Physical Condition (p. 303)**
Axis III: Duodenal ulcer

Stuporous Student

13 An 18-year-old female high-school student was admitted for the first time to the psychiatry service because for three days she had not spoken and would not eat. According to her parents, she had been a "normal" teen-ager, with good grades and friends, until about one year previously when she began to stay at home more, alone in her room, and seemed preoccupied and less animated. Six months before admission, she began to refuse to go to school, and her grades became barely passing. About a month later, she started to talk "gibberish" about spirits, magic, the devil—things that were totally foreign to her background. For the week preceding admission to the hospital she had stared into space, immobile, only allowing herself to be moved from her bed to a chair, or from one room to another.

Discussion of Stuporous Student

The diagnosis of Schizophrenia is justified by the presence of incoherence (started to talk "gibberish") and catatonic stupor (stared into space, immobile) following a one-year history of prodromal symptoms (social withdrawal, deterioration in academic functioning) in the absence of a known organic factor, such as drug use. The course is Subchronic since the disturbance has apparently lasted less than two years. The subtype is Catatonic because these are the most prominent symptoms.

DSM-III Diagnosis:

Axis I: 295.21 Schizophrenic Disorder, Catatonic Type, Subchronic (p. 188)

The Workaholic

14 The patient is a 45-year-old lawyer who seeks treatment at his wife's insistence. She is fed up with their marriage: she can no longer tolerate his emotional coldness, rigid demands, bullying behavior, sexual disinterest, long work hours, and frequent business trips. The patient feels no particular distress in his marriage, and has agreed to the consultation only to humor his wife.

It soon develops, however, that the patient is troubled by problems at work. He is known as the hardest-driving member of a hard-driving law firm. He was the youngest full partner in the firm's history, and is famous for being able to handle many cases at the same time. Lately, he finds himself increasingly unable to keep up. He is too proud to turn down a new case, and too much of a perfectionist to be satisfied with the quality of work performed by his assistants. He finds himself constantly correcting their briefs, displeased with their writing style and sentence structure, and therefore unable to stay abreast of his schedule. People at work complain that his attention to detail and inability to delegate responsibility are reducing his efficiency. He has been through two or three secretaries a year for 15 years. No one can tolerate working for him for very long because he is so critical of any mistakes made by others. When assignments get backed up, he cannot decide which to address first, starts making schedules for himself and his staff, but then is unable to meet them and works 15 hours a day. He finds it difficult to be decisive now that his work has expanded beyond his own direct control.

The patient discusses his children as if they were mechanical dolls, but also with a clear underlying affection. He describes his wife as a "suitable mate" and has trouble understanding why she is dissatisfied. He is punctilious in his manners and dress and slow and ponderous in his speech, dry and humorless, with a stubborn determination to get his point across.

The patient is the product of two upwardly mobile, extremely hard-working parents. He grew up feeling that he was never working hard enough, that he had much to achieve and very little time. He was a superior student, a bookworm, awkward and unpopular in adolescent social pursuits. He has always been competitive and a high achiever. He has trouble relaxing on vacations, develops elaborate activities schedules for every family member, and becomes impatient and furious if they refuse to follow his plans. He likes sports but has little time for them and refuses to play if he can't be at the top of his form. He is a ferocious competitor on the tennis courts and a poor loser.

Discussion of The Workaholic

Although the marital problem is the entry ticket, it is clear that this fellow has many personality traits that are quite maladaptive. He is cold and rigid and excessively perfectionistic. He is indecisive, but insists that others do things his way; his interpersonal relationships suffer because of his excessive devotion to work. It is hard to imagine a more prototypical case of Compulsive Personality Disorder!

The additional notation of the V code Marital Problem is not made in this case since the patient's marital problems are clearly symptomatic of his mental disorder.

DSM-III Diagnosis:

Axis II: 301.40 Compulsive Personality Disorder (p. 327)

Threatening Voices

15 A 44-year-old unemployed male who lived alone in a single-room occupancy hotel was brought to the emergency room by police, to whom he had gone for help, complaining that he was frightened by hearing voices of men in the street below his window talking about him and threatening him with harm. When he looked out the window, the men had always "disappeared."

The patient had a 20-year history of almost daily alcohol use, was commonly "drunk" each day, and often experienced the "shakes" on awakening. On the previous day he had reduced his intake to one pint of vodka, because of gastrointestinal distress. He was fully alert and oriented on mental status examination.

Discussion of Threatening Voices

Vivid auditory hallucinations that occur in a clear state of consciousness following reduction or cessation of alcohol use indicate Alcohol Hallucinosis. This is distinguished from Alcohol Withdrawal Delirium by the absence of clouded sensorium and disturbance in attention.

The additional diagnosis of Alcohol Dependence, Continuous, is made because of the chronic and continuous pathological pattern of alcohol use (daily intoxication) and withdrawal (experiencing morning "shakes"). Alcohol Hallucinosis apparently develops only in people with a long history of Alcohol Dependence.

DSM-III Diagnosis:

Axis I: **291.30 Alcohol Hallucinosis (p. 136)**
303.91 Alcohol Dependence, Continuous (p. 170)

Failing Memory

16 A 73-year-old woman presented with "failing memory," which her husband reported had been gradually developing over the past five years. He considered her only absent-minded, "because we *are* getting older, you know." But when she began to neglect her housework, could no longer balance the household budget, and threw family valuables out in the garbage, he brought her in for medical attention.

The patient minimized her symptoms as part of "aging" and as "nothing serious." She rationalized her actions, e.g., the valuable painting she threw out was one that "no one in their right mind would want and it would be too much bother to put it up for auction."

There were no focal neurological signs, and physical examination and routine laboratory tests were negative.

Discussion of Failing Memory

The impairment in memory, disturbance in intellectual ability (could no longer balance household budget), and poor judgment (threw out family valuables), sufficiently severe to interfere with functioning, indicate the presence of a Dementia. (Since the disturbance is not limited to deficits in memory, the diagnosis of an Amnestic Syndrome is not made.) The diagnosis of Primary Degenerative Dementia is made by exclusion: a normal physical examination and negative routine laboratory tests rule out such causes of Dementia as brain tumor and endocrine disorder. The absence of a stepwise progression of the Dementia and of focal neurological signs excludes Multi-infarct Dementia, that is, Dementia resulting from repeated strokes.

The onset after age 65 and the absence of depression, delirium, or delusions are noted by the subclassifications Senile Onset and Uncomplicated.

DSM-III Diagnosis:

Axis I: 290.00 Primary Degenerative Dementia, Senile Onset, Uncomplicated (p. 126)

Worthless Woman

17 A 50-year-old widow was transferred to a medical center from her community mental health center, to which she had been admitted three weeks previously with severe agitation, pacing, and hand-wringing, depressed mood accompanied by severe self-reproach, insomnia, and a 6–8 kg (15-pound) weight loss. She believed that her neighbors were against her, had poisoned her coffee, and had bewitched her to punish her because of her wickedness. Seven years previously, after the death of her husband, she had required hospitalization for a similar depression, with extreme guilt, agitation, insomnia, accusatory hallucinations of voices calling her a worthless person, and preoccupation with thoughts of suicide. Before being transferred, she had been treated with Doxepin HCL, 200 mg, with only modest effect on the depression and no effect on the delusions.

Discussion of Worthless Woman

The pervasive depressed mood with the characteristic associated symptoms of the depressive syndrome (psychomotor agitation, self-reproach, insomnia, and weight loss) suggests a major depressive episode. The delusions are congruent with the depressed mood, since the content involves the theme of guilt and deserved punishment. In the absence of any specific organic factor to account for the disturbance, the diagnosis is Major Depression. It is further subclassified in the fourth digit as Recurrent, because of the history of a previous episode. The fifth digit indicates the presence of psychotic features (mood-congruent). The absence of any reference to lack of reactivity or pervasive loss of interest or pleasure precludes the subclassification "with Melancholia."

DSM-III Diagnosis:

Axis I: 296.34 Major Depression, Recurrent, with Psychotic Features (Mood-congruent) (p. 213)

Bruised

18 A 25-year-old female graduate student asked for a consultation because of depression and marital discord. The patient had been married for five years, during which time both she and her husband were in school. During the past three years her academic performance had been consistently better than his, and she attributed their frequent, intense arguments to this. She noted that she experienced a feeling of sexual excitement when her husband screamed at her or hit her in a rage. Sometimes she would taunt him until he had sexual intercourse with her in a brutal fashion, as if she were being raped. She experienced the brutality and sense of being punished as sexually exciting.

One year before the consultation the patient had found herself often ending arguments by storming out of the house. On one such occasion she went to a "singles bar," picked up a man, and got him to slap her as part of their sexual activity. She found the "punishment" sexually exciting and subsequently fantasized about being beaten during masturbation to orgasm. The patient then discovered that she enjoyed receiving physical punishment at the hands of strange men more than any other type of sexual stimulus. In a setting in which she could be whipped or beaten, all aspects of sexual activity, including the quality of orgasms, were far in excess of anything she had previously experienced.

This sexual preference was not the reason for the consultation, however. She complained that she could not live without her husband, yet could not live with him. She had suicidal fantasies stemming from the fear that he would leave her.

She recognized that her sexual behavior was dangerous to herself, and felt mildly ashamed of it. She was unaware of any possible reasons for its emergence and was unsure if she wished treatment for "it," because it gave her so much pleasure.

Discussion of Bruised

Fantasies of being bound, beaten, or otherwise humiliated may increase sexual excitement for some individuals whose sexual life is in all other respects unremarkable. In this case the patient has begun to act out these fantasies; and masochistic sexual acts of being beaten, whipped, or punished have become her preferred source of arousal. It is the preference for masochistic sexual acts, not mere fantasy, that justifies the diagnosis Sexual Masochism.

With the limited information available, it is not possible to determine if the patient's marital problem is primarily: (1) a symptom of the Sexual Masochism (Does she provoke arguments in order to be sexually aroused?); (2) a symptom of a Personality Disorder; or (3) a problem unrelated to a mental disorder for which the V code Marital Problem would be appropriate.

DSM-III Diagnosis:

Axis I: 302.83 Sexual Masochism (p. 274)

Coffee Break

19 A 35-year-old secretary sought consultation for "anxiety attacks." A thorough history revealed that the attacks occurred in the mid-to-late afternoon, when she became restless, nervous, and easily excited and sometimes was noted to be flushed, sweating, and, according to co-workers, "talking a mile a minute." In response to careful questioning, she acknowledged drinking five or six cups of coffee each day before the usual time the attacks occurred.

Discussion of Coffee Break

The temporal association of heavy coffee drinking and the anxiety symptoms indicates the etiological significance of caffeine. In the literature this has been referred to as Caffeinism. In DSM-III this organic brain syndrome is an intoxication, that is, maladaptive behavior due to the effect of a specific substance that has been ingested recently and is present in the body. Therefore, the diagnosis is Caffeine Intoxication.

Although the symptoms suggest an Anxiety Disorder, such a diagnosis is not made when the disturbance is due to a known specific organic factor.

DSM-III Diagnosis:

Axis I: 305.90 Caffeine Intoxication (p. 161)

Car Salesman

20 A 29-year-old car salesman was referred by his current girl friend, a psychiatric nurse, who suspected he had an Affective Disorder, even though the patient was reluctant to admit that he might be a "moody" person. According to him, since the age of 14 he has experienced repeated alternating cycles that he terms "good times and bad times." During a "bad" period, usually lasting four to seven days, he oversleeps 10–14 hours daily, lacks energy, confidence, and motivation—"just vegetating," as he puts it. Often he abruptly shifts, characteristically upon waking up in the morning, to a three-to-four-day stretch of overconfidence, heightened social awareness, promiscuity, and sharpened thinking — "things would flash in my mind." At such times he indulges in alcohol to enhance the experience, but also to help him sleep. Occasionally the "good" periods last seven to ten days, but culminate in irritable and hostile outbursts, which often herald the transition back to another period of "bad" days. He admits to frequent use of marijuana, which he claims helps him "adjust" to daily routines.

In school, A's and B's alternated with C's and D's, with the result that the patient was considered a bright student whose performance was mediocre overall because of "unstable motivation." As a car salesman his performance has also been uneven, with "good days" canceling out the "bad days"; yet even during his "good days" he is sometimes perilously argumentative with customers and loses sales that appeared sure. Although considered a charming man in many social circles, he alienates friends when he is hostile and irritable. He typically accumulates social obligations during the "bad" days and takes care of them all at once on the first day of a "good" period.

Discussion of Car Salesman

This patient has had numerous periods during the last two years in which he had some symptoms characteristic of both the depressive and the manic syndromes. Characteristic of the "good days" are overconfidence, heightened social awareness, promiscuity, and sharpened thinking. Although these periods come close to meeting the criteria for a manic esisode, they are not sufficiently severe to justify a diagnosis of Bipolar Disorder. Similarly, the "bad days," characterized by oversleeping and lack of energy, confidence, and motivation, are not of sufficient severity and duration to meet the criteria for a major- depressive episode. Moreover, the brief cycles follow each other with intermittent irregularity on a chronic basis. Therefore, the appropriate diagnosis is Cyclothymic Disorder.

If there were, in addition, a history of a clear-cut manic episode, the *additional* diagnosis of superimposed Bipolar Disorder would be made. If there were a clear history of a major depressive episode, then the *additional* diagnosis of Atypical Bipolar Disorder would be made because of the presence of hypomanic episodes.

Additional diagnoses of Alcohol Abuse and Cannabis Abuse are suspected, but insufficient information is provided.

DSM-III Diagnosis:

Axis I: 301.13 Cyclothymic Disorder (p. 219)

Fraulein Von Willebrand

21 A 29-year-old female laboratory technician was admitted to the medical service via the emergency room because of bloody urine. The patient said that she was being treated for lupus erythematosus by a physician in a different city. She also mentioned that she had had Von Willebrand's disease (a rare hereditary blood disorder) as a child. On the third day of her hospitalization, a medical student mentioned to the resident that she had seen this patient several weeks before at a different hospital in the area, where the patient had been admitted for the same problem. A search of the patient's belongings revealed a cache of anticoagulant medication. When confronted with this information she refused to discuss the matter and hurriedly signed out of the hospital against medical advice.

Discussion of Fraulein Von Willebrand

The circumstances (bloody urine, possession of anticoagulants, history of repeated hospitalizations, leaving the hospital when confronted) strongly suggest that this patient's symptoms were under voluntary control and were not genuine symptoms of a physical disorder.

The differential diagnosis of simulated illness is between Factitious Disorder and Malingering. From what is known of this case, it would appear that there is no obvious understandable goal other than that of assuming the patient role. Therefore, the diagnosis is Chronic Factitious Disorder with Physical Symptoms.

If the facts had suggested, for example, that her goal was primarily to get disability payments, this would have indicated the act of malingering (coded in section V, Codes for Conditions Not Attributable to a Mental Disorder That Are a Focus of Attention or Treatment) rather than a mental disorder.

DSM-III Diagnosis:

Axis I: 301.51 Chronic Factitious Disorder with Physical Symptoms (p. 290)

33

Belligerent Boy

22 A 21-year-old male was interviewed by a psychiatrist while he was being detained in jail awaiting trial for attempted robbery. The patient had a history of multiple arrests for drug charges, robbery, and assault and battery.

Past history revealed that he had been expelled from junior high school for truancy, fighting, and generally poor performance in school. Following a car theft when he was 14 years old, he was placed in a juvenile detention center. Subsequently he spent brief periods in a variety of institutions, from which he usually ran away. At times his parents attempted to let him live at home, but he was disruptive and threatened them with physical harm. After one such incident during which he threatened them with a knife, he was admitted to a psychiatric hospital; but he signed himself out against medical advice, one day later.

The patient has never formed close personal relationships with his parents, his two older brothers, or friends of either sex. He is a loner and a drifter, and has not worked for more than two months at any one job in his life. He was recently terminated, because of fighting and poor attendance, from a vocational training program in which he had been enrolled for about three weeks.

Discussion of Belligerent Boy

The multiple arrests for criminal activity, and the aggressiveness, failure to work consistently, and inability to maintain an enduring attachment to a sexual partner all suggest Antisocial Personality Disorder. A history of antisocial behavior before age 15 (truancy, expulsion from school, fighting, thefts) confirms the diagnosis.

The multiple arrests on drug charges suggest at least a past history of Substance Abuse; but since there is no reference to a current problem in this area, no additional diagnosis is made. Antisocial Personality Disorder is frequently associated with Narcissistic and/or Borderline Personality Disorder. However, this case does not provide the kind of information that would be necessary to make either of these additional Personality Disorder diagnoses.

DSM-III Diagnosis:

Axis II: 301.70 Antisocial Personality Disorder (p. 320)

Heart Attack

23 A 25-year-old married insurance salesman is admitted to the medical service of a hospital by his internist when he arrives at the emergency room, for the fourth time in a month, insisting that he is having a heart attack. The cardiologist's workup is completely negative.

The patient states that his "heart problem" started six months ago when he had a sudden episode of terror, chest pain, palpitations, sweating, and shortness of breath while driving across a bridge on his way to visit a prospective client. His father and uncle had both had heart problems, and the patient was sure he was developing a similar illness. Not wanting to alarm his wife and family, he initially said nothing; but when the attacks began to recur several times a month, he consulted his internist. The internist found nothing wrong and told him he should try to relax, take more time off from work, and develop some leisure interests. In spite of his attempts to follow this advice the attacks recurred with increasing intensity and frequency.

The patient claims that he believes the doctors who say there is nothing wrong with his heart, but during an attack he still becomes concerned that he is having a heart attack and will die.

Discussion of Heart Attack

In the past this clinical presentation might have been referred to as "cardiac neurosis" because of the irrational preoccupation with the fear of having a heart attack. In fact, the concern with the possibility of having a heart attack is merely the patient's incorrect understanding of the frightening symptoms that he is experiencing.

The symptoms consist of the sudden onset of discrete periods of extreme fear, accompanied by chest pain, palpitations, sweating, shortness of breath, and a fear that he will die. These are the symptoms of a panic attack. When panic attacks occur in situations other than during life-threatening circumstances, are precipitated not just by exposure to a circumscribed phobic stimulus (e.g., speaking in public), and occur at least three times within a three-week period, the diagnosis Panic Disorder is made.

The only possible additional diagnosis would be Hypochondriasis. In this case, however, the patient's concern with his heart is clearly a symptom of the Panic Disorder; and the diagnosis Hypochondriasis is not made when the somatic preoccupation is a symptom of another mental disorder.

DSM-III Diagnosis:

Axis I: 300.01 Panic Disorder (p. 231)

Bridge Boy

24 An 18-year-old high-school senior was brought to the emergency room by police after being picked up wandering in traffic on the Triborough Bridge. He was angry, agitated, and aggressive and talked of various people who were deliberately trying to "confuse" him by giving him misleading directions. His story was rambling and disjointed, but he admitted to the police officer that he had been using "speed." In the emergency room he had difficulty focusing his attention and had to ask that questions be repeated. He was disoriented as to time and place and was unable to repeat the names of three objects after five minutes. The family gave a history of the patient's regular use of "pep pills" over the past two years, during which time he was frequently "high" and did very poorly in school.

Discussion of Bridge Boy

The history of regular use of "pep pills" immediately raises the question of the presence of an Organic Brain Syndrome caused by amphetamine. Although persecutory delusions are present, the disorientation, attention disturbance, and increased psychomotor activity indicate a Delirium, which, because it involves a global cognitive disturbance, takes precedence over the diagnosis of an Amphetamine-induced Organic Delusional Disorder. For the same reason, a diagnosis of Amphetamine Intoxication is not made.

The patient's use of amphetamine for a period of over six months probably contributed to his poor school performance, justifying the additional diagnosis of Amphetamine Abuse, Continuous.

DSM-III Diagnosis:

Axis I: 292.81 Amphetamine-induced Delirium (p. 149)
305.71 Amphetamine Abuse, Continuous (p. 174)

Enemies

25 A 40-year-old construction worker believes that his co-workers do not like him and fears that someone might let his scaffolding slip in order to cause him injury on the job. This concern followed a recent disagreement on the lunch line when the patient felt that a co-worker was sneaking ahead and complained to him. He began noticing his new "enemy" laughing with the other men and often wondered if he were the butt of their mockery. He thought of confronting them, but decided that the whole issue might just be in his own mind, and that he might get himself into more trouble by taking any action.

The patient offers little spontaneous information, sits tensely in the chair, is wide-eyed and carefully tracks all movements in the room. He reads between the lines of the interviewer's questions, feels criticized, and imagines that the interviewer is siding with his co-workers. He makes it clear that he would not have come to the personnel clinic at all except for his need for sleep medication.

He was a loner as a boy and felt that other children would form cliques and be mean to him. He did poorly in school, but blamed his teachers — he claimed that they preferred girls or boys who were "sissies." He dropped out of school, and has since been a hard and effective worker; but he feels he never gets the breaks. He believes that he has been discriminated against because of his Catholicism, but can offer little convincing evidence. He gets on poorly with bosses and co-workers, is unable to appreciate joking around, and does best in situations where he can work and have lunch alone. He has switched jobs many times because he felt he was being mistreated.

The patient is distant and demanding with his family. His children call him "Sir" and know that it is wise to be "seen but not heard" when he is around. At home he can never comfortably sit still and is always busy at some chore or another. He prefers not to have people visit his house and becomes restless when his wife is away visiting others.

Discussion of Enemies

Though this patient ostensibly came for treatment only because of trouble sleeping, it is clear that there is a long-standing pattern of suspiciousness and hypersensitivity. His current difficulty at work is merely an exacerbation of a personality disorder rather than an episode of a new illness. He has little insight into his difficulties with others, but he is not delusional: he recognizes that his suspiciousness might be "in his own mind." Therefore, a diagnosis of a psychotic disorder, such as Paranoid Schizophrenia or a Paranoid Disorder, is ruled out.

The long-standing presence of suspiciousness, ideas of reference, hypersensitivity to criticism, avoidance of accepting blame when warranted, absence of a sense of humor, emotional coldness, and inability to relax add up to a diagnosis of Paranoid Personality Disorder.

DSM-III Diagnosis:

Axis II: 301.00 Paranoid Personality Disorder (p. 309)

Math Teacher

26 A 45-year-old mathematics teacher requested medication because he decided to stop smoking and felt that he could not stay off cigarettes without help. After smoking two to three packs a day for 30 years, he abruptly stopped smoking four days before being seen. Since then he has been snapping at his family and students and has been unable to grade papers or do any work that requires sitting at a desk and concentrating. He paces the floor, thinking about smoking—he even dreams about smoking. He has already gained five pounds because of his immensely increased consumption of beer and sweets. He complains of constipation and difficulty sleeping.

Discussion of Math Teacher

No one should have difficulty putting together the abrupt cessation of smoking, the craving for tobacco, irritability, difficulty concentrating, restlessness, and gastrointestinal disturbance to come up with the diagnosis of Tobacco Withdrawal. But there is another diagnosis that should also be given: the Tobacco Withdrawal, by itself, is evidence of Tobacco Dependence. This makes clinical sense, since once the acute problem of Tobacco Withdrawal has been resolved, the long-term problem is going to be Tobacco Dependence.

The choice in coding the course of the Tobacco Dependence is between "Continuous" and "in Remission." We prefer to give the patient the benefit of the doubt, assuming that within the next few days he will not begin to smoke again, and hence assign the subclassification "in Remission." If the patient kicks the habit for good, at some future time the diagnosis Tobacco Dependence in Remission will be changed to No Mental Disorder. (Perhaps this should occur when he stops having dreams about smoking.)

DSM-III Diagnosis:

Axis I: 292.00 Tobacco Withdrawal (p. 159)
           305.13 Tobacco Dependence, in Remission (p. 178)

Trapped

27 A 30-year-old male chemist was referred by his internist because he wanted to talk to someone about his shaky marriage. During five years of courtship and two years of marriage, there have been numerous separations, usually precipitated by his dissatisfaction. Although he and his wife share many interests and, until recently, have had a satisfactory sexual relationship, he thinks that his wife is basically a cold and self-centered person who has no real concern about his career or feelings. His dissatisfaction periodically builds up to a point that leads to fights, which often result in temporary separations. He then feels lonely and comes "crawling back" to her. Their relationship currently is one of "icy separateness," and the patient seems to be seeking support to make a permanent break. Although he is in extreme distress because of his marital situation, frequently choking back tears, there is no evidence that he has difficulties with other interpersonal relationships. He has many good friends, functions well in his job, and denies symptoms other than distress about his marital situation.

Discussion of Trapped

Although this man is very upset about his marital situation and is apparently not able to resolve it as well as he might, his reaction to the situation appears to be well within normal and expectable limits. Therefore, a diagnosis of a mental disorder, such as Adjustment Disorder, is not appropriate.

Despite the fact that the designation of the V code Marital Problem implies that the patient's difficulties are not due to a mental disorder, it might nonetheless be appropriate to offer some form of professional help.

DSM-III Diagnosis:

Axis I: V61.10 Marital Problem (p. 333)

Stubborn Psychiatrist

28 A 34-year-old psychiatrist is 15 minutes late for his first appointment. He had recently been asked to resign from his job in a mental health center because, according to his boss, he had frequently been late for work and meetings, missed appointments, forgot about assignments, was late with his statistics, refused to follow instructions, and seemed unmotivated. The patient was surprised and resentful—he thought he had been doing a particularly good job under trying circumstances and experienced his boss as excessively obsessive and demanding. Nonetheless, he reported a long-standing pattern of difficulties with authority.

The patient had a childhood history of severe and prolonged temper tantrums that were a legend in his family. He had been a bossy child who demanded that other kids "play his way" or else he wouldn't play at all. With adults, particularly his mother and female teachers, he was sullen, insubordinate, oppositional, and often unmanageable. He had been sent to an all-boys' prep school that had primarily male teachers, and he gradually became more subdued and disciplined. He continued, however, to stubbornly want things his own way and to resent instruction or direction from teachers. He was a brilliant but erratic student, working only as hard as he himself wanted to, and he "punished" teachers he didn't like by not doing their assignments. He was argumentative and self-righteous when criticized, and complained that he was not being treated fairly.

The patient is unhappily married. He complains that his wife does not understand him and is a "nitpicker." She complains that he is unreliable and stubborn. He refuses to do anything around the house and often forgets to complete the few errands he has accepted as within his responsibility. Tax forms are submitted several months late; bills are not paid. The patient is sociable and has considerable charm, but friends generally become annoyed at his unwillingness to go along with the wishes of the group: for example, if a restaurant is not his choice, he may sulk all night or forget to bring his wallet.

Discussion of Stubborn Psychiatrist

Whenever this patient feels that demands are being made on him, either socially or occupationally, he passively resists through such characteristic maneuvers as procrastination (e.g., tax returns are late, bills are not paid), stubbornness (e.g., unwillingness to go along with the wishes of his friends), and forgetfulness (e.g., forgets errands for wife and assignments at work). His behavior has resulted in impaired work performance and marital difficulties. Such a long-standing pattern of resistance to demands for adequate performance in role functioning is a prototype of Passive-Aggressive Personality Disorder.

Although passive-aggressive behavior is quite common in situations in which assertive behavior is not encouraged or is actually punished (e.g., in the military service), the diagnosis is made only if the behavior occurs in situations in which more assertive behavior is possible. Passive-aggressive traits may be seen as an associated feature of other Personality Disorders; but the diagnosis Passive-Aggressive Personality Disorder is not made when another personality disorder is present.

This case demonstrates that neither a high IQ nor membership in a mental health profession conveys immunity to this disorder!

DSM-III Diagnosis:

Axis II: 301.84 Passive-Aggressive Personality Disorder (p. 329)

Housepainter

29 A 46-year-old divorced housepainter is admitted to the hospital with a history of 30 years of heavy drinking. He has had two previous admissions for detoxification, but his family states that he has not had a drink in several weeks, and he shows no signs of alcohol withdrawal. He looks malnourished, however, and on examination is found to be ataxic and to have a bilateral sixth-cranial-nerve palsy. He appears confused and mistakes one of his physicians for a dead uncle.

Within a week the patient walks normally, and there is no longer any sign of a sixth-nerve palsy. He seems less confused and can now find his way to the bathroom without direction. He remembers the names and birthdays of his siblings, but has difficulty naming the past five presidents. More strikingly, he has great difficulty in retaining information for longer than a few minutes. He can repeat a list of numbers immediately after he has heard them, but a few minutes later does not recall being asked to perform the task. Shown three objects (keys, comb, ring), he cannot recall them three minutes later. He does not seem worried about this. Asked if he can recall the name of his doctor, he replies, "Certainly," and proceeds to call the doctor "Dr. Masters" (not his name), whom, he claims, he first met in the Korean War. He tells a long untrue story about how he and "Dr. Masters" served as fellow soldiers.

The patient is calm, alert, friendly. One can be with him for a short period and not realize he has a severe memory impairment, in view of his intact immediate memory and spotty but sometimes adequate remote memory. His amnesia, in short, is largely anterograde. Although treated with high doses of thiamine, the short-term memory deficit persists and appears to be irreversible.

Discussion of Housepainter

Confusion, ataxia, and sixth-nerve palsy, with a history of heavy alcohol use, are diagnostic of the neurological disorder Wernicke's Encephalopathy, noted on Axis III. As is often the case, when this responds to treatment with thiamine, the patient is left with an Amnestic Syndrome, Alcohol Amnestic Disorder. This is characterized by short-term (rather than immediate or long-term) memory impairment. In an effort to mask the memory impairment, the individual may confabulate, i.e., fabricate facts or events in response to questions about situations that are not recalled.

If a generalized loss of intellectual functioning rather than memory loss were the predominant disturbance, then a diagnosis of Dementia Associated with Alcoholism would be appropriate.

The history of years of heavy drinking and two admissions for detoxification justifies the additional diagnosis of Alcohol Dependence, Continuous.

DSM-III Diagnosis:

Axis I: 291.10 Alcohol Amnestic Disorder (p. 137)
         303.91 Alcohol Dependence, Continuous (p. 170)
Axis III: Wernicke's Encephalopathy

Frieda

30 A 42-year-old woman, accompanied by her husband, sought psychiatric consultation, primarily at the husband's request. She described a number of marital difficulties of an unexceptional nature and appeared to lapse into periods of daydreaming during the evaluation. Independently her husband reported that on occasion she would leave the house suddenly, dressed in a manner quite different from her customary sedate appearance, and not return for 12 to 36 hours. At other times, after some minor family argument, she would withdraw into a corner of the room, sit on the floor, curl up, and talk as if she were a young girl. Her husband found that he could not bring her out of these episodes easily. His subsequent attempts to discuss them with her were fruitless as she refused to talk about them.

Initially the patient claimed to have no awareness of these incidents; but under hypnosis she acknowledged them openly, giving a highly detailed, vivid, and emotional account. She had been born in 1938 in Poland, shortly before the German invasion. During the war she lived in a variety of orphanages, as her father was killed during the hostilities and her mother fled the country to live in Italy with relatives. The orphanages were run by nuns, who provided institutional care and strong discipline. Food supplies were meager, friendships marginal, and moves frequent, necessitated by wartime conditions. The patient described a make-believe female companion of the same age with whom she engaged in lengthy reveries from about age four. In the face of wartime privation, she would retreat with this companion and imagine playing in a sunny peaceful field with dolls. The girls would run there to get away from family chores. They would dress up in their parents' clothes and impersonate grownups, flaunting the staid customs of their rural village. These reveries continued and, in fact, increased in frequency when she was a young adolescent, especially after she was sexually molested by two Soviet occupation soldiers stationed in Poland after the war.

The patient never saw either of her parents again. She was angry at her mother, whom she perceived as having selfishly abandoned her. Her perception of her father was more complex. She imagined that he had collaborated with German occupation forces as an informant and was killed by residents of his village in retaliation. She felt that her antipathy toward him characterized her relationships with nearly all men, especially after she was molested in adolescence.

Since immigrating to the United States, she had married, but was sexually indifferent to her husband and had difficulty resolving disagreements about money, vacation schedules, and child discipline. When disputes arose, producing clear signs of emotional withdrawal in her husband, she would retreat to the bedroom, dress in flamboyant clothes, and leave the house without a word. During these episodes she would experience herself as Frieda, the girl friend of the Soviet soldier who had molested her. She would meet a man at a nearby bar and propose a sexual liaison, only to belittle his masculinity before any physical involvement occurred. The other incidents, in which she appeared to her husband to curl up on the floor and talk as if she were a young girl, occurred after arguments with her children over issues of discipline, especially their failure to keep their room clean and complete their homework on time. At these times the patient would reexperience, as real, her wartime reveries with her imaginary companion.

Following completion of the interview under hypnosis, the patient had no memory of Frieda.

Discussion of Frieda

Sudden and dramatic changes in behavior can occur in a variety of mental disorders, such as Schizophrenia, Psychogenic Amnesia, and Psychogenic Fugue. In this case, however, there is no evidence of psychotic symptoms; and there are repeated shifts of both identity and complex behavior patterns, neither of which are present in Psychogenic Amnesia or Fugue. The presence of several distinct personalities, each of which at some time determines the patient's behavior, is characteristic of the rare disorder Multiple Personality.

DSM-III Diagnosis:

Axis I: 300.14 Multiple Personality (p. 259)

Binoculars

31 A 25-year-old male business executive requested psychiatric consultation because of his repeated need to peep at women undressing or engaging in sexual activity. The patient had been apprehended for this activity in the past, and the personnel office at his place of work had found out about it. He had been advised that treatment of his problem was mandatory and that he would lose his job if the behavior was repeated. The patient did not seek professional assistance and continued to engage in voyeuristic activity. On one occasion, however, he was almost caught again, and at that point sought consultation.

The patient was an articulate, handsome man who had no difficulty attracting sexual partners. He dated frequently and had sexual intercourse once or twice a week with a variety of partners. In addition, however, he was frequently drawn to certain types of situations he found uniquely arousing. He owned a pair of high-powered binoculars and used these to peep into neighboring apartments. Sometimes he was rewarded for his efforts, but more frequently was not. He would then leave his apartment and go to rooftops of large apartment buildings, where he would search with his binoculars until he found a woman undressing or engaging in sexual activity. He had no desire to enter the apartments he peeped into, and he denied experiencing impulses to rape. If he found a scene in which he could watch a woman undressing or engaging in sexual activity, he would masturbate to orgasm while watching, or immediately afterward, and then return home. He experienced the voyeuristic situation, in its entirety, as uniquely pleasureful, despite the fact that he sometimes encountered potentially hazardous situations. On more than one occasion he had nearly been apprehended by building staff or police, who took him to be a potential burglar or assailant; once he had been chased from a "lovers' lane" by an irate man wielding a tire iron; another time he was discovered peeping into a bedroom window in a rural area and barely escaped being shot.

The patient had been reared in a family that included three older sisters. His father was puritanical, religious, and generally punitive in his attitudes toward the patient. The patient's mother was allegedly warm, expressive, and flirtatious toward men, but not toward the patient. He felt he was his mother's favorite child and wondered whether he would ever fall in love with a woman who measured up to her. By the time of the consultation, he had never been in love, nor had he experienced a durable, deep attachment to a woman.

The patient's family was sexually puritanical. Family members did not disrobe in front of each other, for example; and the parents avoided open displays of activity that could be interpreted as erotic by the children. The patient recalled, between the ages of seven and ten, watching his mother and sisters undress "as much as possible"; but this activity involved seeing only as much as possible within the limits of ordinary family decorum.

The patient had begun "peeping," along with many other boys, at the age of ten, while at summer camp; and he was unable to explain why this particular stimulus subsequently had a unique appeal for him whereas other boys seemed to become progressively interested in sexual intercourse rather than peeping. He had used binoculars to search for erotically stimulating scenes since he was 11, but did not leave his home to do so until age 17.

The patient noticed some relationship between presumed psychological stress and his voyeuristic activity; for example, at times of major life change, such as moving out of his parents' home or finishing a college semester, the activity increased. He was not, however, aware of any relationship between anxiety about having sexual intercourse and the desire to engage in voyeuristic activity. He felt that anxiety was often present *in* the voyeuristic situation, but that it was only a fear of being apprehended. He felt no guilt or shame about his voyeurism and considered it harmless. He was concerned, however, that he might one day go to jail unless he altered his sexual behavior, and had sought help for that reason.

Discussion of Binoculars

There is no question that this patient repeatedly engages in voyeuristic activities for the purpose of achieving sexual excitement. According to DSM-III, when this is a "repeatedly preferred or exclusive method of achieving sexual excitement," the diagnosis of Voyeurism is made. In this case we are told that the patient also enjoys ordinary heterosexual intercourse, so what does "prefer" mean? Perhaps the real question is not whether his problem behavior is repeatedly preferred or exclusive, but whether the behavior itself represents a significant deviation from a normative concept of sexuality.

Voyeurism, because it always involves observing an unsuspecting "victim," violates the normative concept that in human sexuality there should be mutual consent. Whether or not this patient sometimes functions "normally," clearly situations involving a lack of mutual consent play a significant role in his sexual functioning; and it is this that would lead most clinicians to want to make a diagnosis of Voyeurism. On the other hand, no clinician would consider making a diagnosis of Voyeurism of someone who occasionally was sexually aroused by observing an unsuspecting neighbor disrobe or by watching pornography, in which the actors pretend that they are being observed unaware. Obviously, there will be cases (this is not one of them) in which clinical judgment will be required in determining how significant a role the deviant behavior plays in the person's sex life.

We make the diagnosis of Voyeurism in this case using the DSM-III criteria as guidelines and recognizing their intent rather than their literal interpretation.

DSM-III Diagnosis:

Axis I: 302.82 Voyeurism (p. 273)

Blood Is Thicker Than Water

32 The patient is a 34-year-old single man who lives with his mother and works as a draftsman. He presents with feelings of unhappiness after breaking up with his girl friend. His mother had disapproved of their marriage plans, ostensibly because the woman was of a different religion. The patient felt trapped and forced to choose between his mother and girl friend; and since "blood is thicker than water," he had decided not to go against his mother's wishes. Nonetheless, he is angry at himself and at her and believes that she will never let him marry and is possessively hanging on to him. His mother "wears the pants" in the family and is a strongly domineering woman who is used to getting her way. The patient is afraid of her and criticizes himself for being weak, but also admires his mother and respects her judgment — "Maybe Carol wasn't right for me after all." The patient alternates between resentment and a "Mother knows best" attitude. He feels that his own judgment is poor.

The patient works at a job several grades below his education and talent. On several occasions he has turned down promotions because he didn't want the responsibility of having to supervise other people or make independent decisions. He has worked for the same boss for ten years, gets on well with him, and is, in turn, highly regarded as a dependable and unobtrusive worker. The patient has two very close friends who go back to early childhood. He has lunch with one of them every single workday and feels lost if his friend is sick and misses a day.

The patient is the youngest of four children and the only boy. He was "babied and spoiled" by his mother and elder sisters. He had considerable separation anxiety as a child — difficulty falling asleep unless his mother stayed in the room, mild school refusal, and unbearable homesickness when he occasionally tried "sleepovers." As a child he was teased by other boys because of his lack of assertiveness and was often called a baby. He has lived at home his whole life except for one year of college (he returned because of homesickness). His heterosexual adjustment has been normal except for his inability to leave his mother in favor of another woman.

Discussion of Blood Is Thicker Than Water

This patient has allowed his mother to make the important decision as to whether he should marry his girl friend, and this seems to be merely one instance of a pattern of subordinating his own needs and wishes to those of his domineering mother. At work he demonstrates lack of confidence and reluctance to rely on his own judgment and abilities by avoiding promotions and working below his potential. These personality traits are severe enough to interfere significantly with his social and occupational functioning and therefore justify the diagnosis Dependent Personality Disorder.

DSM-III Diagnosis:

Axis II: 301.60 Dependent Personality Disorder (p. 325)

Professor

33 A 33-year-old college professor presented with the complaint that he had never been able to ejaculate while making love. He had no trouble in attaining and maintaining an erection and no difficulties in stimulating his partner to her orgasm, but he could never be stimulated himself to ejaculation and would finally give up in boredom. He has always been able to reach ejaculation by masturbation, which he does about twice a week; but he has never been willing to allow a partner to masturbate him to orgasm. Previously he resisted all of his girl friend's attempts to persuade him to seek medical or psychological help, as he felt that intravaginal ejaculation was unimportant unless one wanted children.

The patient's current relationship is in jeopardy because his girl friend is eager to marry and have children. He has never wanted to have children and is reluctant to become a father, but the pressures from his current girl friend have forced him to seek therapy. Throughout the interview his attitude toward the problem is one of distance and disdain. He describes the problem as though he were a neutral observer, with little apparent feeling.

Discussion of Professor

This professor has an unusual sexual problem. He is able to have an erection without any difficulty, has no problem in sustaining the erection during intercourse (as would be the case in Inhibited Sexual Excitement), but is unable to have an orgasm during intercourse. Significantly, he has no trouble having an orgasm when he masturbates, which excludes the possibility that a physical disorder accounts for the problem. Persistent inhibition of the male orgasm phase not caused by an organic factor is called Inhibited Male Orgasm.

There is a suggestion of coldness and hyperintellectualization, traits often present in individuals with this disorder. Perhaps on the basis of more information a diagnosis of Compulsive Personality Disorder might also be warranted.

DSM-III Diagnosis:

Axis I: 302.74 Inhibited Male Orgasm (p. 280)

Factory Foreman

34 A 51-year-old factory foreman began to have difficulty remembering details necessary for performing his job. At home he was having problems keeping accurate financial records and, on several occasions, forgot to pay bills. It became increasingly difficult for him to function properly at work, and eventually he was forced to retire. Intellectual deterioration continued, and behavioral problems appeared. He became extremely stubborn and, if thwarted, would become verbally and physically abusive.

When seen by a neurologic consultant after five years of illness, the patient was fully alert and cooperative, but obviously anxious and fidgety. He thought he was at his place of employment and the year was "1960 or something" (it was actually 1979). He could not remember any one of six objects after an interval of ten minutes, even when prompted by multiple-choice answers. He knew his birthplace and high school, but not the names of his parents or siblings. He said he had two children, whereas in fact he had only one. Although he insisted he was still working, he could not describe his job. He did not know the current President and could not explain the resignation of President Nixon or remember the assassination of President Kennedy. His speech was well-articulated, but vague and circuitous, with many empty, meaningless phrases. He had difficulty naming common objects and repeating sentences. He could not do even the simplest arithmetic calculations. He could not write a proper sentence, copy a two- or three-dimensional figure, or draw a house. He interpreted proverbs concretely and had difficulty finding similarities between related objects.

An elementary neurologic examination revealed nothing abnormal. All laboratory studies were normal, including B-12, folate, T4 levels, and serology; but a computerized tomography (CT) scan showed marked cortical atrophy.

Discussion of Factory Foreman

The difficulty with memory, abstract thinking (difficulty finding similarities between related objects), and other higher cortical functions (e.g., inability to name common objects, to do arithmetic calculations, or copy a figure), all severe enough to interfere with social and occupational functioning and occurring in a clear state of consciousness, indicates a Dementia.

The insidious onset with a uniformly progressive deteriorating course, the absence of focal neurological signs, the absence of a history of trauma or stroke, the normal blood tests, and the cortical atrophy evident from the CT scan add up to the diagnosis of Primary Degenerative Dementia. In the past this would have been called Presenile Dementia, but the evidence indicates that in most cases the underlying brain disease is the same whether the onset is before or after age 65. It is only for the sake of compatibility with other classification systems that the subclassification Presenile Onset is used.

DSM-III Diagnosis:

Axis I: **290.10 Primary Degenerative Dementia, Presenile Onset (p. 126)**

Too Far from Home

35 This 32-year-old, white, married housewife comes to the clinic because of fear of losing her balance and either falling or fainting. (She has, in fact, never fallen or fainted.) The current difficulties began one year ago, shortly after she and her family moved away from her mother's neighborhood. Her husband went into his own business, which kept him away from home a lot. Before the move she could walk to her mother's and sister's houses. Now she lives so far from them that she knows they can't come over immediately if she needs them. At first she avoided going out of her new house, but she eventually could go alone to small neighborhood stores and supermarkets if they were not crowded. Two months ago a man of 41, who was her friend, died of a brain cyst. Since then she has been continuously anxious, unable to go out, and comfortable at home only when she is with her husband.

The patient's present condition is a recurrence of symptoms she first experienced 12 years ago, immediately after her marriage. She began to fear losing her balance and falling. The more frightened she became, the more unsteady she felt. She became unable to go anywhere. She remembers thinking, "Now that I don't want to die, God is going to answer my childhood prayers, and I will die." At that time she consulted an internist, who was unable to help her; then a psychiatrist, whom she saw three times, with no improvement; and finally, a hypnotist. After hypnosis, her symptoms subsided.

She denies ever having such symptoms as palpitations or chest pain, sweating, or difficulty breathing.

Discussion of Too Far from Home

This woman is terrified of leaving her house because of a fear that she may fall or faint. This fear has kept her housebound, and she is also afraid of being alone, even at home. This marked constriction of activity from a fear of being alone is Agoraphobia.

Ordinarily this disorder is preceded by panic attacks, which the patient associates with being in public places and, finally, with leaving his or her own home. More rarely, as in this case, there is no such history. Therefore, the diagnosis is Agoraphobia without Panic Attacks.

DSM-III Diagnosis:

Axis I: 300.22 Agoraphobia without Panic Attacks (p. 227)

Emilio

36 Emilio is a 40-year-old man who looks ten years younger. He is brought to the hospital, his 12th hospitalization, by his mother because she is afraid of him. He is dressed in a ragged overcoat, bedroom slippers, and a baseball cap and wears several medals around his neck. His affect ranges from anger at his mother — "She feeds me shit . . . what comes out of other people's rectums" — to a giggling, obsequious seductiveness toward the interviewer. His speech and manner have a childlike quality, and he walks with a mincing step and exaggerated hip movements. His mother reports that he stopped taking his medication about a month ago and has since begun to hear voices and to look and act more bizarrely. When asked what he has been doing, he says "eating wires and lighting fires." His spontaneous speech is often incoherent and marked by frequent rhyming and clang associations.

Emilio's first hospitalization occurred after he dropped out of school at 16, and since that time he has never been able to attend school or hold a job. He lives with his elderly mother, but sometimes disappears for several months at a time, and is eventually picked up by the police as he wanders in the street. There is no known history of drug or alcohol abuse.

Discussion of Emilio

The combination of a chronic illness with marked incoherence, inappropriate affect, auditory hallucinations, and bizarre behavior leaves little doubt that the diagnosis is Chronic Schizophrenia, with an acute exacerbation. The absence of systematized delusions or prominent catatonic symptoms and the presence of the disorganization of speech and silly affect indicate the Disorganized Type.

DSM-III Diagnosis:

Axis I: 295.14 Schizophrenia, Disorganized Type, Chronic with Acute Exacerbation (p. 188)

Unrecognized Genius

37 A 25-year-old, single, graduate student complains to his psychoanalyst of difficulty completing his Ph.D. in English Literature and expresses concerns about his relationships with women. He believes that his thesis topic may profoundly increase the level of understanding in his discipline and make him famous, but so far he has not been able to get past the third chapter. His mentor does not seem sufficiently impressed with his ideas, and the patient is furious at him, but also self-doubting and ashamed. He blames his mentor for his lack of progress, and thinks that he deserves more help with his grand idea, that his mentor should help with some of the research. The patient brags about his creativity and complains that other people are "jealous" of his insight. He is very envious of students who are moving along faster than he and regards them as "dull drones and ass-kissers." He prides himself on the brilliance of his class participation and imagines someday becoming a great professor.

He becomes rapidly infatuated with women and has powerful and persistent fantasies about each new woman he meets, but after several experiences of sexual intercourse feels disappointed and finds them dumb, clinging, and physically repugnant. He has many "friends," but they turn over quickly, and no one relationship lasts very long. People get tired of his continual self-promotion and lack of consideration of them. For example, he was lonely at Christmas and insisted that his best friend stay in town rather than visit his family. The friend refused, criticizing the patient's self-centeredness; and the patient, enraged, decided never to see this friend again.

Discussion of Unrecognized Genius

This patient's narcissistic personality traits are clear: grandiosity about the importance of his thesis, entitlement in expecting his mentor to do some of his work, and overidealization and devaluation of women. Because these traits significantly interfere both with his academic achievement and with friendships and heterosexual relations, a diagnosis of Narcissistic Personality Disorder is appropriate.

Although it is not specifically stated that these traits are of long duration, this is a reasonable assumption. (There is no description in the literature of episodic narcissism!)

DSM-III Diagnosis:

Axis II: 301.81 Narcissistic Personality Disorder (p. 317)

Emphysema

38 A 50-year-old mother of two was admitted to the hospital for evaluation of a suspicious-looking density on her chest X-ray. Her internist had recently urged her to give up or reduce her 30-year, 2-pack-a-day cigarette habit because of early signs of emphysema, but she continued to smoke. She worked in a women's clothing store of which she was co-owner, and claimed that she would not be able to "keep up the pace" if she did not have a cigarette in her hand most of the day. The psychiatric consultant was asked to speak with her, since she continued chain smoking in her hospital room. She admitted that she was aware of the "destructive" aspects of her behavior, but said that she was "too nervous" in the hospital to give up the habit.

Discussion of Emphysema

Not all heavy cigarette smoking is regarded as evidence of a mental disorder in DSM-III. However, evidence of tobacco withdrawal, unsuccessful attempts to stop smoking, or (as in this case) smoking despite the knowledge that one has a serious physical disorder that is exacerbated by tobacco use is evidence of the mental disorder Tobacco Dependence. Although purists might argue that this patient's Tobacco Dependence began only when she was told that she had emphysema and should stop smoking, we prefer to code the course of her illness as Continuous, since very likely she had been aware of the symptoms of emphysema and the contribution of smoking to those symptoms for quite some time.

The reason for the psychiatric referral was this woman's noncompliance with the medical recommendation to stop smoking. Her noncompliance is symptomatic of her Tobacco Dependence. Therefore, it would not be appropriate to use the V code for Noncompliance with Medical Treatment, as V codes are used only for conditions *not* attributable to a mental disorder.

DSM-III Diagnosis:

Axis I: 305.11 Tobacco Dependence, Continuous (p. 178)

Lovely Rita

39 A 36-year-old London meter maid was referred for psychiatric examination by her solicitor. Six months previously, moments after she had written a ticket and placed it on the windshield of an illegally parked car, a man came dashing out of a barbershop, ran up to her, swearing and shaking his fist, swung, and hit her in the jaw with enough force to knock her down. A fellow-worker came to her aid and summoned the police, who caught the man a few blocks away and placed him under arrest.

The patient was taken to the hospital, where a hairline fracture of the jaw was diagnosed by X-ray. The fracture did not require that her jaw be wired, but the patient was placed on a soft diet for four weeks. Several different physicians, including her own, found her physically fit to return to work after one month. The patient, however, complained of severe pain and muscle tension in her neck and back that virtually immobilized her. She spent most of her days sitting in a chair or lying on a bedboard on her bed. She enlisted the services of a solicitor since the Workmen's Compensation Board was cutting off her payments and her employer was threatening her with suspension if she did not return to work.

The patient shuffled slowly and laboriously into the psychiatrist's office and lowered herself with great care into a chair. She was attractively dressed, well made up, and wore a neck brace. She related her story with vivid detail and considerable anger directed at her assailant (whom she repeatedly referred to as that "bloody foreigner"), her employer, and the compensation board. It was as if the incident had occurred yesterday. Regarding her ability to work, she said that she wanted to return to the job, would soon be severely strapped financially, but was physically not up to even the lightest office work.

She denied any previous psychological problems and initially described her childhood and family life as storybook perfect. In subsequent interviews, however, she admitted that as a child she had frequently been beaten by her alcoholic father, and had once suffered a broken arm as a result, and that she had often been locked in a closet for hours at a time as punishment for misbehavior.

Discussion of Lovely Rita

In this case the first question is: Can this woman's pain be entirely accounted for by the nature of her very real physical injury? Evidently, the answer is no, given the extensive assessment by several physicians. The next question is: Is this woman *simply* attempting to get continued financial support from Workman's Compensation so that she will no longer have to earn a living? If the answer to this is yes, this would be an instance of malingering, that is, the voluntary production and presentation of false symptoms in pursuit of a goal that is obviously recognizable. The apparent genuineness of her suffering and her desire to return to work make this unlikely.

This leaves us with the possibility of undiagnosed physical pain or Psychogenic Pain Disorder, a Somatoform Disorder. Our diagnosis, Psychogenic Pain Disorder, is made only when there is positive evidence of the role of psychological factors in the development of the pain, such as a temporal relationship between an environmental stimulus that is related to a psychological conflict and the initiation of the pain. In this case such evidence is the history of the patient's having been physically abused by her father as a child, which probably produced psychological conflict that was revived by the recent assault. This would presumably account for the continuation of the pain beyond what would be accounted for by her injury.

DSM-III Diagnosis:

Axis I: 307.80 Psychogenic Pain Disorder (p. 249)

Forgetful Widow

40 The patient is an 82-year-old widow referred by a friend who contacted a geriatrics team when the patient no longer seemed able to take care of her apartment or her personal hygiene. Over the previous five years she had been hospitalized for three minor strokes, from which she recovered except for some slurred speech and right-sided weakness. Over the past year her friend had noticed an apathetic attitude toward her previously meticulously maintained apartment, some loss of memory about things such as having gone shopping, having changed clothes, and having bathed, and certain lapses in judgment. When visited by the team in her home, the patient was cooperative, cheerful, and denied any problems, but showed evidence of recent memory loss, disorientation to time, and concrete interpretation of proverbs.

Discussion of Forgetful Widow

The salient features of this case are: loss of intellectual abilities of sufficient severity to interfere with functioning (no longer able to maintain her apartment or personal hygiene), loss of memory, impaired abstract thinking (concrete interpretation of proverbs), personality change (apathetic attitude toward her apartment), and impaired judgment, all occurring in a clear state of consciousness.

Although memory disturbance is prominent, this is not an Amnestic Syndrome, but rather a more global disturbance, a Dementia.

In the absence of evidence for an etiology other than those associated with aging (such as a neoplasm or endocrine disturbance), the differential is between Primary Degenerative Dementia and Multi-infarct Dementia. The latter is most likely because of the stepwise deterioration with focal neurological signs that suggest that the strokes were the cause of the Dementia. The absence of either delirium, delusions, or depression, often associated with Dementia, is noted in the fifth digit as Uncomplicated.

In the elderly, apathy, loss of interest, and apparent memory loss may indicate a major depressive episode. However, in this case the patient's cheerful mood rules this out.

DSM-III Diagnosis:

Axis I: **290.40 Multi-infarct Dementia, Uncomplicated (p. 128)**

Writer's Block

41 A 19-year-old male college sophomore was referred to a West Coast mental health service because of difficulties completing school assignments. He apparently is able to complete a first paragraph that is well written and of high quality, but is unable to go further, and consequently is now in danger of flunking two or three of his courses. He has also had difficulty getting to class because he oversleeps. He states that the difficulty began about two years ago and created problems for him during his freshman year, but he somehow managed to get his papers done and to pass his courses.

The patient attended a private secondary school and did well there until his senior year, when he began to have academic difficulties after his mother had a recurrence of cancer and died. He has no conflict about being in college at this time and very much wants to be able to overcome his difficulty and continue his education toward an eventual career in law.

Discussion of Writer's Block

This disturbance in academic functioning is clinically significant because of its persistence and potentially damaging effect on the patient's career. On the basis of the limited information available, however, the disturbance does not meet the criteria for any other specific mental disorder. Therefore, it is classified in the residual category of Adjustment Disorder with Academic Inhibition.

Most cases of work (or academic) inhibition are chronic manifestations of a Personality Disorder, usually Compulsive Personality Disorder. But in this case, the disturbance apparently marked a sudden change in functioning in response to a psychosocial stressor, and there is no information to support a diagnosis of a Personality Disorder.

There is also the possibility that with more time and information available, a diagnosis of Depressive Disorder would be warranted; but on the basis of the initial evaluation, Adjustment Disorder seems appropriate.

DSM-III Diagnosis:

Axis I: **309.23 Adjustment Disorder with Academic Inhibition (p. 300)**

Antique Dealer

42 An internist requested consultation on a 59-year-old antique dealer who had been admitted to the hospital for workup of severe hypertension. On the third hospital day he appeared "depressed." The consultant found the patient dozing in his bed; it was apparent that he had spilled some of his lunch on the sheets. The patient was difficult to arouse; and although he responded to his name and looked at the consultant, he did not appear to understand simple questions such as where he was or what the date was. He mumbled incoherently and, when tested, had obvious weakness in his right arm and leg. A neurological consultation confirmed the diagnosis of a stroke.

Discussion of Antique Dealer

Clouding of consciousness (dozing in bed and being difficult to arouse), reduced capacity to sustain attention (did not appear to understand simple questions), and disorientation, in the presence of evidence of an organic etiology (right-sided weakness) indicate an Organic Brain Syndrome, Delirium. Although in the past the term *delirium* had the connotation of an agitated or excited confusional state, in DSM-III it is more broadly defined to include the rapid development of clouding of consciousness, disorientation, and memory impairment, even when not associated with psychomotor agitation (as in this case).

Although neurologists would generally agree that technically this patient had a Delirium when he was seen by the psychiatric consultant, they would very likely not note it in their own diagnostic formulation, as they would focus diagnostically on the etiological process, the cerebrovascular accident (stroke).

In a DSM-III diagnosis the Delirium is coded according to Section 2 of the Organic Mental Disorders, since the etiology (cerebrovascular accident) is outside the mental disorders section of the ICD-9-CM classification. The physical disorder (etiology) is noted on Axis III.

DSM-III Diagnosis:

Axis I: 293.00 Delirium (p. 107)
Axis III: Cerebrovascular accident

Bookkeeper

43 A 27-year-old, single, male bookkeeper was referred to a consulting psychologist because of a recent upsurge in anxiety that seemed to begin when a group of new employees were assigned to his office section. He feared that he was going to be fired, though his work was always highly commended. A clique had recently formed in the office and, though very much wanting to be accepted into this "in group," the patient hesitated to join them unless explicitly asked to do so. Moreover, he "knew he had nothing to offer them" and thought that he would ultimately be rejected anyway.

The patient spoke of himself as having always been a shy, fearful, quiet boy. Although he had two "good friends" whom he continued to see occasionally, he was characterized by fellow workers as a loner, a nice young man who usually did his work efficiently, but on his own. They noted that he always ate by himself in the company cafeteria and never joined in the "horsing around."

Discussion of Bookkeeper

The presenting symptons of anxiety suggest an Anxiety Disorder. However, the predominant disturbance does not appear to be symptoms of anxiety, but rather a long-standing pattern of difficulty in relating to others because of low self-esteem and anticipation of rejection. These characteristics, which are obviously sufficiently severe to interfere with social functioning, indicate a personality disorder. The social isolation does not stem from a basic emotional coldness and indifference to others, such as would be seen in Schizoid Personality Disorder; the strong desire for affection and acceptance indicate Avoidant Personality Disorder.

A person with a personality disorder can have a superimposed adjustment disorder, but only if the current episode includes new clinical features not characteristic of his or her personality. There is no evidence in this case that the anxiety is qualitatively different from that which the patient has always experienced in social situations—it is just more intense. Therefore, an additional diagnosis of Adjustment Disorder with Anxious Mood is not made. Some clinicians might consider the possibility of a diagnosis of a Social Phobia because of the anxiety in social situations; but in this case it is relationships in general, rather than a specific situation, such as public speaking, that are avoided.

DSM-III Diagnosis:

Axis II: 301.82 Avoidant Personality Disorder (p. 324)

The Bully

44 J.P. is a muscular 24-year-old man who presented himself to the admitting office of a state hospital. He told the admitting physician that he had taken 30 200-mg tablets of Thorazine in the bus on the way over to the hospital. After receiving medical treatment for the "suicide attempt," he was transferred to the inpatient ward.

On mental-status examination the patient told a fantastic story about his father's being a famous surgeon who had a patient die in surgery and whose husband then killed his father. J.P. then stalked his father's murderer several thousand miles across the United States and he found him, but was prevented from killing him at the last moment by the timely arrival of his 94-year-old grandmother. He also related several other intriguing stories involving his $14,000 sports car, which had a 12-cylinder diesel engine, and about his children, two sets of identical triplets. All these stories had a grandiose tinge, and none of them could be confirmed. The patient claimed that he was hearing voices, as on the TV or in a dream. He answered affirmatively to questions about thought control, thought broadcasting, and other Schneiderian first-rank symptoms; he also claimed depression. He was oriented and alert and had a good range of information except that he kept insisting that it was the Germans (not the Russians) who had invaded Afghanistan. There was no evidence of any associated features of mania or depression, and the patient did not seem either elated, depressed, or irritable when he related these stories.

It was observed on the ward that the patient bullied the other patients and took food and cigarettes from them. He was very reluctant to be discharged, and whenever the subject of his discharge was brought up, he renewed his complaints about "suicidal thoughts" and "hearing voices." It was the opinion of the ward staff that the patient was not truly psychotic, but merely feigned his symptoms whenever the subject of disposition was brought up. They thought that he wanted to remain in the hospital primarily so that he could bully the other patients and be a "big man" on the ward.

Discussion of The Bully

Although this patient would have us believe that he is psychotic, his story, almost from the start, seems to conform to no recognizable psychotic syndrome. That his symptoms are not genuine is confirmed by the observation of the ward staff that he seemed to feign his symptoms whenever the subject of disposition was brought up.

Why does this fellow try so hard to act crazy? His motivation is not to achieve some understandable goal, such as, for instance, avoiding the draft, as would be the case in Malingering; this goal becomes understandable only with knowledge of his individual psychology (the suggestion that he derives satisfaction from being the "big man" on the ward). The diagnosis is, therefore, Factitious Disorder with Psychological Symptoms.

DSM-III Diagnosis:

Axis I: 300.16 Factitious Disorder with Psychological Symptoms
(p. 287)

Toy Designer

45 A 45-year-old toy designer was admitted to the hospital following a series of suicidal gestures culminating in an attempt to strangle himself with a piece of wire. Four months before admission his family had observed that he was becoming depressed: when at home he spent long periods sitting in a chair, he slept more than usual, and he had given up his habits of reading the evening paper and puttering around the house. Within a month he was unable to get out of bed each morning to go to work. He expressed considerable guilt, but could not make up his mind to seek help until forced to do so by his family. He had not responded to two months of outpatient antidepressant drug therapy, and had made several half-hearted attempts to cut his wrists before the serious attempt that precipitated the admission.

Physical examination revealed signs of increased intracranial pressure, and a computerized tomography (CT) scan showed a large frontal-lobe tumor.

Discussion of Toy Designer

Depressed mood, suicidal gestures, increased sleep, loss of interest, and guilt all suggest a major depressive episode. Although the patient's symptoms are identical with those seen in a major depressive episode, it is reasonable to infer that the disturbance is caused by the frontal-lobe tumor; thus, the diagnosis is Organic Affective Syndrome, from Section 2 of the Organic Mental Disorders.

Some clinicians might prefer to consider this diagnosis "provisional," pending the results of surgery. If the depression lifts after removal of the brain tumor, the diagnosis of an Organic Affective Syndrome would be supported. If the depression persists following surgery, the diagnosis would remain equivocal, since there would be no way to definitely rule out a Major Depression that developed coincidentally.

The frontal-lobe tumor, of course, is noted on Axis III.

(Minor point: It is helpful to indicate in parentheses that the Organic Affective Syndrome, in this case, was "depressed.")

DSM-III Diagnosis:

Axis I: **293.83 Organic Affective Syndrome (Depressed) (p. 118)**
Axis III: **Frontal-lobe tumor**

Former Toy Designer

46 A 47-year-old former toy designer was evaluated during a routine two-year postneurosurgical follow-up. Two years previously he had been severely depressed and had made a suicide attempt. A frontal-lobe tumor had been diagnosed and removed. According to the patient's wife, the depression had lifted after the surgery, but he had been uninterested in returning to work since that time.

Although the patient makes few complaints, his wife describes him as no longer depressed, but lacking his former enthusiasm and "spark." In addition, he seems to have trouble concentrating while reading the paper.

Discussion of Former Toy Designer

This is a follow-up of case #45. The predominant disturbance is a marked change in personality, as manifested by the patient's apathy and indifference. Personality changes are common in Dementia; but in this patient, despite some difficulty in concentrating, there is no evidence of a global deterioration in intellectual functioning. Thus, the diagnosis Organic Personality Syndrome, from Section 2 of the Organic Mental Disorders, is appropriate.

The physical condition, postsurgical removal of the frontal-lobe tumor, is noted on Axis III.

DSM-III Diagnosis:

Axis I: 310.10 Organic Personality Syndrome (p. 119)
Axis III: Postsurgical removal of frontal-lobe tumor

Charles

47 A 25-year-old patient, who called himself Charles, requested a "sex change operation." He had for three years lived socially and been employed as a man. For the last two of these years he had been the housemate, economic provider, and husband-equivalent of a bisexual woman who had fled from a bad marriage. Her two young children regarded Charles as their stepfather, and there was a strong affectionate bond between them.

In social appearance the patient passed as a not very virile man whose sexual development in puberty might be conjectured to have been extremely delayed or hormonally deficient. His voice was pitched low, but not baritone. His shirt and jacket were bulky and successfully camouflaged tightly bound, flattened breasts. A strap-on penis produced a masculine-looking bulge in the pants; it was so constructed that, in case of social necessity, it could be used as a urinary conduit in the standing position. Without success the patient had tried to obtain a mastectomy so that in summer he could wear only a T-shirt while working outdoors as a heavy construction machine operator. He had also been unsuccessful in trying to get a prescription for testosterone, to produce male secondary sex characteristics and suppress menses. The patient wanted a hysterectomy and oophorectomy, and as a long-term goal looked forward to obtaining a successful phalloplasty.

The history was straightforward in its account of progressive recognition in adolescence of being able to fall in love only with a woman, following a tomboyish childhood that had finally consolidated into the transsexual role and identity.

Physical examination revealed normal female anatomy, which the patient found personally repulsive, incongruous, and a source of continual distress. The endocrine laboratory results were within normal limits for a female.

Discussion of Charles

The diagnosis of Transsexualism is certainly suggested by the first sentence, but this case also demonstrates the other features of this disorder that are necessary to make the diagnosis: subjective distress about one's anatomic sex, living as a member of the opposite sex for a period of time, and no evidence of physical intersex, genetic abnormality, or another mental disorder that would account for the disturbance.

The fifth-digit coding refers to the predominant prior sexual history, in this case relationships with persons of the same anatomic sex. This is coded as "homosexual," although such individuals, because of their gender identity, do not perceive it as such.

DSM-III Diagnosis:

Axis I: 302.52 Transsexualism, with homosexual history (p. 263)

Useful Work

48 An 85-year-old man is seen by a social worker at a senior citizens' center for evaluation of health-care needs for himself and his bedridden wife. He is apparently healthy, with no evidence of impairment in thinking or memory. He has been caring for his wife, but has been reluctantly persuaded to seek help because her condition has deteriorated and his strength and energy have decreased with age.

A history is obtained from the subject and his daughter. He has never been treated for mental illness, and in fact has always claimed to be "immune to psychological problems" and to act only on the basis of "rational" thought. He had a moderately successful career as a lawyer and businessman. He has been married for 60 years, and his wife is the only person for whom he has ever expressed tender feelings, and is probably the only person he has ever trusted. He has always been extremely careful about revealing anything of himself to others, assuming that they are out to take something away from him. He refuses obviously sincere offers of help from acquaintances because he suspects their motives. He never reveals his identity to a caller without first questioning him as to the nature of his business. Throughout his life there have been numerous occasions on which he has displayed his exaggerated suspiciousness, sometimes of almost delusional proportions (e.g., storing letters from a client in a secret safe deposit box so that he could use them as evidence in the event that the client attempted to sue him for mismanagement of an estate).

He has always involved himself in "useful work" during his waking hours, and claims never to have time for play, even during the 20 years he has been retired. He spends many hours monitoring his stock market investments, and has had altercations with his broker when he has suspected that an error on a monthly statement was evidence of the broker's attempt to cover up some fraudulent deal.

Discussion of Useful Work

This gentleman demonstrates pervasive and unwarranted suspiciousness (assuming others are out to take something from him; first questioning callers before giving his identity), readiness to counterattack (storing evidence against possible enemies), inability to relax (never has time for play), and restricted affectivity (pride in being "rational"). These lifelong features, in the absence of any evidence of persistent persecutory delusions or any other psychotic symptoms, characterize Paranoid Personality Disorder.

This case also illustrates the ego-syntonic nature of the disturbance. For this reason, treatment is rarely sought.

This man has many schizoid features, but there is no mention of indifference to the feelings of others, a requirement for a diagnosis of Schizoid Personality Disorder. Since these features, such as social isolation and emotional coldness, are also characteristic of Paranoid Personality Disorder, there is nothing gained by also listing schizoid personality traits.

DSM-III Diagnosis:

Axis II: 301.00 Paranoid Personality Disorder (p. 309)

The Mayor's Friend

49 A 33-year-old advertising executive was picked up by police at 4:00 A.M. following a traffic accident in which the car he was driving struck a parked vehicle. The police observed him to be extremely talkative and agitated and brought him to the emergency room for evaluation. There he was noted to be sweaty and to have a rapid pulse and widely dilated pupils. At first he threatened to call his lawyer, "who is a friend of the Mayor"; but later he admitted that he had been using cocaine at a local disco.

Discussion of The Mayor's Friend

The poor judgment (reckless driving), loquacity, irritability, agitation, and possible grandiosity (lawyer is a friend of the Mayor) all suggest a manic episode. The physical findings (sweaty, rapid pulse, dilated pupils), however, raise the question of a drug intoxication, which in this case was confirmed by the admission of recent use of cocaine. This clinical picture is quite characteristic of intoxication with either an amphetamine or cocaine.

DSM-III acknowledges that not all use of drugs to alter mood or behavior is necessarily pathological. In this case the clear presence of maladaptive behavioral effects (poor judgment leading to a traffic accident) distinguishes the disorder from mere recreational drug use.

DSM-III Diagnosis:

Axis I: 305.60 Cocaine Intoxication (p. 146)

Grumpy

50 A 36-year-old electrical engineer was "dragged" to a marital therapist by his wife because of his unwillingness to join in family activities, failure to take an interest in his children, lack of affection, and disinterest in sex. Few demands of an interpersonal nature were made of him on his job; he was characterized by some of his associates as reticent and shy, and by others, as cold and aloof.

The patient's history revealed long-standing social indifference, with only an occasional and brief friendship here and there and little emotional responsivity. He recalled being indifferent to the idea of marriage, but went along with it to please his parents. His wife reported making repeated efforts to arrange situations that might be of potential interest to him, but these had proved to be of no avail, and seemed to make the patient "grumpy" and antagonistic.

Discussion of Grumpy

A personality disorder is indicated by the long history of a maladaptive pattern of relating to others that is sufficiently severe to cause significant impairment in social functioning. As is frequently the case with individuals with personality disorders, this patient does not regard his behavior as a problem. It is his effect on his wife that prompts the evaluation.

In the case of an individual with a personality disorder characterized by chronic social isolation, the differential diagnosis is between Schizoid, Schizotypal, and Avoidant Personality Disorders. In this case there are none of the eccentricities associated with Schizotypal Personality Disorder and no strong desire for social relations, which is required for a diagnosis of Avoidant Personality. The patient's emotional coldness and aloofness, indifference to others, and lack of close friends indicate a diagnosis of Schizoid Personality Disorder.

Despite the reference to his being "grumpy" and emotionally unresponsive, there is no complaint of depressed mood or a loss of interest or pleasure to support an additional diagnosis of Dysthymic Disorder.

DSM-III Diagnosis:

Axis II: 301.20 Schizoid Personality Disorder (p. 311)

Form Examiner

51 A 51-year-old single woman was brought to the hospital by her elderly parents — "My parents think I need to be here, but I'm not sick." About a year before admission the patient had begun seeing her family physician for painful breasts, and was receiving male hormone injections. She began to believe that her doctor was maliciously trying to change her into a man, and wrote several letters to him complaining of this.

Shortly thereafter, she began to believe that her stepfather and certain government officials were involved in a plan to get her to give up a piece of land she owned in the country. She also accused her stepfather of telling various garages to perform improper repairs on her car and to overcharge her, as a means of harassment. She accused the neighbors of putting substances in her water that damaged the trees and grass. Drinking this water, she believed, caused her and her pets to have problems with receding gums. She wrote numerous letters to public officials complaining of these events, and sent soil and water samples off to the agriculture department to be tested. Yet all the while she worked efficiently at her job examining real-estate tax forms.

She had no previous contact with mental health professionals. The mental status examination revealed no hallucinations, incoherence, or loosening of associations.

Discussion of Form Examiner

Persecutory delusions are the central feature of this illness. In the absence of evidence of a known organic factor, an affective disturbance, or hallucinations, incoherence, or loosening of associations, a diagnosis of a Paranoid Disorder is made.

In DSM-III the diagnosis of Paranoia is used for any Paranoid Disorder of more than six months' duration, even though historically the term has been used in a more limited sense to describe an intricate and elaborate chronic paranoid system that is based on misinterpretation of an actual event.

As is characteristic of a Paranoid Disorder, this woman's emotion and behavior are appropriate to the content of the delusional system.

DSM-III Diagnosis:

Axis I: 297.10 Paranoia (p. 197)

Leather

52 A 35-year-old married writer sought consultation because he feared he might kill someone by acting upon sexually sadistic impulses.

The patient has been married for 15 years, and during the last year has had sexual intercourse with his wife approximately every other week. The patient's fantasy life is predominantly homosexual, however, and has been so since age nine. He has felt sexually attracted to males since childhood, but resisted acting on these impulses until mid-adulthood, long after he married. Before that, he felt sexually aroused by homosexual pornography (to which he was exposed from mid-adolescence), particularly by pornography with sadistic content. Although somewhat responsive to heterosexual pornography, his interest in it was much less intense than in homosexual pornography, and he was never excited by heterosexual pornography with sadistic content.

The patient had married for reasons of social propriety, and also because he consciously hoped that initiation into regular heterosexual activity would lead to diminution of his sadistic homosexual impulses. This was not the case, however. These impulses continued periodically to form the basis of the patient's masturbation fantasies. Typical masturbation fantasies were of a man bound, tortured, and killed. Sometimes the men in his fantasies were people he knew, such as colleagues or teachers, and sometimes movie stars or strangers. These fantasies were more intense at certain times than at others. The patient recalls, for example, that he was "wildly" aroused when he read about the activities of a homosexual lust murder as described in a detective magazine. Immediately following this, he masturbated many times a day, always with sadistic homosexual fantasies. After a few weeks, this period of intense arousal subsided, but the patient used the scenario of the events described in this magazine in subsequent masturbation fantasies.

About eight years ago, the patient went to a gay bar with an associate from his office. At the time, he was under much pressure, and his work was being closely supervised by an aggressive, demanding male superior. The patient's associate was openly homosexual, and the patient allegedly went to the bar with him "as a lark." En route to the particular bar they visited, they passed other bars that, the patient's friend told him, were for "the leather crowd who like S and M." The patient had a brief homosexual encounter with someone he picked up in the bar they visited, following which he "put sex out of my mind." Some months later, however, following a week of intense work at his office, the patient impulsively sought out one of the "S and M" bars he had previously walked past. There he met a man who was sexually aroused by being beaten, and the patient engaged in pleasureful sadistic activity with the understanding that the severity of the beating, administered with a belt, was under the control of his masochistic partner. That incident, occurring when he was 28 years old, was the first episode in a series of sexually sadistic activities, ultimately leading to his consultation. About once a month the patient would frequent a homosexual sadomasochistic bar. He would dress in a leather jacket and wear a leather cap. Once in the bar, he would seek out a masochist and engage in a variety of activities, all of which the patient experienced as sexually exciting. The activities included binding the partner with ropes, whipping him, threatening to burn him with cigarettes, forcing him to drink urine, forcing him to "beg for mercy." The patient would experience orgasm during these activities, usually by "forcing" his partner to commit fellatio.

During the year before the consultation, the patient's wife had become progressively dissatisfied with their marriage. She was unaware of her husband's homosexual interest and of his sadistic tendencies. She felt, however, that his sexual involvement with her was desultory, and she wondered whether he had a mistress. She became confronting and also more hostile and demanding toward the patient. He realized that he "needed" his wife, and he did not wish the relationship to end, yet he felt unable to deal with her dissatisfactions directly. He avoided her as much as possible and argued with her when she insisted on talking to him. The patient's work pressures increased and he found, to his dismay, that the intensity of his sadistic impulses also increased.

On one occasion the patient convinced a partner to agree to being burned. Afterward, he felt guilty and ashamed. Just before the consultation, he bound a partner and cut the man's arm. At the sight of blood he experienced a powerful desire to kill his partner. He restrained himself, and alarmed that his sadistic impulses were out of control, sought psychiatric consultation.

Discussion of Leather

This man had first been aroused by sadistic homosexual fantasies in mid-adolescence. The fantasies had persisted, and eventually he had begun to act on them. He married, hoping that marriage would be an antidote to his sadistic homosexual impulses, but found that this was not the case. He now enters treatment fearful that the sadistic impulses may become so strong that he will lose control and kill a sexual partner.

This is a fairly typical history of a person with severe Sexual Sadism.

DSM-III Diagnosis:

Axis I: 302.84 Sexual Sadism (p. 275)

The Ripper's Wife

53 A 27-year-old female was admitted to a neurology service for an evaluation of a movement disorder thought to be tardive dyskinesia. She described a history of four hospitalizations over the past six years and virtually continuous treatment with phenothiazines. Her most recent psychiatric admission had been approximately one year previously. The hospital chart noted that at that time she believed that her husband was a notorious killer then being sought by the police, and that she had marked loosening of associations. Her delusion was based on similarities she saw between newspaper speculations about the personality of the killer and certain characteristics of her husband.

During the present examination the patient acted silly and asked the doctors about their personal lives. She described plans to put her powerful intuitive senses to work by becoming a counselor for other patients like herself. Although her speech was digressive and circumstantial, it was not incoherent.

The patient, once a nursing student, had tried to be a waitress at McDonald's, but got confused by the customers' orders. Her husband both worked and took care of the household.

Discussion of The Ripper's Wife

The patient's previous hospitalization, during which she had prominent psychotic symptoms, delusions, and marked loosening of associations, together with her long history of illness and no mention of an affective disturbance, justifies the diagnosis of Schizophrenia.

Currently the patient has no psychotic symptoms, but does display inappropriate affect ("silly"), eccentric behavior (asking the doctors about their personal lives), and severe impairment in functioning. Some clinicians might consider her plans to become a counselor for other patients evidence of a grandiose delusion; but we regard this as a sign of poor judgment rather than a false belief about a factual matter, and therefore not a delusion. The subtype Residual is specified when a patient with continuing manifestations of Schizophrenia is currently without any prominent psychotic symptoms. The course is noted as Chronic since the patient has been ill for more than one year.

DSM-III Diagnosis:

Axis I: **295.62 Schizophrenia, Residual Type, Chronic (p. 188)**
Axis III: **Movement Disorder (Tardive Dyskinesia?)**

Sleeping Pills

54 A disheveled, 27-year-old man walked into an emergency room shortly after midnight asking to be hospitalized. He stated that he was depressed and would kill himself if not admitted so that he could get a good night's rest. He was observed to be anxious and tremulous, sweaty, and had a rapid pulse. He became angry when the interviewer tried to ask him questions, denied heavy drug use, but said that he would settle for "a few pills" to help him sleep. The intern suspected drug dependence and gave a barbiturate tolerance test, which indicated daily use of 1,200–1,600 mg.

Discussion of Sleeping Pills

The patient came to the emergency room complaining of depression, but it was soon apparent that depression—even if present—was not the most pressing problem. The intern correctly put together the patient's anxiety, tremulousness, rapid pulse, and sweating and entertained the possibility of Barbiturate Withdrawal. Wisely ignoring the patient's denial of a history of heavy drug use, the intern confirmed the diagnosis of Barbiturate Dependence by demonstrating tolerance. The acute physical symptoms were then easily understood as symptoms of Barbiturate Withdrawal.

In listing the diagnoses, Barbiturate Withdrawal is noted first, because it is the focus of clinical attention. The course of the Barbiturate Dependence is Unspecified, since the duration is unknown.

Perhaps the patient was malingering when he complained of depression in order to gain admission to the hospital with the expectation of receiving drugs, but even if this were the case, it would seem unnecessary to record the V code Malingering in addition to the other Axis I conditions. A diagnosis of a depressive disorder is not appropriate because there is no evidence of either a full depressive syndrome or a chronic depressed mood.

DSM-III Diagnosis:

Axis I: 292.00 Barbiturate Withdrawal (p. 141)
          304.10 Barbiturate Dependence, Unspecified (p. 171)

Pushed Around

55 A 26-year-old homosexual presented for treatment with a chief complaint of difficulty having an erection. He has been in a relationship for the past two years with a partner who insists totally on a dominant sexual role and is unwilling to be responsive to the patient's sexual needs. The patient's previous liaison was with a passive individual about three years ago. That relationship terminated when the partner brought home another male who beat up the patient severely enough for him to require a week's hospitalization. The patient then broke up with his partner, left his home with only a few of his belongings, quit his job, and moved to another town. It was in this town that he met his current partner. During the past two years, the new partner has supported the patient financially, the patient taking only occasional part-time jobs. Sexually, he has accepted his passive role, though he wishes he could be more assertive. He has tried to be sexually assertive with some casual acquaintances (without his partner's knowledge), but has discovered that outside of his relationship with his partner, he is unable to achieve an erection. With his partner alone, he is able to achieve an erection, maintain it, and reach climax. Every two or three weeks, however, his partner arranges a "group sex activity" during which the patient finds himself relegated to a totally passive role, and feels he is being used. On these occasions he is unable to achieve an erection or climax, feels himself "used," and finds the experience completely distasteful.

After discussion with the therapist, the patient realizes he has gotten himself into an untenable situation and seeks help to assume a more assertive role in his relationships, both generally and sexually.

Discussion of Pushed Around

The diagnosis of this patient's sexual difficulties is rather straightforward. In certain situations he has complete failure to attain an erection, despite the likelihood that sexual activity is adequate in focus, intensity, and duration. Thus, the diagnosis is Inhibited Sexual Excitement.

The patient himself is apparently aware that his problems are not limited to simple sexual difficulties. He is unable to extricate himself from a relationship in which he is abased and abused. He does not assert himself, allowing his sexual partner to ignore his needs. This suggests a Personality Disorder. Dependent behavior is clearly present in his current relationship, but there is inadequate information to determine whether this is characteristic of his long-term functioning.

We would therefore make a provisional diagnosis of Dependent Personality Disorder.

DSM-III Diagnosis:

Axis I: **302.72 Inhibited Sexual Excitement (p. 279)**
Axis II: **301.60 Dependent Personality Disorder (p. 325) (Provisional)**

Runaway

56 A 40-year-old man was interviewed on an inpatient service. He claimed to be an accountant who had encountered some business difficulties and had come to the hospital "to get some help." His story was coherent, but seemed lacking and inconsistent in specific details. Concerning the details of his hospitalization, first he said he had been in for "just a few days," then later said "several weeks." He stated that his doctor's name "just slipped my mind."

On formal mental-status testing, the patient was unable to recall three objects in five minutes or to repeat a story told to him, but he did fairly well on simple calculations and in defining words and concepts and finding similarities and differences. His chart revealed that he had a long history of Alcohol Dependence and had been living in a nursing home for the past three years until he had been admitted one week previously, following several incidents in which he wandered off and had to be returned to the nursing home by the police.

Discussion of Runaway

The predominant disturbance is impairment in memory, as evidenced by the patient's inability to be consistent in his story, remember his doctor's name, and poor performance on mental-status memory questions. In addition, the patient confabulated his occupation and reason for being in the hospital.

Significant memory loss suggests a Dementia, but the mental-status examination did not indicate a general loss of major intellectual abilities. Memory loss is also seen in a Delirium, but this man was fully alert and did not demonstrate any clouding of consciousness. The predominance of short- and long-term memory disturbance, in the absence of a Dementia or Delirium, indicates an Amnestic Syndrome.

The long history of heavy alcohol use supports the notion that alcohol is etiologically related to the disturbance—hence the diagnosis of Alcohol Amnestic Disorder. We note the additional diagnosis of Alcohol Dependence, in Remission, to emphasize the potential for future problems with alcohol. Some clinicians might find it unnecessary to add this diagnosis since the patient apparently had not been drinking for several years and Alcohol Dependence is irrelevant to his current treatment.

DSM-III Diagnosis:

Axis I: **291.10 Alcohol Amnestic Disorder (p. 137)**
           303.93 Alcohol Dependence, in Remission (p. 170)

Loan Sharks

57 A 48-year-old male attorney was interviewed while he was being detained awaiting trial. He had been arrested for taking funds from his firm, which he stated he had fully intended to return after he had a "big win" at gambling. He appeared deeply humiliated and remorseful about his behavior, although he had a previous history of near-arrests for defrauding his company of funds. His father had provided funds to extricate him from these past financial difficulties, but refused to assist him this time. The patient had to resign his job under pressure from his firm. This seemed to distress him greatly since he had worked diligently and effectively at his job, although he had been spending more and more time away from work in order to pursue gambling.

He had gambled on horse racing for many years. He had been losing heavily recently, had resorted to illegal borrowing, and was now being pressured for payment. He stated that he embezzled the money to pay off these illegal debts because the threats of the "loan sharks" were frightening him so that he could not concentrate or sleep. He admitted to problems with his friends and wife since he had borrowed from them. They were now alienated and giving him little emotional support. His wife had decided to leave him and live with her parents.

During the interview the patient was tense and restless, at times having to stand up and pace. He said he was having a flare-up of a duodenal ulcer. He was somewhat tearful throughout the interview, and said that although he realized his problems stemmed from his gambling, he still had a strong urge to gamble.

Discussion of Loan Sharks

This man was arrested for embezzlement, has defaulted on debts, and has disrupted his marriage by gambling. This is beyond the bounds of "recreational gambling" and indicates a disturbance in impulse control, Pathological Gambling.

Although he has engaged in antisocial behavior, a diagnosis of Antisocial Personality Disorder is not appropriate because the antisocial behavior is limited to attempts to obtain money to pay off gambling debts, and there is neither a childhood history of antisocial behavior nor evidence of impaired occupational and interpersonal functioning other than that associated with his gambling.

DSM-III Diagnosis:

Axis I: **312.31 Pathological Gambling (p. 292)**

Flashbacks

58 A 23-year-old-former Vietnam veteran was admitted to the hospital at the request of his wife after he began to experience depression, insomnia, and "flashbacks" of his experiences in Vietnam. He had been honorably discharged two years previously, having spent nearly a year in combat in Vietnam. He had only minimal difficulties in returning to civilian life, resuming his college studies, and then marrying within six months after his return. His wife had noticed that he was always reluctant to talk about his military experience, but she wrote it off as a natural reaction to unpleasant memories.

The patient's current symptoms began, however, at about the time of the fall of Saigon. He became preoccupied with watching TV news stories about this at home. He then began to have difficulty sleeping and at times would awaken at night in the midst of a nightmare in which he was reliving his past experiences. His wife became particularly concerned one day when he had a flashback experience while out in the back yard: as a plane flew overhead, flying somewhat lower than usual, the patient threw himself to the ground seeking cover, thinking it was an attacking helicopter. The more he watched the news on TV, the more agitated and morose he became. Stories began to spill out about atrocities that he had seen and experienced, and he began to feel guilty that he had survived while many of his friends had not. At times he also seemed angry and bitter, feeling that the sacrifices he and others had made were all wasted. His wife expressed concern that his preoccupation with Vietnam had become so intense that he seemed to be losing touch with the reality of his present life, instead living almost completely in a world of events experienced two years earlier.

Discussion of Flashbacks

This veteran has become totally preoccupied with his painful year in Vietnam. His combat experience was obviously a stressor that would generally be outside the range of usual human experience and evoke significant symptoms of distress in almost anyone. He relives this trauma through dreams and flashbacks. His responsiveness to his current environment is diminished, and he is "living almost completely in a world of events experienced two years earlier." In addition, his sleep is disturbed, and he feels guilty about having survived when many of his buddies died. This is the full picture of Post-traumatic Stress Disorder. The disorder is further subclassified as Delayed to indicate that the onset of the symptoms occurred at least six months after the trauma.

DSM-III Diagnosis:

Axis I: 309.81 Post-traumatic Stress Disorder, Delayed (p. 238)

New Face

59 The patient, a single, unemployed, 19-year-old male was referred for psychiatric evaluation prior to orthognathous surgery for a protruding mandible. The procedure was to create a new facial look and improve both function and aesthetics. The evaluation was requested to determine if there were any psychiatric contraindications to surgery.

The patient says that his jaw has been protruding since childhood: he feels it may have protruded because as a child he frequently stuck his tongue out, and "maybe this stretched my jaw." He knows his molars are in place, but the teeth on the side are "pointed." His friends don't tease him about his jaw, but they do say "You got a mug," and this upsets him. He describes himself as shy and feels it is partly from his self-consciousness about his jaw. He has difficulty talking and eating, as his teeth underbite and his tongue protrudes; thus, he cannot bite, but has to tear, his food. He has wanted to have his jaw fixed for a long time, but was "too shy" to ask about it. He says that, as a result, he hasn't seen a dentist for the last four years. He is aware that some teeth will have to be removed and that he will have his jaw wired for six weeks and will be on a liquid diet. He is uneasy about being unable to eat solid food. He hopes the surgery will correct his chewing problem, and that he will feel better about his face, enabling him to be more comfortable with other people.

The patient did well in school until he reached high school; then he started to cut classes and dropped out of the tenth grade. He worked for two years as a security guard. He is now unemployed, but wants to go back to school and become an auto mechanic.

The patient is the third in a family of eight children. His parents separated when he was 14 years old. He lives with his mother and siblings. He argues with his siblings about doing household chores and, as a result, doesn't spend much time with his family; he just comes and goes and spends time with friends. He describes himself as shy and quiet. He restrains himself from telling his friends not to comment on his "mug," preferring to "keep it inside." He hopes that if the operation is successful, his friends will stop remarking on his looks.

When examined, the young man was noted to have mild acne and a very visibly protruding jaw with an underbite. His manner was somewhat awkward. There were no gross abnormalities of thinking, perception, or overt behavior. He denied ever having any problems with mood, sleeping, eating, or in the use of alcohol or other drugs.

Discussion of New Face

The complaint of a defect in some aspect of one's physical appearance requires a clinical judgment on whether or not the complaint is out of proportion to any actual physical abnormality that may exist. A gross discrepancy suggests the possibility of an Atypical Somatoform Disorder, or what has sometimes been referred to in the literature as "Dysmorphophobia." In this case, however, the interviewer notes the visibly protruding jaw and underbite, ruling out such a diagnosis.

The next question is whether or not the patient's reaction to his physical appearance is maladaptive, leading, for example, to marked social withdrawal, preoccupation, or depression. This does not appear to be the case. The young man is shy, and sensitive to his friends' comments about his appearance, but this hardly indicates significant psychopathology.

On the basis of the limited information provided, there is no reason to suspect a mental disorder. Thus, the appropriate designation on Axes I and II is "No Diagnosis." His protruding jaw and underbite *may* be recorded on Axis III as relevant to understanding this young man, but the intent of Axis III is really to facilitate the recording of physical conditions relevant to a person with a mental disorder, which does not apply in this case.

DSM-III Diagnosis:

Axis I: **V71.09 No Diagnosis or Condition**
Axis II: **V71.09 No Diagnosis**

Saturday Night Fever

60 A 19-year-old female secretary was transferred from the medical clinic to the psychiatric inpatient service. At age 16 she had first been diagnosed as having systemic lupus erythematosis and had begun steroid treatment. About three months before admission she developed kidney complications, and her cortisone was gradually increased to 70 mg/day. One month before admission her mother reported a change in the patient's usual shy and cooperative disposition. She had started staying out very late at night, often "discoing" until early morning; she dressed in wild and inappropriate costumes.

On the day of admission the patient paced the clinic, could not wait for the doctor, was alternately abusive and seductive to male staff, and talked incessantly about a range of loosely related topics: her future as a go-go dancer, how she was going to marry one of the Bee Gees (a rock group), and the lack of style in the dress of the female employees.

Discussion of Saturday Night Fever

The patient presents with a manic syndrome: poor judgment (wearing wild and inappropriate clothing), pressure of speech (talks incessantly), physical restlessness (pacing), and grandiosity (talk of marrying one of the Bee Gees). One can infer that her mood is alternately irritable and expansive.

In view of the temporal association between the increased dose of cortisone and the behavioral changes, it is reasonable to assume that steroids have caused an Organic Affective Syndrome. Since steroids are not listed as a specific substance class in DSM-III, the diagnosis is

Other (or Unspecified) Substance-induced Affective Disorder, but the name of the specific substance is substituted for the "Other."

DSM-III Diagnosis:

Axis I: **292.84 Cortisone-induced Affective Disorder (Manic) (p. 118)**

The Heiress

61 A wealthy and beautiful 34-year-old woman presented with a "marital problem." She was an heiress of a wealthy European family, and her husband was the president of a small importing company. She felt he was insensitive and demanding; and he, apparently, accused her of being self-centered, impulsive, and a "compulsive" liar. Over the course of their ten-year marriage each had had numerous affairs, most of which eventually came out into the open. Both would resolve to deal with their marital frustrations and to stop having affairs, and a brief period of reconciliation would follow; but soon one or the other would again surreptitiously begin an affair.

The patient also described a special problem that worried her and that she had never disclosed to her husband. Periodically she experienced the urge to walk into one of the more elegant department stores in the city and steal an article of clothing. Over the course of the previous three or four years she had stolen several blouses, a couple of sweaters, and a skirt. Since her husband's income alone was over $150,000 a year and her investments worth many times that, she recognized the "absurdity" of her acts. She also indicated that what she stole was rarely very expensive and sometimes not even enough to her liking for her to wear. She would become aware of the desire to steal something several days before she actually did it. The thoughts would increasingly occupy her mind until, on impulse, she walked into the store, plucked an item off the rack, and stuffed it into a bag she happened to be carrying or under her coat. Once out the door she felt a sense of relaxation and satisfaction; but at home she experienced anxiety and guilt when she realized what she had done. She was caught on one occasion, but gave a long, involved story about intending to pay after she had gone elsewhere in the store and then "forgetting." She was released by the store security officers with a warning and suspiciously raised eyebrows.

She spent considerable time describing her own accomplishments, talents, and abilities. Her affairs, she said, proved that she was indeed beautiful and of superior "stock." She thought that she and her husband, who was handsome, aggressive, and successful, should be a perfect match. According to her, the problems with her husband stemmed from the little attention he paid her and the expectations he seemed to have that she would be at his beck and call. The frequent arguments they had upset her greatly, and thus it was her idea that they seek professional help. Regarding the charge that she was a compulsive liar, she admitted that she often found it easier to tell "white lies" than to face up to something "stupid" that she had done.

Discussion of The Heiress

Although not the reason for seeking treatment, the stealing that this woman describes has the classic features of Kleptomania. She has recurrent impulses to steal objects she does not like and does not need. There is a mounting sense of tension that builds until she gives in to the impulse to steal; this is followed by a sense of release, and then remorse at what she has done. The act of stealing occurs without planning and when she is alone.

Her marital problem, which is the reason for her seeking professional help, is apparently unrelated to the Kleptomania. It may be related to certain narcissistic personality traits, such as her exaggerated sense of her own importance (belief that she is of superior stock), her disregard of the rights of others (her lying), and her apparent lack of empathy (totally blaming her husband for their marital problems). Her need to have affairs may be because she requires constant admiration and attention. Since there is no evidence of a characteristic response to criticism or indifference from others, the diagnosis of Narcissistic Personality Disorder is not made, but the presence of narcissistic traits is noted on Axis II.

Since the marital problem is the focus of attention, rather than the Kleptomania, and it is related to the narcissistic personality traits, the V code Marital Problem is the first condition noted on Axis I.

DSM-III Diagnosis:

Axis I: **V61.10 Marital Problem (p. 333)**
              312.32 Kleptomania (p. 294)
Axis II: **Narcissistic traits**

Not So Gay

62 A 23-year-old unmarried male schoolteacher presents for help with his distress about his preoccupation with homosexuality. He has had almost no dating experience with women. He has felt "unmasculine" since childhood and "different from most boys" as he was growing up. He was frail and unsuccessful in sports, and he became a loner in most activities, concentrating particularly on his education, in which he excelled.

Since puberty he has felt fearful of girls, expecting to be rejected. He began at that time to fantasize about dominating and being appreciated by strong, handsome boys his age or older. He would masturbate to this fantasy and find the ideas increasingly pleasurable. Now, although he has not yet had any overt homosexual experience, he is constantly preoccupied with a physical desire for homosexual contact. Yet, in a social sense, he is repulsed by the idea, finds it totally shameful and unacceptable to his social and cultural goals. He wants to rid himself of these homosexual ideas and be able to make love to a woman. He has intense fear that he will be impotent with women and further humiliated.

During childhood he felt close to his mother, who, he felt assured, loved him, but distant and isolated from his father. He felt he "never measured up" to his father's standards, and was unable to discuss much with him. He feels both respect and intense resentment toward him.

He chronically has low self-esteem and is often depressed, even at times suicidal when faced with the "emptiness of the future." On the few occasions on which he has dated women, the patient had only weak sexual feelings and an intense feeling of "inadequacy and failure." Therefore, he goes to elaborate efforts to avoid being introduced to new women for fear of being unable to follow through, yet he hates himself for this. He feels he has no one with whom he can talk openly.

Discussion of Not So Gay

This young man complains that although he wishes he could have heterosexual relationships, since adolescence he has had an exclusively homosexual arousal pattern. His wish to be heterosexual is internalized (his homosexuality has become unacceptable to his social and cultural goals), and his distress is not just because of societal discrimination against homosexuality. Furthermore, the ego-dystonic nature of his homosexual feelings is not a transient symptom of a Depressive Disorder; rather, his depressive symptoms seem secondary to his sexual problem. Therefore, the diagnosis of Ego-dystonic Homosexuality is made.

Since there is mention of chronic low self-esteem, periodic suicidal thoughts, and pessimism about the future, a diagnosis of Dysthymic Disorder needs to be ruled out. There is not enough information to know whether or not he has been bothered over at least the past two years for most or nearly all of the time by depressive symptoms, a requirement for Dysthymic Disorder. If this proved to be the case, the diagnosis would be made, even if the clinician believed that the Dysthymic Disorder was a reaction to the Ego-dystonic Homosexuality.

DSM-III Diagnosis:

Axis I: **302.00 Ego-dystonic Homosexuality (p. 282)**
R/O Dysthymic Disorder

Traction

63 The patient is a previously healthy 32-year-old carpenter from Nevada who was involved in a motor vehicle accident as he was returning from a three-month trip to Mexico. He was found by the state police and taken to the hospital. On admission he was found to have multiple fractures involving his pelvis, toes on his right foot, and several ribs on his left side. He also sustained two small cuts on his head that required stitches. The patient reported that he had a period of amnesia of about fifteen minutes and that he lost consciousness during the accident, but this was not witnessed. He was alert and complained of severe back pain; he was not disoriented. He was treated with Demerol, 125 mg IM every 3 hours; Seconal, 100 mg at bedtime; and Phenergan, 25 mg IM every 3 hours. The following day his back pain was unimproved, and his pain medication was changed to morphine and Phenergan.

Two days later he spiked a fever and was sweaty and tremulous. Because a history of drinking five to six beers per day had been elicited, the diagnosis of Alcohol Withdrawal was considered, and Valium, 5 mg po every 6 hours, was added to his daily medication regimen, which at this time included Tylox, 1 or 2 capsules po every 3–4 hours, and Seconal, 100 mg at bedtime. The next day he was described as anxious, agitated, and constantly scratching. Two days later he was still febrile. Blood cultures, urine analysis, and chest X-ray were negative. Atarax, 25 mg po four times a day, was given to relieve itching.

The next day, one week after admission, the patient was noted to be disoriented. He complained that it took him some time to realize where he was upon awakening. His temperature was still elevated. He was receiving morphine, 3–10 mg every 3 hours; Valium, 5 mg po every 6 hours; and Dalmane, 30 mg po at bedtime. The next day his pain medication was again changed, this time to Percodan, 1–2 tablets every 3 hours, and Demerol, 75 mg IM every 4 hours.

One day later the patient underwent an open reduction for a fractured left acetabulum. The surgery, done under general anesthesia, was tolerated well; but immediately following the procedure he was disoriented to time and place and was noted to be picking at things in the air. His temperature was still elevated, and there was no documented source of infection. At this time the patient was taking Demerol, 75–100 mg IM every 4 hours; Vistaril, 75 mg every 3 hours; and Tylenol, every 4 hours.

Over the next few days the patient's mental status improved, although he was still disoriented at times and confessed, "You know, sometimes I can't comprehend what you're saying." His temperature was still moderately elevated. Medication consisted of Dilaudid, 2–4 mg every 3–4 hours. The continuing periods of disorientation disturbed his doctors, and a psychiatric consultation was requested.

Upon initial interview, now 17 days after the accident, the patient was alert, fully oriented, and in good spirits. Mental status testing was normal. He admitted to having had difficulties in thinking and "hallucinations" at times during the previous couple of weeks. He described them as "opiate dreams," caused by his pain medication.

Over the next few days his condition was generally improved during the daylight hours, but at night he was frequently found to be taking his traction apparatus apart. When discovered, he would sometimes admit to removing the traction, but if quizzed the next day, he always denied having dismantled the equipment. At this time he was taking Tylox, 2 capsules every 6 hours, for pain. He often complained of severe pain, many times arguing with his doctors in an attempt to persuade them to give him Tylox more often. The psychiatrist was called in again to help, and the Tylox dose was given more frequently. It was felt that his addiction potential was not very high at that time.

Several days later he was found to be playing with fecal material in his bed and once again dismantling his traction apparatus. When discovered he admitted to these acts, as he had previously. However, this time he was very disturbed by his actions and did not sleep the remainder of the night. The next day he did not deny these acts, but instead was very upset and asked to see a psychiatrist. When interviewed he appeared anxious and angry. He stated that he did not understand what was happening to him and was very upset with himself about his behavior. He said he had not been sleeping more than two to three hours a night for at least two weeks. He was very frightened by the thought that his mind was doing things he was not aware of and could not control. He asked for a "game plan" to stop this behavior and even suggested stopping all pain medication if necessary. Over the next few days pain medication was reduced. The patient appeared alert and oriented, and there were no further episodes of disturbed behavior at night.

Discussion of Traction

Beginning with the second day of hospitalization and continuing for several weeks, this man intermittently was disoriented; had clouding of consciousness (took him some time to realize where he was upon awakening), visual hallucinations (picked at things in the air, had "opiate dreams"), and disturbance in the sleep-wakefulness cycle (trouble sleeping); and engaged in bizarre behavior (playing with his feces, dismantling his traction equipment). These are the characteristic features of a Delirium, and in this case there is no difficulty in identifying several physical factors that could have contributed to the development of the disturbance. The difficulty is in deciding the relative roles of withdrawal from alcohol, infection, and the large number of analgesics and sedatives that he received. Delirium, from Section 2 of the Organic Mental Disorders, since the cause is unknown, is noted on Axis I; fever of unknown origin, as a possible contributing factor, is listed on Axis III.

DSM-III Diagnosis:

Axis I: 293.00 Delirium (p. 107)
Axis III: Fever of unknown origin

Empty Shell

64 The patient is a 23-year-old veterinary assistant admitted for her first psychiatric hospitalization. She arrived late at night, referred by a local psychiatrist, saying "I don't really need to be here."

Three months before admission the patient learned that her mother had become pregnant. She began drinking heavily, ostensibly in order to sleep nights. While drinking she became involved in a series of "one-night stands." Two weeks before admission she began feeling panicky and having experiences in which she felt as if she were removed from her body and was in a trance. During one of these episodes she was stopped by the police while wandering on a bridge late at night. The next day, in response to hearing a voice repeatedly telling her to jump off a bridge, she ran to her supervisor and asked for help. Her supervisor, seeing her distraught and also noting scars from a recent wrist-slashing, referred her to a psychiatrist, who then arranged for her immediate hospitalization.

At the time of hospitalization the patient appeared as a disheveled and frail, but appealing, waif. She was cooperative, coherent, and frightened. Although she did not feel hospitalization was needed, she welcomed the prospect of relief from her anxiety and depersonalization. She acknowledged that she had had feelings of loneliness and inadequacy and brief periods of depressed mood and anxiety since adolescence. Recently she had been having fantasies that she was stabbing herself or a little baby with a knife. She complained that she was "just an empty shell that is transparent to everyone."

Her parents divorced when she was three, and for the next five years she lived with her maternal grandmother and her mother, who had a severe drinking problem. The patient had night terrors during which she would frequently end up sleeping with her mother. At age six she went to a special boarding school for a year and a half, after which she was withdrawn by her mother against the advice of the school. When she was eight her maternal grandmother died, and she recalls trying to hide her grief about this from her mother. She spent most of the next two years living with various relatives, including a period with her father, whom she had not seen since the divorce. When she was nine, her mother was hospitalized with a diagnosis of Schizophrenia. From age ten through college she lived with an aunt and uncle, but had ongoing and frequent contacts with her mother. Her school record was consistently good.

In adolescence she dated regularly, having an active but rarely pleasurable sex life. Her relationships with men usually end abruptly after she becomes angry with them when they disappoint her in some apparently minor way. She then concludes that they were "no good to begin with." She has had several roommates, but has had trouble establishing a stable living situation because of her jealousy of sharing her roommates with others and her manipulative efforts to keep them from seeing other people.

After college she worked steadily and well as a veterinary assistant. At the time of admission she was working a night shift in a veterinary hospital and living alone.

Discussion of Empty Shell

In the last three months, since hearing of her mother's pregnancy, this young woman has begun drinking heavily, has had several episodes of what appears to be depersonalization, and has been anxious, depressed, and suicidal. In addition, she briefly had auditory hallucinations telling her to kill herself. In the absence of a previous history of significant psychopathology, these symptoms would suggest one or more Axis I diagnoses, such as Major Depression with Psychotic Features, Alcohol Abuse, or even Adjustment Disorder. However, the long-standing history of interpersonal difficulties and a variety of other symptoms, such as loneliness, depression, feelings of inadequacy, etc., suggests that she has a Personality Disorder and that the current disturbance merely represents an exacerbation of this, not a separate illness.

In fact, she demonstrates enough of the characteristic features of Borderline Personality Disorder to warrant that diagnosis. She clearly has a pattern of unstable and intense interpersonal relationships with men, with marked shifts of attitude. She is described as "manipulative" with her roommates. Affective instability is suggested by the reference to her having brief periods of depressed mood and anxiety since adolescence. She reports that she is "an empty shell," evidence of chronic feelings of emptiness. In addition, at least during the present episode, she demonstrates impulsivity (drinking and sex) and physically self-damaging acts (slashing her wrists). It is quite likely that these characteristics have also been present during periods of stress in the past.

The diagnosis of a psychotic disorder, such as Atypical Psychosis, for the current episode is not warranted since the brief hallucination and her reaction to it as ego-dystonic are an example of the transient psychotic experiences that are often a feature of Borderline Personality Disorder.

DSM-III Diagnosis:

Axis II: 301.83 Borderline Personality Disorder (p. 322)

Fear of Flying

65 The patient, a 25-year-old female laboratory technician, has been married to a 32-year-old cabdriver for 5 years. The couple has a two-year-old son, and the marriage appears harmonious.

The presenting complaint is the wife's lifelong inability to experience orgasm. She has never achieved orgasm, although during sexual activity she has received what should have been sufficient stimulation. She has tried to masturbate, and on many occasions her husband has manually stimulated her patiently for lengthy periods of time. Although she does not reach climax, she is strongly attracted to her husband, feels erotic pleasure during lovemaking, and lubricates copiously. According to both of them, the husband has no sexual difficulty.

Exploration of her thoughts as she nears orgasm reveals a vague sense of dread of some undefined disaster. More generally, she is anxious about losing control over her emotions, which she normally keeps closely in check. She is particularly uncomfortable about expressing any anger or hostility.

Physical examination reveals no abnormality.

Discussion of Fear of Flying

This woman's sexual difficulties are limited to the orgasm phase of the sexual response cycle (she has no difficulty in desiring sex or in becoming excited). During lovemaking there is what would ordinarily be an adequate amount of stimulation. The report of a ''vague sense of dread of some undefined disaster'' as she approaches orgasm is evidence that her inability to have orgasms represents a pathological inhibition. There is no suggestion of any other Axis I disorder or any physical disorder that could account for the disturbance. Thus, the diagnosis is Inhibited Female Orgasm.

If with treatment it became apparent that the fear of loss of control were a symptom of a Personality Disorder, such as Compulsive Personality Disorder, the diagnosis of a psychosexual dysfunction would nonetheless prevail. It is only when a sexual disturbance is judged to be symptomatic of another Axis I disorder, such as Major Depression, that the diagnosis of a psychosexual dysfunction is not made.

DSM-III Diagnosis:

Axis I: 302.73 Inhibited Female Orgasm (p. 279)

Coma

66 A 34-year-old, white, male, former schoolteacher lives in a halfway house. For the last two years he has been unemployed and separated from his wife and children, who avoid him. Two years ago he was in a serious auto accident which resulted in a coma, from which he made a gradual recovery with only supportive medical treatment. Now he has no significant neurological signs except for very minor loss in one visual field. Verbal and performance IQ is about 120.

According to the family he has changed since the accident. He is frequently impulsive and argumentative, often misses buses and trains to familiar places, and gets lost. He displays poor social judgment and financial irresponsibility, e.g., he makes long-distance phone calls (including one to the Pope at the Vatican) and then sends the bills to his family.

When seen, the patient was disheveled and joked frequently, but with an undercurrent of bitterness and hostility. A computerized tomography (CT) scan demonstrated large areas of brain tissue destruction, principally in the frontal lobes.

Discussion of Coma

The apparent abrupt change in this man's functioning following his recovery from coma secondary to head trauma obviously indicates an Organic Brain Syndrome. Although there is some evidence of memory impairment (often misses buses and trains and gets lost), his high IQ is inconsistent with the generalized loss in intellectual functioning of a Dementia. Instead, the most prominent features are impulsivity, argumentativeness, poor judgment, and deterioration in self-care, all of which have led to severe occupational and social impairment. These changes in personality, associated with a specific organic factor known to be etiologic to the disturbance (history of trauma and CT scan indicating frontal-lobe brain damage), indicate an Organic Personality Syndrome. Because the etiologic factor is not from the Mental Disorders section of the ICD-9-CM, the diagnosis of Organic Personality Syndrome is from Section 2 of Organic Mental Disorders, and the etiologic factor is noted on Axis III.

DSM-III Diagnosis:

Axis I: 310.10 Organic Personality Syndrome (p. 119)
Axis III: Frontal-lobe brain damage secondary to trauma

Thunderstorms

67 This 28-year-old housewife sought psychiatric treatment for a fear of storms that had become progressively more disturbing to her. Although frightened of storms since she was a child, the fear seemed to abate somewhat during adolescence, but had been increasing in severity over the past few years. This gradual exacerbation of her anxiety, plus the fear that she might pass it on to her children, led her to seek treatment.

She is most frightened of lightning, but is uncertain about the reason for this. She is only vaguely aware of a fear of being struck by lightning, and recognizes that this is an unlikely occurrence. When asked to elaborate on her fears, she imagines that lightning could strike a tree in her yard; the tree might fall and block her driveway, thus trapping her at home. This frightens her, but she is quite aware that her fear is irrational. She also recognizes the irrational nature of her fear of thunder. She begins to feel anxiety long before a storm arrives. A weather report predicting a storm later in the week can cause her anxiety to increase to the point that she worries for days before the storm. Although she does not express a fear of rain, her anxiety increases even when the weather becomes overcast because of the increased likelihood of a storm.

During a storm, she does several things to reduce her anxiety. Since being with another person reduces her fear, she often tries to make plans to visit friends or relatives or go to a store when a storm is threatening. Sometimes when her husband is away on business she stays overnight with a close relative if a storm is forecast. During a storm she covers her eyes or moves to a part of the house far from windows, where she cannot see lightning should it occur.

The patient is married and has three young children. She describes her marriage as a happy one and states that her husband has been supportive of her when she is frightened and has encouraged her to seek psychiatric treatment. She is in good physical health, and at the time she entered treatment there were no unusually stressful situations in her life or other psychiatric difficulties. Her parents separated shortly after she began treatment. Although she found this distressing, she felt her personal supports were adequate and that this occurrence did not necessitate psychiatric attention.

She describes her past history as generally unremarkable in terms of any obvious psychiatric problems, except for her fear of storms. She feels that she may have learned this fear from her grandmother, who also was frightened of storms. She denies panic attacks, or any other unusual or incapacitating fears.

Discussion of Thunderstorms

Many people feel uncomfortable during thunder and lightning storms; but this woman's fear is clearly excessive, causes her considerable distress, and is acknowledged to be irrational. She goes to great lengths to avoid situations in which she might be alone and exposed to the feared stimulus, storms. These features indicate the presence of a Phobic Disorder. Although she is afraid of being alone during storms, there is apparently no general fear of being alone or in public places away from home, as in Agoraphobia. Her fear of storms does not involve a fear of humiliation or embarrassment in certain social situations, as in Social Phobia. Therefore, the diagnosis of Simple Phobia is appropriate.

DSM-III Diagnosis:

Axis I: 300.29 Simple Phobia (p. 229)

Chief Petty Officer

68 A medical student on rotation at a chronic-disease hospital was assigned to present at rounds a 56-year-old retired chief petty officer. The patient was a long-time heavy consumer of alcoholic beverages. Following his divorce many years previously, his drinking had become exceptionally heavy, and he underwent a change in personality. He was often belligerent, even when sober, and on several occasions had assaulted members of his family. This disturbing behavior had necessitated two brief admissions to mental hospitals. The patient persisted in his heavy drinking, and on several other occasions had been admitted to hospitals for tremulousness and hallucinations associated with Alcohol Withdrawal. As far as was known, he had never had major trauma or a stroke. Finally, because of his inability to care for himself properly, he had been sent to live in a nursing home; but because of his belligerent and disruptive behavior, admission to this hospital had been found necessary seven years earlier.

When examined by the student, the patient was somewhat peevish and inattentive. His consciousness was not clouded, however, and he was not hallucinating. He knew the name of the hospital, but not the correct date. He could not retain the names of five objects after a brief interval of distraction. He remembered events of his youth and young manhood, but not those of more recent years. He remembered the dispute between President Truman and General MacArthur, but had no recollection of the Watergate affair. His language was normal, but he could not copy the drawing of a two- or three-dimensional figure. He could not do even the simplest of calculations, and he interpreted proverbs very concretely. Neurological examinations revealed somewhat diminished ankle jerks, and there was mild unsteadiness of gait. Laboratory tests failed to reveal any positive evidence for the etiology of the disturbance.

Discussion of Chief Petty Officer

The short-term and recent memory disturbances suggest an Amnestic Syndrome; but the marked loss of intellectual abilities, the personality change, the poor judgment, and other disturbances of higher cortical functioning (e.g., inability to copy drawings and do calculations, and concrete responses to proverbs) all indicate the presence of the more global disturbance, a Dementia.

The differential diagnosis of Dementia involves a search for specific causes, such as trauma (particularly important with a history of Alcohol Dependence) and brain tumor. In this case, the absence of a history of trauma and the failure of the laboratory tests to reveal the etiology of the Dementia make prolonged heavy drinking the most likely etiologic agent; thus, the diagnosis is Dementia Associated with Alcoholism. Primary Degenerative Dementia is ruled out because the course has remained relatively stable over many years.

DSM-III Diagnosis:

Axis I: 291.20 Dementia Associated with Alcoholism (p. 138)

Vertigo

69 A 46-year-old married housewife was referred by her husband's psychiatrist for consultation. In the course of discussing certain marital conflicts that he was having with his wife, the husband had described "attacks" of dizziness that his wife experienced that left her quite incapacitated.

In consultation, the wife described being overcome with feelings of extreme dizziness, accompanied by slight nausea, four or five nights a week. During these attacks, the room around her would take on a "shimmering" appearance, and she would have the feeling that she was "floating" and unable to keep her balance. Inexplicably, the attacks almost always occurred at about 4:00 P.M. She usually had to lie down on the couch and often did not feel better until 7:00 or 8:00 P.M. After recovering, she generally spent the rest of the evening watching TV; and more often than not, she would fall asleep in the living room, not going to bed in the bedroom until 2:00 or 3:00 in the morning.

The patient had been pronounced physically fit by her internist, a neurologist, and an ENT specialist on more than one occasion. Hypoglycemia had been ruled out by glucose tolerance tests.

When asked about her marriage, the patient described her husband as a tyrant, frequently demanding and verbally abusive of her and their four children. She admitted that she dreaded his arrival home from work each day, knowing that he would comment that the house was a mess and the dinner, if prepared, not to his liking. Recently, since the onset of her attacks, when she was unable to make dinner he and the four kids would go to McDonald's or the local pizza parlor. After that, he would settle in to watch a ballgame in the bedroom, and their conversation was minimal. In spite of their troubles, the patient claimed that she loved her husband and needed him very much.

Discussion of Vertigo

This woman complains of a variety of physical symptoms (dizziness, nausea, visual disturbances, loss of balance) that all suggest a physical disorder; but thorough examinations by a number of medical specialists have failed to detect a physical disorder that could account for the symptoms. With a specific physical disorder ruled out, the differential diagnosis is between undiagnosed physical symptoms and a mental disorder.

The context in which these symptoms occur suggests the role of psychological factors in their development: they recur at virtually the same time each day, closely associated with the husband's arrival home from work; the symptoms enable the patient to avoid both her husband's angry tirades and her responsibility for preparing evening meals. Since there is no evidence that the patient is voluntarily producing the symptoms (e.g., taking a drug that would induce such symptoms or claiming to have the symptoms when they are not present), diagnoses of a Factitious Disorder or Malingering are ruled out. The disorder is a Somatoform Disorder—a mental disorder with physical symptoms that suggest a physical disorder.

Since the patient's complaints are not part of a long-standing polysymptomatic disturbance involving many organ systems, Somatization Disorder is excluded. The symptoms are all limited to an alteration in physical functioning; hence, the diagnosis is Conversion Disorder.

DSM-III Diagnosis:

Axis I: 300.11 Conversion Disorder (p. 247)

Panties

70 A 32-year-old, single, male, free-lance photographer presented with the chief complaint of "abnormal sex drive." The patient related that although he was somewhat sexually attracted by women, he was far more attracted by "their panties."

To the best of the patient's memory, sexual excitement began at about age seven, when he came upon a pornographic magazine and felt stimulated by pictures of partially nude women wearing "panties." His first ejaculation occurred at age 13 via masturbation to fantasies of women wearing panties. He masturbated into his older sister's panties, which he had stolen without her knowledge. Subsequently he stole panties from her friends, and from other women he met socially. He found pretexts to "wander" into the bedrooms of women during social occasions and would quickly rummage through their possessions until he found a pair of panties to his satisfaction. He later used these to masturbate into, and then "saved them" in a "private cache." The pattern of masturbating into women's underwear had been his preferred method of achieving sexual excitement and orgasm from adolescence until the present consultation.

The patient first had sexual intercourse at age 18. Since then he had had intercourse on many occasions, and his preferred partner was a prostitute paid to wear panties, with the crotch area cut away, during the act. On less common occasions when sexual activity was attempted with a partner who did not wear panties, his sexual excitement was sometimes weak.

The patient felt uncomfortable dating "nice women," since he felt that friendliness might lead to sexual intimacy and that they would not understand his sexual needs. He avoided socializing with friends who might introduce him to such women. He recognized that his appearance, social style, and profession all resulted in his being perceived as a highly desirable bachelor. He felt anxious and depressed because his social life was limited by his sexual preference.

He sought consultation shortly after his mother's sudden and unexpected death. Despite the fact that he complained of loneliness, he admitted that the pleasure he experienced from his unusual sexual activity made him unsure about whether or not he wished to give it up.

Discussion of Panties

This man's first remembered sexual arousal was in response to pictures of women wearing "panties." Ever since that time panties, alone or worn by a woman, have been his preferred source of sexual arousal. He does not wear the panties in an effort to dress like a woman, as would be the case with Transvestism. This use of nonliving objects (fetishes) as a repeatedly preferred or exclusive method of achieving sexual excitement is Fetishism.

As is generally the case with the Paraphilias, the deviant sexual act itself gives only pleasure, and it is the secondary consequences (humiliation, fear of exposure or criminal prosecution) that cause the person to seek treatment. In contrast, the symptoms of both the Gender Identity Disorders and the Psychosexual Dysfunctions are generally distressing in themselves.

DSM-III Diagnosis:

Axis I: 302.81 Fetishism (p. 269)

Clairvoyant

71 The patient is a 32-year-old unmarried, unemployed woman on welfare who complains that she feels "spacey." Her feelings of detachment have gradually become stronger and more uncomfortable. For many hours each day she feels as if she were watching herself move through life, and the world around her seems unreal. She feels especially strange when she looks into a mirror. For many years she has felt able to read people's minds by a "kind of clairvoyance I don't understand." According to her, several people in her family apparently also have this ability. She is preoccupied by the thought that she has some special mission in life, but is not sure what it is; she is not particularly religious. She is very self-conscious in public, often feels that people are paying special attention to her, and sometimes thinks that strangers cross the street to avoid her. She is lonely and isolated and spends much of each day lost in fantasies or watching TV soap operas. She speaks in a vague, abstract, digressive manner, generally just missing the point, but she is never incoherent. She seems shy, suspicious, and afraid she will be criticized. She has no gross loss of reality testing, such as hallucinations or delusions. She has never had treatment for emotional problems. She has had occasional jobs, but drifts away from them because of lack of interest.

Discussion of Clairvoyant

Although the patient's symptoms have become more distressing to her recently, they are manifestations of a long-standing maladaptive pattern that suggests a Personality Disorder rather than the new development of an Axis I disorder. Her symptoms include depersonalization (feelings of detachment and feeling as if she were watching herself), derealization (". . . the world . . . seems unreal"), magical thinking (clairvoyance), ideas of reference (strangers cross the street to avoid her), social isolation, odd speech (vague, abstract, digressive), suspiciousness, and hypersensitivity to criticism. These are the hallmarks of Schizotypal Personality Disorder.

Is her belief in her ability to read people's minds a delusion rather than merely magical thinking, which would indicate a psychotic disorder? Her statement that she herself "doesn't understand" the process suggests that it is probably not a belief that is firmly held, as in a delusion.

The clinician might be concerned about the likelihood of a previous psychotic episode in this patient, in which case the current symptoms would be indicative of the residual phase of Schizophrenia. In the absence of such a history, however, a diagnosis of Schizotypal Personality Disorder is most appropriate.

DSM-III Diagnosis:

Axis II   301.22 Schizotypal Personality Disorder (p. 312)

Mr. and Ms. B.

72 Mr. and Ms. B. have been married for 14 years and have 3 children, aged 8 through 12. They are both bright and well educated. Both are from Scotland, from which they moved ten years ago because of Mr. B.'s work as an industrial consultant. They present with the complaint that Ms. B. has been able to participate passively in sex "as a duty" but has never enjoyed it since they have been married.

Before their marriage, although they had intercourse only twice, Ms. B. had been highly aroused by kissing and petting and felt she used her attractiveness to "seduce" her husband into marriage. She did, however, feel intense guilt about their two episodes of premarital intercourse; and during their honeymoon she began to think of sex as a chore that could not be pleasing. Although she periodically passively complied with intercourse, she had almost no spontaneous desire for sex. She never masturbated, had never reached orgasm, thought of all variations such as oral sex as completely repulsive, and was preoccupied with a fantasy of how disapproving her family would be if she ever engaged in any of these activities.

Ms. B. is almost totally certain that no woman she respects in any older generation has enjoyed sex, and that despite the "new vogue" of sexuality, only sleazy, crude women let themselves act like "animals." These beliefs have led to a pattern of infrequent sex, or sex that at best is accommodating and gives little or no pleasure to her or her husband. Whenever Ms. B. comes close to having a feeling of sexual arousal, numerous negative thoughts come into her mind, such as "What would my mother say about this?"; "What am I, a tramp?"; "If I like this, he'll just want it more often"; or "How could I look myself in the mirror after something like this?" These thoughts almost inevitably are accompanied by a cold feeling and an insensitivity to sensual pleasure. As a result, sex is invariably an unhappy experience. Almost any excuse, such as fatigue or being busy, is sufficient for her to rationalize avoiding intercourse.

Yet, intellectually Ms. B. wonders "Is something wrong with me?" She is seeking help to find out if she is normal or not. Her husband, although extraordinarily tolerant of the situation, is in fact very unhappy about their sex life and is very hopeful that help may be forthcoming.

Discussion of Mr. and Ms. B.

This couple seeks help for the wife's long-standing sexual problem. Clearly this woman's lack of sexual desire is due to her many negative attitudes toward sexuality, and cannot be accounted for by a nonsexual Axis I disorder, such as Major Depression. Therefore, she receives the diagnosis of Inhibited Sexual Desire. Moreover, most likely, on the rare occasions when she does have sexual intercourse, she does not become sexually excited. If additional information confirmed this, the supplementary diagnosis of Inhibited Sexual Excitement would be made. The diagnosis of Inhibited Orgasm would be added only if there were many occasions when during intercourse she failed to have an orgasm but had no disturbance in sexual excitement — extremely unlikely in this case.

The absence of any significant complaint on the part of the husband is reflected in the notation of No Diagnosis or Condition on Axis I for him. '

DSM-III Diagnosis:

Wife:
Axis I: 302.71 Inhibited Sexual Desire (p. 278)
**   R/O Inhibited Sexual Excitement**
Husband:
Axis I: V71.09 No Diagnosis or Condition

Hungarian Opera Singer

73 B.B., a 39-year-old Hungarian opera singer, is readmitted to a psychiatric hospital after keeping her family awake for several nights with a prayer and song marathon. She is flamboyantly dressed in a floor-length red skirt and peasant blouse, and is adorned with heavy earrings, numerous necklaces and bracelets, and medals pinned to her bosom. She speaks very rapidly and is difficult to interrupt as she talks about her initimate relationship with God. She often breaks into song, explaining that her beautiful singing voice is a special gift that God has given her to compensate for her insanity. She uses it to share the joy she feels with others who are less fortunate.

B.B. has had at least ten admissions to this hospital in the past 20 years, some because of serious suicide attempts made when she was depressed, some because she was manic, and some, in her words, "just because I was crazy." Although she does have a lovely voice, she has not been able to organize herself to work professionally during the past 15 years, and has spent much of her time at the local community mental health center. She has seen the same therapist weekly for many years and believes that he communicates with her through a local radio station, giving her instructions on how to conduct her life between therapy sessions. She also receives illuminations from Kahlil Gibran and Adele Davis, whose conversations she is able to overhear.

Discussion of Hungarian Opera Singer

There should not be much difficulty recognizing that this woman is currently in a manic episode. She has expansive mood (singing, flamboyant dress), with pressure of speech (difficult to interrupt), decreased need for sleep, and grandiosity (intimate relationship with God). In the past she has had similar episodes, as well as depressions with suicide attempts. The diagnosis of Bipolar Disorder is made, and would be made even in the absence of a history of depressive episodes.

The current episode is manic and is further characterized in the fifth digit to indicate the presence of mood-congruent psychotic features (receiving illuminations from famous people). Some clinicians might interpret the delusion that she receives messages from her therapist through the local radio station as unrelated to any typical manic theme. It seems to us, however, that this delusion also has a grandiose theme.

DSM-III Diagnosis:

Axis I: **296.44 Bipolar Disorder, Manic, with Psychotic Features (Mood-congruent) (p. 208)**

Reluctant Home Buyer

74 A 30-year-old accountant was referred by his internist to a psychiatric consultant because of a 6-month history of recurrent bouts of extreme fear accompanied by sweating, shortness of breath, palpitations, chest pain, headache, muscular tension, and the thought that he was going to die. His internist had given him a complete physical, an EKG, and glucose tolerance and other blood tests, and had found no abnormalities.

The patient has been married for five years; he has no children. He went to night school while working to get a master's degree in business administration and was quite successful and well liked at his firm. He and his wife, a teacher, generally got along well and had several couples with whom they enjoyed going out.

Because of the attacks, which occurred in a variety of situations, the patient started to avoid driving his car and going into department stores, lest he have an attack in these situations. He began to coax his wife to accompany him on errands, and during the last month he felt comfortable only at home with his wife. Finally he could not face the prospect of leaving home to go to work, and took a medical leave of absence.

When asked about the onset of his attacks, the patient said that he and his wife had been discussing buying a house and moving from their apartment. He admitted that the responsibilities of home ownership intimidated him and related the significance of the move to similar concerns his mother had had that prevented his parents from ever buying a house.

Discussion of Reluctant Home Buyer

The diagnosis of Agoraphobia is justified in this case by the patient's increasing constriction of his normal activities (he could not face the prospect of leaving home to go to work) because of a fear of being alone or in situations in which help might not be available if he suddenly became incapacitated (he avoided driving his car or going into department stores). As is often the case, the Agoraphobia was preceded by panic attacks (recurrent bouts of extreme fear, with sweating, shortness of breath, palpitations, chest pain, headache, muscular tension, and the thought that he was going to die). The history of panic attacks is coded in the fifth digit.

DSM-III Diagnosis:

Axis I: 300.21 Agoraphobia with Panic Attacks (p. 227)

Burt Tate

75 The patient is a 42-year-old white male who was brought to the emergency room by the police. He was involved in an argument and fight with a customer at the diner where he is employed. When the police arrived and began to question the patient, he gave his name as Burt Tate, but had no identification. Burt had drifted into town several weeks earlier and begun working as a short-order cook at the diner. He could not recall where he had worked or lived before his arrival in this town. There were no charges against him, but the police convinced him to come to the emergency room for an examination.

When questioned in the emergency room, "Burt" knew what town he was in and the current date. He admitted that it was somewhat unusual that he could not recall the details of his past life, but he did not appear very upset about this. There was no evidence of alcohol or drug abuse, and a physical examination revealed no head trauma or any other physical abnormalities. He was kept overnight for observation.

When the police ran a description check on the patient, they found that he fit the description of a missing person, Gene Smith, who had disappeared a month before from a city 200 miles away. A visit by Mrs. Smith confirmed the identity of the patient as Gene Smith. His wife explained that for the 18 months before his disappearance, her husband, who was a middle-level manager at a large manufacturing company, had been having considerable difficulty at work. He had been passed over for a promotion, and his supervisor had been very critical of his work. Several of his staff had left the company for other jobs, and the patient found it impossible to meet production goals. Work stress made him very difficult to live with at home. Previously an easygoing, gregarious person, he became withdrawn and critical of his wife and children. Immediately preceding his disappearance, he had had a violent argument with his 18-year-old son. The son had called him a "failure" and stormed out of the house to live with some friends who had an apartment. It was two days after this argument that the patient disappeared.

When brought into the room where his wife was waiting, the patient stated that he did not recognize her. He appeared noticeably anxious.

Discussion of Burt Tate

The police brought this man to the emergency room because of his amnesia concerning where he had previously lived and worked. Although this impairment in memory suggests an Organic Mental Disorder, ordinarily in Organic Mental Disorders the disturbance in memory is more marked for recent than for remote events. The lack of any disturbance in attention or orientation also weighs against the presence of an Organic Mental Disorder.

The functional nature of the patient's amnesia becomes more apparent when we learn that just before the development of his symptoms, on top of increasing difficulties at work, he had a violent argument with his son. The additional features of sudden travel away from his home and the assumption of a new identity justify the diagnosis of Psychogenic Fugue.

DSM-III Diagnosis:

Axis I: 300.13 Psychogenic Fugue (p. 257)

Eggs

76 The patient is a 19-year-old white male who, until admission, was working in a mailroom while waiting to apply to college. The onset of his illness is not clear. According to him, he has not been "the same" since his mother died of a cerebral hemorrhage nine months before his admission. According to his father, however, he exhibited a normal mourning response to his mother's death and changed only three months ago. At that time, shortly after his girl friend had rejected him for another man, he began to think that male co-workers were making homosexual advances to him. He began to fear that he was homosexual and that his friends believed he was homosexual. He finally developed the conviction that there was a disorder of his reproductive system: he had one normal testicle that produced sperm and his other testicle was actually an ovary that produced eggs. He thought this was evidence that a "woman's body resides inside my man's body." He began to gamble and was convinced that he had won $400,000 and was not paid by his bookie, and that he was sought after by talk-show hosts to be a guest on their shows and tell his unusual story (all not true). He claimed that he had a heightened awareness, an "extra sense," and that sounds were unusually loud. He had difficulty sleeping at night, but no appetite disturbance.

On admission his speech was somewhat rapid, and he jumped from topic to topic. His affect was neither irritable, euphoric, nor expansive. He said he was now seeking treatment because "there is a war between my testicles, and I prefer to be a male."

When he was ten, his pediatrician became concerned that he had an undersized penis. This led to a complete endrocrine workup and examinations of his genitals every four months for the next four years. At that time it was concluded that there were no significant abnormalities.

During high school he was a poor student with poor attendance. He claims always to have had many friends. He has never received psychiatric treatment. He admits to occasional marijuana and phencyclidine use in the past, but denies any use of hallucinogens.

The patient is the oldest child in a family of six children. His parents met when they were both patients in a psychiatric hospital.

Discussion of Eggs

The significant features of this man's illness include bizarre somatic delusions, grandiose delusions, and disorganization in his speech (jumped from topic to topic). Although the grandiose delusions and pressured speech suggest the possibility of a manic episode, this is ruled out by the absence of either an elevated, expansive, or irritable mood.

When did his illness begin? Although he says he has not been the same since his mother died nine months ago, he does not describe any change in himself that is out of keeping with normal bereavement. Furthermore, his father claims that his abnormal behavior began only three months ago. Giving the patient the benefit of the doubt, we date the onset of the illness at three months before admission. The presence of the characteristic symptoms of Schizophrenia in an illness of more than two weeks' but less than six months' duration indicates Schizophreniform Disorder.

DSM-III Diagnosis:

Axis I: **295.40 Schizophreniform Disorder (p. 200)**

The Cold War

77 A beautiful, successful, 34-year-old interior designer is brought to the clinic by her 37-year-old husband, a prominent attorney. The husband laments that for the past three years his wife has made increasingly shrill accusations that he is unfaithful to her. He declares that he has done everything in his power to convince her of his innocence, but there is no shaking her conviction. A careful examination of the facts reveals that there is actually no evidence that the man has been unfaithful. When his wife is asked what her evidence is, she becomes vague and mysterious, declaring that she can tell such things by a faraway look in his eye.

She is absolutely sure that she is right, and feels highly insulted by the suggestion that she is imagining the disloyalty. Her husband reports that for the last year she has been increasingly bitter, creating a kind of "cold war" atmosphere in the household. Militantly entrenched against her husband, she refuses to show him any affection except at social gatherings. She seems intent on giving the impression socially that they have a good relationship; but when they are alone, the coldness reenters the picture. She has physically assaulted her husband on occasion, but her account obscures the fact that she initiated the assaults; her description of the tussles actually begins at the point at which the husband attempted to interrupt her assault by holding her arms. She declares that she will never forgive him for holding her down and squeezing her arms, and her account makes it appear that she was unfairly pinned down.

The patient experiences no hallucinations; her speech is well organized; she interprets proverbs with no difficulty; she seems to have a good command of current events and generally displays no difficulty in thinking aside from her conviction of the disloyalty. She describes herself as having a generally full and effective life, with a few close friends and no problems except those centering on her experiences of unhappiness in the marriage. The husband reports that his wife is respected for her skills, but that she has had difficulties for most of her life in close relationships with friends. She has lost a number of friends because she seems to be intolerant of differences in opinion. The patient reports that she does not want to leave the marriage, nor does she want her husband to leave her; instead, she is furious about the "injustice," and she demands that the injustice be confessed and redeemed.

Discussion of The Cold War

Not all complaints of infidelity are unfounded, but in this case the evidence supports the notion that the wife's jealousy is delusional. Delusional jealousy may be seen in Schizophrenia; but in the absence of hallucinations or disorganized speech, they are symptoms of a Paranoid Disorder. A chronic and stable Paranoid Disorder of at least six months' duration is called Paranoia. As is commonly the case in Paranoia, this woman's impairment due to her delusion does not involve her daily functioning apart from her relationship with her husband.

DSM-III Diagnosis:

Axis I: 297.10 Paranoia (p. 197)

Thunderbird

78 A 43-year-old divorced carpenter is examined in the hospital emergency observation ward. The patient's sister is available to provide some information. The sister reports that the patient has consumed large quantities of cheap wine daily for over five years. Evidently the patient had a reasonably stable home life and job record until his wife left him for another man five years previously. The sister indicates that the patient drinks more than a fifth of wine a day, and that this has been an unvarying pattern since the divorce. He often has had blackouts from drinking and has missed work; consequently, he has been fired from several jobs. Fortunately for him, carpenters are in great demand, and he has been able to provide marginally for himself during these years. However, three days ago he ran out of money and wine and had to beg on the street to buy a meal. The patient has been poorly nourished, eating perhaps one meal a day and evidently relying on the wine as his prime source of nourishment.

The morning after his last day of drinking (three days ago), he felt increasingly tremulous, his hands shaking so grossly that it was difficult for him to light a cigarette. Accompanying this was an increasing sense of inner panic, which had made him virtually unable to sleep. A neighbor became concerned about the patient when he seemed not to be making sense and clearly was unable to take care of himself. The neighbor contacted the sister, who brought him to the hospital.

On examination, the patient alternates between apprehension and chatty, superficial warmth. He is quite keyed up and talks almost constantly. At times he recognizes the doctor, but at other times he thinks the doctor is his older brother. Twice during the examination he calls the doctor by his older brother's name and asks when he arrived, evidently having lost track entirely of the interview up to that point. He has a gross hand tremor at rest, and there are periods when he picks at "bugs" he sees on the bed sheets. He is disoriented for time and thinks that he is in a supermarket parking lot rather than in a hospital. He indicates that he feels he is fighting against a terrifying sense that the world is ending in a holocaust. He is startled every few minutes by sounds and scenes of fiery car crashes (evidently provoked by the sound of rolling carts in the hall). Efforts at testing memory and calculation fail because his attention shifts too rapidly. An electroencephalogram indicates a pattern of diffuse encephalopathy.

Discussion of Thunderbird

This carpenter, with a long history of heavy alcohol use, develops severe withdrawal symptoms after he stops drinking. He has a gross hand tremor, anxiety, disorientation to time and place, misinterpretations (thinking the doctor is his brother), visual hallucinations (picking at "bugs" on the bed sheets), difficulty sustaining attention, and synesthesias (he sees scenes of car crashes provoked by the sound of rolling carts in the hall).

Although the treatment will initially be directed at the Alcohol Withdrawal Delirium, the additional diagnosis of Alcohol Dependence is warranted by the pathological pattern of use (need for daily use, consumption of more than a fifth of alcohol each day, blackouts) and the patient's social and occupational impairment (fired from several jobs). The course of the Alcohol Dependence is noted as Continuous because of regular maladaptive use for more than six months.

DSM-III Diagnosis:

Axis I: **291.00 Alcohol Withdrawal Delirium (p. 135)**
          303.91 Alcohol Dependence, Continuous (p. 170)

Fidgety

79 A 32-year-old mother of four presented at the clinic with complaints of anxiety, irritability, temper outbursts, and concentration problems. She wept continuously throughout the first interview, claiming that her life had brought her little happiness. She had come to the clinic on the recommendation of a child psychiatrist, who, while evaluating one of her sons for a learning problem, had observed emotional difficulties in her.

Although she recalls that her mother described her as a "difficult" child, the patient had no substantial problems until she entered elementary school. During the first two years she did well in arithmetic, but reading and spelling were problems. She remembers being so "fidgety" in the first and second grades that she could not stay seated for long and the teacher had to turn the pages of books, since she could not do this herself. She daydreamed frequently and failed to complete classwork unless closely supervised. She had difficulty organizing both her schoolwork and her chores at home (the latter improved with constant supervision) and had the problem, which continues to the present day, of speaking before thinking. As she grew older, her academic problems worsened and she developed behavioral problems (fighting with other children, disrupting the class); in the third grade she was placed in a special school for children with learning difficulties (her IQ in adulthood was 115). Despite the transfer, she continued to have difficulties, not only academically but with her peers, because of her quick temper.

There was some improvement in high school, where the patient began to have friends. Reading continued to be difficult, and she avoided it as much as possible. She attributed her reading problems to continuing difficulty in attention. She stated that it was difficult for her to keep her mind on movies or TV programs unless they were unusually spellbinding. Although she participated in many social activities, she had the nagging feeling that she derived less pleasure from them than other people did. She made and severed interpersonal relations impulsively.

She had married her husband after a few weeks' courtship when she was 22, and they frequently argued from the very beginning. Their problems had been compounded by the birth of four children in rapid succession. These children displayed behavioral difficulties similar to those the patient had had as a child; and their problems were aggravated by their mother's inability to set reasonable limits, be consistent, and maintain a relatively even temper. Since their marital problems persisted, both she and her husband began psychotherapy. Despite intermittent individual and couple therapy over a ten-year period, there had been little improvement in their marital relationship. The severity of the problem had diminished somewhat when her husband learned the efficacy of leaving her alone when she became angry, since arguments only made things worse.

Discussion of Fidgety

This woman demonstrates that even when diagnosing an adult, one should consider the possibility of a residual form of a disorder that usually is seen in children. As a child this woman often was fidgety, could not stay seated, had difficulty organizing her work, spoke out in class impulsively, failed to complete her classwork, and often appeared to have trouble listening or concentrating (daydreaming). All of these suggest the hyperactivity, impulsivity, and inattention associated with Attention Deficit Disorder with Hyperactivity. During adolescence many of these difficulties continued, and as an adult the patient continues to be impulsive (temper outbursts) and to have attentional difficulties (trouble concentrating).

When, as in this case, there is a childhood history of Attention Deficit Disorder with Hyperactivity and the attentional problems and impulsivity persist into adult life and cause some social or occupational impairment, the diagnosis of Attention Deficit Disorder, Residual Type, is made.

DSM-III Diagnosis:

Axis I: 314.80 Attention Deficit Disorder, Residual Type (p. 44)

Mr. and Ms. A.

80 Mr. and Ms. A. are an attractive, gregarious couple, married for 15 years, who present in the midst of a crisis over their sexual problems. Mr. A., a successful restaurateur, is 38. Ms. A., who since marriage has devoted herself to child-rearing and managing the home, is 35. She reports that throughout their entire marriage she has been extremely frustrated because sex has "always been hopeless for us." She is now seriously considering leaving her husband.

The difficulty is the husband's rapid ejaculation. Whenever any lovemaking is attempted, Mr. A. becomes anxious, moves quickly toward intercourse, and reaches orgasm either immediately upon entering his wife's vagina or within one or two strokes. He then feels humiliated, recognizes his wife's dissatisfaction, and they both lapse into silent suffering. He has severe feelings of inadequacy and guilt, and she experiences a mixture of frustration and resentment toward his "ineptness and lack of concern." Recently they have developed a pattern of avoiding sex, which leaves them both frustrated, but which keeps overt hostility to a minimum.

Mr. A. has always been a perfectionist, priding himself on his ability to succeed at anything he sets his mind to. As a child he had always been a "good boy" in a vain effort to please his demanding father. His inability to control his ejaculation is a source of intense shame, and he finds himself unable to talk with his wife about his sexual "failures." Ms. A. is highly sexual, easily aroused by foreplay, but has always felt that intercourse is the only "acceptable" way to reach orgasm. Since intercourse with her husband has always been brief, she holds him completely responsible for her sexual frustration. Since she cannot discuss the subject without feeling rage, she usually avoids talking about it. As a result, they have not developed other techniques for pleasing each other, and sex has always been a disaster.

In other areas of their marriage, including rearing of their two children, managing the family restaurant, and socializing with friends, these two are highly compatible. Despite these strong points, however, they are near separation because of the tension produced by their mutual sexual disappointment.

Discussion of Mr. and Ms. A

This couple presents with a sexual problem that is threatening their marriage. Since DSM-III does not include a classification of disturbed dyadic units, it is necessary, when focusing on this type of diagnostic problem, to consider each marital partner separately. (This does not preclude the clinician's focusing on the relationship when considering both how the problem arose and its possible treatment.)

The husband's sexual difficulty is that he lacks a reasonable degree of voluntary control over ejaculation, so that he invariably ejaculates almost immediately upon penetration during intercourse. As a result, his wife is never sexually satisfied, and he feels extremely inadequate. Since the lack of control is not limited to novel situations and does not occur only after long periods of abstinence, and since there is no evidence of a nonsexual Axis I mental disorder that might account for the disturbance, such as Generalized Anxiety Disorder, the Axis I diagnosis of Premature Ejaculation is made. Because the husband's "perfectionism" is mentioned and this might be related to either the development or the perpetuation of the sexual problem, compulsive personality traits are noted on Axis II.

There is little information about the wife's difficulties, other than that she clearly has a marital problem. With this limited information, the V code Marital Problem is appropriate; it should be understood, however, that with more information it may need to be changed to, for example, a Personality Disorder. The husband, of course, does not receive the V code Marital Problem since his marital problem apparently is due to his Axis I mental disorder.

Some clinicians might consider the diagnosis of Adjustment Disorder for either the husband, the wife, or both. In the husband's case, the diagnosis would not be made since the distress that he is experiencing seems to be an associated feature of the Premature Ejaculation rather than a separate illness. In the wife's case, an Adjustment Disorder diagnosis would imply that her reaction to her husband's sexual problem (her rage and threatening separation) is excessive and indicates significant psychopathology. This might be the case, but such a judgment would require more information than is available.

DSM-III Diagnosis:

Husband:
Axis I: **302.75 Premature Ejaculation (p. 280)**
Axis II: **Compulsive personality traits**

Wife:
Axis I: **V61.10 Marital Problem (p. 333)**

Embarrassed

81 A 46-year-old married male was referred for evaluation in 1966 because of unremitting tics. At age 13 he had developed a persistent eye blink, soon followed by lip-smacking, head-shaking, and barking-like noises. Despite these symptoms, he functioned well academically, and eventually graduated from high school with honors. He was drafted during World War II. While in the army his tics subsided significantly, but were still troublesome, and eventually resulted in a medical discharge. He married, had two children, and worked as a semiskilled laborer and foreman. At the age of 30 his symptoms included tics of the head, neck, and shoulders, hitting his forehead with his hand and various objects, repeated throat clearing, spitting, and shouting out "Hey, hey, hey; la, la, la." Six years later noisy coprolalia started: he would emit a string of profanities such as "Fuck you, you cocksucking bastard" in the middle of a sentence and then resume his conversation.

Various treatments, all without benefit, were tried from 1951 to 1957, including insulin shock therapy, electroshock treatment, and administration of various phenothiazines and antidepressants. His social life became increasingly constricted because of his symptoms. He was unable to go to church or to the movies because of the cursing and noises. He worked at night to avoid social embarrassment. His family and friends became increasingly intolerant of his symptoms, and his daughters refused to bring friends home. He was depressed over his enforced isolation and the seeming hopelessness of finding effective treatment. At the age of 46 he sought a prefrontal lobotomy; but after psychiatric evaluation, his request was denied. This led to the 1966 referral for treatment with a new experimental drug, haloperidol. Treatment with haloperidol effectively controlled 99% of his symptoms. For the next 14 years his dosage was 1 mg/day. He resumed a normal social life and was no longer depressed.

Discussion of Embarrassed

This patient has the characteristic features of Tourette's Disorder: onset before age 15, recurrent motor and vocal tics (involuntary cursing or shouting), and a chronic waxing and waning course. It is largely for historical reasons that this disorder is classified as a mental rather than a neurological disorder. Originally the coprolalia and other bizarre symptoms were thought to represent pregenital conversion symptoms. Now, most investigators believe that the etiology of the disorder is organic and that whatever psychological disturbance may be present is best understood as a reaction to the chronic, incapacitating symptoms. In this case, when the symptoms of Tourette's Disorder were brought under control, the patient was no longer depressed.

When the patient was evaluated, he was described as being "depressed over his enforced isolation and the seeming hopelessness of finding effective treatment." This raises the question of Adjustment Disorder with Depressed Mood or of a Major Depression. The concept of Adjustment Disorder generally does not include situations in which the patient is distressed because of the consequences of the symptoms of, or the reaction of others to, his or her mental disorder. Such distress is commonplace in chronic illnesses and is better thought of as an associated feature of the illness rather than as Adjustment Disorder. On the other hand, if the depression were so severe as to meet the criteria for a major depressive episode, then the additional diagnosis of Major Depression would be appropriate. In this case there is no information about the other features of a depressive syndrome that would be necessary to make such a diagnosis.

DSM-III Diagnosis:

Axis I: 307.23 Tourette's Disorder (p. 77)

Hurting

82 A 26-year-old unemployed woman was referred for admission to a hospital by her therapist because of intense suicidal preoccupation and urges to mutilate herself by cutting herself with a razor.

The patient was apparently well until her junior year in high school, when she became preoccupied with religion and philosophy, avoided friends, and was filled with doubt about who she was. Academically she did well, but later, during college, her performance declined. In college she began to use a variety of drugs, abandoned the religion of her family, and seemed to be searching for a charismatic religious figure with whom to identify. At times massive anxiety swept over her and she found it would suddenly vanish if she cut her forearm with a razor blade. Three years ago she began psychotherapy, and initially rapidly idealized her therapist as being incredibly intuitive and empathic. Later she became hostile and demanding of him, requiring more and more sessions, sometimes two in one day. Her life centered on her therapist, by this time to the exclusion of everyone else. Although her hostility toward her therapist was obvious, she could neither see it nor control it. Her difficulties with her therapist culminated in many epidoses of her forearm cutting and suicidal threats, which led to the referral for admission.

Discussion of Hurting

This is a textbook case of Borderline Personality Disorder. Characteristic of the patient's long-term functioning is impulsivity (use of drugs and self-mutilation), unstable and intense interpersonal relations (idealization and devaluation of her therapist), inappropriate, intense anger (hostility toward therapist), identity disturbance (filled with doubt about who she was), affective instability (episodes of massive anxiety), and physically self-damaging acts (cutting self with razor).

Although this woman is suicidal, there is no description of other depressive symptoms that would justify a diagnosis of Dysthymic Disorder or Major Depression.

DSM-III Diagnosis:

Axis II: 301.83 Borderline Personality Disorder (p. 322)

Foggy Student

83 A 20-year-old male college student sought psychiatric consultation because he was worried that he might be going insane. For the past two years he had experienced increasingly frequent episodes of feeling "outside" himself. These episodes were accompanied by a sense of deadness in his body. In addition, during these periods he was uncertain of his balance and frequently stumbled into furniture; this was more apt to occur in public, especially if he was somewhat anxious. During these episodes he felt a lack of easy, natural control over his body, and his thoughts seemed "foggy" as well, in a way that reminded him of having received intravenous anesthetic agents for an appendectomy some five years previously.

The patient's subjective sense of lack of control was especially troublesome, and he would fight it by shaking his head and saying "stop" to himself. This would momentarily clear his mind and restore his sense of autonomy, but only temporarily, as the feelings of deadness and of being outside himself would return. Gradually, over a period of several hours, the unpleasant experiences would fade. The patient was anxious, however, about their return, since he found them increasing in both frequency and duration.

At the time the patient came for treatment, he was experiencing these symptoms about twice a week, and each incident lasted from three to four hours. On several occasions the episodes had occurred while he was driving his car and was alone; worried that he might have an accident, he had stopped driving unless someone accompanied him. Increasingly he had begun to discuss this problem with his girl friend, and eventually she had become less affectionate toward him, complaining that he had lost his sense of humor and was almost totally self-preoccupied. She threatened to break off with him unless he changed, and she began to date other men.

The patient's college grades remained unimpaired — they had, in fact, improved over the past six months, since the patient was spending more time studying than had previously been the case. Although discouraged by his symptoms, the patient slept well at night, had no change in appetite, and showed no impairment in concentration. He was neither fatigued nor physically "edgy" because of his worry.

Because he had had a cousin hospitalized for many years with severe mental illness, the patient had begun to wonder if a similar fate might befall him, and he sought direct reassurance on the matter.

Discussion of Foggy Student

Depersonalization—that is, alteration in the perception or experience of the self so that the usual sense of one's own reality is lost — can be a symptom of a variety of mental disorders, such as Schizophrenic, Anxiety, and Affective, Personality, and Organic Mental Disorders. Mild depersonalization, without functional impairment, occurs at some time in a large proportion of young adults, and does not by itself warrant diagnosis as a mental disorder. When, as in this case, the symptom of depersonalization occurs in the absence of a more pervasive disorder and is sufficiently severe to lead to impairment in social or occupational functioning, the diagnosis Depersonalization Disorder is made.

DSM-III Diagnosis:

Axis I: 300.60 Depersonalization Disorder (p. 260)

Disabled Vet

84 The patient is a 32-year-old man who admitted himself to a mental hospital after attempting suicide by taking sleeping pills. He said nothing in particular had prompted this attempt, but that he had been this depressed, with only minor fluctuations, for the last ten years, ever since he returned from Vietnam.

He describes a reasonably normal childhood and adolescence. "I never in my life felt like this before I got to Nam." He had friends through high school, always got at least average grades, and never was in trouble with the law or other authorities. He has had many girl friends, but has never married. After high school he went to technical school, was trained as an electrician, and was working in this occupation when he was drafted to go to Vietnam. He loathed the violence there; but on one occasion, evidently swept away by group spirit, he killed a civilian "for the fun of it." This seems to him totally out of keeping with his character. The memory of this incident continues to haunt him, and he is wracked with guilt. He was honorably discharged from the army, and has never worked since, except for three weeks when an uncle hired him. He has been living on various forms of government assistance.

In the army he began to drink heavily and to use whatever drugs he could get his hands on, abusing most of them; but in the last few years he has turned to alcohol almost exclusively. He has been drinking very heavily and nearly continually for the past 12 years, with blackouts, frequent arrests for public intoxication, and injuries in barroom brawls. He has acquaintances, but no friends. Whenever he "dries out" he feels terribly depressed (as he also does when he drinks), and he has made four suicide attempts in the last seven years. For the month before his latest suicide attempt he had been living in an alcohol-treatment residence, the longest dry period he can remember.

He presents as a very sad, thoughtful, introspective man with a dignified bearing, and in informal conversation appears to be of at least normal intelligence. He is not interested in anything and confides that when he sees others enjoying themselves, he is so jealous he wants to hit them; this urge is never evident from his unfailingly courteous behavior. There is no evidence of delusions, and no history of hallucinations except during several bouts of Alcohol Withdrawal Delirium in the past. His appetite is normal, as is his sex drive, "but I don't enjoy it." He has trouble falling asleep or staying asleep without medication. He is not psychomotorically slow. He complains of "absentmindedness," and immediate and short-term memory are grossly impaired. After two weeks, he still has trouble finding his way around the ward. He seemed very well motivated to cooperate with neuro-psychological testing, and was extremely distressed by his disabilities.

Testing revealed severely pathological functioning, with apraxias, agnosias, peripheral neuropathy, and constructional difficulties; his IQ measured 66.

The patient has not responded to antidepressant medication. He is sorry that his suicide attempt did not succeed, and he says that if things aren't going to get any better, he definitely wants to die.

Discussion of Disabled Vet

What occasioned this patient's hospital admission was a suicide attempt, a symptom of his long-standing depression. A ten-year period of depressed mood with such associated symptoms as sleep difficulties and recurrent suicidal acts, in the apparent absence of the full depressive syndrome, warrants the first-listed diagnosis of Dysthymic Disorder.

There is a history of heavy drinking, for the past 12 years, with a pathological pattern of use (blackouts) and social impairment (frequent arrests and injuries in barroom brawls). These, together with the history of episodes of withdrawal (Alcohol Withdrawal Delirium), indicate the presence of Alcohol Dependence. Since the patient has not been drinking for the past month, the course is noted as in Remission, although with such a brief period of remission the likelihood of relapse is extremely high.

Furthermore, he has severe memory loss and evidence of impairment of higher cortical functioning (apraxias, agnosias, constructional difficulties) and a decrement in intellectual abilities (IQ of 66) that interferes with functioning. Since this is apparently due to the long history of Alcoholism and is not limited to memory loss (as in Alcohol Amnestic Disorder), the diagnosis of Dementia Associated with Alcoholism is given. Because this diagnosis is more relevant to his current condition than the Alcohol Dependence, in Remission, it is listed as the second diagnosis.

DSM-III Diagnosis:

Axis I: 300.40 Dysthymic Disorder (p. 222)
291.20 Dementia Associated with Alcoholism (p. 138)
303.93 Alcohol Dependence, in Remission (p. 170)

Miriam and Esther

85 Miriam was hospitalized after her mother called the police because she feared Miriam might hurt both of them. Miriam claimed she was 56 years of age and lived with her 76-year-old "assumed" or "estranged" mother, Esther, and her 12-year-old daughter, Alice. She described Esther as a family friend who had given her and her daughter a room some years ago, but who had increasingly angered her by acting as a mother and a grandmother, invading her privacy, attacking her in her sleep, and jealously turning Alice against her. The night of admission, domestic squabbling had threatened to become violent, she said, which caused Esther to send her to the hospital "for hygiene." The patient expected to leave as soon as the ward social worker could relocate her and Alice in a "condominium or other suitable environment in which to rear my own child, who is coming of age as a young lady." She admitted to a recent sense of confusion, but denied sleep and appetite changes, mood disturbance, and hallucinations. However, she did describe a "whooshing" sound in her "cranium" intermittently over the past several years, which she felt resulted from fluid in her ear; at other times she had felt "very aware" of her own thoughts, but she denied hearing voices.

Miriam gave a vague but complex past history, as follows: She was born 56 years ago in Italy, on November 15, 1924. Her "biologic parents" (as she put it), Louise and William, were wealthy from oil. They took her to their country house in Mt. Vernon, New York, where she spent her childhood. Esther, a family friend, visited often. Miriam recalled people driving Packards and Rolls Royces. She stated she later lived in Europe and North Africa, and was present in Hiroshima when the atom bomb was dropped. This event left her with a steel plate in her head and an "atom brain." She lived with Louise and William from 1957 to 1968. She said she had three husbands and seven children. Her youngest, Alice, fathered by her last husband, was born in 1968, four years after his death. When asked how this could be, she explained that a "tubal infection" had delayed the baby's conception in a "technical way."

According to Miriam, after the birth of Alice she moved in with Esther and enrolled at Hunter College in a special program for middle-aged students, where she excelled in Romance languages. She became an alcoholic, consuming up to a pint of whiskey daily. Once when she didn't drink, she became shaky and broke into a sweat. Following the death in 1973 of her "biologic mother," Louise, Miriam became depressed and lost weight. A "nervous breakdown" landed her in a state mental hospital for three months, where she stopped drinking and improved with medication. For several years thereafter a local "mental hygiene" clinic gave her medication for "stability," including Prolixin, which made her hair fall out. Since then she had worked steadily, first for the Board of Education, and then as a home health aide. For the last year she had remained home to care for her child.

Miriam's mother, Esther, related quite a different history, corroborated by family members and clinic staff. Miriam is actually 30 years old and was born October 8, 1950. Esther is 56 and is, in fact, her biologic mother. When Miriam was seven, her father walked out on the family. The next year she and her older sister were sent to Mt. Vernon to live with Esther's middle-class Aunt Louise and Uncle William, probably for financial reasons. Esther visited on weekends.

Miriam was a good student, but had few friends and kept to herself. In 1968, at 17 years of age, she became pregnant by a cousin from Trinidad, whom she never saw again. She finished high school but, shamed, returned to her mother's home to have the baby. Esther cared for them both and took responsibility for rearing her granddaughter, Alice. Miriam attended night classes in business skills for two years at Hunter College, but did poorly. She then worked for a year as a home health aide, but quit because she thought people were against her. She began to hear voices that commented about her actions, and was finally admitted to a state hospital in 1973, where she improved with medication. The voices ceased several months after discharge. She lived at home and worked occasionally as a secretary, but failed a stenography and typing course. In 1977 her mother paid for her to have her own apartment. Miriam mismanaged her money, and was evicted after a year. The stress apparently caused her to become psychotic again (details are not known). She moved back to her mother's, and improved greatly on antipsychotics. She worked inconsistently for a year, again as a home health aide, but then stopped her medication and quit work. She began to call her mother "Esther," rather than "Mother," and began to say she was not her real mother. Friction developed because of Esther's disappointment in Miriam and Miriam's jealousy of the continued mothering role taken by Esther toward Miriam's child. The child clearly preferred Esther.

Miriam spent more time alone in her room, friendless, venturing out only for shopping trips in which she would spend her disability check on expensive clothes. Relatives say she was often belligerent when talking about her mother. She became unkempt and unable to help with the household chores. She began yelling at imaginary people to leave her alone and not touch her. On several occasions, by the time police had been summoned, Miriam had calmed down. However, the night of admission she was out of control, threatening to throw herself and her mother out the window, and was forcibly handcuffed and brought to the hospital.

According to her mother and family members, there is no history of alcohol (or drug) abuse.

Miriam's mental status in numerous interviews was characterized by calm, socially appropriate behavior. She was obese and homely but tastefully dressed. Speech and movement were of normal tempo and quantity. Her affect was constricted, although at times she seemed pedantic and slightly haughty. Contained anger and sarcasm were apparent during a joint interview with her mother. Thought processes were slightly loose, vague, and circumstantial. Most striking was her odd language, ranging from idiosyncratic usage — "my assumed mother," "my estranged mother"—to neologisms. ("Medicine makes me incognizant. I am not correlative enough." "My mother does not accreditize me." "The hospital will have my records if they are consortive; they must have a litigation department." "My cousin was a devasive schizoid.").

When confronted with inconsistencies in her account of her life, Miriam only smiled or giggled. While hospitalized she admitted neither to currently hearing the "whooshing" sound nor to any hallucinations. Nurses reported that when unknowingly observed, she acted as if she were aware of nonexistent beings.

Discussion of Miriam and Esther

This woman clearly has an illness with prominent psychotic features, the most notable being a delusion that the woman who claims to be her mother is actually only a family friend. (This delusion seems to be a variant of the Capgras syndrome, in which the individual believes that one or more people in his or her environment are actually imposters who either look exactly or almost exactly like the people whose roles they have assumed.) Other bizarre delusions include the belief that the conception of her youngest child was delayed several years beyond the death of the biologic father and that she was in Hiroshima when the atom bomb was dropped, leaving her with a steel plate in her head.

Although she denies hallucinations, the sound in her head probably is an auditory hallucination; her mother claims that she has heard voices in the past.

The absence of a known organic factor that could account for the symptoms, the deterioration in functioning over several years, and the bizarre delusions and hallucinations clearly establish the diagnosis as Schizophrenia. The prominence of the persecutory delusions indicates the Paranoid subtype. The course of her illness is characterized as chronic (ill for more than two years) with a current acute exacerbation (reemergence of prominent psychotic symptoms).

An unusual feature of this case is what is sometimes referred to as pseudologia fantastica, the presentation of fantastic and elaborate details about oneself that are completely false but that the patient appears to believe. In Miriam's case this is illustrated by her account of her past history, being born in Italy, growing up with wealthy parents, later living in Europe and North Africa, and her claim of having had a serious alcohol problem (which her family denied).

DSM-III Diagnosis:

Axis I: **295.34 Schizophrenia, Paranoid Type, Chronic with Acute Exacerbation (p. 191)**

The Fashion Plate

86 Mr. A., a 65-year-old security guard, formerly a fishing-boat captain, is distressed about his wife's objections to his wearing a nightgown at home in the evening now that his youngest child has left home. His appearance and demeanor, except when he is dressing in women's clothes, are always appropriately masculine, and he is exclusively heterosexual. Occasionally over the past five years he has worn an inconspicuous item of female clothing even when dressed as a man, sometimes a pair of panties, sometimes an ambiguous pinkie ring. He always carries a photograph of himself dressed as a woman.

His first recollection of an interest in female clothing was putting on his sister's bloomers at age 12, an act accompanied by sexual excitement. He continued periodically to put on women's underpants—an activity that invariably resulted in an erection, sometimes a spontaneous emission, sometimes masturbation, but was never accompanied by fantasy. Although he occasionally wished to be a girl, he never fantasized himself as one. He was competitive and aggressive with other boys and always acted "masculine." During his single years he was always attracted to girls, but was shy about sex. Following his marriage at 22, he had his first heterosexual intercourse.

His involvement with female clothes was of the same intensity even after his marriage. Beginning at age 45, after a chance exposure to a magazine called *Transvestia*, he began to escalate his cross-dressing activity. He learned there were other men like himself, and he became more and more preoccupied with female clothing in fantasy and progressed to periodically dressing completely as a woman. More recently he has become involved in a transvestite network, writing to other transvestites contacted through the magazine and occasionally attending transvestite parties. Cross-dressing at these parties has been the only time that he has cross-dressed outside his home.

Although still committed to his marriage, sex with his wife has dwindled over the past 20 years as his waking thoughts and activities have become increasingly centered on cross-dressing. Over time this activity has become less eroticized and more an end in itself. He always has an increased urge to dress as a woman when under stress; it has a tranquilizing effect. If particular circumstances prevent him from cross-dressing, he feels extremely frustrated.

The patient's parents belonged to different faiths, a fact of some importance to him. He was the eldest of three children, extremely close to his mother, whom he idolized, and angry at his "whoremaster," "alcoholic" father. The parents fought constantly. He is tearful, even now at age 65, when he describes his mother's death when he was 10. He was the one who found her dead (of pleurisy), and he says he has been "not the same from that day . . . always [having] the feeling something's not right." The siblings were reared by three separate branches of the family until the father remarried. When the patient was 20, his father died, a presumed suicide; but Mr. A. believes he may have been murdered, since he could not figure out a suicide motive. His brother also died traumatically, drowned in his teens.

Because of the disruptions in his early life, he has always treasured the steadfastness of his wife and the order of his home. He told his wife about his cross-dressing practice when they were married, and she was accepting so long as he kept it to himself. Even so, he felt guilty, particularly after he began complete cross-dressing and periodically attempted to renounce it, throwing out all his female clothes and makeup. His children served as a barrier to his giving free rein to his impulses. Following his retirement from fishing, and in the absence of his children, he finds himself more drawn to cross-dress, more in conflict with his wife, and more depressed.

Discussion of The Fashion Plate

This man demonstrates the characteristic development and course of Transvestism. Initially he is sexually aroused by cross-dressing. He is, however, never in doubt about his gender identity as a male or his heterosexual orientation. As he becomes more involved in cross-dressing, it becomes "less eroticized and more an end in itself." His urge to cross-dress increases under stress, and the cross-dressing has a calming effect. If the behavior is prevented, he feels intensely frustrated.

DSM-III Diagnosis:

Axis I: **302.30 Transvestism (p. 270)**

Beasts

87 A white male in his mid-thirties, in prison for molesting prepubescent girls, volunteered for an interview with a sex researcher. He had been reared in a rural area by lower-middle-class parents with a grammar-school education. His mother, who was extremely prudish, frightened her son with tales of venereal disease and the dire consequences of masturbation, and impressed upon him that all sexual activity was nasty and that men were "beasts" *(sic)*. He therefore felt guilty about his heterosexual urges and his preadolescent heterosexual play, and with puberty at age 12 ceased all heterosexual activity. Masturbation had begun a year before puberty and ceased a year after puberty, evidently because of the maternal warnings. During adolescence he was shy and fearful of females, although desiring them. Girls accused him of being "tied to his mother's apron strings."

He had always been sexually aroused by the sight of stallions and mares copulating and sometimes fantasied animal contact while masturbating. He had heard of animal contact from his peer group and substituted for masturbation coitus with cows, which he performed almost daily from ages 13 to 18. Some affectional component developed, such as one might have for a pet animal. However, he never found the idea of sexual activity with an animal as exciting as the idea of sexual activity with a girl. When he was 18 an epidemic of brucellosis appeared among the farm animals in the region, and the young man associated this in his mind with venereal disease — concerning which he had a deep horror, instilled by his mother. He therefore terminated his animal contacts. Lacking any adult heterosexual activity, afraid to masturbate or engage in animal contacts, the young man reverted to his preadolescent pattern (which had been very gratifying) and began seeking contact with prepubescent girls. This led to his arrest and imprisonment.

Discussion of Beasts

The Institute for Sex Research at Indiana University, founded by Alfred C. Kinsey, was asked to submit a case of Zoophilia. A computer search of their extensive files of thousands of individuals interviewed between 1938 and 1963 revealed 96 cases involving extensive sexual activity with animals, but in not a single case was the animal contact or the fantasy of contact with animals the *preferred* source of achieving sexual excitement. However, this case was submitted since it involved exclusive sexual contact with an animal for several years.

Because this man's sexual activity was exclusively with animals for several years, his diagnosis at that time would certainly have been Zoophilia. Unlike the other Paraphilias, sexual activity with animals may always be a second choice, as it was in this case. Apparently there are no cases in which the idea of sexual activity with an animal is more exciting than the idea of sexual activity with a human.

DSM-III Diagnosis:

Axis I: 302.10 Zoophilia (p. 270)

The behavior that led to his incarceration involved sexual activity with prepubescent girls. Because this was his exclusive, if not necessarily his preferred, method of achieving sexual excitement, the diagnosis at the time of his arrest was Pedophilia.

DSM-III Diagnosis:

Axis I: 302.20 Pedophilia (p. 271)

Mental Disorders in Children and Adolescents

Mental Disorders in Children and Adolescents

Echo

88 Richard, aged three and a half, a firstborn child, was referred at the request of his parents because of his uneven development and abnormal behavior. Delivery had been difficult, and he had needed oxygen at birth. His physical appearance, motor development, and self-help skills were all age-appropriate; but his parents had been uneasy about him from the first few months of life because of his lack of response to social contact and the usual baby games. Comparison with their second child, who, unlike Richard, enjoyed social communication from early infancy, confirmed their fears.

Richard appeared to be self-sufficient and aloof from others. He did not greet his mother in the mornings, or his father when he returned from work, though, if left with a baby-sitter, he tended to scream much of the time. He had no interest in other children and ignored his younger brother. His babbling had no conversational intonation. At three years he could understand simple practical instructions. His speech consisted of echoing some words and phrases he had heard in the past, with the original speaker's accent and intonation; but he could use one or two such phrases to indicate his simple needs. For example, if he said "Do you want a drink?" he meant he was thirsty. He did not communicate by facial expression or use gesture or mime, except for pulling someone along and placing his or her hand on an object he wanted.

He was fascinated by bright lights and spinning objects, and would stare at them while laughing, flapping his hands, and dancing on tiptoe. He also displayed the same movements while listening to music, which he had liked from infancy. He was intensely attached to a miniature car, which he held in his hand, day and night; but he had no imaginative, pretend play with this or any other toy. He could assemble jigsaw puzzles rapidly (with one hand because of the car held in the other), whether the picture side was exposed or hidden. From age two he had collected kitchen utensils and arranged them in repetitive patterns all over the floors of the house. These pursuits, together with occasional periods of aimless running around, made up his whole repertoire of spontaneous activities.

The major management problem was Richard's intense resistance to any attempt to change or extend his interests. Removing his toy car, disturbing his puzzles or patterns, including retrieving, for example, an egg whisk or a spoon for its legitimate use in cooking, or even trying to make him look at a picture book, precipitated temper tantrums that could last an hour or more with screaming, kicking, and biting himself or others. These tantrums could be cut short by restoring the *status quo*. Otherwise, playing his favorite music or a long car ride were sometimes effective.

His parents had wondered if Richard could be deaf, but his love of music, his accurate echoing, and his sensitivity to some very soft sounds, such as that made by unwrapping a chocolate in the next room, convinced them that this was not the cause of his abnormal behavior. Psychological testing gave him a mental age of 3 years in non-language-dependent skills (fitting and assembly tasks), but only 18 months in language comprehension.

Discussion of Echo

Richard demonstrates a lack of responsiveness and gross impairment that began in the first few months of life. His speech has continued to be peculiar in that it consists entirely of echoing the words and phrases of others. His responses to the environment are often bizarre (flapping his hands and dancing on tiptoe in response to bright lights or spinning objects, temper tantrums when his routines are interfered with). These behaviors, beginning before 30 months of age, are the characteristic signs of Infantile Autism.

The DSM-III criteria for Infantile Autism and Childhood Onset Pervasive Developmental Disorder preclude the presence of incoherence or marked loosening of associations, characteristic symptoms of Schizophrenia. The disturbance of speech in this case is typical of Infantile Autism; but, because it is often ungrammatical and inappropriate in relation to the situation, it could be described as "incoherent." This term describes disorganized speech in other conditions, including Schizophrenia and Organic Brain Syndromes, although the phenomena to which it refers in each case differ in detail. Therefore, perhaps "incoherence" should not be used in the differential diagnosis of Pervasive Developmental Disorders.

DSM-III Diagnosis:

Axis I: Infantile Autism, Full Syndrome Present (p. 90)

Dressing Up

89 The following is a transcript of an interview with the parents of a seven-year-old boy:

Mother: Well, my husband doesn't feel there's a problem as much as I do. . . . When I really realized there was a problem is when he was four years old and he wanted to put a picture of a little girl by his bed. He cut the picture out of a magazine. It was a very pretty girl. I didn't think anything of it and said go ahead. And when I went to tuck him in bed he said, "Mommy, if I look at her hard enough, will I turn into her?"

He leans toward feminine type of behavior. He follows me around constantly with the baby; he likes her ruffled panties, and he comes in when I comb her hair. He loves the little bows. He's very interested in female things. His natural singing voice is a deeper voice, but he prefers to use a high voice.

Stepfather: I feel it's just that most of his life he was thrown into playing with girls. Wherever he lived he had nothing but girls to play with. Competing with girls is very easy, and he liked it. When we moved, he got thrown in with a bunch of boys, and competing was a lot harder. Without girls he didn't want to compete because the boys are too rough.

Mother: He gives up playing with boys for a girl. If he had his choice and no one would ridicule him, he would go in the room and play with the girls and be more comfortable.

Stepfather: At four years old they were playing with dolls; he never picked up a ball, knew how to throw a ball.

Mother: He didn't have any kind of relationship at all with his father. . . . My mother and I were actually competing for him. She wanted to be his mother, and I wanted to be his mother. She would take him for the day and he would go visit her girl friends, and he would sit with the women at the table . . . he was a little old lady with the little old ladies. I can honestly say I just didn't know how to relate to a boy. I played with him. I didn't realize I was playing with him like a girl . . . I realize now I was playing with him as a girl.

Doctor: How do you mean?

Mother: Combing his hair a lot, dressing him twenty times a day, telling him how pretty he was all the time. When he started wearing pants I called them bloomers. . . . The first time I went to see his kindergarten teacher, she said he played in the girls' corner all the time, and she had a really hard time getting him with the boys.

Stepfather: He always acted a little bit feminine. He played so placidly. When the other boys would come over to the house, he wouldn't play well with them. He would always kind of back off; and if they hit him, he would come and hide behind my legs rather than hit them back. He was wanting more to be with the girls or wanting to be with the women and not play rough and tough.

Mother: If he could get into the makeup, he'd put the makeup on. If he could get into my clothes, he'd put them on from when he could first start putting something on. He always leaned more toward copying me than anyone else . . . he would just follow me around the house copying everything that I do.

Doctor: How far back did his interest in getting into your clothes go?

Mother: As early as he could start putting something on himself. He would take scarves, and underwear he loved to put on . . . he was taking something of mine and putting on shoes, whatever. He loved jewelry. He used to love my wigs.

Doctor: How did you feel about the behavior?

Mother: In the beginning I laughed at it; it was funny and cute. My mother laughed at it and in a way encouraged it. We didn't think it was anything . . . a phase; it was cute and we laughed.

Doctor: Did he at any time improvise or make up women's clothes from other materials?

Mother: Yes. To this day he wears my husband's old pajamas, and he loves to wear just the tops . . . it's like a little dress . . . I remember his taking scarves and using them to make dresses.

Doctor: You mentioned his interest in wigs. When did he begin to show that interest?

Mother: From day one . . . I would take my wig and prop it on his head. As a young baby if I was wearing a wig I would take the wig off and put the wig on him . . .

Stepfather: 99% of the books that he read . . . little girl books . . . Jane went . . . Jane baked a cake . . .

Doctor: Does he imitate characters from books or television when he would role play?

Stepfather: Yes. Women. Girls.

Mother: I have to be completely honest. This son, when he was one, was my life, my whole world. I found something to pour it all out in, a possession and ownership. His brother, at one, I was indifferent to. It wasn't mother love; it was smother love.

Stepfather: From the time I came into the picture, all I heard from her is, "I wish I had a girl. I wish I had a girl. I love to buy girl clothes. Oh, how nice it would be to have a girl." She'd sit and talk to her sisters about how it would be to have a girl, and he hears all that stuff. I think his desire to change into a girl was to please her.

Mother: He had this head full of curly hair, and many times he got mistaken for a girl, which I think he kind of enjoyed. Then when I bought him a christening dress instead of the pants, everyone told me they would have preferred pants. But I preferred the dress and did it my way.

Doctor: Did you buy other clothing that people commented on?

Mother: I would buy him little sunsuits; they had elastic, people told me they're for girls. But I still feel I would rather see a boy with the elastic around the legs.

Stepfather: It was a standard joke . . . you and your sister would laugh how you dressed him as a baby like a girl and you would say, "Oh, he's getting more like a girl every day," and they'd laugh. And he'd walk in.

Mother: He's already been called names. His brother calls him a faggot.

Discussion of Dressing Up

From the report of the parents, there is clear evidence of a conflict in gender identity early in the life of this child. There was a wish to be a girl, as well as behavior by his mother that could be seen as feminizing. He asked his mother if he would turn into a girl if he looked hard enough at a picture he had cut out of a magazine and placed by his bed. He is preoccupied with female stereotypical activities. He prefers to play with girls at school and in the neighborhood, plays in the doll corner at school, enjoys wearing his mother's clothes, jewelry, and wig, and improvises female clothing from his stepfather's pajamas. When imitating characters from books or television, he always takes the female role.

This is the characteristic picture of Gender Identity Disorder of Childhood as seen in a male. When this disorder is diagnosed in a female, the desire to be a male, because of a profound discontent in being a female, needs to be distinguished from the desire merely to have the cultural advantages associated with being a man.

DSM-III Diagnosis:

Axis I: 302.60 Gender Identity Disorder of Childhood (p. 266)

Shoelaces

90 George is a 16-year-old who was admitted to the hospital from a juvenile detention center following a serious suicide attempt. He had, in some way, wrapped shoelaces and tape around his neck, causing respiratory impairment. When found he was cyanotic and semiconscious. He had been admitted to the detention center earlier that day; it had been noted there that he was quite withdrawn.

On admission he was reluctant to speak, except to say that he would kill himself and nobody could stop him. He did, however, admit to a two-week history of depressed mood, difficulty sleeping, decreased appetite, decreased interest, guilt feelings, and suicidal ideation.

According to his parents, George was without emotional difficulties until, at age 13, he became involved in drugs, primarily LSD, marijuana, and other nonopioid substances. His grades dropped drastically, he ran away from home on several occasions after arguments with his parents, and he made a suicide gesture by overdosing on aspirin. A year later he was expelled from school following an argument with the principal. Unable to control his behavior, his parents had him declared a child in need of assistance. He was then evaluated in a mental health clinic, and a recommendation was made for placement in a group home. He apparently did well in the group home, and his relationships with his parents improved immensely with family counseling. He was quite responsible in holding a job and attending school and was involved in no illegal activities, including use of drugs. However, six months ago he again became involved in drugs and, over a course of two weeks, engaged in ten breaking-and-enterings, all of which he did alone. He remembers being depressed at this time, but cannot recall whether the mood change was before or after reinvolvement with drugs. He was then sent to the juvenile detention center, where he did well, so that he had been discharged to his parents' care three weeks ago. One day after returning home, he impulsively left with his buddies in a stolen car for a trip to Texas. His depression began shortly thereafter; and, according to him, his guilt about what he had done to his parents led to his suicide attempt.

Discussion of Shoelaces

The serious suicide attempt that occasioned admission to the hospital is clearly a symptom of a major depressive episode. There is a two-week history of depressed mood with many of the associated symptoms of the depressive syndrome. Although there is mention of the patient's being depressed six months previously, it is not clear whether at that time he had the full depressive syndrome. There is also a reference to his having made a suicide gesture by overdosing on aspirin at age 13, but it is also unclear whether that represented a major depressive episode. Thus, the first-listed diagnosis would be Major Depression, Single Episode. Since there is no mention of the characteristic symptoms of Melancholia, such as lack of reactivity and diurnal mood variation, the fifth-digit subclassification would be without Melancholia.

Since age 13 there has been a repeated and persistent pattern of conduct in which the basic rights of others or major age-appropriate societal norms or rules have been violated. This has included behavior leading to being expelled from school, purchasing illegal drugs, and running away from home, culminating in the ten breaking-and-enterings and the stealing of a car. The antisocial behavior justifies the diagnosis of a Conduct Disorder. The mention of some peer-group relations suggests the Socialized subtype. Finally, breaking-and-entering is regarded in DSM-III as an example of the Aggressive subtype, since it does involve some physical destruction of property.

There have been many episodes of maladaptive use of substances, including LSD, marijuana, and other nonopioid substances. These have caused academic and social impairment, thus justifying the diagnosis of Substance Abuse. Since the substances abused have been from several nonalcoholic substance categories (cannabis, a hallucinogen, and others), the diagnosis of Mixed Substance Abuse is made. Since the patient currently is not using these drugs, the course is specified as in Remission. The likelihood of relapse and resumption of use is high.

DSM-III Diagnosis:

Axis I: **296.22 Major Depression, Single Episode, without Melancholia (p. 213)**
312.23 Conduct Disorder, Socialized, Aggressive (p. 49)
305.93 Mixed Substance Abuse, in Remission

Janet

91 Janet, 13 years old, has a long history of school problems. She failed first grade, supposedly because her teacher was "mean," and was removed from a special classroom after she kept getting into fights with the other children. Currently in a normal sixth-grade classroom, she is failing reading, barely passing English, arithmetic, and spelling, but doing satisfactory work in art and sports. Her teacher describes Janet as a "slow learner with a poor memory" and states that she doesn't learn in a group setting and requires a great deal of individual attention.

Janet's medical history is unremarkable except for a tonsillectomy at age five and an early history of chronic otitis. She sat at 6 months, walked at 12 months, and began talking at 18 months. Examination revealed an open and friendly girl who was very touchy about her academic problems. She stated that she was "bossed around" at school, but had good friends in the neighborhood. Intelligence testing revealed a full-scale intelligence quotient of 97, and wide-range achievement testing produced grade-level scores of 4.8 for reading, 5.3 for spelling, and 6.3 for arithmetic.

Discussion of Janet

The differential diagnosis of academic problems includes consideration of poor schooling, Mental Retardation, Attention Deficit Disorder, Oppositional Disorder, Conduct Disorder, and a Specific Developmental Disorder. In this case, because other children in her class are apparently passing when she is not, it is reasonable to rule out inadequate schooling as an explanation for Janet's academic difficulties. Her average intelligence rules out a diagnosis of Mental Retardation. Although there is a mention of "fights with other children" and inability to "learn in a group setting," there is certainly no description of other behaviors that would justify a diagnosis of either Attention Deficit Disorder, Oppositional Disorder, or Conduct Disorder.

There is positive evidence suggesting a Specific Developmental Disorder: she not only seems to have particular difficulty with reading in school but also performs significantly below her expected level on a reading achievement test. Her reading score of 4.8 is more than one year below her expected reading level. Given the diagnosis of Developmental Reading Disorder, it is reasonable to regard the fighting and difficulty learning in a group as associated features of the Specific Developmental Disorder.

There is now considerable research evidence suggesting that early, chronic otitis may be associated with later learning and/or language difficulties.

DSM-III Diagnosis:

Axis II: 315.00 Developmental Reading Disorder (p. 94)

Space Cadet

92 An eight-year-old boy, a second-grade student, was brought to a mental health clinic because of increasing difficulty at school. His teacher reported that he often seemed to be in a "fog" or a world of his own in which he appeared "not to be listening." He did not finish classroom assignments unless the teacher continuously supervised his performance. When she succeeded in gaining his attention, he was able to deal with academic tasks easily, which was not surprising since he had learned to read at the age of four in a Montessori nursery school. His writing was usually illegible. He spent a good deal of time drawing spaceships. The child was somewhat obese and awkward (appearing to be the size of an 11- or 12-year-old), and his physical awkwardness resulted in his being chosen last in baseball or volleyball. He tended to be bossy with his peers, and often abruptly quit games because he could not tolerate waiting for his turn.

The patient was the product of a difficult breech delivery at term. His mother reported that he had been an irritable baby and that she had had a difficult time establishing sleeping and eating routines. She stated that, as a toddler, he was "always into everything" and was difficult to control. For example, at age two she told him a dozen or more times not to go into the street, yet he often did; this situation was finally controlled by putting him in a fenced backyard. As he grew older, he had a proclivity for getting into other dangerous situations. For instance, he often ran off to play without telling his parents. At various times they had found him walking the railroad tracks or playing on the thin ice of a not-quite-frozen reservoir.

Even now the patient requires fairly consistent parental supervision. He does not like to watch TV, but enjoys being read to, knows many books by heart, and, as mentioned, learned to read at an early age. His play patterns have been relatively immature, and his room is generally cluttered with his things. When requested to clean his room or perform chores, he is often noncompliant. In fact, he seems incapable of organizing his activities and, as a result, approaches them in a haphazard manner, leaving much undone. At home he is a friendly, cuddly child who is absentminded and sometimes disobedient.

On a Wechsler Intelligence Scale for Children the patient's performance IQ was 110 and his verbal IQ, 140. A screening neurologic examination revealed impaired balance and impaired fine-motor coordination. Eye contact is good, and his thought content is typical for an eight-year-old boy.

Discussion of Space Cadet

Academic difficulties in a child may be symptomatic of many different disorders. This child's normal intelligence and demonstrated competence in all academic tasks rule out Mental Retardation or a Specific Developmental Disorder. The primary disturbance is clearly his difficulty attending to academic tasks. He often fails to finish things he starts, does not seem to listen, and apparently has trouble concentrating (at school he appears "not to be listening"). In addition, he shows various signs of impulsivity: he has difficulty organizing his work ("seems incapable of organizing his activities"), he needs a lot of supervision, often acts before thinking (he has a proclivity for getting into dangerous situations), and has difficulty waiting his turn in games. All of these features indicate Attention Deficit Disorder.

As a toddler the patient was "always into everything." Very likely, at that time he was hyperactive; but the description of his current behavior does not include hyperactivity. Thus, the diagnosis is Attention Deficit Disorder without Hyperactivity.

Some clinicians might want to note the soft neurological signs (impaired balance and impaired fine-motor coordination) on Axis III.

DSM-III Diagnosis:

Axis I: 314.00 Attention Deficit Disorder without Hyperactivity (p. 44)

Chubby

93 Mary is a gaunt 15-year-old high-school student evaluated at the insistence of her parents, who are concerned about her weight loss. She is 5'3", and obtained her greatest weight of 100 pounds a year ago. Shortly thereafter she decided to lose weight to be more attractive. She felt chubby and thought she would be more appealing if she were thinner. She first eliminated all carbohydrate-rich foods and gradually increased her dieting until she was eating only a few vegetables a day. She also started a vigorous exercising program. Within six months she was down to 80 pounds. She then became preoccupied with food and started to collect recipes from magazines and prepare gourmet meals for her family. She had difficulty sleeping and was irritable and depressed, having several crying spells every day. Her menses started last year, but she has had only a few normal periods.

Mary has always obtained high grades in school and has spent a great deal of time studying. She has never been active socially and has never dated. She is conscientious and perfectionistic in everything she undertakes. She has never been away from home as long as a week. Her father is a business manager. Her mother is a housewife who for the past two years has had a problem with hypoglycemia and has been on a low-carbohydrate diet.

During the interview Mary said she felt fat even though she weighed only 80 pounds, and described a fear of losing control and eating so much food that she would become obese. She did not feel she was ill and thought hospitalization unnecessary.

Discussion of Chubby

The intense fear of becoming obese, the disturbance in body image (feeling fat when actually gaunt), and the profound weight loss in the absence of a known physical illness make up the clinical picture of Anorexia Nervosa.

This case also demonstrates such frequently associated features as vigorous exercise in order to lose weight, preoccupation with the preparation of food, and compulsive personality traits, such as perfectionism.

There are features of the depressive syndrome, such as crying spells, difficulty sleeping, depressed and irritable mood. Because these are common associated features of Anorexia Nervosa, an additional diagnosis of an Affective Disorder seems unnecessary.

DSM-III Diagnosis:

Axis I: 307.10 Anorexia Nervosa (p. 69)

Andy

94 Andy, four years and three months old, is brought in by his mother with a complaint of speech problems. His speech development was somewhat delayed, his first words being spoken at 20 months and sentences formed at 30 months; but other milestones were normal. At the age of two and a half he had been hospitalized with pneumonia and began to stutter. Upon release from the hospital, his mother consulted a speech pathologist and was told that the child's problem was a common one and that he would outgrow it. However, the stuttering has continued, and in fact has increased in frequency, with the child beginning to complain of fear of speaking as well.

There have been a number of serious psychosocial problems in the child's environment, including multiple arrests and jail terms of his father for burglaries, his mother's frequent losses of jobs, and multiple separations of his parents, who have never married.

During the examination Andy made few spontaneous remarks. He seemed shy and not too friendly, but he did cooperate with tasks and showed good concentration. When speaking he repeated the initial sounds of most words. His grammar and intonation were good. Breathing pattern and rate of speech were normal.

Discussion of Andy

What else could this be but Stuttering? Spastic dysphonia is ruled out by the normal breathing pattern, and Cluttering is ruled out by the normal rate of speech.

Developmental Language Disorder is ruled out by the current good grammar, although the rather late speech milestones suggest that this may have been an earlier problem. Stuttering is frequently associated with early language delays.

DSM-III Diagnosis:

Axis I: 307.00 Stuttering (p. 79)

Lady Macbeth

95   *Interviewer:* Tell me about when things were the hardest for you. When was that?

Patient: It was around Christmas time last year.

I: And you were how old then?

P: 13.

I: You're 14 now, right?

P: Yes.

I: When things were really at their worst, can you tell me what it was that was disturbing to you at that time?

P: Well, the major part about it was that like all these things that I did, they were really stupid, and they didn't make any sense; but I'm still gonna have to do it and, it was sort of like being scared of what would happen if I didn't do it.

I: What were the things that you were doing?

P: In the morning when I got dressed, I was real afraid that there'd be germs all over my clothes and things, so I'd stand there and I'd shake them for half an hour. I'd wash before I did anything — like if I was gonna wash my face, I'd wash my hands first; if I was gonna brush my teeth, I'd wash my hands first; and if I was gonna get dressed, I'd wash my hands first; and then it got even beyond that point. Washing my hands wasn't enough, and I started to use rubbing alcohol. It was wintertime and cold weather, and this really made my hands bleed. Even if I just held them under water, they'd bleed all over the place, and they looked terrible, and everyone thought I had a disease or something.

I: And when you were doing that much washing, how much time every day did that take if you added up all the different parts of it?

P: It took about six hours a day. In the morning I didn't have a whole lot of choice, because I had to get up at 6:00 and get ready for school. All I'd do was get dressed and go to the bathroom and brush my teeth and wash my face. I didn't even have time to brush my hair. At the time I never ate breakfast, so all these things — it was just so complex that I didn't have time to do anything.

I: You also told me about other things in addition to the washing and worrying about dirt: that you would have plans about how you would do other things.

P: Okay, well, they were like set plans in my mind that if I heard the word, like, something that had to do with germs or disease, it would be considered something bad, and so I had things that would go through my mind that were sort of like "cross that out and it'll make it okay" to hear that word.

I: What sort of things?

P: Like numbers or words that seemed to be sort of like a protector.

I: What numbers and what words were they?

P: It started out to be the number 3 and multiples of 3 and then words like "soap and water," something like that; and then the multiples of 3 got really high, and they'd end up to be 124 or something like that. It got real bad then. . .

I: At any time did you really believe that something bad would happen if you didn't do these things? Was it just a feeling, or were you really scared?

P: No! I was petrified that something would really happen. It was weird, because everyone would always say how sensible I was and intelligent. But it was weird because I tried to explain it in order to really make them understand what I was trying to say and they'd go, you know, like "Well, that's stupid," and I *knew* it; but when I was alone, things would be a lot worse than when I was with this group, because if I was around friends, that would make me forget about most of this. But when I was alone it . . . like, my mind would wander to all sorts of things and I'd get new plans and new rituals and new ideas, and I'd start worrying more and more about people that could get hurt that I cared about and things that could really go bad if I didn't.

I: Who were the people you'd worry most would get hurt?

P: My family, basically my family.

I: Any particular people in your family?

P: Well, like my grandmother — she's 83 and you know, I was just worried that . . . I know that she's old and she's not gonna be around much longer, but I was worried that maybe something *I* did could cause her to get really, really sick or something.

I: Had anything like this ever been on your mind before you were 13, when this started?

P: Well, let's see . . . my mother, her family has always been mostly real neat people and extremely clean and so that could have affected it, because I was growing up in that sort of background. But I always like to be clean and neat, and I was never really allowed to walk around the house with muddy shoes or anything like that, so. . .

I: But your concerns about clean, about how many times you did things—have they ever gotten in the way of your doing things that you wanted to do?

P: Uh-huh. Many times. Like, I was supposed to go somewhere with a friend, and we were gonna leave at 11:00 and I wanted to take a shower before I left. So I had to get up about 6:00 in the morning, and sometimes I just won't even make it with five hours to do it. . .

I: And that was since you were 13. But what about any time in your life before that—had anything like this ever happened? Or as far as you know was this the first?

P: It was the first time.

I: Have you at any time felt that you had some other special idea about forces beyond you . . . about your being able to control things magically or be in control?

P: I'm really scared of supernatural things. I don't like to say that I believe in superstitions and things, but I guess I really do 'cause they frighten me. When I was little they weren't really bothering me or anything, but now I avoid it as much as I can. Like, the number 13 now, if it came up, you know, it wouldn't bother me, but I'd rather have the number 7 instead.

I: So you are superstitious, but you've never heard any special voice talking to you or. . .

P: Yeah, I have. It's like . . . if I try to describe it, people would think that I saw little people dancing around or something, and that was wrong because all it was, it wasn't like a voice, it was just like a thought.

I: More like being able to hear yourself think?

P: Right.

I: Have you ever seen things that other people couldn't see?

P: No.

I: I know you are doing very well here in school and on the ward here at the hospital. Do you have any signs left of the problems that you used to have with your rituals and compulsions?

P: Well, everyone is compulsive to a point. I can see little things that I'll do. Like I will go over something twice, or three times, because that's a special number. Like, if I read something and I really don't understand it, maybe I would go over it one more time and then, say, one more time will make it three. But nothing really big. It's been really good, because I have gotten out and taken a shower, and gotten dressed, and washed my face and brushed my teeth, and all that stuff in like a half an hour! That's really good for me because I wasn't able to do that before.

I: So, in general it's fair to say it's things that just *you* would notice now, and probably someone sharing the room with you wouldn't be able to tell the other things you are doing even though you know these little things are there. Good . . . Well, thank you very much.

Discussion of Lady Macbeth

This adolescent girl articulately and vividly describes what it is like to have a severe form of Obsessive Compulsive Disorder. This patient has both obsessions and compulsions, and both are a significant source of distress to her and interfere with her functioning.

The obsessions consist of ideas that intrude themselves into her consciousness and are experienced as senseless (ego-dystonic). For example, she gets the idea that maybe she did something that could cause her grandmother to get sick. Another example is the thought that there are germs on her clothes. These obsessions lead to various compulsions that are designed to prevent some future event. For example, if she washed or showered enough, then she could avoid becoming infected by the germs. If she heard a word that suggested germs or disease, she had to undo it ("cross that out") by saying the number 3 and multiples of 3 or words like "soap and water." The compulsive acts were not pleasurable in themselves (like eating, or sexual activity), but were followed by a decrease in anxiety. Although emotionally she reacted as if the dangers were real ("I was petrified that something would really happen"), intellectually she always knew that her fears were irrational (her friends would say that it was stupid, and she *knew* that it was).

Obsessional thoughts need to be distinguished from auditory hallucinations. This patient recognized that if she described some of her obsessional thoughts to people, they might think that she was hallucinating ("if I tried to describe it, people would think that I saw little people dancing around or something"). However, she is quite clear that it was just her own thoughts, not a voice.

Obsessive Compulsive Disorder is sometimes associated with Compulsive Personality Disorder. Whereas Obsessive Compulsive Disorder involves true obsessions and compulsions, Compulsive Personality Disorder involves such personality traits as perfectionism, indecisiveness, and restricted ability to express warm and tender emotions. There is no evidence in this case of Compulsive Personality Disorder.

Individuals with Obsessive Compulsive Disorder also often have a Major Depression, either before or during the course of Obsessive Compulsive Disorder. In fact, on further questioning this patient did describe an episode of Major Depression that occurred early in the course of her Obsessive Compulsive Disorder.

DSM-III Diagnosis:

Axis I: 300.30 Obsessive Compulsive Disorder (p. 235)

Angelo

96 Angelo, seven years old, was referred to the clinic by his parents because of wetting himself at night and during the day. His parents were also concerned about his temper tantrums and other behavior problems.

Angelo has never been consistently dry. He is now wet most nights, often several times each night, although he is usually dry for a few days when sleeping over at his grandparents' house. The longest period during which he has been continuously dry at night was two weeks when, two years ago, he was in a hospital because of a fractured leg.

Angelo has never been dry through the day. Since starting at a new school three months ago, he has managed to be dry during school hours. However, he invariably wets himself once he returns home from school and again before bedtime.

His parents have tried a variety of methods to stop the wetting. They have praised him, offered him rewards if he would stay dry, told him off in private and in public, and, on one occasion, even gave him a mild spanking. He has received various forms of medication from his pediatrician, but has never stuck with this for very long; his parents feel that the medication has never been very helpful. His parents have tried waking him up to urinate after he has gone to sleep but before they go to bed, but this has seemed to have no predictable effect on whether he would be wet later at night or not.

Before wetting himself during the daytime, Angelo often seems to become agitated, crosses his legs, and hops up and down. If his parents notice him doing this and tell him to go to the toilet, they feel that they can avert his wetting. During family outings in an automobile, Angelo seems to need to urinate more often than other children of his mother's acquaintance.

The boy has been evaluated by a urologist, who found no urinary infection or other genitourinary abnormality.

His mother describes Angelo as having frequent temper tantrums. This occurs two to three times a week, and is precipitated by only minor frustrations. For example, the day before his first attendance at the clinic, he had a temper tantrum when he could not find his jacket before going outside in the cold weather. At such time he jumps up and down and shrieks, or sits or lies down and kicks his legs. The tantrums last for up to ten minutes, and then everything seems to be forgotten. Angelo's parents describe him as also being generally stubborn and very persistent in trying to get something he wants. Often he is oppositional and refuses to do as he is told — "He always thinks he knows best."

Angelo enjoys sports, and his parents have started to let him take ski-jumping lessons. He does this very well, and has won several competitions. However, he invariably gets upset if he does not win, even if he comes in second. He sometimes talks of breaking the winner's skis, or running away from home, and also once said that he planned to try an impossibly high jump. If he loses a competition, he sulks for several hours; the same is true of any other game played at home.

In other ways Angelo's behavior is essentially normal. He eats and sleeps well, enjoys going to school, and has many friends, although his friendships often are short-lived. He rarely gets into a fight. His teachers always regard him as being precocious in his ability to talk about grownup things.

He is very close to his mother and spends a lot of time telling her everything that he has been doing during the day. He also enjoys his father's company. He ignores his 1½-year-old sister, and regards her as a nuisance.

Angelo had normal motor milestones, sitting at seven months and walking at one year. His parents believe that he was slow to speak and recall that he only started to say single words at 16 months and was not putting sentences together until at least the age of 2. He stopped soiling himself during the day at three years of age.

On examination, Angelo was a pleasant-looking, slim, blond boy with no physical abnormalities. His intravenous pyelogram was reviewed and found to be normal. His IQ had previously been tested, and he was known to have a full-scale IQ of 110, with verbal and performance scores close to that. The psychologist who tested him reported that he was anxious about his performance and easily became distressed if he could not do an item or feared that he might have done it wrong.

During the interview Angelo was active in exploring the room, talked readily, and had good rapport with the interviewer. He seemed confident and mature for his age and discussed his bed-wetting without seeming concern. He often approached aggressive themes during play, but very rarely followed through on them.

Discussion of Angelo

Persistent enuresis at the age of seven is clearly abnormal. The absence of any physical explanation for the enuresis suggests the diagnosis of Functional Enuresis.

There are several references to behavior that is suggestive of Oppositional Disorder — the child's frequent temper tantrums, stubbornness, and frequent refusal to do as he is told — but in the absence of evidence that his oppositional behavior is pervasive (e.g., also seen at school and with other authority figures), one would be reluctant to give an additional diagnosis of Oppositional Disorder, although it would need to be ruled out.

DSM-III Diagnosis:

Axis I: 307.60 Functional Enuresis (p. 80)

Brrr

97 Kevin is an attractive six-year-old boy whose mother brought him to the emergency room because she was frightened that she could not prevent the child from setting fires, which he had done several times in the last year and a half. Although he had so far managed to put out all the fires he set himself, his mother was afraid that he would set the house afire while she and his sister were asleep. She complained that he was sneaky about setting the fires, making it impossible for her to control him or to know how many fires he had actually set.

Kevin says that he has set fires because a "man in his head tells him to do so." This "man" stays in his room when he is awake and "goes away" when he is asleep. The man makes a noise ("brrr"), which Kevin interprets as a command to "set fires." He is afraid to talk to anyone about the man or not to obey his commands, "because he might beat me up." His mother apparently does not take the voice seriously, stating that he has offered a variety of different reasons for setting fires, depending on whom he talked to. Both agree that he sets fires in retaliation against his mother when he is angry with her.

Kevin has been fascinated with setting fires for the last two years. His mother remembers that he and a friend set the first fire by burning holes in the plastic sheets on his and his sister's bed. His mother found out about the incident later and reacted by hitting him on his hands and telling him how dangerous fires were. During the next fire-setting incident, Kevin used a lighter to try to burn a door frame that his mother had just painted. This time he was not hit, but was forbidden to ride his bicycle for a week. His mother was sleeping during a third episode, in which he lit the garbage with a table lighter. He then took a broom and beat out the fire. His mother awoke to a funny smell and remembers that he was running all over the house in a peculiar manner. She related this incident with amusement at the child's antics.

The last two fires took place three weeks ago, when Kevin first tried to burn a dishtowel on a gas flame. After he burned the fringe, he rolled up the towel and threw it in the garbage. His mother, who was just outside the apartment at the time, sent him to bed and later explained to him again about the dangers of fire-setting. During the last incident, he took a stretch monster toy that was kept in a styrofoam box and burned holes with a lighter on the sides of the box that corresponded to the monster's arms and feet.

Apart from these incidents, his mother remembers that Kevin would often find matches or go into the bathroom with a lighter to try to smoke. His mother has talked to him at length about fires, how they get bigger with alcohol, and can be put out with water. He becomes excited during these discussions, but then promises never again to play with fire.

At the present time his mother reports that Kevin is unhappy in school and misses his former friends from the neighborhood the family moved from three months before admission. She says that he has made no new friends outside school, and that he and his sister complain frequently of boredom.

Aside from the fire-setting, there is no history of any other aggressive or antisocial behavior. His mother reports that he has been difficult to discipline, but mainly because he ignores her. Kevin's schoolteacher was surprised to hear of his fire-setting. She described him as a lovely, bright, obedient child who played and worked well with both the teacher and his peers. Upon further inquiry, she could say only that at times he became a "little wild" in play.

Kevin lives with his 10-year-old sister and 26-year-old mother, who herself was hospitalized as an adolescent after she had been truant from school for seven months in retaliation for her mother's remarriage. In an initial discussion with the interviewer, she acknowledged that at times she becomes violently angry, to the point where she is unable to control herself.

The findings of Kevin's physical examination were within normal limits except for a second-degree burn on his hand, which his mother initially said came from her attempts to "teach him that fire hurts" by insisting that he put his hand in a gas flame. (She later denied this, but Kevin insisted that she had done it.)

When interviewed, Kevin was somewhat guarded and distrustful at first. This seemed to be a manifestation of shyness and fear of what his mother would say or do. Over the course of several evaluation sessions, Kevin's play revolved around themes of fires getting bigger and out of control. He knows that he can get burned and that a big fire could burn his house and "I would die." When talking about fires, his affect was either inappropriate (laughter) or blunted. When discussing the "man" and his command hallucinations, Kevin seemed to be genuinely frightened, as if he regarded the man as real and threatening. He denied suicidal ideation, although his mother reported that he had recently said that he wished to die.

Discussion of Brrr

Recurrent setting of fires may be a symptom of Conduct Disorder; Kevin, however, is described by his teacher as a "lovely, bright, obedient child who play[s] and work[s] well with both the teacher and his peers," and he apparently engages in no antisocial activities other than the fire-setting. Political extremists may set fires to make a political statement. We doubt this is what Kevin is up to.

It does seem that Kevin has recurrent, irresistible impulses to set fires, that he derives pleasure from the fire-setting, and that there is no understandable goal, such as monetary gain from insurance. The diagnosis is therefore the Impulse Control Disorder Pyromania.

Some readers may notice that the DSM-III diagnostic criteria for this disorder require "an increasing sense of tension before setting the fire and an experience of intense pleasure, gratification, or release at the time of committing the act." It is true that these features can only be inferred from the available information. These criteria emphasize a subjective experience that is often not easily documented in a very young patient.

Other readers may be bothered by the "command hallucinations." We tend to accept his mother's evaluation that the "man" in his head is one of a number of stories that he provides to explain his behavior. If the hallucination were genuine, one would certainly expect other signs of disorganized or psychotic behavior.

DSM-III Diagnosis:

Axis I: 312.33 Pyromania (p. 295)

Wewwow Fwowers

98 Bob is a four-year-old who is tall for his age and extremely good-looking. His mother reports that he has no physical health problems, gets along well at nursery school and at home, but seems restless, has trouble staying asleep, and has a "speech problem." The school reports that the boy is difficult to understand and has a short attention span.

Examination revealed a bright, pleasant youngster who played well and chatted happily while drawing and playing. Some of the boy's utterances included "Wook at the wewwow fwowers in duh gaden"; and "Zis is where I hurt my fumb on de hot tove."

Discussion of Wewwow Fwowers

Bob's speech difficulties are not part of impaired *language* development (as might be seen in Developmental Language Disorder, Mental Retardation, or Infantile Autism), since they are apparently limited to problems in articulating certain speech sounds. The example of his speech indicates difficulty pronouncing *r, y, l, th,* and *s.* This is quite characteristic of Developmental Articulation Disorder. There is no evidence of any other cause of his articulation difficulties, such as hearing impairment or dysarthria (articulation disturbance due to a disorder of the oral speech mechanism or to neurological abnormalities).

The reference to trouble staying asleep, restlessness, and having a short attention span also suggests the possibility of Attention Deficit

Disorder, which should be ruled out or, at most, considered a "provisional" diagnosis on Axis I.

DSM-III Diagnosis:

Axis II: 315.39 Developmental Articulation Disorder (p. 98)

Refrigerator Raider

99 Alice is a single 17-year-old who lives with her parents, who insisted that she be seen because of binge eating and vomiting. She achieved her greatest weight of 180 pounds at 16 years of age. Her lowest weight since she reached her present height of 5'9'' has been 150 pounds, and her present weight is about 160 pounds.

Alice states she has been dieting since age ten and says she has always been very tall and slightly chubby. At age 12 she started binge eating and vomiting. She was a serious competitive swimmer at that time, and it was necessary for her to keep her weight down. She would deprive herself of all food for a few days and then get an urge to eat. She could not control this urge, and would raid the refrigerator and cupboards for ice cream, pastries, and other desserts. She would often do this at night, when nobody was looking, and would eat, for example, a quart of ice cream, an entire pie, and any other desserts she could find. She would eat until she felt physical discomfort and then would become depressed and fearful of gaining weight, following which she would self-induce vomiting. When she was 15 she was having eating binges and vomiting four days a week. Since age 13 she has gone through only one period of six weeks without gaining weight or eating binges or vomiting. She quit school this year (at age 17) for a period of five months, during which she just stayed home, overeating and vomiting. She then went back to school and tried to do better in her schoolwork. She has obtained average or below-average grades in junior high and high school.

For the past two years Alice has been drinking wine and beer on weekends. She drinks mostly with girl friends; she dates infrequently. Alice states that she wants to date, but is ashamed of the way she looks. At times in the past she has taken Dexedrine to lose weight. Several months ago she was hospitalized for two weeks to control her binge eating. During this time she was very depressed and cut her wrists several times while hospitalized.

Alice is neatly dressed, well oriented, and answers inquiries rationally. During the interview she indicates that she realizes she has a serious problem with binge eating and vomiting, but feels rather hopeless about getting the behavior under control.

Discussion of Refrigerator Raider

Clearly Alice has a gross disturbance in eating behavior, an Eating Disorder. She consumes large quantities of food over a short period of time (binge eating). The food she eats during the binges is typically high in calories (ice cream, pastries, and other desserts), she eats it in secret (at night when nobody is looking), and the binge ends in self-induced vomiting and feelings of self-reproach. Alice has had frequent fluctuations in weight due to the binges, and dieting and control of her weight have been a chronic preoccupation. Furthermore, she is aware that the eating pattern is abnormal and that she is unable to control it. These are the characteristic features of Bulimia.

Although binge eating can be an associated feature of Anorexia Nervosa, there is no suggestion here of the severe weight loss characteristic of that disorder. Since depressive symptoms are typically associated with Bulimia, we see no advantage in adding the diagnosis of Adjustment Disorder with Depressed Mood to characterize the more recent depressive episode, triggered, perhaps, by Alice's hospitalization; but we would not quarrel with a clinician who added this diagnosis.

Mention is made of Alice's drinking wine and beer and using Dexedrine. There is, however, no clear pattern of maladaptive use or resulting impairment in social or occupational functioning to justify a diagnosis of Substance Abuse.

DSM-III Diagnosis:

Axis I: 307.51 Bulimia (p. 70)

*Cartographer**

100 A psychiatric evaluation is requested by the teachers of C.B., a 13-year-old boy. He is of average intelligence, according to the Wechsler Intelligence Scale for Children (WISC), with better verbal than performance skills. He does well on

*Wing, Lorna: "Asperger's Syndrome. A Clinical Account." *Psychological Medicine*, Feb. 11: 115-130, 1981.

tasks needing rote learning, but his teachers are deeply puzzled and concerned about his poor comprehension of abstract ideas and his social naiveté. They find him appealing, but sadly vulnerable to the hazards of everyday life.

His mother dates C.'s problems from the age of six months, when his head was accidentally bruised. From that time he became socially aloof and isolated, and spent most of his time gazing at his hands, which he moved in complicated patterns in front of his face. At one year old he began to watch the passing traffic, but still ignored people. He continued to be remote, with poor eye contact, until five years of age. He passed his motor milestones at the usual ages and, as soon as he was physically able, he spent hours running in circles with an object in his hand, and would scream if attempts were made to stop him. At the age of three he began to be able to recognize letters of the alphabet, and rapidly acquired skill in drawing; he drew the salt and pepper pots, correctly copying the names written on them, over and over again. For a time this was his sole activity. Following this he became fascinated with pylons and tall buildings, and would stare at them from all angles and draw them.

He did not speak till age four, and then for a long time used only single words. After this he acquired repetitive phrases and reversed pronouns. C. performed many stereotyped movements as a young child, including jumping, flapping his arms, and moving his hands in circles.

After age five, C.'s speech and social contact markedly improved. Until age 11, he attended a special school, where they tolerated a range of bizarre, repetitive routines. At one point, for example, he insisted that, before lessons could begin, all his class and the teacher should wear watches he made from plasticine. Despite all the problems, he proved to have excellent rote memory, absorbed all he was taught, and could reproduce facts verbatim when asked. C. was transferred to a regular public school at age 11. He uses good grammar and has a large vocabulary, but his speech is naive and immature and concerned mainly with his own special interests. He has learned not to make embarrassing remarks about other people's appearance, but tends to ask repetitive questions. He is not socially withdrawn, but prefers the company of adults to that of children his own age, finding it difficult to understand the unwritten rules of social interaction. He says of himself, "I am afraid I suffer from bad sportsmanship." He enjoys simple jokes, but cannot understand more subtle humor. He is often teased by his classmates.

C.'s main interest is in maps and road signs. He has a prodigious memory for routes and can draw them rapidly and accurately. He also makes large, complicated, abstract shapes out of any material that comes to hand and shows much ingenuity in ensuring that they hold together. He has never engaged in pretend play, but is deeply attached to a toy panda, to which he talks as if it were an adult when he needs comfort.

His finger dexterity is good, but he is clumsy and ill-coordinated in large movements and therefore is never chosen by the other children for sports and team games.

Discussion of Cartographer

C.B.'s many problems apparently began at an early age. Before 30 months he demonstrated lack of responsiveness to people (he became socially aloof and isolated, ignored people), had gross deficits in language development and peculiar speech patterns (did not speak until age four and then, for a long time, used single words and reversed pronouns), and exhibited bizarre reactions to the environment (flapped his arms and moved his hands in circles, insisted that his classmates wear plasticine watches). In the absence of delusions, hallucinations, and incoherence, these characteristics indicate the Pervasive Developmental Disorder Infantile Autism.

C.B.'s condition has improved considerably. He no longer exhibits bizarre behavior and gross distortions in language. Although he still retains some residual signs of the illness (his speech is naive and immature, he has difficulty understanding the unwritten rules of social interaction), the full syndrome of Infantile Autism is no longer present. Hence, the diagnosis is Infantile Autism, Residual State.

DSM-III Diagnosis:

Axis I: 299.01 Infantile Autism, Residual State (p. 90)

Zombie

101 An 11-year-old girl asked her mother to take her to a psychiatrist because she feared she might be "going crazy." Several times during the last two months she has awakened confused about where she is until she realizes she is on the living-room couch or in her little sister's bed, even though she went to bed in her own room. When she recently woke up in her older brother's bedroom, she became very concerned and felt quite guilty about it. Her younger sister says that she has seen the patient walking during the night, looking like "a zombie," that she didn't answer when she called her, and that she has done that several times, but usually goes back to her bed. The patient fears she may have "amnesia" because she has no memory of anything happening during the night. There is no history of seizures or of similar episodes during the day. An electroencephalogram (EEG) and physical examination are normal. The patient's mental status is unremarkable except for some anxiety about her symptom and the usual early adolescent concerns. School and family functioning are excellent.

Discussion of Zombie

This girl is not going crazy, but rather is experiencing the characteristic features of Sleepwalking Disorder: episodes of arising from bed during sleep and walking about, appearing unresponsive during the episodes, amnesia for the episode upon awakening, and no impairment in consciousness several minutes after awakening. Psychomotor epileptic seizures are ruled out by the normal EEG and the absence of any seizurelike behavior during the waking state.

Although the process of dissociation is involved in Sleepwalking Disorder, since the disturbance begins during sleep it is not classified as a Dissociative Disorder.

DSM-III Diagnosis:

Axis I: 307.46 Sleepwalking Disorder (p. 84)

Jumping Jim

102 The school referred Jim, six years of age, because "he requires constant supervision to keep him from disrupting classroom activities." He is also described as "stubborn, defiant, and quarrelsome," and as having a very short attention span. Every school he has attended has had the same complaints about his behavior: he is overactive, uncontrollable, disruptive, and impulsive.

His mother states that at home Jim never keeps still for any length of time; he is always running, jumping, rocking, or fiddling with something. She describes him as doing three or four things at a time without completing anything. He has very poor judgment and goes off anywhere by himself and does whatever he wants to do. He is extremely intrusive and disrupts any activity in which others are attempting to engage. His mother feels that he demands her undivided attention. Furthermore, she says, he is always provoking his older brother, and has a "wild" temper, which erupts very dramatically and suddenly and disappears in the same fashion.

As an infant Jim was constantly climbing out of his crib and high-chair, and couldn't be contained. As a toddler he was into everything, and his parents made many visits to the emergency room because of his minor accidents. He climbed a lot, jumped all over the furniture, and refused to stay in his playpen.

During the evaluation Jim spent most of the time walking around the office or tilting a chair, leaning on its back, and rocking back and forth. He jumped from subject to subject and talked incessantly. He acknowledged having some difficulty in school, but felt it was strictly because the other children picked on him.

Discussion of Jumping Jim

Jim displays extensive evidence of problems with attention, impulsivity, and hyperactivity. His attention difficulties include not completing tasks and his short attention span for schoolwork. Evidence of impulsivity includes his doing "whatever he wants to do" and his being extremely intrusive and disruptive. Hyperactivity is shown by his inability to sit still and his "always running, jumping, rocking. . . ." These are the characteristic symptoms of Attention Deficit Disorder with Hyperactivity, which seems to have begun in infancy in this case.

DSM-III Diagnosis:

Axis I: 314.01 Attention Deficit Disorder with Hyperactivity (p.43)

Dirty Pictures

103 A well-developed 15-year-old boy in a training school entered the office of a woman staff member, closed the door, and directed her to pull down the window shade. When she did not do so, he produced a bread knife, placed the point against her chest with her back to the wall, and tried to intimidate her into having sex. She advised him to put the knife away, which he did, but then he seized her forcefully. She broke away and ran from the office.

The boy had come to the training school at age 13, after two daylight attacks on girls, whom he had knocked down. His behavior in the training school was highly variable; on the one visit home that he earned, he had been involved in a car theft before he was returned. He was sensitive to older boys' teasing him about being too little and too young for sexual experiences. He developed a little trade ("almost a racket," he said), along with several of his friends, of drawing pornographic pictures and selling them to other boys. He seemed to be loyal to and protective of his own "gang," but was quite amoral in his attitude toward outsiders ("If you thought you could get away with something, wouldn't you try it?").

Discussion of Dirty Pictures

This young man came to the training school after he had attacked two girls. He has now physically threatened a female staff member. He has also been involved in car thefts. These incidents are clearly reflective of a repetitive and persistent pattern of conduct in which the basic rights of others are violated. This pattern of aggressive conduct indicates the Aggressive type of Conduct Disorder. His loyalty toward and protectiveness of members of his gang are evidence of the Socialized type.

If this pattern of antisocial behavior persists beyond the age of 18 (as well it might), a diagnosis of Antisocial Personality Disorder should be considered.

DSM-III Diagnosis:

Axis I: 312.23 Conduct Disorder, Socialized, Aggressive (p. 49)

Omnivorous George

104 George, a thin, pale, five-year-old, was admitted to the hospital for a nutritional anemia that seemed to be due to his ingestion of paint, plaster, dirt, wood, and paste. He had had numerous hospitalizations under similar circumstances, beginning at 19 months of age, when he had ingested lighter fluid.

George's parents subsisted on welfare, and were described as immature and dependent. He was the product of an unplanned but normal pregnancy. His mother began eating dirt when she was pregnant, at 16 years of age. His father periodically abused drugs and alcohol.

Discussion of Omnivorous George

Eating non-nutritive substances may be seen in such pervasive disorders as Infantile Autism, Schizophrenia, or the neurologic disorder Klein-Levin syndrome. When not symptomatic of such a disorder, the diagnosis of Pica is made. As in this case, it is commonly associated with a similar history in the mother and low socioeconomic status.

DSM-III Diagnosis:

Axis I: 307.52 Pica (p. 72)

Killer

105 A ten-year-old boy was brought before juvenile authorities on charges that he had pushed a six-year-old girl from a rooftop to her death. Although initially it was thought to be an accident, the boy was later overheard bragging about the incident. Another neighborhood child, who cared very little for the boy, told his parents, who encouraged the girl's mother to go to the police.

The boy was known to be a peculiarly solitary and destructive child. Since age eight he had been caught several times in his neighborhood setting fires and breaking windows. When questioned by police, he readily admitted to pushing the girl, stating that she refused to give him money. On arrest he expressed no concern or remorse about what he had done. The judge remanded the boy to the hospital for psychiatric consultation.

Discussion of Killer

This child's pattern of antisocial behavior began with setting fires and breaking windows and culminated in his killing a young girl. Such a pattern of antisocial behavior that involves physical violence against people and property indicates the Aggressive type of Conduct Disorder. His social isolation and lack of remorse are symptomatic of the Undersocialized type.

The V code Childhood or Adolescent Antisocial Behavior is obviously not appropriate since a pattern, rather than an isolated episode, of antisocial behavior is involved. Although this child may well grow up to have Antisocial Personality Disorder, for now that diagnosis is excluded because it is given only to individuals over 18.

DSM-III Diagnosis:

Axis I: **312.00 Conduct Disorder, Undersocialized, Aggressive (p. 48)**

Timothy

106 Tim, six years old, was referred to the clinic by his general practitioner because of persistent soiling, for which no organic cause could be found.

Tim had never gained control of his stools. He was not constipated as an infant; but after a febrile illness at age two, he had become constipated. Six months later he had impacted feces, and was seen by a surgeon, who prescribed laxatives and suppositories. Following this there was a pattern of alternating constipation, when he did not go to the toilet for several days, and runny diarrhea, when he soiled his pants many times a day. At age four he took laxatives regularly, and his stool became softer and more regular. At about the same time his mother first attempted to toilet train him. He was made to sit on the toilet every evening until he "performed." Although he usually managed this, producing a tiny amount or, rarely, a normal stool, he continued to soil his pants frequently during the day. His mother said that within half an hour of changing his pants, he would be soiled again, and this pattern has continued until the present time.

Tim himself has been distressed about the soiling since starting school. He hates taking his clothes off for gym or on the beach. He worries that people will notice if, as occasionally happens, feces drop out of his pants. He is anxious when sitting on the toilet in the evenings and at first would do so only if bribed. Now he insists his mother stay in the bathroom with him. Tim is also enuretic at night. He became dry by day at three and a half, but has continued to wet at night; and, as waking him at night has not prevented his wetting, his mother still puts him in diapers.

For the last month, since seeing a puppet show, Tim has awakened frequently with nightmares about witches. He often asks about witches, and his mother has tried to assure him that they do not exist. He has had a light on all night in his room for the past month. He never comes into his parents' bed, as they do not allow this because of his being wet. His mother says that he has seemed rather preoccupied with death. He often asks why people have to die and if he or his parents will die first. He then works out how old he might be when his parents die. He has said that he doesn't want to be buried because then people would walk over him.

Apart from the problems of soiling and wetting, his mother feels he is a normal little boy who is happy and outgoing. He is very affectionate with his mother and likes to have lots of kisses and hugs. His mother implied that this might be excessive for a boy. He is attached to his father, but not as much as to his mother. He likes to play and go out with his father, but with his mother he is clinging and likes to stay close to her.

Up until the age of four he had worried his parents because of seeming rather effeminate. He liked to dress in girl's clothes and talked of "when I grow up to be a girl." Now when playing he likes to take traditionally male roles such as policemen or bus conductors.

There was initially some difficulty over his adjustment at school. He used to scream when his mother left him, and he was reported to be very timid and afraid of other children. This lasted most of the first term; but he eventually began "to stand up for himself," and has been quite happy at school since then. He has several friends there, and the school is satisfied with his progress.

Developmental milestones were all a little behind those of his two older sisters, but his mother could not recall them exactly. He sat at about 6 months, shuffled on his bottom and did not crawl, and walked at about 18 months. He spoke his first words at about that time.

Tim's mother is a smartly dressed, 35-year-old, laboratory technician who seems timid and speaks quietly, but at the same time is quite forceful and articulate in what she says. She seems to feel unsure of herself with Tim and thinks that bringing up a boy is much more difficult than bringing up her daughters. She is embarrassed, as a professional person, not to have sought help earlier. She recalls how she, too, had in childhood hated to use lavatories away from home.

Tim's father is a 40-year-old, intelligent, distinguished-looking contractor. He was reticent during the interview. He readily admitted that he did not take an active part in the rearing of the children, but enjoyed them and was very fond of them. He explained that he was rather disgusted by the soiling and tried to keep out of the situation for fear of being too punitive.

In the interview Tim appeared rather small for his age and had a babyish, full face. At first he was very timid and shy and clung to his mother. However, he did allow his mother to leave the room after a short period and became much more assertive and outgoing once she had left. He played with family figures in the dollhouse and soon had the little boy figure on the toilet and all the other members of the family watching him. His speech was immature and difficult to understand but his vocabulary was extensive.

The patient was also seen by a pediatrician. On physical examination a fecal mass the size of a melon could be palpated in the lower abdomen, and soft feces could be felt in his rectum.

Discussion of Timothy

Encopresis can sometimes be caused by physical disorders, such as aganglionic megacolon and anal fissure. Since these have been ruled out in Tim's case, the diagnosis of Functional Encopresis is appropriate. In addition, he continues to have nighttime wetting, warranting an additional diagnosis of Functional Enuresis.

For the last month Tim has had nightmares about witches and has been scared of the dark and preoccupied with death. Since this is likely to be only a transient reaction, it does not warrant an additional diagnosis. If it persists or becomes more severe, however, then an additional diagnosis, such as Adjustment Disorder with Anxious Mood, should be considered.

Tim apparently went through a phase during which he showed some signs of possible disturbance in gender identity, but he now seems to have a clear sense of himself as a male.

DSM-III Diagnosis:

Axis I: 307.70 Functional Encopresis (p. 82)
           307.60 Functional Enuresis (p. 80)

Ed Hates School

107 Ed, nine and a half years old, is failing in school, as evidenced by extensive school reports from his teacher and from a school psychologist. The teacher reports that he is failing in arithmetic, spelling, and science, and that he is doing average work in reading, art, history, and sports. She states that he does not work well on his own, but that he tries.

The psychologist reports that Ed has been tested frequently over the past several years with the Wechsler Intelligence Scale for Children, and was given the Stanford Achievement Test in the third grade (intelligence score of 95, reading achievement score of grade level 3.0, and math achievement score of grade level 1.0); the Wide-Range Achievement Test in the fourth grade (grade-level scores of 4.4 for reading, 3.9 for spelling, and 2.8 for arithmetic); and, two months ago, in the fifth grade, the Peabody Individual Achievement Test (with age-level scores of 10 years, 3 months, for reading; 8 years, 6 months, for math; and 9 years, 2 months, for spelling).

Examination revealed a quiet but personable boy who expressed concern about his schoolwork and "just really hating to go to school."

Discussion of Ed Hates School

Why is Ed failing in school? He has a normal intelligence, is motivated, and there is no evidence that schooling is inadequate.

The extensive achievement testing consistently reveals that he has the greatest difficulty with arithmetic, and it is only in this area that both his school performance and test results indicate a level of achievement significantly below expected levels. This suggests a diagnosis of Developmental Arithmetic Disorder.

Although the teacher reports that the boy is failing also in spelling and science, a diagnosis of Mixed Specific Developmental Disorder is not appropriate since the achievement testing indicates that the boy is not performing significantly below the expected level in spelling.

DSM-III Diagnosis:

Axis II: 315.10 Developmental Arithmetic Disorder (p. 95)

Goose Pimples

108 An eight-year old boy was taken by his parents to the pediatric emergency room at 12:30 A.M. The parents were very concerned because the child woke them up with a sudden, intense, bloodcurdling scream. They went to his room and found him sitting up in bed perspiring copiously, anxious, and trembling, with rapid breathing and "goose pimples." He kept putting his forefinger in his nose (an unusual gesture for him), and was quite disoriented and anxious, as if something terrible were going to happen. His speech could not be understood. He remained in this state for about ten minutes, despite his parents' efforts to calm him. Once in the car enroute to the hospital, he calmed down and became quite sleepy again.

When seen, the child was asleep and when awakened, resisted being examined. Physical examination was negative except for a pulse rate of 110/min and mildly wet pajamas due to excessive sweating.

The child's mother is afraid he may have had an epileptic fit, as an uncle of hers had; but she noticed he did not bite his tongue or wet himself during the episode, as her uncle used to do. There is no history of seizures or febrile convulsions. The child had occasional nightmares, at the age of four and a half, for a few months; but the mother thinks "this is different."

Discussion of Goose Pimples

This boy's mother is probably correct in ruling out epilepsy. In fact, what he has are the characteristic features of an episode of Sleep Terror Disorder: abrupt awakening from sleep with a scream; intense anxiety during the episode, with sweating, rapid breathing, and piloerection; relative unresponsiveness to efforts of others to comfort him; and disorientation, confusion, and perseverative motor movements (kept putting his finger in his nose).

Since the criteria for Sleep Terror Disorder require "repeated" episodes, the diagnosis is provisional after this first episode.

DSM-III Diagnosis:

Axis I: 307.46 Sleep Terror Disorder (Provisional) (p. 86)

Silent Sister

109 A 16-year-old high-school junior was referred by a teacher to the mental health clinic with the complaint that she was unable to make any verbal contributions in her classes. Her inability to speak had begun one year previously, following the death of her mother. It took school personnel some time to realize that she did not speak in any of her classes. She had kept up with her assignments, handing in all her written work and receiving better than average grades on tests.

The patient's father is a hardworking janitor in a large apartment building. He usually comes home late and is rather passive and indifferent toward the patient and her six younger siblings. He has never responded to school requests for visits to discuss his daughter's problems. Since her mother's death, the patient has assumed the mothering of her siblings: cooking the meals, cleaning, and listening to their requests and complaints.

When seen, the patient was a thin, neatly dressed girl who was alert but responded only with brief nods of her head at first. With reassurance she began to whisper monosyllabic answers to questions. Her responses were rational and logical, but she denied that her failure to speak was much of a problem. A younger sibling reported that the patient had no difficulty speaking at home.

Discussion of Silent Sister

Under ordinary circumstances this girl will not talk to anyone except her family. With considerable reassurance and coaxing, the interviewer manages to get whispered monosyllabic answers to questions. Mutism may be a symptom of many mental disorders, such as Major Depression, Social Phobia, or Schizophrenia. In this case, however, it is the predominant — in fact, as far as we know, the only—symptom. Hence, the diagnosis is Elective Mutism.

The diagnostic criteria for this disorder require refusal to talk in "almost all social situations." Since in this disorder the child commonly will talk at home with the immediate family or with one or two friends, this criterion should perhaps be "refusal to talk in most social situations, including at school."

DSM-III Diagnosis:

Axis I: 313.23 Elective Mutism (p. 63)

Nathan

110 Nathan, a 14-year-old boy, was brought in by his mother because of trouble in his special classroom, including restlessness, fidgeting, and being difficult to understand. He had been adopted from a Latin American country, and little was known of his early history, except that he had suffered from malnutrition. His mother provided a detailed history for the boy since the time of his adoption, noting that he sat at age 19 months, stood at age 40 months, walked at age 4 years, 2 months, and said "bye-bye," his first word, at age 30 months. Extensive medical workup, including an electroencephalogram, pneumoencephalograms, and chromosome studies, provided no clues to the etiology of the boy's delayed development.

Nathan's teacher described him as "meaning well, but causing a lot of problems." His mother reported that he was "very aware of relationships and vibes," but unable to deal with the abstract. She stated that he had very limited speech, daydreamed, became easily frustrated, and was difficult to take to stores because he liked to run up to people and touch them, often frightening them.

During examination the boy stared at the examiner, grabbed his hand, and tried to pull him to the toy chest. The boy made a few sounds —"da," "ah," and "wa"—but none could be considered real words. However, he used gestures to indicate his understanding of words such as "telephone," "car," "cookie," and "spoon." He was able to follow four-step commands, but did not seem to comprehend questions such as "How are you feeling?" His play was what might be expected from a much, much younger child.

Discussion of Nathan

Nathan has had markedly delayed developmental milestones and has current evidence of significantly subaverage intellectual functioning, as evidenced by his limited speech and ability to comprehend abstract questions. This is associated with markedly impaired adaptive functioning (troubles in school and in normal social interactions). These all indicate Mental Retardation. Since there is no mention of IQ testing, the level of retardation cannot be determined; hence, it is noted as Unspecified.

DSM-III Diagnosis:

Axis I: 319.00 Unspecified Mental Retardation (p. 40)

Broken Home

111 Don, 3 years and 7 months old, has a complicated early medical history, including being born 11 weeks prematurely with hyaline membrane disease and later having bilateral hernia repairs. He began sitting at 6 months, crawling at 10 months, walking at 13 months, and saying words at 12 months. At three years his parents noted that his speech seemed far less well developed than that of his playmates, although most of them were younger than he was. He did not attend nursery school, and had been subjected to a number of moves because of parental problems and divorce.

During the examination Don was slow to warm up. He was extremely difficult to understand, and had to augment most of his utterances with gestures to make himself understood. Most of his sentences consisted of single words that were mispronounced — for example, "gun" was "dub," "scissors" was "duhduh," and "fish" was "pet." The boy could follow commands such as "Get the red book and bring it to the table," could point out body parts and objects in the room, and could produce drawings that seemed quite sophisticated for his age.

Discussion of Broken Home

Normal developmental milestones rule out Mental Retardation as an explanation for Don's speech difficulties. Significantly, Don's speech difficulties are not in articulating certain speech sounds, but rather in finding the proper words to express himself. This rules out Developmental Articulation Disorder and suggests a Developmental Language Disorder. The fact that he apparently has no difficulty understanding language indicates an Expressive Type of Developmental Language Disorder. (The two subtypes, Expressive and Receptive, use the same code.)

DSM-III Diagnosis:

Axis II: 315.31 Developmental Language Disorder, Expressive Type (p. 96)

Dolls

112 The patient is a six-year-old boy for whom his parents seek treatment because "he wants to be a girl."

The patient's major playmate is his younger sister; and although his parents are trying to foster friendships with other boys, he prefers to play with girls or to be with his mother or a female baby-sitter. He particularly dislikes rough play with boys and physical fighting, although he is well built, above average in height for his age, and well coordinated. At home he engages in much role-playing, invariably assuming female roles. When playing house with his younger sister, he plays the "mother" or "big sister" role and leaves the male role to her. He likes to imitate female TV figures, such as the oldest daughter from the Brady Bunch, the adult wives of the Flintstones, or Wonder Woman. Similarly, he likes to playact female characters from various children's books.

He has never been interested in toy cars, trucks, or trains, but is an avid player with dolls (baby, Barbi, and family dolls) and enjoys playing with kitchen toys. He also likes to play wedding, pregnancy, a female teacher, or a lady doctor. He is good at drawing and is very interested in drawing female figures. Although his parents try to restrict the activity, he engages in a lot of cross-dressing. Sometimes he uses a quilt or a towel around his middle for skirts, or a T-shirt or nightgown for a dress. He does not use any female underwear or bathing suits. He likes bows in his hair, and may use an underskirt or a veil on his head to imitate long hair. He loves dancing, preferably in dresses. He is very interested in jewelry, has plastic necklaces, and pretends at times to wear earrings. Also, he pretends to apply lipstick (with chapstick), and would use real lipstick and perfume if his mother would let him. He states, "I want to be a girl," often when he is unhappy, for instance, when he started kindergarten, or has felt in competition with his younger sister.

On examination, the boy is found to be clearly not effeminate. His intellectual development is apparently normal. Although somewhat reluctant, he is able to describe much of what his parents have related about his toy and game preferences. He says that he does not want to be a boy because he is afraid he will have to play with soldiers or play army with other boys when he grows bigger. He wishes a fairy could change him into a girl. What he likes about being a girl is wearing dresses, long hair, and jewelry. His drawings are all of female figures.

Family history, pregnancy, birth, and early development are all normal. The parents do not show any overt psychopathology. The patient's problems seem to have started with the birth of his younger sister, when he was two years old. For the first four months of her life his sister suffered from digestive problems and required a great deal of parental attention and care. The patient then began to display definite signs of regression—played the baby role again, wanted to drink from a bottle, and to be held and carried. His mother gave in to some extent. Both parents and baby-sitters think that cross-dressing and wanting to be a girl date back to that time, although, before the birth of his sister, there were already some instances of the patient's imitating long hair by wearing a towel on his head. When the patient was four years old, his sister got a baby doll, which he took from her. Around this same time he spent a vacation with his sister at their grandparents' and complained that his sister got more attention than he, ending with the familiar "Why can't I be a girl? Why didn't God make me a girl? Girls get to dress up, get to wear pretty things."

From age three on, he was enrolled in nursery school, and initially showed much separation anxiety. He appeared more sensitive than the other children, always seemed to feel threatened by them, and did not stand up for himself. His teacher noted from the beginning that he dressed up very frequently, said that he wanted to be a mother when he grew up, and was reluctant to engage in rough-and-tumble activities. In the second year he was so good at imitating a girl (batting his eyes, voice inflection, walking) that the teacher wondered if he were an intersex. In the third year his classroom teacher closed the doll corner because of his preoccupation with doll play.

Discussion of Dolls

There should be little question about the diagnosis in this case. This boy has a persistent and frequently stated desire to be a girl. He is preoccupied with female stereotypical activity and openly expresses a desire to be turned into a girl — not merely to play a female role. These are the essential features of Gender Identity Disorder of Childhood in a male.

DSM-III Diagnosis:

Axis I: 302.60 Gender Identity Disorder of Childhood (p. 266)

California Earthquake

113 The patient was a handsome boy, nine years, three months of age, presenting with the complaint of speech difficulties, which had appeared suddenly, at the age of six years, when he had been frightened in one of the major California earthquakes. The pediatrician reported a history of allergies, poor coordination, and mixed eye–hand dominance, and noted that the boy appeared to be a "slow thinker." The mother reported that there were sibling rivalry problems with a younger sister, that the boy had a very poor self-image, and that he had speech difficulties during stress. The school reported that the boy was well-behaved and had only minor problems with academic subjects.

During the interview the boy complained of learning problems, peer problems, and fear of school. He also stated that he had a speech problem that made it very difficult for him to speak in public. During the discussion of this, and of the earthquake that allegedly precipitated the problems, the boy's speech became marked by pauses and occasional repetitions of sound, but his speech was normal the rest of the time. Intelligence testing revealed a performance IQ of 114 and a verbal IQ of 133.

Neurologic examination disclosed difficulties with fine finger movements, hopping, and skipping.

Discussion of California Earthquake

There is reference to many problems: speech difficulties, learning problems, poor coordination, peer problems, and fear of school. However, the only disorder diagnosable on the basis of the information available is Stuttering (speech marked by pauses and occasional repetitions of sounds).

Although this boy's problems apparently began suddenly following a frightening earthquake, the diagnosis of Adjustment Disorder would not be made since it is a residual category and is used only if the disturbance does not meet the criteria for a more specific disorder. Although there is mention of problems of coordination (difficulties with fine finger movements, hopping, and skipping), there is no suggestion of problems of attention or impulsivity that would justify a diagnosis of Attention Deficit Disorder. Soft neurological signs such as these are noted on Axis III.

DSM-III Diagnosis:

Axis I: **307.00 Stuttering (p. 79)**
Axis III: **Soft neurological signs (poor coordination)**

Baby Loretta

114 Loretta, age seven and one-half months, was referred with her mother, Crystal, age 30, by the mother's attorney and by Loretta's pediatrician because Loretta did not respond to her name or to ordinary conversation. Her hearing, according to tests, was normal.

The mother's pregnancy had been planned and uneventful until two weeks before birth, when placenta previa was diagnosed. Delivery was by Caesarean section. Birth weight was 7½ pounds; length was 21 inches. Loretta was discharged from the hospital at two days. Her mother, however, remained in the hospital for seven days because of fever, which responded to antibiotics, while Loretta was cared for at home by her father and a variety of other relatives. The mother was weak and unable to care for her child and developed a spiking fever that required rehospitalization. She was referred for surgery for removal of a sponge that had been left in the abdomen at the time of the Caesarean section. The mother's recovery was again slow, and she did not return home until six weeks postpartum.

At two months Loretta was extremely quiet, apathetic, and weak and was not gaining weight. At home her mother became severely depressed and had dreams of Loretta's dying through some form of violence. She avoided holding Loretta until the baby was five months old, at which time her depression lifted and she began caring for the infant regularly.

When first seen, Loretta was well nourished and apparently well developed. However, she had a constantly serious expression and an extremely immature smile, with a partly open mouth and no upturning at the corners of the mouth. She did not respond to her name. She made few sounds, and it was difficult for her to maintain eye contact. According to her mother, Loretta had made no notable gains in physical development since she (the mother) has resumed care of the child when Loretta was five months of age.

Further follow-up of Loretta at nine months of age showed that her development had begun to proceed much more rapidly, and she was almost up to age level in fine-motor movements and socialization responses. She was beginning to show some evidence of separation anxiety. Her affect, however, remained blunted; and she was still a quiet, serious-looking, unresponsive child. She was not playful and did not show anticipatory extension of the arms when her mother reached for her.

Discussion of Baby Loretta

For the first seven and one-half months of her life, Loretta showed numerous signs of a lack of developmentally appropriate social responsivity. These include lack of visual tracking of eyes and face, lack of smiling in response to faces, and lack of alerting and turning toward the caretaker's voice. She was also noted to be quiet, apathetic, physically weak, and not gaining expected weight.

The pediatrician apparently recognized that all of these symptoms could not be accounted for by any physical disorder, that they were probably related to the inadequate care that Loretta had received in the first five months of her life, because of her mother's complicated postpartum obstetrical course and subsequent postpartum depression.

The failure to thrive that is due to a lack of the type of care that ordinarily leads to the development of affectional bonds to others, occurring in an infant before eight months of age, is diagnosed as Reactive Attachment Disorder of Infancy. The DSM-III criteria for the disorder note that "The diagnosis is confirmed if the clinical picture is reversed shortly after institution of adequate caretaking . . ." In fact, the follow-up record notes that Loretta's development proceeded more rapidly once her mother had resumed care. Nevertheless, there were still signs of the disturbance ("Her affect, however, remained blunted; and she was still a quiet, serious-looking, unresponsive child"; and she did not yet display anticipatory reaching when approached by her mother). Clinicians working in this area believe that total recovery does not always occur, as implied by the DSM-III criteria. Perhaps this criterion should be modified to indicate that a significant degree of recovery is to be expected following reinstitution of adequate caretaking.

DSM-III Diagnosis:

Axis I: 313.89 Reactive Attachment Disorder of Infancy (p. 59)

"Wabbit"

115 Arthur, a six-year-old first-grader, came with his mother, who reported that the boy was humming and making odd noises, and was having problems speaking properly and with letter reversals when writing. The schoolteacher sent a report stating that the boy was a "very good" student in reading readiness, phonics, and sports, was average in art, and seemed to have problems only in speech.

Examination revealed a friendly and handsome boy who conversed intelligently on a number of topics. Speech errors were noted during conversation, including "wabbit" for "rabbit," "bwown" for "brown," "dis" for "this" and "lellow" for "yellow." The boy was given the Wechsler Preschool Primary Intelligence Test, and the Wide-Range Achievement Test (WRAT) and received the following scores: performance intelligence, 135; verbal intelligence, 120; reading grade level, 1.8; spelling grade level, 1.4; arithmetic grade level, 1.8. It was noted on the WRAT that the boy spelled "cat" "ɔat."

Discussion of "Wabbit"

Arthur's problem is that he has difficulty articulating various sounds, particularly r's, l's, and th's, the later-acquired speech sounds. His ability to understand language and to express himself rules out a Developmental Language Disorder; his above-average intelligence rules out Mental Retardation; and his normal social development rules out a Pervasive Developmental Disorder. Thus, a diagnosis of Developmental Articulation Disorder is made on Axis II.

The frequent letter reversals raise the question of an additional diagnosis of Developmental Reading Disorder. However, a certain number of letter reversals are normal at this age, and this diagnosis is given only if an individually administered test reveals scores significantly below expected level. In this case, Arthur's reading grade level is not below that of the other achievement tests and is consistent with his IQ.

DSM-III Diagnosis:

Axis II: 315.39 Developmental Articulation Disorder (p.98)

Open Door Policy

116 Michael, seven and a half years old, is brought in by his mother, who had read an article in a local newspaper about a clinic that treated children with anxiety disorders. She believed that the description in the newspaper article of anxiety symptoms fit her child to a "T."

The presenting complaint is that Michael does not sleep in his own bed. He falls asleep in his parents' bed, is put in his own bed during the night in a room he shares with his five-year-old brother, but is never found in his own bed in the morning. During the night he makes his way into his parents' bed. If they remove him from their bed, they find him huddled in a corner of their room, or in a chair in their bedroom.

In addition, his mother describes herself as "a prisoner in my own home." Michael is afraid to stay home alone, and will not even go out of the apartment by himself to do simple things such as take out the garbage. He does not let his mother go into any room by herself, but insists upon staying with her. Because the mother does not allow Michael to be with her while she dresses or is in the bathroom, he stands outside the door, continuously asking when she will be out. She has learned to take care of her grooming in five-minute periods, which are the maximum he tolerates without becoming extremely upset. These difficulties began when, at age two, he started having tantrums when she went to the bathroom.

Furthermore, Michael has many numerous physical symptoms, such as stomachaches and headaches, that usually occur in the morning and are often accompanied by complaints that he is going to die and should be taken to the hospital. These never occur on weekends or during the summer, but only on school days. Yet he has never refused to go to school.

His teacher describes Michael as doing little work in class and not turning in homework. She states, "He appears dejected, not a happy child and not a confident one. His work is messy and could be much better; he seems to have the capabilities of doing better." His performance in all subjects is considered at average or above-average level.

At the clinic Michael separates easily from his mother but wants to keep the office door open while being interviewed. He relates well initially, laughing easily while talking about school, which he says he likes and in which he feels he is doing well. His affect changes markedly when the topic turns to his feelings. He becomes difficult to draw out and states that he misses his mother in school, especially while staying with a baby-sitter after school until his mother comes home from work. He constantly worries about whether his mother will pick him up from the baby-sitter's house. He says that at night he is plagued by scary thoughts about something happening to his parents and reports "I'm afraid I'll never see them again." During the day he often worries about getting lost and what would happen to him if his mother died.

Discussion of Open Door Policy

This child has the full-blown picture of Separation Anxiety Disorder. He refuses to go to sleep except in his parents' bed; he avoids being alone in his home and becomes extremely upset if not allowed to follow his mother as she moves about the apartment. He has physical complaints on school days, has difficulty concentrating on his work at school, and has many "scary thoughts" about some harm befalling his parents or some event's separating him from them. The only common feature of this disorder that is not present in this case is school refusal.

Although this child shows many of the features of Agoraphobia, that diagnosis is not given if the individual is under 18 and shows the characteristic features of Separation Anxiety Disorder. If this child had generalized and persistent anxiety that involved concerns *other* than separation, such as about competence or physical symptoms, the diagnosis of Overanxious Disorder would be considered.

DSM-III Diagnosis:

Axis I: 309.21 Separation Anxiety Disorder (p. 53)

Cases for
Multiaxial Evaluation

Cases for
Multiaxial Evaluation

This chapter includes cases that illustrate the use of the DSM-III multiaxial system, which is described in DSM-III Chapter 2, Use of This Manual.

Radar Messages

117 The patient was first admitted to the hospital at the age of 22. For three or four months before admission she felt depressed and had anorexia, with a weight loss of about ten pounds, and both initial and terminal insomnia. About two months before admission she began to feel increasingly energetic, requiring only two to five hours of sleep at night, and to experience her thoughts as racing. She began to see symbolic meanings in things, especially sexual meanings, and experienced marked ideas of reference, involving, particularly, innocent comments on television shows. During the month preceding admission she became increasingly euphoric and irritable and began experiencing both visual and auditory hallucinations. She believed that there was a hole in her head through which radar messages were being sent to her. These messages could control her thoughts or produce emotions of anger, sadness, or the like, that were beyond her control. She also believed that her thoughts could be read by people around her and that alien thoughts from other people were intruding themselves via the radar into her own head. She described hearing voices, which sometimes spoke about her in the third person and at other times ordered her to perform various functions, particularly sexual activity.

Before her recent illness the patient had been asymptomatic and had been a successful student at a prestigious university. There she had done well academically and had had a large circle of friends of both sexes. She could not recall any particular precipitants of her symptoms, saying that they seemed to arise almost at random in the midst of an uneventful period in her second year of college.

Upon admission to the hospital the patient was started on chlor-promazine and lithium carbonate. Over the course of about three weeks she experienced a fairly rapid reduction in hyperactivity, euphoria, pressured speech, delusions, and hallucinations. After four weeks the chlorpromazine dosage was gradually reduced and then discontinued. She was maintained thereafter on lithium carbonate alone. At the time of her discharge, her manic symptoms had disap-peared, but she displayed hypersomnia of about ten hours per night; mild anorexia; definite diurnal variation, worse in the mornings; and mild psychomotor retardation. These symptoms, however, were not severe enough to require hospitalization, and the patient was dis-charged to live with friends.

Approximately eight months after her discharge, the patient was taken off lithium carbonate by her psychiatrist at college. She con-tinued asymptomatic for approximately three or four weeks, but then began to experience a gradual reappearance of symptoms similar to those that had precipitated her previous hospitalization. About two weeks after this she was readmitted to the hospital with a syndrome almost identical with that which had characterized her on her first admission. She again responded uneventfully to a regimen of chlor-promazine and lithium initially, with her medication gradually being reduced to lithium alone. At the time of her discharge she again displayed mild depressive symptoms.

The patient's father had had a severe episode of depression, charac-terized by hypersomnia, anorexia, profound psychomotor retardation, and suicidal ideation, when in his 40s. The patient's paternal grand-mother had committed suicide during what also appeared to be a depressive episode.

Discussion of Radar Messages

This woman was functioning at a high level before the develop-ment of a depressive period, followed shortly by an episode with characteristic manic symptoms: increased energy, less need for sleep, racing thoughts, euphoria, and irritability. At the height of the illness she developed bizarre delusions (her emotions were con-trolled by radar messages sent through a hole in her head) and hallucinations (voices commanding her to perform sexual acts). In the absence of any evidence of a specific organic factor that could account for the disturbance, such as the use of a stimulant, this disturbance is a manic episode. The occurrence of a manic episode (even in the absence of a full depressive episode) is sufficient for a diagnosis of Bipolar Disorder, Manic. Because the content of the delusions and hallucinations has no apparent relationship to such typical manic themes as inflated worth or identity, the fifth-digit subclassification is "with Psychotic Features (Mood-incongruent)."

There is no evidence of any Personality Disorder or of a physical disorder that is relevant to the Axis I diagnosis. According to the patient, the illness developed "almost at random in the midst of an uneventful period." Therefore, the severity of psychosocial stressors is noted as 1 — None. Her previously excellent academic and social functioning at college justifies the Axis V rating of 2 — Very good, for the highest level of her adaptive functioning during the past year.

DSM-III Diagnosis:

Axis I: **296.44 Bipolar Disorder, Manic, with Psychotic Features (Mood-incongruent) (p. 208)**

Axis II: **V71.09 No diagnosis on Axis II (p. 335)**

Axis III: **None**

Axis IV: **Psychosocial stressors: none**
           Severity: 1 — None

Axis V: **Highest level of adaptive functioning past year: 2 — Very good**

Nailbiter

118 A 12-year-old, pubertal girl came for a consultation because of a one-year history of "nervousness." About a year before the consultation, her parents had separated. Their marriage had been apparently stable and outwardly satisfactory up until that time, and their child-rearing practices were unremarkable. Following her parents' separation, the patient developed several fears and a relatively persistent state of anxiety. She began to bite her nails and to worry about the excellence of her school performance; she became afraid of the dark and appeared to live in a relatively constant state of apprehension. Her worries were mostly realistic, but greatly exaggerated. She was concerned about her appearance, felt awkward, and her shyness in social situations became more pronounced. She reported relatively constant feelings of nervousness and anxiety, which seemed to be exacerbated by almost any event in her life. She experienced no panic attacks and no specific fears upon separation from her parents, although she was occasionally worried about their safety without good reason.

The patient is a shy girl who often has difficulty making friends, though she has developed lasting and close relationships with several peers. Her school performance has ranged from adequate to outstanding and has not declined in the past year.

During the interview her palms were sweating, it was hard for her to look at the examiner, and she was rather inhibited and tense. She denied persistent feelings of sadness and lack of interest in her environment, and she said she was able to enjoy things except for the times when her anxiety peaked. When questioned about guilt, she reported with difficulty that sometimes she felt that somehow she was responsible for her parents' separation or divorce, although she really couldn't say how. Physical examination findings were unremarkable. Specifically, she had no goiter or exophthalmos, and thyroid indices were within normal limits. Neurologic findings were unremarkable except for a mild tremor of extended hands during the examination, but this did not interfere with fine-motor skills.

Discussion of Nailbiter

Anxiety and its various manifestations are the central features of this girl's illness. She has none of the circumscribed symptoms that would suggest such Anxiety Disorders as Phobic Disorder, Obsessive Compulsive Disorder, or Panic Disorder. Even though the precipitating event was the separation of her parents and she "occasionally worried about their safety," she is not particularly concerned about separation from them. This would seem to rule out Separation Anxiety Disorder.

She demonstrates a variety of symptoms of generalized anxiety: unrealistic worrying about her parents' safety, overconcern about her academic performance, marked self-consciousness, and inability to relax. These have all persisted for more than six months, and thus add up to a diagnosis of Overanxious Disorder. (The diagnosis of Generalized Anxiety Disorder is not considered because she is younger than 18.)

There is no evidence of an Axis II Specific Developmental Disorder or of an Axis III physical disorder.

On Axis IV we would note the parents' separation as a moderate psychosocial stressor that apparently is related to the development of the Axis I disorder.

On Axis V we would code her highest level of adaptive functioning during the past year as good, taking into account her good academic performance and several close friendships.

DSM-III Diagnosis:

Axis I: 313.00 Overanxious Disorder (p. 56)
Axis II: V71.09 No diagnosis on Axis II
Axis III: None
Axis IV: Psychosocial stressors: separation of parents
             Severity: 4 — Moderate
Axis V: Highest level of adaptive functioning past year: 3 — Good

Sad Sister

119 The patient is a 26-year-old teacher's aide who seeks counseling. For several years she has been feeling increasingly lonely and "lost," particularly since her two-year-older sister married and moved out of town three months ago. This sister and one close friend from high school have been the patient's only real social contacts; otherwise she has no other girl friends, and she is extremely afraid of men. As far back as she can remember, she has felt she has very little to offer others. She has always anticipated that men, even if attracted to her, would quickly find fault with her and "drop" her. Although she would like to be married, she characteristically cuts off potential relationships with men after two or three dates because of her fear of eventual rejection. Her relationships with others are superficial and usually structured through work with civic groups or her church club. She is rarely critical of others or able to get angry at them, except concerning social or political issues. She champions the causes of minorities, ecology, and liberalism against the rich and the powerful, but she is more likely to volunteer to spend a Saturday stuffing leaflets in envelopes than canvassing door to door to collect money.

At work the patient is regarded as competent and responsible and apparently does not demand the kind of unconditional acceptance from her four-year-old students that she demands from adults. She has for several years considered seeing a counselor, but this is her first attempt to get professional help.

Discussion of Sad Sister

Although the exacerbation of the patient's long-standing problems since her sister moved away has caused her to seek treatment at this time, this does not represent a new illness (such as Adjustment Disorder). The absence of an Axis I diagnosis is coded as V71.09, No diagnosis on Axis I.

Throughout most of her life this patient has had significant difficulty establishing relationships with other people. Social isolation is commonly seen in Schizotypal Personality Disorder, but the absence of oddities of behavior and thinking rules out that diagnosis. In Schizoid Personality Disorder the isolation is apparently the result of a basic emotional coldness and indifference to others. In this case, however, there is obviously a strong desire for affection and acceptance, which is inhibited by anticipation of rejection — the characteristic features of Avoidant Personality Disorder. The patient also displays low self-esteem (she feels she has little to offer others), another characteristic feature of this disorder.

On Axis III the absence of any significant physical disorder is noted.

For most people, the departure of a married sister to another city would not be a major psychosocial stressor. Therefore, this stressor is coded 3 — Mild on Axis IV. It is only because of the patient's Personality Disorder that she was particularly vulnerable to this stressor.

This patient clearly functions more effectively at work than socially. Because of her good occupational functioning and her poor social relations, a rating of 4—Fair would seem appropriate for Axis V.

DSM-III Diagnosis:

Axis I: V71.09 No diagnosis on Axis I (p. 335)
Axis II: 301.82 Avoidant Personality Disorder (p. 324)
Axis III: None
Axis IV: Psychosocial stressors: sister marries and moves away
            Severity: 3—Mild
Axis V: Highest level of adaptive functioning past year: 4 — Fair

Altar Boy

120 A nine-year-old boy was referred by his parents and school after getting kicked off the school bus for arguing and fighting. He is now repeating the second grade after being expelled from public school and is currently in parochial school. School personnel like him, but find him frustrating. They know he can do the work, but he is "just not motivated." He is always "into it" with other children and cannot keep his hands to himself. The child himself says, "Sometimes I get into trouble for sassing and I talk back. The teacher says, 'Sit in the corner' and I'll say, 'Why?' or 'No,' and then I get sent to the principal's office." He has few friends and fights with other children. When asked who starts the fights, he says, "Most of the time I start them. But nobody ever gets hurt."

At the school conference there were numerous complaints about the patient's negativistic behavior. On the first day at the new school he told a nun, "I'm not going out on any dumb-shit fire drill." In class he insisted that his way of doing long division was better than the teacher's, even though it did not give the correct answer. He tends to be self-righteous and is often overly concerned with injustices done to him. He performs beautifully as an altar boy and, in spite of the problems, is well liked by his teachers. He is not seen as a "bad" boy, just a stubborn, frustrating one. He argues even when there is no point in it; logic and persuasion do not change him, and he resists any attempt by an adult to change him. His parents are equally frustrated by his stubbornness, his "short fuse," and his swearing.

This child has had lifelong, well-controlled epilepsy. Psychological testing at school has revealed a hint of visual/motor problems (mostly motor); but his IQ is normal, and achievement-test results are slightly above grade level. His drawings show poor small-muscle coordination.

Discussion of Altar Boy

This young man's behavior is a trial to his teachers and parents. He fights with others, talks back to his teachers, and stubbornly refuses to do what is asked of him. These characteristics immediately suggest a Conduct Disorder, but this is ruled out because his behavior, although objectionable, does not violate either the basic rights of others or major age-appropriate societal norms or rules—that is, the boy neither inflicts serious physical harm during his fights, steals, destroys property, lies, nor runs away from home or school. His pattern of disobedience and his negativistic and provocative opposition to authority figures are characteristic of Oppositional Disorder.

Children with this disorder often also have Attention Deficit Disorder, but other than the reference to his having a "short fuse," there is nothing to suggest either the inattention or the impulsivity that are characteristic of that disorder.

Although there is a reference to "visual/motor problems," with the information available there is no evidence for a Specific Developmental Disorder, which would be coded on Axis II.

The patient's epilepsy should be noted on Axis III, both because of its obvious importance in management and because the underlying central nervous system disturbance may contribute to the Oppositional Disorder.

The stimulus for this referral, getting kicked off the school bus, was just one in a series of disciplinary acts by school authorities. Thus, there does not seem to be any particular psychosocial stressor that is provoking an exacerbation of his chronic difficulties. On Axis IV, then, the level of psychosocial stressors would be noted as 1—None.

On Axis V, highest level of adaptive functioning past year, we would give a rating of 5 — Poor, in view of his poor academic performance and his difficulties not only with school authorities and his parents but with friends (he has few friends and fights with other children).

DSM-III Diagnosis:

Axis I: 313.81 Oppositional Disorder (p. 64)
Axis II: V71.09 No diagnosis on Axis II (p. 335)
Axis III: Epilepsy
Axis IV: Psychosocial stressors: none
            Severity: 1 — None
Axis V: Highest level of adaptive functioning past year: 5 — Poor

Motorman

121 The patient is a 65-year-old retired subway motorman who was admitted to an inpatient service for treatment of depression. He dates the onset of the depression to two months before admission, when his wife entered the hospital for an exacerbation of her chronic depression. He is very worried about her, says that he would not want to live without her, and hints that he will kill himself if she does not get well. Since her hospitalization he has been unable to sleep, waking up many times during the night and early in the morning, averaging only three or four hours of sleep a night. He has been extremely fatigued, slow in his movements, unable to concentrate, and uninterested in anything but his wife's condition. When his wife feels better, his mood noticeably improves.

The patient was, for many years, active in local politics, often serving as an elected delegate to state conventions. He used to be a voracious reader of historical novels. Since his wife has become sick, he does neither of these things. He has no appetite, and has lost five pounds. When he was 55, he had a similar episode of illness after being involved in a serious accident in which he was not injured, but was badly frightened.

The patient's wife gives a somewhat different account of his current illness. According to her, immediately before her current depression, he was recovering from a prostatectomy. He was so "elated" at having survived the surgery that he made plans to enjoy life to the fullest, took a trip to Ireland with his wife, bought her expensive and unnecessary presents, plunged into local politics, and made several enemies because he insisted on control of the political club and bullied club officials into spending a lot of money on sound equipment. According to his wife, he was "high," and his overactivity and excessive spending precipitated her depression. She does not recall accelerated speech or decreased need for sleep. The patient feels guilty about his role in her illness, but denies being "high," saying he was just "glad to be alive."

Discussion of Motorman

In view of the depressed mood, sleeplessness, fatigue, psychomotor retardation, poor concentration, loss of interest, and poor appetite, there is no problem in recognizing that at present this patient has a major depressive episode. The difficulty is in evaluating the period immediately preceding the depression, during which his wife claims that he was "high," but he says he was only feeling glad to be alive. If one accepts the *patient's* account, then the diagnosis is merely Major Depression, Recurrent, without Melancholia, and the wife's account can be seen as a distortion influenced by her own depression. On the other hand, if one accepts the *wife's* account (which we are inclined to accept because of the detail), then the period preceding her husband's depression represents a hypomanic episode — a period of elevated mood with poor judgment and hyperactivity that is apparently not sufficiently severe to meet the criteria for a manic episode. Although DSM-III does not code hypomanic episodes as such, they are given as an example of Atypical Bipolar Disorder, the Axis I disorder in this case.

There is no history suggesting a Personality Disorder, hence no diagnosis is given on Axis II. Similarly, the absence of any physical disorder affecting the patient's management or treatment is reflected on Axis III.

For most people a mental illness in a spouse that requires hospitalization would be a severe stressor—hence a rating of 5—Severe, on Axis IV. The patient has previously been functioning at a high level, as evidenced by his political and recreational activity. We give the rating of 2—Very good, rather than 1—Superior, on Axis V, since there is no evidence of unusually good social relationships.

DSM-III Diagnosis:

Axis I: 296.70 Atypical Bipolar Disorder (p. 223)
Axis II: V71.09 No diagnosis on Axis II
Axis III: None
Axis IV: Psychosocial stressors: illness and hospitalization of wife
Severity: 5 — Severe
Axis V: Highest level of adaptive functioning past year: 2 — Very good

Bereaved

122 A 17-year-old high-school junior was brought to the emergency room by her distraught mother, who was at a loss to understand her daughter's behavior. Two days earlier the patient's father had been buried; he had died of a sudden myocardial infarction earlier in the week. The patient had become wildly agitated at the cemetery, screaming uncontrollably and needing to be restrained by relatives. She was inconsolable at home, sat rocking in a corner, and talked about a devil that had come to claim her soul. Before her father's death she was a "typical teen-ager , popular, and a very good student, but sometimes prone to overreacting." There was no previous psychiatric history.

Discussion of Bereaved

Grief is an expected reaction to the loss of a loved one. This young woman's reaction, however, not only is more severe than would be expected (wildly agitated, screaming uncontrollably) but also involves psychotic symptoms (the belief that a devil has come to claim her soul). The sudden onset of a florid psychotic episode immediately following a marked psychosocial stressor, in the absence of increasing psychopathology preceding the stressor, indicates the Axis I diagnosis of Brief Reactive Psychosis. Typically the psychotic symptoms last for more than a few hours but less than two weeks. The diagnosis can be made before the two-week period—the maximum duration of symptoms consistent with this diagnosis—has elapsed. It is anticipated that the symptoms will subside and the patient will return to her usual level of good functioning. If the symptoms persist beyond that time, the diagnosis would be changed to another psychotic disorder, such as Schizophreniform Disorder.

Axis II indicates the absence of a Personality Disorder but the presence of the histrionic traits her mother describes as "overreacting."

Axis III notes the absence of any physical disorder or condition.

Axis IV rates the severity of the father's death as an extreme psychosocial stressor.

Axis V, based on the limited information that she was a "typical teen-ager, popular, and a very good student," rates the highest level of adaptive functioning during the past year as very good.

DSM-III Diagnosis:

Axis I: **298.80 Brief Reactive Psychosis (p. 201)**
Axis II: **Histrionic traits**
Axis III: **None**
Axis IV: **Psychosocial stressor: death of father**
            Severity: 6 — Extreme
Axis V: **Highest level of adaptive functioning past year:**
            2 — Very good

Narcolepsy

123 This agitated 42-year-old businessman was admitted to the psychiatric service after a two-and-one-half-month period in which he found himself becoming increasingly distrustful of others and suspicious of his business associates. He was taking their statements out of context, "twisting" their words, and making inappropriately hostile and accusatory comments; he had, in fact, lost several business deals that had been "virtually sealed." Finally, the patient fired a shotgun into his backyard late one night when he heard noises that convinced him that intruders were about to break into his house and kill him.

One and one-half years previously the patient had been diagnosed as having narcolepsy and had been placed on Ritalin. He became asymptomatic and was able to work quite effectively as the sales manager of a small office-machine company and to participate in an active social life with his family and a small circle of friends. In the four months before admission he had been using increasingly large doses of Ritalin to maintain alertness late at night because of an increasing amount of work that could not be handled during the day.

Discussion of Narcolepsy

The primary symptoms are persecutory delusions about co-workers, delusions of reference (the patient believed that noises indicated the presence of intruders who were about to kill him), and psychomotor agitation. Because of the temporal relationship between the increasing doses of Ritalin, an amphetaminelike stimulant, and the development of these symptoms, it is reasonable to assume that the disturbance represents an Organic Delusional Syndrome, more specifically, Ritalin-induced Delusional Disorder. The additional diagnosis of Ritalin Abuse is given because of the pathological pattern of use over a period of longer than one month (using increasingly large doses to maintain alertness late at night).

Since there is no evidence of any personality problems, the code on Axis II is V71.09, No diagnosis on Axis II.

The narcolepsy is noted on Axis III. The increased demands at work are noted as a mild psychosocial stressor on Axis IV. At his best, in the preceding year the patient's functioning in both work and social relations was apparently very good. This is noted as 2 — Very good, on Axis V.

DSM-III Diagnosis:

Axis I: 292.11 Ritalin-induced Delusional Disorder (p. 149)
           305.70 Ritalin Abuse, Unspecified (p. 174)
Axis II: V71.09 No diagnosis on Axis II (p. 335)
Axis III: Narcolepsy
Axis IV: Psychosocial stressors: increased demands at work
           Severity: 3 — Mild
Axis V: Highest level of adaptive functioning past year:
           2 — Very good

Bye-bye

124 A five-year-old boy was evaluated by a psychologist because of problems in school. He had begun kindergarten eight months earlier, and had had problems getting along with the other children and the teacher from the beginning. The teacher had called numerous parent conferences throughout the school year to report that the boy seemed angry and frustrated, had great trouble handling the natural conflicts that occur among children, seemed at times not to understand her instructions, and was difficult to understand. Very recently there had been some improvement, however, in that the boy was now playing with the other children, whereas he had started out staying mostly by himself. The parents reported that the boy was on phenobarbital for a seizure disorder, but was otherwise healthy, and that there were no problems at home.

During the examination the boy was very quiet and shy, and his mother had to remain in the room. The boy stared at the examiner, seemingly agreeable, but often not responding to questions or demands. Sometimes he produced inappropriate responses, and the examiner was unsure of the boy's grasp of the task. For example, when given a pencil and a toy car and told to "put the pencil on the car," the boy stared at the examiner, put the car on the floor, and began to draw with the pencil. In general, verbalizations from the boy were very limited: he did tell the examiner his name, but generally pointed to objects when asked to name them. When asked to define objects (car, pencil, etc.), he only gestured to show their use. When leaving the examination room, the boy said "me go" and "bye-bye" to the examiner.

Discussion of Bye-bye

This child has difficulty understanding what people say and in making himself understood. Such disturbance in language development can be seen in Mental Retardation or Pervasive Developmental Disorders (Axis I) or as a Specific Developmental Disorder (Axis II). The absence of any reference to delayed developmental milestones or deficits in adaptive functioning, such as late walking or inability to dress himself, suggests normal intelligence. His ability to grasp the purpose of common objects (such as pencils and cars) suggests the presence of inner language and, along with the absence of bizarre behavior, rules out a Pervasive Developmental Disorder. Thus, the diagnosis of Developmental Language Disorder, involving both comprehension and expression, is made on Axis II.

On Axis III the seizure disorder requiring medication would be noted.

There is no suggestion of a recent psychosocial stressor that might have contributed to the development of the Axis II disorder. Although the language difficulty first became a focus of attention when he started kindergarten, most likely it was present before. Furthermore, there is no mention of an exacerbation. Thus, a rating of 1–None would be made on Axis IV.

With the limited information available, the highest level of adaptive functioning during the past year would seem to be only fair, in view of the troubles the child had for most of the year in kindergarten.

DSM-III Diagnosis:

Axis I: **V71.09 No diagnosis on Axis I**
Axis II: **315.31 Developmental Language Disorder, Expressive and Receptive Types (pp. 96, 97)**
Axis III: **Seizure disorder**
Axis IV: **Psychosocial stressors: none**
  Severity: 1–None
Axis V: **Highest level of adaptive functioning past year: 4–Fair**

Sickly

125 A 38-year-old married woman came to a mental health clinic with the chief complaint of depression. In the last month she has been feeling depressed, suffering from insomnia, crying, and been aware of poor concentration and diminished interest in activities.

She relates that she was sickly as a child and has been depressed since childhood because her father deserted the family when she was approximately ten. Apparently she was taken to a doctor for this, and the family doctor recommended that her mother give the patient a little wine before each meal. Her adolescence was unremarkable, although she describes herself as having been shy. She graduated from high school at age 17 and began working as a clerk and bookkeeper at a local department store. She married at about the same time, but the marriage was not a success: she had frequent arguments with her husband, in part related to her sexual indifference and pain during intercourse.

At age 19 she began to drink heavily, a behavior pattern she claims started after the desertion by her father. With the heavy drinking she went on benders, had morning shakes, and had guilt feelings because she was not caring well for her children. At 21 she was admitted to a local mental hospital, where she was diagnosed as having alcoholism and depression. She was treated with antidepressants. After discharge she continued to drink almost continually up until age 29; she did have a one-year period of abstinence in this time. At 29 she was again hospitalized, this time in an alcohol treatment unit. Since that time she has remained abstinent. She has subsequently been admitted to psychiatric hospitals for a mixture of physical and depressive symptoms, and she has been treated with electroconvulsive therapy (ECT), without much relief.

She describes nervousness since childhood; she also spontaneously admits to being sickly since her youth with a succession of physical problems doctors often indicated were due to her nerves or depression. She, however, believes that she has a physical problem that has not yet been discovered by the doctors. Besides nervousness, she has chest pain, and has been told by a variety of medical consultants that she has a "nervous heart." She also goes to doctors for abdominal pain, and has been diagnosed as having a "spastic colon." She has seen chiropractors and osteopaths for backaches, for pains in the extremities, and for anesthesia of her fingertips. Three months ago she had vomiting, chest pain, and abdominal pain, and was admitted to a hospital for a hysterectomy. Since the hysterectomy she has had repeated anxiety attacks, fainting spells that she claims are associated with unconsciousness that lasts more than thirty minutes, vomiting, food intolerance, weakness, and fatigue. She has had several medical hospitalizations for workups of vomiting, colitis, vomiting blood, and chest pain. She has had a surgical procedure for an abcess of the throat.

The patient is one of five children. She was reared by her mother after her father left. Her father was said to be an alcoholic who died at age 53 of liver cancer. Despite a difficult childhood financially, the patient graduated from high school and worked two years. She tried to work a second time, but was forced to quit because of her sickliness. She married her present husband at 17 and has remained married. Her husband is said to be an alcoholic who has had some periods of work instability. They have argued over sex and finances. She has five children, ranging in age from 2 to 20. She currently admits to feeling depressed, but thinks that it is all because her "hormones were not straightened out." She is still looking for a medical explanation for her physical and psychological problems.

Discussion of Sickly

If the reader appreciates all of the nuances of making a multiaxial evaluation of this case, he or she is well on the way to becoming a supernosologist!

It is first necessary to separate the immediate problem that is the reason for the patient's current consultation (depression) from her long-standing problems (physical symptoms and excessive use of alcohol). She is apparently now having a recurrence of a major depressive episode (depressed mood accompanied by insomnia, poor concentration, and diminished interest). The criteria for a major depressive episode require four associated symptoms, yet there is reference to only three. Nevertheless, in view of the history of several previous episodes apparently severe enough to require hospitalization, the use of the criteria as guidelines justifies making a diagnosis of Major Depression, Recurrent, without Melancholia.

Nearly all of the patient's many physical symptoms that have plagued her for so many years are apparently without an organic basis. This is consistent with the two "physical" diagnoses mentioned: "nervous heart" and "spastic colon." This suggests a Somatoform Disorder, and the large number of symptoms involving multiple organ systems suggests Somatization Disorder. This diagnosis requires, in a woman, 14 symptoms that she reports cause her to see a physician, take medicine, or otherwise alter her life pattern. Let us count them: admits to being sickly most of her life, sexual indifference, pain during intercourse, chest pain, abdominal pain, backaches, extremity pain, anesthesia of fingertips, vomiting, fainting spells, periods of "unconsciousness," food intolerance, weakness, and diarrhea (colitis). Although we count 14, the diagnosis would still be made clinically if a few less were noted, on the assumption that she probably had others not noted, since the characteristic picture of Somatization Disorder is clearly present.

She has also had periods of heavy alcohol consumption that have included "benders," "morning shakes," and difficulty functioning as a mother. The presence of a pattern of pathological use, impairment in occupational functioning, and evidence of withdrawal all indicate a diagnosis of Alcohol Dependence. Since she is apparently currently not having difficulties attributable to alcohol use, the course is noted as in Remission. (We would prefer "in Remission" to not noting the history of Alcohol Dependence because of the high probability of relapse in this case.) The order in which these diagnoses have been discussed indicates their order when listed on Axis I and reflects their relative importance as factors determining the current evaluation.

On Axis II we are tempted to note Mixed Personality Disorder (Provisional) to indicate our suspicion that her pattern of relating to herself and others (apart from the Axis I diagnoses) is maladaptive. However, the chronic and pervasive psychopathology described in this case can be entirely accounted for by her Axis I diagnoses. Therefore, we would note "Diagnosis deferred" on Axis II.

On Axis III we would list those current physical symptoms of the Somatization Disorder that might require clinical attention or treatment in their own right, such as vomiting and fainting. (The DSM-III discussion of Axis III does not include listing physical symptoms that are part of an Axis I diagnosis. Nevertheless, we think it will prove clinically useful to note such symptoms according to the above principle, despite the apparent redundancy.)

This woman's life situation is probably always associated with considerable stress. Arguments with her husband and his alcoholism and work instability are mentioned. However, the only recent significantly stressful event mentioned is the hysterectomy three months earlier, which may well have played a role in precipitating a recurrence of her Major Depression. The hysterectomy would be listed on Axis IV, with a severity rating of 4—Moderate. (A serious physical illness is given as an example of a rating of 5—Severe, but this seems too high a rating in this case, given the patient's history of chronic physical illness.)

Owing to her inability to work because of her "sickliness" and the interpersonal problems with her husband, a rating of 4—Fair would be made on Axis V, highest level of adaptive functioning past year, to indicate some impairment in both social and occupational functioning.

DSM-III Diagnosis:

Axis I: 296.32 Major Depression, Recurrent, without Melancholia (p. 213)
300.81 Somatization Disorder (p. 243)
303.93 Alcohol Dependence, in Remission (p. 170)
Axis II: 799.90 Diagnosis deferred
Axis III: Vomiting, fainting
Axis IV: Psychosocial stressors: recent hysterectomy
Severity: 4—Moderate
Axis V: Highest level of adaptive functioning past year: 4—Fair

Down's Syndrome

126 A 15-year-old boy was brought to the emergency room by his mother, who, clutching the on-call resident's arm, pleaded, "You've got to admit him; I just can't take it anymore." The patient had been taken home from a special school by his mother six months previously. The mother showed the resident papers from the school that indicated that the patient's IQ was 45. He had had several placements, beginning at age eight. After a year or so away, the patient would be brought home by his mother, who had always been racked by guilt over his retardation and her inability to manage him in the home. The patient was an only child whose parents had been divorced for the past four years. The father had moved to another city.

During the last six months at home, the patient had increasingly become a behavior problem. He was about 5'9" and weighed close to 200 pounds. He had become destructive of property at home — breaking dishes and a chair during angry tantrums — and then, more recently, physically assaultive. He had hit his mother on the arm and shoulder during a recent scuffle that began after she tried to get him to stop banging a broom on the apartment floor. The mother showed her bruises to the resident and threatened to call the mayor's office if the hospital refused to admit her son.

On examination the boy had the typical signs of Down's syndrome, including thick facial features, slightly protruding tongue, epicanthal fold of the eyelids, and Simian crease of the palms of the hands. With indistinct and slurred speech, the boy insisted that he "didn't mean to hurt anybody."

Discussion of Down's Syndrome

The IQ of 45 indicates significantly subaverage general intellectual functioning. The need for placement in a special school since age eight suggests that there have been severe concurrent deficits or impairments in adaptive behavior. These two features, with onset before the age of 18, indicate the Axis I diagnosis of Mental Retardation. Since the IQ level is between 35 and 49, the subtype is Moderate.

This child, as is often the case, presents for admission because of destructive and aggressive behavior, not because of impairment in intellectual functioning. Presumably, this aggressive behavior is a persistent pattern. Should one therefore make an additional diagnosis of Conduct Disorder? We think not. The DSM-III criteria for Conduct

Disorder do not rule out Moderate or Severe Mental Retardation; but since most clinicians would regard this boy's aggressive behavior as qualitatively different from the aggressive behavior of a child with Conduct Disorder, perhaps the criteria for Conduct Disorder should rule out Moderate or Severe Mental Retardation (as Severe Mental Retardation is ruled out in the diagnosis of Antisocial Personality Disorder).

In the presence of significant Mental Retardation, the issue of a Specific Developmental Disorder is moot. Therefore, the Axis II notation would be V71.09, No diagnosis on Axis II.

In this case the Mental Retardation is apparently due to Down's syndrome, which would be noted on Axis III.

A possible contribution of psychosocial stressors to an exacerbation of his behavioral problems is unclear from the available information. Perhaps returning home from the special school or a change in the mother's behavior, because of her guilt feelings, was a factor in triggering the boy's recent episodes of assaultive behavior. In the absence of more information, the Axis IV level of psychosocial stressors is noted as "0," unspecified.

The patient's highest level of adaptive functioning in the past year is determined by comparing his functioning with what would be expected of a hypothetical normal child of his age — not a similarly retarded child. By this standard of reference, his level of adaptive functioning is very poor, owing to marked impairment in all areas of functioning.

DSM-III Diagnosis:

Axis I: 318.00 Moderate Mental Retardation (p. 40)
Axis II: V71.09 No diagnosis on Axis II
Axis III: Down's syndrome
Axis IV: Psychosocial stressors: undetermined
            Severity: 0 — Unspecified
Axis V: Highest level of adaptive functioning past year: 6 — Very poor

Diagnostic Dilemmas

Diagnostic Dilemmas

In preparing this book, we encountered some cases for which DSM-III does not easily provide the definitive diagnosis. This will come as no surprise to clinicians, who appreciate the difficulty of summarizing the complexities of abnormal human behavior by means of a diagnosis. In some of these cases there is no doubt that a mental disorder exists, but it does not correspond to any of the specific DSM-III categories. In other cases a diagnosis of a specific DSM-III category seems evident, but the diagnostic criteria for that category do not allow the diagnosis to be made. In a few of these cases we offer suggestions about how the diagnostic criteria might be modified in the future to improve their value for clinical and research use. Finally, certain cases present with features of several mental disorders. In these cases supernosologists, in particular, will appreciate the difficulty that we had in making the differential diagnosis.

The Men's Room

127 A 26-year-old, single, male grocery clerk complained: "I have a problem with shit." The patient was referred to a mental health clinic by a pastoral counselor who has been seeing him for the past six months for interpersonal problems. Over the past three to four years, during periods of low sexual activity, the patient becomes sexually frustrated and goes to public restrooms. He turns off the water to the toilets and then waits for a male whom he finds sexually attractive to enter. He waits until this person uses a toilet and then "retrieves" the feces and takes them home in a plastic bag. He warms the feces by placing the bag in boiling water and subsequently plays with the feces, which sexually excites him. He then masturbates to orgasm. This behavior has occurred about once a month. He admits to a great deal of guilt and concern over his habit because "it is not socially acceptable."

The patient is homosexual but is extremely reluctant to frequent "gay" bars. When he does, he stays only a few minutes: if he is not approached within the first 15 to 20 minutes, he leaves. He shares an apartment with a roommate, but is not emotionally involved with him. He has a limited circle of friends.

He has had an attraction for restrooms since early adolescence. Some of his earliest sexual contacts occurred in restrooms. Once he was excited by urine; however, this is not currently the case.

The patient recalls having been a "loner" throughout his childhood. At an early age he realized that this sexual attraction to other boys made him different from his peers. This led him to be socially isolated. His first sexual activity occurred at age ten with group masturbation. At age 11 he began engaging in homosexual activity. This has continued throughout his life, and he has had no history of heterosexual arousal or activity.

The patient is a short, stocky, rather masculine male who is meticulously dressed and groomed. During the interview he was somewhat tense and stiff, especially when describing his sexual behavior. His affect was somewhat constricted. He complained of feeling depressed, but he has no associated symptoms of depression. His speech tends to be rather overinclusive and circumstantial. There is no evidence of psychotic symptoms.

Discussion of the Men's Room

How should the use of feces for achieving sexual excitement be classified? In DSM-III Coprophilia is given as an example of Atypical Paraphilia. In Coprophilia the individual is excited by observing the act of defecation or by being defecated upon. In this case, however, it is the feces themselves that serve as the stimulus. Therefore, it seems to us no different from the use of other parts of the body, such as hair or nails, for sexual excitement, and as such should be classified as Fetishism. (Unfortunately, we cannot claim that classifying this disorder as Fetishism rather than as Atypical Paraphilia has profound treatment implications.)

In view of the history of social isolation and inability to initiate relationships with people, it seems reasonable to give an Axis II diagnosis of Atypical Personality Disorder (Provisional), R/O Schizoid or Avoidant Personality Disorder.

DSM-III Diagnosis:

Axis I: 302.81 Fetishism (p. 269)
Axis II: 301.89 Atypical Personality Disorder (Provisional)
(p. 329)
R/O Schizoid or Avoidant Personality Disorder

Supply Sergeant*

128 The patient, a black man, was a supply sergeant in the military during the late 1950s. He was caught by the military police stealing a deodorant stick from the post exchange. The army, which had reason to suspect the sergeant of other thefts and was undeterred by constitutional restraints on search and seizure, went to his home and reclaimed every piece of army property the sergeant could not account for. The pile of supplies — uniforms, blankets, picks and shovels, cartons of canned goods, mess kits, etc. — could have filled a trailer truck. It was all photographed on the sergeant's front lawn, and that photo became part of his army medical file. The army was determined to courtmartial the sergeant; but he had been examined by a civilian psychiatrist, who decided that much of what was stolen was of no use to the sergeant and, on the basis of an understanding of the sergeant's psychodynamics, had diagnosed him as having Kleptomania. This civilian psychiatrist was prepared to testify at a courtmartial that the stealing was due to unconscious and irresistible impulses. Unhappy with the civilian psychiatrist's report, the army sent this man to be evaluated at an army hospital. There he was told repeatedly that anything he said could be used against him at the courtmartial. The sergeant took the warning rather impassively, and the army psychiatrist set to work gathering a detailed history.

The sergeant, a very intelligent man, got caught up in telling the story of his life. He had grown up in a southern city during the days of racial segregation. A good and serious student from a deeply religious family, he had done well in school and had gone to a small college, where he studied literature. After graduation, despite his hopes and dreams, he had found no appropriate work, and eventually was drafted into the Korean War. After the war, seeing no alternatives, he remained in the army to serve his 20 years. As the years passed, he became increasingly bitter. He was convinced that life had cheated him because he was black and that the army, in the work and position it

*Taken from Stone A: (Presidential address): Conceptual ambiguity
and morality in modern psychiatry. Am J Psychiatry 137:887-894, 1980

gave him, continued to discriminate against him. Out of this sense of being cheated grew a sense of entitlement, and he came to feel that he was justified in taking whatever he could, whenever he could. He had no sense of being impulsively driven to steal army property; instead, he stole with a sense of entitlement and reparation in protest against the racist world that had deprived him of his hopes.

It is not clear why, despite being warned, the sergeant told all this to the army psychiatrist. At any rate, he did; and the army psychiatrist, after puzzling over the diagnostic possibilities, which included Paranoid Personality and Depression, concluded that the sergeant did not have Kleptomania or any other mental disorder that should excuse him from responsibility. Subsequently the army psychiatrist, trying to avoid the sergeant's eyes, testified to this at the courtmartial. The sergeant sat there in his dress uniform with his medals, his wife, and their small children. He was sentenced to five years at hard labor.

Discussion of Supply Sergeant

This poignant case illustrates that some maladaptive behavior is not encompassed by the concept of mental disorder offered in standard classifications such as DSM-III. Although stealing in an adult may occur in many disorders (e.g., Schizophrenia, Dementia, Bipolar Disorder), there are only two in which it is likely to be the predominant symptom: Antisocial Personality Disorder and Kleptomania.

The civilian psychiatrist attempted to make a case for the diagnosis of Kleptomania. The army psychiatrist had no difficulty in demonstrating the absence of the characteristic signs of the disorder: Kleptomania is an Impulse Control Disorder in which the stealing represents a failure to resist an impulse; it is always preceded by an increasing sense of tension and is followed by the experience of pleasure or release. In this case the sergeant "had no sense of being impulsively driven to steal army property; instead, he stole with a sense of entitlement and reparation in protest against the racist world that had deprived him of his hopes." A diagnosis of Antisocial Personality Disorder would make no sense in the view of the absence of any childhood history of antisocial behavior, the sergeant's good work and family functioning in adulthood, and the lack of a pervasive pattern of adult antisocial behavior.

There is a suggestion that this man stole some things that he did not need and that the extent of his stealing probably invited his being caught. In addition, once caught he made no attempt to protect himself either by distorting his story to lend credence to the diagnosis of Kleptomania or by refusing to cooperate with the army psychiatrist. All this indicates a self-destructive, and therefore maladaptive, aspect to his behavior.

Does the maladaptive nature of his behavior indicate a mental disorder—albeit unspecified, since it does not correspond to any of the specific mental disorders included in the DSM-III classification? To classify it as such would so broaden the concept of mental disorder that virtually all criminal acts (murder, rape, grand larceny) could be interpreted as symptoms of mental disorder. There is no doubt that careful psychological study of any individual who has engaged in a criminal act would reveal the psychological origins of the maladaptive behavior—in this case, the sergeant's sense of entitlement as a reaction to his life in a racist society.

DSM-III does provide a code for indicating that antisocial behavior in an adult is the focus of attention, but is not due to a mental disorder —the V code Adult Antisocial Behavior.

DSM-III Diagnosis:

Axis I: **V71.01 Adult Antisocial Behavior (p. 332)**

Sex Problem

129 Ms. B. is a 43-year-old married housewife who entered the hospital in 1968 with a chief complaint of being concerned about her "sex problem"; she stated that she needed hypnotism to find out what was wrong with her sexual drive. Her husband supplied the history; he complained that she had had many extramarital affairs, with many different men, all through their married life. He insisted that in one two-week period she had had as many as a hundred different sexual experiences with men outside the marriage. The patient herself agreed with this assessment of her behavior, but would not speak of the experiences, saying that she "blocks" the memories out. She denied any particular interest in sexuality, but said that apparently she felt a compulsive drive to go out and seek sexual activity despite her lack of interest.

The patient had been married to her husband for over twenty years. He was clearly the dominant partner in the marriage. The patient was fearful of his frequent jealous rages, and apparently it was he who suggested that she enter the hospital in order to receive hypnosis. The patient maintained that she could not explain why she sought out other men, that she really did not want to do this. Her husband stated that on occasion he had tracked her down, and when he had found her, she acted as if she did not know him. She confirmed this and believed it was due to the fact that the episodes of her sexual promiscuity were blotted out by "amnesia."

When the physician indicated that he questioned the reality of the wife's sexual adventures, the husband became furious and accused the doctor and a ward attendant of having sexual relations with her.

Neither an amytal interview nor considerable psychotherapy with the wife was able to clear the "blocked out" memory of periods of sexual activities. The patient did admit to a memory of having had two extramarital relationships in the past, one 20 years before the time of admission and the other just a year before admission. She stated that the last one had actually been planned by her husband, and that he was in the same house at the time. She continued to believe that she had actually had countless extramarital sexual experiences, though she remembered only two of them.

Discussion of Sex Problem

One's first impression is that an Amnestic Syndrome, either psychogenic or organic, should be considered. However, the plot thickens as evidence accumulates that the husband, the chief informant, has persecutory delusions that his wife is repeatedly unfaithful to him. Apparently, under his influence, his wife has accepted this delusional belief, explaining her lack of memory of the events by believing that she has "amnesia." It would seem that she has adopted his persecutory delusion and does not really have any kind of "amnesia." Since there are none of the essential features of Schizophrenia (e.g., bizarre delusions, hallucinations, or incoherence), the diagnosis is a Paranoid Disorder. Because the delusional system developed as a result of a close relationship with another person who had an established disorder with persecutory delusions, the diagnosis is Shared Paranoid Disorder, formerly called *Folie à deux*.

An interesting twist to this case is that it is the patient who, by virtue of her alleged extramarital activity, is the source of the persecution of the husband. It is more common in a Shared Paranoid Disorder for the person who has adopted the other's delusional system to believe that he or she is also being persecuted.

DSM-III Diagnosis:

Axis I: 297.30 Shared Paranoid Disorder (p. 197)

Exercises

130 Jenny, age four, was referred by her pediatrician for a psychiatric evaluation. Her parents are concerned about the girl's "obsession" with her own and her father's genitals. This takes the form of spending a considerable amount of time every day masturbating, which she calls doing her "exercises," asking to see her father's genitals several times a day, and running upstairs with him to watch him urinate.

Her parents feel that she has always been very interested in her genitals and began to masturbate for apparent pleasure when she was six months old. They did not think much of it but became concerned when she increased the intensity and length of her masturbation at about one year of age. At that time she would spend up to three hours a day masturbating, often doing it while she was also playing with toys or watching her parents. The masturbation decreased somewhat at about 18 months, but flared up again when her baby sister was born two years ago. At that time she also began to soil again; she smeared feces on the wall. She was openly angry with the new baby, sometimes had to be forcibly restrained from hurting her (e.g., putting a pillow over her face), and could virtually never be left alone with the baby.

About eight months ago she began spending more time masturbating and became fascinated with male genitals. She has approached other men to see their genitals, and two months ago asked a five-year-old boy to take his pants down. Although her parents did not consider this abnormal, the boy's parents were extremely upset, and have forbidden the boy to play with her. Currently, she masturbates mostly when she goes to bed, for about 20 to 30 minutes, and while she speaks to people or watches TV. There have also been times when she has masturbated by lying on the staircase sideways and rubbing her genitals against the stairs.

Jenny is the oldest of two children of an upper-middle-class family. The father comes from an island in the Mediterranean and is an outgoing, personable man. Her mother is from Australia, is much more reserved, and cannot show her feelings easily. They have a somewhat impoverished sexual relationship, the mother acknowledging that "Since the last baby I don't feel like it anymore." Regarding Jenny's problem, her father thinks that it is okay for him to let her look at his genitals, but he has tried to get her to stop asking to see other men's. The mother stresses that she "doesn't mind her doing her exercises," as she herself calls it, although she seemed quite upset and tense about it. The father, on the other hand, seems mainly concerned about the future of this behavior, especially when Jenny enters school.

Jenny has always been a very active child who has demanded much attention and generally has a hard time sticking to any activity for more than two to three minutes. Her mother says that she is impulsive and flits from activity to activity without seeming to enjoy herself at anything. When her mother confronts her about this, Jenny often has severe temper tantrums.

Jenny was evaluated for two hours, during which she played cheerfully and eagerly with the interviewer. She concentrated well on the tasks she set herself to do. Her drawings were of long snakes and race tracks for cars. Her mother found her attentiveness surprising and commented repeatedly that it was "the first time she had ever done that." Jenny's speech and general knowledge were quite advanced for her age. There were no signs of gross psychopathology.

Discussion of Exercises

It is now recognized that as part of normal development many children engage in masturbation. However, the amount of time that Jenny spends every day masturbating and her preoccupation with her father's and other men's genitals seem outside the normal range. Excessive masturbation in a child may be a symptom of Mental Retardation or a Pervasive Developmental Disorder, but there is certainly no suggestion of either subaverage intellectual development or grossly bizarre behavior or gross impairment in social and language development in Jenny's case.

Her parents refer to her preoccupation with genitals as an "obsession," but there is no evidence either that this preoccupation is a true obsession or that her masturbation is a compulsion. Obsessions are persistent thoughts that intrude themselves into consciousness and are experienced as senseless or repugnant. There is no evidence that Jenny feels this way about them. A compulsion is a repetitive and seemingly purposeful behavior that generally does not include activities that are inherently pleasurable, such as eating or masturbation.

If the excessive masturbation and preoccupation with men's genitals developed after a specific psychosocial stressor, such as frequent arguments between the parents, this might be conceptualized as an Adjustment Disorder. However, there is no evidence of this in this case. One could make a case for considering this an atypical form of a Disorder of Impulse Control. Presumably Jenny is unable to resist an increasing sense of tension, and experiences pleasure when she gives in to the impulse to masturbate. Generally, however, in Impulse Control Disorders the resulting behavior has severely negative consequences for the patient and others. At the present time, except for the incident with the five-year-old boy and her parents' distress, there is no evidence of serious negative consequences. If the same behavior persists into school (her father's fear), then the consequences will undoubtedly be more significant.

Jenny is described as "a very active child" who is "impulsive and flits from activity to activity." This raises the question of Attention Deficit Disorder, but there is no evidence of the full clinical picture.

Many readers will wonder if Jenny's behavior is best understood as a manifestation of a disturbance in the relationship between the parents and the child. More substantial evidence for this would suggest the appropriateness of the V code Parent–Child Problem.

Since this unusual behavior does not conform to any of the specific mental disorders included in DSM-III, and since there is insufficient information to make a diagnosis of any of the mental disorders that are slightly suggested, we would recommend that the diagnosis be deferred until more information is available. In the introduction to the section on Disorders Usually First Evident in Infancy, Childhood, or Adolescence, it is acknowledged that certain disturbances in development are not easily classified. We would therefore not quarrel with a diagnosis of Unspecified Mental Disorder, nonpsychotic. We would also not quarrel with the use of the V code Parent–Child Problem by clinicians who believe that, with the available information, it would be most useful to conceptualize the unusual behavior not as a symptom of a mental disorder, but rather as a symptom of a disturbed parent–child relationship, possibly requiring family intervention.

DSM-III Diagnosis:

Axis I: 799.90 Diagnosis deferred on Axis I

The Heavenly Vision*

131 An obese 34-year-old woman was brought to a local hospital by the police. She had removed her clothing and, standing naked beside her car in a gas station, had ostentatiously engaged in fellatio with her five-month-old son. She later claimed that she did this in response to a vision: "I felt I had been instructed to step out of the car, remove my clothes as a sort of shocking, attention-getting episode depicting the stripping that this

*Adapted from Spitzer RL, Gibbon M, Skodol A, Williams JBW, Hyler S: The heavenly vision of a poor woman: A down-to-earth discussion of the DSM-III differential diagnosis. J Operational Psychiatry 11 (2):169–172, 1980

nation is to be going through soon." She explained that the depiction of oral sex was in order to draw attention to the abuse of children in vile ways in this country, as in prostitution and pornography. She described her own behavior as a "bizarre act" and understood that it was viewed as evidence of a "mental aberration." But in her own words, "There's method to my madness."

The patient had apparently, for the past 20 years, been having "different levels of visionary states" during which she both saw and heard God. Recently she had been receiving religious and political messages from God and believed that "The Communist Party and the Nazi Party in America have joined hands and will be occupying the country . . . the strike of the invasion point will come over Canada down through the Midwest to the point of St. Louis."

The patient's description of her visionary experiences and her history was coherent and articulate and delivered in a matter-of-fact manner, although with many vivid and startling details.

Records from a previous hospitalization noted that the patient had a completely positive review of physical symptoms. Her presenting complaint at that time was migraine headaches; but as each physician examined her, the symptom list grew longer and longer. Records from a psychiatric outpatient evaluation nine years before the current admission noted that she complained of extreme shakiness, which had gone on for a number of years; of a painful "knot" growing at the lower part of the back of her head; and of blackout spells. After these spells she said she frequently went into a deep sleep. Several electroencephalograms (EEGs) were negative. A neurologist who examined her did not think she had epilepsy and recommended that she see a psychiatrist.

During her current hospitalization the patient had some physical complaints, particularly back pain, which she attributed to a fall at age 18 and to arthritis of the lower spine. She had difficulty walking and had consulted many doctors about this. She had a 100% disability rating for "nerves and arthritis."

On physical examination the patient was noted to be overweight. She had several small lipomas on her back and arm. Palpation of her abdomen revealed a poorly localized right lower quadrant tenderness. She complained of polymenorrhea. A Pap smear and endometrial biopsy were normal. An electrocardiogram (EKG) showed a right bundle branch block and left ventricular hypertrophy. Radiological examination of her skull revealed microcephaly (greater than two standard deviations below the lower limits of normal) and osteosclerosis. A rheumatology consultant diagnosed mechanical low back pain exacerbated by obesity.

Her personal history was obtained from the patient alone. She reported that her father was a fundamentalist Christian minister, and she had been deeply involved in the church from an early age. She was baptized at 12, and was "speaking in tongues." At that age she "felt a call to the ministry." She completed high school with above-average grades. At 18, after a broken engagement (which she describes very dramatically, as she does every event in her history), she joined the WACs, against her parents' wishes; and she has been alienated from her family ever since. She claims to have been raped while in the service, and later to have fallen down, hit her head on concrete, and been "unconscious for nine days," after which she was "very weak" and had "bouts of amnesia." She left the WACs after 13 months and married a man who turned out to be a bigamist. She lived with him for 12 years, had 4 children, and separated from him when she discovered that he had molested her daughters. She has worked only sporadically since then.

After her marital separation, the patient left town with her children, because she was being "harassed" by gossiping neighbors. She moved to another town, but the harassment continued. At one point she took the children to Israel, with no money and no plans other than to settle there, claiming that she had traced a "Jewish bloodline" in her ancestry. She gives the impression of having been "on the road" a good deal of the time since her separation (four years ago). For at least part of that time, she placed her children in state foster homes.

Fourteen months before admission she had slept with a stranger in a motel. She claims that this was her only sexual contact in four years; it resulted in the birth of her son, five months previously.

During her hospital stay the patient was quite verbal, and the staff noted her to be "hostile and histrionic." She held firmly to her religious beliefs, and referred to many prophecies that, she claimed, had come true. She produced tape cassettes from various people throughout the country who shared her religious beliefs. In these tapes she was generally praised for her steadfast faith and her gift of prophecy. In some tapes "speaking in tongues" was prominent. The staff had the impression she experienced brief "psychotic episodes," which centered on feelings of persecution by the government.

The patient was discharged after a month. She refused any follow-up care and told a few people that she was heading West in the hope of matriculating in an evangelistic training school. Her children remained in the custody of the appropriate state social service agency. Several days after her discharge she was sought by law-enforcement officials because she allegedly had written about $650 in bad checks and had apparently stolen the car she had been driving before admission.

Discussion of The Heavenly Vision

The central question in the differential diagnosis in this case is whether or not the visions, voices, unusual beliefs, and bizarre behavior are symptoms of a true psychotic disorder — a disorder in which there is gross impairment in reality testing. By definition, a delusion is a belief that is not ordinarily accepted by other members of the person's culture or subculture. This patient has a long history of association with fundamentalist religious sects in which such experiences as speaking in tongues and having visions of God are not uncommon. Can this woman's unusual perceptual experiences and strange notions be entirely accounted for by her religious beliefs? We think not. It is true that receiving messages from God and instructions to do various things to carry out God's will are common among such groups. However, this patient's elaborate notions of a combined invasion by Communist and Nazi forces and her instructions to reveal the sexual depravity of this country seem to us well beyond the range of even extreme fundamentalist beliefs. Thus, we doubt that this woman's behavior is merely the reflection of a culture-bound pattern of beliefs and behavior and without true psychopathological significance.

Having ruled out subcultural identification as an explanation for her "symptoms," we must ask whether the symptoms are genuine (i.e., true delusions and hallucinations) or in some way voluntarily produced, or whether they fall at some interim point along a genuine-fake continuum. There is some evidence that at least some of the symptoms, particularly the bizarre behavior that occasioned her admission to the psychiatric hospital, were produced for dramatic effect. The patient seemed particularly aware of the likely reactions to what she was saying and doing. Such awareness is generally not seen in an individual who is currently in a psychotic state. In the interview itself, the patient described events in her life that strained credulity and suggested that many of them might be at least consciously exaggerated or outright fabrications (pseudologia fantastica). Was she unconscious for nine days? Were her children sexually molested by her husband? Did she trace her lineage back to a Jewish ancestor? Did she conceive during a single occasion of intercourse?

Further evidence suggesting that her "psychotic" symptoms may not be genuine is the long history of physical complaints that appear not to be symptomatic of genuine physical illness. The patient has had episodes of amnesia and blackout "spells," yet her EEGs were negative. She has been noted to have a completely positive review of physical symptoms, many of which presumably cannot be traced to organic pathology. Finally, both the interviewer and the ward staff are apparently impressed with her histrionic manner and presentation.

The DSM-III concept of Factitious Disorder is meant to encompass the murky area between the act of malingering to achieve an easily understandable goal (e.g., feigning illness to avoid military duty) and a genuinely psychotic experience over which the individual has no control whatever. The two critical judgments involved in making a diagnosis of a Factitious Disorder are that the "symptoms" are under voluntary control and that the motivation is not for an easily understandable goal. Since the sense of voluntary control is subjective and can only be inferred by an outside observer, what circumstances would favor such a judgment? Examples would include the "patient" who appears to be hallucinating only when he believes that he is being observed, or the patient who claims to have a cluster of symptoms that generally do not coexist (e.g., a severe Dementia with systematized persecutory delusions).

The judgment that the motivation is not for an easily understandable goal is based on the assumption that in a Factitious Disorder the "patient" is motivated to achieve some benefit that is subsumed within the concept of the patient role. This might be the obvious benefit of treatment and being taken care of in a hospital, or the less obvious benefit of being absolved of certain responsibilities that are normally part of adult life, such as having to work for a living, even though it means being a "patient" for life.

What evidence do we have that this patient's crazy behavior is motivated by the desire to assume some benefits of the patient role? There is the possibility that she realized that her sexual behavior with her infant son would result in her being hospitalized in a mental hospital. Furthermore, whether or not she deliberately sought to have her children removed from her care, this did occur, divesting her of the responsibility for their care and making it possible for her to take off more easily on her own pursuits. We regard this "evidence" as equivocal.

If one accepts the authenticity of the delusions and hallucinations in this case, then the following specific DSM-III categories need to be considered: Schizophrenia (or Schizophreniform Disorder), a Bipolar Disorder, and a Paranoid Disorder. Schizophrenia (and Schizophreniform Disorder) requires a deterioration from a previous level of functioning in such areas as work, social relations, and self-care. There is no evidence of this in our patient. Furthermore, such common features of Schizophrenia as flat affect and loosening of associations are not present. A Paranoid Disorder is ruled out by the prominent hallucinations. Although the patient is grandiose and expansive, none of the other characteristic symptoms of the manic syndrome were noted by either the interviewer or the ward staff; therefore, the diagnosis of Bipolar Disorder seems unlikely.

In DSM-III the diagnosis of Atypical Psychosis may be used when the clinician judges that the patient has a psychotic disorder but the clinical picture does not conform to any of the specific mental disorders. Thus, in this case we are left with either a diagnosis of Factitious Disorder with Psychological Symptoms (if one judges the psychotic symptoms to be factitious) or Atypical Psychosis (if one judges the psychotic symptoms to be genuine).

Although this woman has real physical illness, it is unlikely that this accounts for her amnesia, menstrual symptoms, and probable conversion seizures, reported during a previous hospitalization. This suggests the need to rule out Somatization Disorder, an illness characterized by recurrent and multiple somatic complaints which apparently are not due to any physical disorder but for which medical attention is sought. In this case we count only about 9 symptoms, whereas 14 are required to make the diagnosis.

In view of the long history of disturbed interpersonal relationships, a diagnosis of a Personality Disorder would certainly seem appropriate. The patient's history reveals prominent histrionic features and a suggestion of significant antisocial traits (car theft, passing bad checks, possible abandonment of children). In the absence of more information, a diagnosis of Mixed Personality Disorder with histrionic and antisocial traits seems appropriate.

DSM-III Diagnosis:

Axis I: 298.90 Atypical Psychosis (p. 202) (Provisional, R/O Factitious Disorder with Psychological Symptoms and Somatization Disorder)

Axis II: 301.89 Mixed Personality Disorder (p. 329) with Histrionic and Antisocial Traits

Blinker

132 A seven-year-old boy was referred by a pediatric neurologist who had failed to find any organic basis for his repeated blinking eye movements. His parents report that the eye-blinking began with the birth of his younger sister three years ago. His mother was seized by abdominal pains in the ninth month of pregnancy, in the middle of the night; and labor progressed so rapidly that she delivered at home half an hour later. The commotion awakened the child, who heard his mother's screams and saw his father going in and out of the room in a frantic manner. He saw several bloodstained sheets. The parents, though under stress at the moment, made sure that the child "didn't see anything" and afterward did not allow him to verbalize his reaction to the event, but "just rejoiced with him" about the birth of the baby. Two days later he began to blink his eyes frequently; this blinking was sometimes accompanied by grimacing.

The parents report that the tics became more frequent and were especially so two months after the delivery of the baby. After that they progressively decreased and did not appear at all for several years except under conditions of great anxiety, which were rare.

Five months ago the mother became pregnant again, and two months ago, she informed the patient. Shortly thereafter his tics reappeared; they have been increasing in frequency ever since. No other tics have been noted. In neither of the two episodes has the child displayed grunting noises, repetitive throat-clearing, or other abnormal movements. The parents report that when the child was five, for three months he was very afraid of dogs.

Upon entering the office the child went straight for the dolls and quickly engaged in play that was filled with the theme of pregnancy and birth. His eye-blinking was present throughout the examination. Mild anxiety and agitation were apparent as he proceeded into the play. After he announced that a baby had been born, he just sat on a chair, pensive.

Discussion of Blinker

Experts in movement disorders who have reviewed this case believe that it is unusual in several respects. Although the parents report that both episodes of the disturbance were associated with the birth of a younger sibling, precipitating events are rarely associated with the development of tic disorders. Furthermore, it is very unlikely that the tics in this child were present only during periods of great anxiety. Tics are characteristically exacerbated during periods of stress, but are virtually always present at other times as well.

This boy does not have the recurrent multiple motor and vocal tics that are characteristic of Tourette's Disorder, although some cases of Tourette's Disorder begin with intermittent motor tics only. The intensity of the tics varies considerably, with long periods during which they are absent; this rules out Chronic Motor Tic Disorder. We are left with the diagnosis of Transient Tic Disorder, but the onset at age four and the recurrence after several years are unusual. The most common age at onset for Transient Tic Disorder is seven and, typically, there are no recurrences. According to the diagnostic criteria, the disorder lasts "at least one month, but not more than one year." We could view this boy's illness as two separate episodes — each lasting less than one year—and therefore in strict conformity with the diagnostic criteria. But since the course of the illness is unusual, perhaps the better diagnosis is Atypical Tic Disorder.

DSM-III Diagnosis:

Axis I: 307.20 Atypical Tic Disorder (p. 77)

Slim and Trim

133 A very slim, attractive, articulate, 22-year-old graduate student consulted the counseling service about an eating problem. Since age 17 she has been preoccupied with her weight. Between the ages of 17 and 21 she dieted and reduced her weight from 127 to 94 pounds. Her weight has been stable for the last year.

The patient is not afraid of becoming obese, but feels angry and guilty if she gains a few pounds. She often goes on what she calls "binges," during which she typically consumes two or three sandwiches and a salad, and then feels guilty. During the late afternoons or early mornings she becomes ravenous, and has gone into classrooms searching through trashcans for any leftover food, which she will eat. At times she has experienced excitement at the thought that she might be seen doing this. When she was finally "caught" by a classmate, she was very embarrassed; and this was the stimulus to seek treatment.

She denies persistent anxiety or depression, and has always functioned well both academically and interpersonally. She has not used laxatives or excessive exercise to lose weight, and has never been amenorrheic, although her periods have often been irregular.

Discussion of Slim and Trim

This young woman has a problem with food! There are suggestions in this case of both Anorexia Nervosa and Bulimia, but she does not have the full syndrome of either disorder. She does not have the fear of becoming obese or the disturbed body image that are characteristic of Anorexia Nervosa. She refers to her loss of control of the impulse to eat as a "binge," but she apparently does not consume enormous amounts of food in a short period of time as in a true binge. What she does have is preoccupation with her weight and her eating behavior and a morbid thrill at the prospect of being seen eating garbage. The residual diagnosis of Atypical Eating Disorder is therefore appropriate.

DSM-III Diagnosis:

Axis I: 307.50 Atypical Eating Disorder (p. 73)

Man's Best Friend

134 The patient is a 50-year-old retired policeman who seeks treatment a few weeks after his dog has been run over and died. Since that time he has felt sad, tired, and has had trouble sleeping and concentrating.

The patient lives alone and has for many years had virtually no conversational contacts with other human beings beyond a "Hello" or "How are you?" He prefers to be by himself, finds talk a waste of time, and feels awkward when other people try to initiate a relationship. He occasionally spends some time in a bar, but always off by himself and not really following the general conversation. He reads newspapers avidly and is well informed in many areas, but takes no particular interest in the people around him. He is employed as a security guard, but is known by fellow workers as a "cold fish" and a "loner." They no longer even notice or tease him, especially since he never seemed to notice or care about their teasing anyway.

The patient floats through life without relationships except for that with his dog, which he dearly loved. At Christmas he would buy the dog elaborate gifts and in return would receive a wrapped bottle of scotch that he bought for himself as a gift from the dog. He believes that dogs are more sensitive and loving than people, and he can in return express toward them a tenderness and emotion not possible in his relationships with people. The loss of his pets are the only events in his life that have caused him sadness. He experienced the death of his parents without emotion, and feels no regret whatever at being completely out of contact with the rest of his family. He considers himself different from other people and regards emotionality in others with bewilderment.

Discussion of Man's Best Friend

This man's intense reaction to the death of his dog would not be regarded as abnormal if the deceased were a family member or close friend. In such a case the V code Uncomplicated Bereavement would probably apply. However, the facts that the deceased is a dog and that the patient's symptoms have lasted several weeks and are severe enough to make him seek treatment indicate that his reaction is in excess of what would be considered normal. Thus, we are dealing with a mental disorder. (Clinicians with particular fondness for "man's best friend" may disagree with this conclusion and prefer instead the designation Uncomplicated Bereavement.) Since a full depressive syndrome is not present, the diagnosis is Adjustment Disorder with Depressed Mood rather than Major Depression.

The patient's long-standing pattern of social isolation, inability to express tenderness or emotion for people, and indifference to others, coupled with an absence of oddities and eccentricities of behavior, speech, or thought, is indicative of Schizoid Personality Disorder. It is the presence of the Schizoid Personality Disorder that has made him particularly vulnerable to the stress of his pet's death.

If there were evidence of unusual perceptions or thinking, such as recurrent illusions or ideas of reference, the diagnosis Schizotypal Personality Disorder would have to be considered.

DSM-III Diagnosis:

Axis I: 309.00 Adjustment Disorder with Depressed Mood (p. 300)
Axis II: 301.20 Schizoid Personality Disorder (p. 311)

Inhibited

135 A 24-year-old female was referred by her therapist to a sexual dysfunction clinic because she was no longer able to achieve orgasm. She has been married for five years and previously was able to reach orgasm and enjoyed a regular, sexually satisfying relationship with her husband.

Two years ago she had a classic Major Depression with melancholic and psychotic features, which responded to imipramine and Parnate. She now has no associated symptoms of the depressive syndrome, such as loss of appetite or trouble sleeping, yet she still feels "down" and does not think she has fully recovered her normal, healthy ebullience. For this reason her therapist has continued to give her Parnate, 15 mg three times a day.

She often initiates sexual encounters, finds pleasure in sexual activity, and claims her husband is a "good and satisfactory lover." However, she has to use a lubricant as she finds she does not lubricate enough for him to penetrate without causing her discomfort; and more disturbingly, she has been unable to have an orgasm since her depression. She has tried to masturbate herself to orgasm without success.

Discussion of Inhibited

According to the history, this woman had a major depressive episode from which she has recovered, but not entirely. The issue is whether her difficulty with sexual excitement (does not lubricate enough) and orgasm should be regarded as residual symptoms of the depressive episode or side effects from her medication. Since MAO inhibitors, such as Parnate, are known to cause both impairment in sexual arousal and, more commonly, difficulty in orgasm, it is more practical to regard these symptoms first as drug side effects (noted on Axis III), since reducing the dose somewhat might alleviate the sexual symptoms.

On Axis I we would diagnose Major Depression, Single Episode, in Remission. This is justified even though there are still some residual symptoms (still feels "down" and not her normal, healthy, ebullient self), since she apparently has no other specific depressive symptoms (such as loss of appetite or trouble sleeping).

DSM-III Diagnosis:

Axis I: 296.26 Major Depression, Single Episode, in Remission (p. 213)

Axis III: Impaired sexual excitement and orgasm secondary to Parnate

Fits of Rage

136 A 38-year-old mother of four was referred to a psychiatrist by her priest, to whom she had confided that every few months she was subject to intense fits of rage in which she struck her children and threw things at her husband, sometimes needing to be physically restrained. The children had learned to run off to their rooms and lock the doors when she began to rant "Did you do your homework?" or "Look at this messy house!" She had overheard them referring to her to their father as "crazy Mommy" and "looney." Her husband would not talk to her for several days after such an incident. The patient herself felt very guilty and ashamed.

Detailed questioning revealed that each episode was apparently associated with the patient's sneaking only a swallow or two from a bottle of bourbon she kept hidden from her husband in the trunk of her car.

Discussion of Fits of Rage

This case was submitted as an example of Alcohol Idiosyncratic Intoxication. The clinician accepted (as we did initially) his patient's claim that each episode was initiated by only "a swallow or two" of bourbon. If this were the case, the maladaptive behavior would be seen as the effect on the central nervous system of an amount of alcohol insufficient to cause intoxication in most people, and the diagnosis would be Alcohol Idiosyncratic Intoxication.

On further reflection, it seemed to us that an individual experiencing such an extreme reaction would very quickly learn to avoid alcohol. Why, then, is she hiding the bottle of bourbon? We suspect that she minimizes the amount of alcohol she actually uses and that, in all likelihood, the more prosaic diagnosis of Alcohol Abuse, Episodic, is appropriate. Because we lack clear evidence of a pattern of pathological use, such as daily drinking, binges, or "blackouts," we make a provisional diagnosis.

DSM-III Diagnosis:

Axis I: 305.02 Alcohol Abuse, Episodic (Provisional) (p. 169)

Schoolbus Driver

137 A 45-year-old married schoolbus driver, the father of four, sought psychiatric consultation prior to appearing before a judge following arrest for having committed sexual acts with children.

The patient reported that he frequently had children between the ages of four and six, of both sexes, stimulate him sexually to the point of orgasm. Manual and oral stimulation were preferred, and the patient denied attempting intercourse with the children. He felt equally motivated to have sexual activity with children of both sexes, depending on the practical circumstances involved. He had engaged in this activity with children he picked up and delivered home in his bus for about a year before being apprehended. The combination of small gifts to the children, threats, and selection of children from home environments that were chaotic, indifferent, or lax in supervision had enabled him to pursue his sexual activity without coming to the attention of authorities.

He stated that he had engaged in similar sexual activity with prepubertal children during his late adolescence and early adulthood. His first ejaculation occurred at age 12 via masturbation accompanied by adult heterosexual fantasies. He had severe acne and was moderately obese, and attributed his adolescent failures to obtain either a romantic or a sexual partner to these faults. His family lived in a two-story house, and he often visited the neighbors who lived on the first floor. One night when he was 16 years old, he found himself alone in a room with a 5-year-old child from that family and had her fondle his genitals. This was the first time he experienced sex with another person. Following that encounter, he experienced apprehension lest he be caught, but not guilt. This response was typical of him thereafter. He masturbated regularly with fantasies of having sexual activity with children of both sexes, but did not attempt to have sex with his original partner because he felt anxious about being apprehended.

The patient lived in his parents' home until age 32. His mother, a devout fundamentalist, had outspokenly antisexual attitudes. His father, an alcoholic sailor in the Merchant Marines, was allegedly "neutral" regarding sexuality. The father was away from home for long periods of time, and when home, he was withdrawn. An older sister and younger sister, both unmarried, still lived with the parents at the time of the patient's consultation.

His sexual activity was confined exclusively to masturbation until age 25, when he was introduced to prostitutes by a friend. He visited prostitutes frequently until age 33. Nevertheless, masturbation fantasies involving children persisted.

When he was 32 years old, he married a friend of his sister's, and the couple moved to their own apartment. During the first years of his marriage, his preferred sexual stimulus was his wife, who was fully sexually responsive. The couple had intercourse many times a week, and self-masturbation stopped.

After the birth of his third child, the patient was laid off from his job as a semiskilled worker. A six-month period of unemployment followed, during which his wife had to take a part-time job at night. The couple stopped having regular sexual intercourse, and both became irritable, anxious, and depressed. The patient's sexual fantasies involving children returned, at first during self-masturbation, then at other times as well. He was able to obtain a series of temporary jobs, but was not able to get a permanent job for three more years. During this time he began to drink at least a half bottle of whiskey a day; and when he drank, he sometimes became abusive at home. At his wife's behest, the couple had their fourth child, allegedly because of her conviction that it would improve their relationship.

Shortly after the birth of this child, he began to engage in sexual activity with small children. He was not aware why he had decided to act on the basis of his fantasies at the time he did. The circumstances were varied, and the children were of both sexes. After pursuing this activity for some months, he was apprehended, arrested, and served a jail term, during which his usual sexual fantasies persisted. Following release from jail, the family moved to another city. His wife decided, after much soul searching, not to leave her husband, on condition that he get professional help.

The patient was treated with supportive psychotherapy. For about a year and a half he was stably employed at an unskilled job; and his usual sexual fantasies, although present, were infrequent and of low intensity. Sexual intercourse with his wife occurred about twice a week and was mutually satisfying. The patient then became involved in a bar fight while intoxicated and suffered an injury requiring a brief hospitalization. He lost his job and discontinued therapy. After much searching, he had finally been able to obtain employment as a schoolbus driver, a little over a year ago. This employment facilitated his acting upon the basis of his again frequent and intense sexual fantasies, which in turn led to his present consultation.

Discussion of Schoolbus Driver

This individual's lifelong pattern of sexual arousal has primarily involved fantasies of prepubertal children. Overt sexual acts with children have occurred, but sporadically, depending on his level of tension and the availability of the children. It is clear that during the periods when he acts upon these impulses, as during the past year, this method of achieving sexual excitement is clearly preferred, if not exclusive. Therefore, in this case, the diagnosis of Pedophilia is unambiguous.

Suppose that this individual, as is often the case, had periods during which he acted on his pedophiliac impulses while at the same time maintaining an active sexual life with his wife. According to the DSM-III criteria, the diagnosis of Pedophilia requires that the "sexual activity with children is a repeatedly preferred or exclusive method of achieving sexual excitement." A strict interpretation of this criterion might well preclude the diagnosis in such a case, although most clinicians would certainly regard any significant sexual arousal to children as pathological. This clinical judgment reflects the recognition that the more deviant the sexual pattern is from the norm, the fewer instances there need to be of the behavior to indicate psychopathology. Being turned on by ladies' underwear (Fetishism) a few times may not mean much, but once with a corpse (Necrophilia) is too much!

The second-listed diagnosis of Alcohol Abuse, Episodic, is rather straightforward, given the history of episodes of a pattern of pathological alcohol use (drinking at least a half bottle of whiskey per day), social impairment (being abusive at home), and occupational impairment (having lost his job following injury suffered in a bar fight).

DSM-III Diagnosis:

Axis I: 302.20 Pedophilia (p. 271)
305.02 Alcohol Abuse, Episodic (p. 169)

Three Voices

138 A 23-year-old man was admitted to the hospital. He was almost totally mute. His parents reported that he had been apparently well until about four years ago when he broke off with his girl friend. Since then he had been living at home, spending much time by himself, holding various odd jobs, and unable to pursue any long-term goals. About four months before his hospital admission he decided to go to California to find a new job and change his environment. However, shortly after he had arrived there, his parents received a telephone call from him in which he "sounded bad." His father flew to California and found him vigilant, paranoid, and frightened, seemingly having not eaten for several days. The father brought him home, where he saw a neurologist and was found to be essentially normal neurologically. Shortly thereafter he saw a psychologist, who recommended admission.

On admission the patient was sleeping 10–12 hours a night, had little appetite, and had lost perhaps 20 pounds in weight over the last couple of months. He reported a profound loss of energy and said nothing except for occasional monosyllabic answers to the interviewer's questions. During his first few days in the hospital he showed virtually no interest or pleasure in any activities and spent most of the time sitting on his bed and staring into space. On questioning he did not complain of any specific feelings of worthlessness, self-reproach, or guilt, nor did he mention thoughts of death or suicide, although it was difficult to be certain on any of these points because of his paucity of speech.

In the hospital he was seen daily by a medical student who took a great interest in him and gradually gained his trust. Eventually the patient revealed to the student that he was hearing three distinct voices — the voice of a child, the voice of a woman, and the voice of a man impersonating a woman. The three voices talked among themselves and sometimes talked to him directly. At times they spoke about him in the third person and on some occasions they seemed to echo his thoughts. The voices spoke about many different subjects and did not focus on any specific depressive themes, such as guilt, sin, or death.

On the second day after admission to the hospital the patient was started on a regimen of molindone, 50 mg/day, and imipramine, at a dose that was being gradually increased to 150 mg/day. For the first two weeks there was virtually no visible improvement. However, by the second week he displayed some increased restlessness. The dose of molindone was reduced to 25 mg/day and eventually stopped entirely by about the third week. On the 23rd hospital day the patient began to experience a marked improvement in his energy level, and by the end of the fourth week he was smiling, talkative, sleeping and eating well, and able to reminisce about the hallucinations, which he stated had now completely disappeared. A week later he was discharged home on imipramine, 150 mg/day, but no other psychotropic medication.

Some months after his discharge he ran out of imipramine and did not obtain more from his pharmacy. His symptoms reappeared rapidly over the course of a few days. After a phone call from his parents to his doctor, the imipramine treatment was hastily resumed, and the patient again reverted essentially to normal after another week or so.

The patient's mother had had a postpartum depressive episode of about a year's duration that had gradually remitted spontaneously without treatment. In addition, the mother's sister had had a "nervous breakdown," when she was in her forties, that had required her to be hospitalized; she had been treated with a course of 12 electroconvulsive treatments. Since that time the aunt had had a complete remission, and was described as functioning normally.

Discussion of Three Voices

This young man apparently had a four-year period during which he had some nonspecific difficulties (social withdrawal and inability to pursue long-term goals) followed by an episode of illness with paranoid behavior, bizarre auditory hallucinations, loss of interest and pleasure, anorexia and a 20-pound weight loss, hypersomnia, loss of energy, and psychomotor retardation (paucity of speech and spending most of his time sitting on the bed staring into space).

In the past this might well have been diagnosed as Schizophrenia, the four-year period being viewed as prodromal to the acute psychotic phase. The loss of interest and pleasure and the other nonpsychotic symptoms would have been considered as merely associated features. According to DSM-III, the loss of interest and pleasure and the other nonpsychotic symptoms actually constitute a full depressive syndrome. Since the psychotic symptoms apparently have been present only when the patient had a depressive syndrome, they are considered a psychotic feature of Major Depression. This is true in spite of the fact that the content of the delusions and hallucinations is not consistent with such usual depressive themes as personal inadequacy, guilt, or deserved punishment. Thus, on admission the diagnosis would be Major Depression, Single Episode, with Psychotic Features (Mood-incongruent), a diagnosis that is certainly supported by the response to a tricyclic antidepressant and the family history of Affective Disorder.

What are we to make of the four-year period reported by his parents? Did this represent mild depressive symptomatology or identity problems? These would not be inconsistent with our recommended diagnosis. Mild depressive symptoms frequently are early manifestations of a major depressive episode. If indeed mild depressive symptoms were present for more than two years, the additional diagnosis of Dysthymic Disorder would be made. On the other hand, if closer examination revealed more malignant symptoms, such as ideas of reference or bizarre behavior that preceded the depressive symptoms, this would suggest that the psychotic episode was not Major Depression and present the possibility of Schizoaffective Disorder.

Another question raised by this case is the appropriate subclassification of Major Depression at the time of the reappearance of the depressive syndrome when medication was discontinued. Should this be regarded as Major Depression, Recurrent, or as the continuation of the single episode, the symptoms of which had been suppressed by medication? DSM-III offers no guidelines. Most clinicians would consider the length of the symptom-free period and the rapidity with which the symptoms developed after discontinuation of the medication. In our view the several-month period of remission favors a diagnosis of Recurrent whereas the rapid development of symptoms following discontinuation of the medication favors a diagnosis of Single Episode. We are therefore equally comfortable (and uncomfortable) with either diagnosis.

DSM-III Diagnosis:

Axis I: 296.24 Major Depression, Single Episode, with Psychotic Features (Mood-incongruent) (p. 213)

Minister's Daughter

139 The 22-year-old daughter of a fundamentalist minister was brought for treatment by her parents because of their concern that over the last three years "she has become a different person." Although always somewhat "shy" and "quiet," she apparently was "completely normal" and had gotten "O.K." grades in high school. Her troubles seemed to begin when she dropped out of college after the first semester and came home to live. Since that time she had held several jobs, but each for only a few weeks. Recently she had just been sitting at home, wanting only to go shopping, using her parents' money. She had no goals, had gained considerable weight, and insisted on dressing like a little girl. On several occasions she had been verbally abusive to her parents, at least once to the extent that they had had her put in jail for a week when she threatened her father.

On examination, the patient was found to have flat affect, with occasional inappropriate smiling. She avoided eye contact. She rarely answered questions with more than "yes" or "no," but did admit to feeling "unhappy," which she said was only because "they won't give me what I want." There was no evidence of delusions, hallucinations, loosening of associations, or incoherence.

Discussion of Minister's Daughter

This clinical picture strongly suggests the prodromal phase of Schizophrenia and does not correspond to any specific DSM-III diagnosis. The diagnosis of Schizophrenia cannot now be made since there is no clear evidence of psychotic features, although the patient may be experiencing delusions or hallucinations that she is not revealing. In this ambiguous situation we would recommend noting both Unspecified Mental Disorder (nonpsychotic) and a statement that Schizophrenia needs to be ruled out. Perhaps in subsequent interviews the patient will acknowledge having psychotic symptoms, thus confirming the diagnosis of Schizophrenia.

Although schizoid and eccentric features are prominent in this patient, a diagnosis of Schizoid Disorder of Childhood or Adolescence or Schizotypal Personality Disorder would not seem appropriate because both of these diagnoses imply enduring patterns of behavior rather than a marked change, which seems to be present in this case.

DSM-III Diagnosis:

Axis I: 300.90 Unspecified Mental Disorder (nonpsychotic) (p. 335)
R/O Schizophrenia

Stewardess

140 A 31-year-old stewardess asked for a consultation because of a recent experience she had had while flying. Without warning she had suddenly begun to feel panicky, dizzy, had trouble breathing, started to sweat, and trembled uncontrollably. She excused herself and sat in the back of the plane, and within ten minutes the symptoms had subsided. Two similar episodes had occurred in the past: the first, four years previously, when the plane had encountered some mild turbulence; the second, two years earlier, during an otherwise uneventful flight, as in this episode. Her main concern was that if these attacks recurred, she might be unable to continue at her job.

The patient also complained of "nervousness" of about one year's duration, beginning shortly after her marriage to an airline engineer. She attributed her nervousness to concerns about her marriage, which, from the start, had been beset with difficulties. She denied other signs of persistent anxiety, such as motor tension, restlessness, or insomnia.

Discussion of Stewardess

The patient describes the characteristic symptoms of a panic attack: sudden onset of anxiety, dizziness, trouble breathing, sweating, and trembling. This suggests the diagnosis of Panic Disorder. This diagnosis, however, requires at least three attacks within a three-week period, and this patient's three attacks were widely separated in time.

Since she fears that future attacks will occur while she is flying, the diagnosis of a Simple Phobia might be considered. But what she fears is not flying itself (as would be the case in a phobia), but rather the occurrence of another panic attack. Her complaint of nervousness suggests Generalized Anxiety Disorder, but other features required for a diagnosis of that disorder are not present (she denies having motor tension, restlessness, and insomnia). Because the predominant symptoms are anxiety, yet the criteria for no specific anxiety disorder are met, the diagnosis is Atypical Anxiety Disorder.

A case can be made for the additional diagnosis of Adjustment Disorder with Anxious Mood, to account for the nervousness of the last year (following her marriage), which may be unrelated to the panic attacks. The V code Marital Problem could be added if the clinician believed that the patient's marital difficulties warranted attention and treatment but were not symptomatic of a mental disorder.

DSM-III Diagnosis:

Axis I: 300.00 Atypical Anxiety Disorder (p. 239)

Star Wars

141 Susan, a 15-year-old, was seen at the request of her school district authorities for advice on placement. She had recently moved into the area with her family and, after a brief period in a regular class, was placed in a class for the emotionally disturbed. She proved very difficult, with a very poor understanding of schoolwork at about the fifth-grade level, despite an apparently good vocabulary; and she disturbed the class by making animal noises and telling fantastic stories, which made the other children laugh at her.

At home Susan is aggressive, biting or hitting her parents or brother if frustrated. She is often bored, has no friends, and finds it difficult to occupy herself. She spends a lot of time drawing pictures of robots, spaceships, and fantastic or futuristic inventions. Sometimes she has said she would like to die, but she has never made any attempt at suicide, and apparently has not thought of killing herself. Her mother says that from birth she has been different, and that the onset of her current behavior has been so gradual that no definite date can be assigned to it.

Susan's prenatal and parental history are unremarkable. Her milestones were delayed, and she did not use single words until four or five years of age. Ever since she entered school there has been concern about her ability. Repeated evaluations have suggested an IQ in the lower 70s, with achievement somewhat behind even that expected at this level of ability. Because her father was in the military, there have been many moves; and results of her earlier evaluations are not available.

The parents report that Susan has always been difficult and restless, and that several doctors have said she is not just mentally retarded but suffers from a serious mental disorder. The results of an evaluation done at the age of 12, because of difficulties in school, showed "evidence of bizarre thought processes and fragmented ego structure." At this time she was sleeping well at night and was not getting up with nightmares or bizarre requests, though this apparently had been a feature of her earlier behavior. Currently she is reported to sleep very poorly and tends to disturb the household by getting up and wandering around at night. Her mother emphasizes Susan's unpredictability, the funny stories that she tells, and the way in which she will talk to herself in "funny voices." Her mother regards the stories Susan tells as childish make-believe and preoccupation and pays little attention to them. She says that since Susan went to see the movie *Star Wars* she has been obsessed with ideas about space, spaceships, and the future.

Her parents are in their early 40s. Her father, having retired from military service, now works as an engineer. Susan's mother has many unusual beliefs about herself. She claims to have grown up in India and to have had a very bizarre early childhood full of dramatic and violent episodes. Many of these episodes sound highly improbable. Her husband refuses to let her talk about her past in his presence and tries to play down this material and Susan's problems. The parents appear to have a rather restricted relationship in which the father plays the role of a taciturn, masterful head of household and the mother bears the brunt of everyday family duties. The mother, in contrast, is loquacious and very circumstantial in her history-giving. She dwells a great deal on her strange childhood experiences. Susan's brother is now 12 and apparently is a normal child with an average school career. He does not spend much time in the house or with the family, but prefers to play with his friends. He is ashamed of Susan's behavior and tries to avoid going out with her.

In the interview Susan presented as a tall, overweight, pasty-looking child, dressed untidily and with a somewhat disheveled appearance. She complained vociferously of her insomnia, though it was very difficult to elicit details of the sleep disturbance. She talked at length about her interests and occupations. She says she made a robot in the basement that ran amok and was about to cause a great deal of damage, but she was able to stop it by remote control. She claims to have built the robot from spare computer parts, which she acquired from the local museum. When pressed on details of how this worked, she became increasingly vague, and when asked to draw a picture of one of her inventions, drew a picture of an overhead railway and went into what appeared to be complex mathematical calculations to substantiate the structural details, but which in fact consisted of meaningless repetitions of symbols (e.g., plus, minus, divide, multiply). When the interviewer expressed some gentle incredulity, she blandly replied that many people did not believe that she was a supergenius. She also talked about her unusual ability to hear things other people cannot hear, and said she was in communication with some sort of creature. She thought she might be haunted, or perhaps the creature was a being from another planet. She could hear his voice talking to her and asking her questions; he did not attempt to tell her what to do. The voice was outside her own head, but was inaudible to others. She did not regard the questions being asked her as upsetting. They did not make her angry or frightened.

Her teacher comments that although Susan's reading is apparently at the fifth-grade level, her comprehension is much lower. She tends to read what is not there and sometimes changes the meaning of the paragraph. Her spelling is at about the third-grade level, and her mathematics, a little bit below that. She works hard at school, though very slowly. If pressure is placed on her, she becomes upset, and her work deteriorates.

Discussion of Star Wars

At the present time Susan exhibits several psychotic symptoms. She apparently is delusional in that she believes that she has made a complicated invention and that she is in communication with "some sort of creature." She has auditory hallucinations of voices talking to her and asking her questions. The presence of delusions and hallucinations, in the absence of a specific organic etiology or of a full affective syndrome, raises the question of Schizophrenia.

The DSM-III criteria for Schizophrenia require "deterioration from a previous level of functioning in such areas as work, social relations, and self-care." The major intent of this particular criterion was to exclude cases in which the illness did not seem to be associated with any impairment in functioning. For example, there are rare instances in which an individual may harbor a bizarre delusion for many years without any noticeable impairment in functioning, and it seemed advisable to differentiate such a condition from Schizophrenia. (Such an unusual case would probably end up with a diagnosis of Atypical Psychosis.) The problem in this case is not the absence of functional impairment, but whether or not there has been deterioration. Susan's mother says that she was "different" from birth, her developmental milestones were delayed, and she did not use single words until four or five years of age. Is her current psychotic behavior a deterioration from this level of functioning? Perhaps it is difficult or impossible to make such a judgment when serious psychopathology is present at a very early age. Should such cases not be diagnosed as Schizophrenia, even if the characteristic schizophrenic symptoms are present at a later age? Some would argue that Schizophrenia should be diagnosed only when a psychotic illness develops in an individual with a relatively intact personality. According to this view, Susan should not be diagnosed as having Schizophrenia. Others would argue that frequently, as in Susan's case, the prodromal phase of severe forms of Schizophrenia may be evident in early childhood. We take the latter view, partly because we think that a history of severe disturbance at an early age may not be that unusual in cases that later seem to develop a typical schizophrenic illness. Therefore, our diagnosis of Susan is Schizophrenia, Chronic. Although her delusions have a grandiose quality, they seem too diffuse to justify Paranoid Type. In the absence of prominent catatonic features or frequent incoherence, we are left with Undifferentiated Type.

Susan's IQ level above 70 mercifully spares her from the additional diagnosis of Mild Mental Retardation. One could argue for the V code Borderline Intellectual Functioning. However, it is not Susan's limited intellectual capacity, but rather her bizarre behavior, that is creating difficulties at school.

DSM-III Diagnosis:

Axis I: **295.92 Schizophrenia, Chronic, Undifferentiated Type (p. 188)**

Calisthenics

142 A 31-year-old housewife sought help because of a two-to-three-year history of temper outbursts associated with increasing marital discord. During the past few years she had had increasing difficulty with her husband, whom she suspected of having an affair with his secretary. She ruminated angrily about his possible deception whenever he claimed to be working late. During such ruminative episodes, she felt her tension "building up," and would often attempt to "discharge it" by calisthenics; but she still found herself "exploding" when her husband eventually came home. On one occasion she threw a glass at him; on another, she banged on the walls of her house with her high-heeled shoes, causing the plaster to crumble; and on yet another occasion she put her hand through a window when her husband left abruptly after one of her outbursts. Before each outburst she tried to remain calm, but often experienced a headache and a feeling of "strangeness" when she saw her husband coming home. At this point she would usually lose control and become violent. Following the outburst she felt depressed and remorseful, recognizing that her outbursts were "crazy" — even if her suspicions were justified. She also admitted that when the children cried or were impatient when she was in one of her ruminative periods, she was overzealous in her discipline and often found herself slapping them or punishing them more harshly than she ordinarily would. On one occasion she had lost her temper when one of her children would not go to sleep and had slapped him hard enough to cause a bruise on his face.

The episodes of loss of control occurred one to two times a month, but had seemed to be increasing over the past year. In between these episodes the patient was generally calm and displayed no signs of aggressiveness.

Past history revealed that at the age of eight the patient had been knocked unconscious for a short period of time in a roller-skating accident, but had no medical intervention for this injury. Apparently she had sustained repeated head injuries, to the point where the family urged her to "wear a football helmet" because she was so clumsy.

An electroencephalogram (EEG) was done after the patient entered therapy and revealed a nonspecific abnormality, a 6–14-second dysrhythmia. During the course of her treatment she confronted her husband, who finally acknowledged that he was having an affair with his secretary.

Discussion of Calisthenics

This woman entered therapy because she realized that, even if her suspicions about her husband were warranted, her angry outbursts were inappropriate and markedly at variance with her normally unaggressive behavior. Each outburst was preceded by a mounting sense of tension and followed by feelings of remorse. These features suggest an Impulse Disorder, specifically, Intermittent Explosive Disorder.

The diagnosis in this case hinges on two issues. Do the outbursts result in "serious assault or destruction of property," and is the behavior "grossly out of proportion to any precipitating psychosocial stressor"? The patient had on one occasion broken a window with her fist and on another bruised her child's face. These acts just make it past our threshold for serious assault and destruction of property, although some more worldly clinicians might be unimpressed. (One could argue that no degree of rage is "out of proportion" to the provocation of a lying, unfaithful husband.) But what about her losing control with her child when he refused to go to sleep? We are inclined to think that this behavior is grossly out of proportion to the provocation. Therefore, we propose the provisional diagnosis Intermittent Explosive Disorder, because of our own uncertainty about the boundary between this disorder and the "normal" temper outbursts to which relations between spouses and between parents and children may give rise. In this case, particularly because of the potential for child abuse, we think it better to err on the side of making a diagnosis that justifies treatment directed at the patient's loss of impulse control.

The EEG abnormality suggests an underlying disorder of the central nervous system, as is often the case in patients with this disorder. This is the basis for noting on Axis III the history of head injury and the EEG abnormality.

DSM-III Diagnosis:

Axis I: 312.34 Intermittent Explosive Disorder (Provisional) (p. 297)
Axis III: History of head injury and nonspecific EEG abnormality

Seizure

143 A 16-year-old female junior-high-school student was hospitalized on the psychiatric service for behavior problems. She had been in trouble with school authorities since age 12 for truancy and petty thefts. More recently, she was expelled from junior high school for smoking marijuana in the locker room. Finally, a series of thefts from neighborhood stores and an incident in which she and a companion set a fire in a vacant lot brought her into court and prompted a judge to remand her to a psychiatric ward for evaluation. Her parents said they were unable to control her.

On the ward, she befriended other adolescent kids. The staff found her to be demanding and affectively volatile. She frequently stormed out of community meetings when decisions were made that did not go her way. She tried to have the ward recreational activities revolve around her, and would be very enthusiastic about them at first, but later would appear angry and pouting when she was not permitted to monopolize the activity. Beneath her superficial bravado, however, the nursing staff found her to be insecure and dependent.

One evening about a week into her hospitalization, after being refused a pass to go out of the hospital, the patient stormed down the hall to her room. Minutes later, a scream was heard; and when the first nurse reached her, the patient was writhing on the floor on her back, making jerking movements of her pelvis, arms, and legs and rolling her eyes upward. When the staff and patients had congregated near her room, her violent shaking stopped. She lay nearly still, eyes closed, with a slight trembling visible over her body. She had not bitten her tongue or voided urine or feces. An arm placed over her face repeatedly fell to the side of her head each time, rather than on her face. Finally, the nurse, noting her to be fully alert, asked her some questions, which she answered appropriately, although she stated that she could not yet move. Fifteen minutes later she walked to the examining room to be evaluated by the doctor on call.

Discussion of Seizure

The doctor on call would have no difficulty in making a diagnosis of the behavioral problems that led to this girl's hospitalization. For at least four years she has been getting into trouble. She has repeatedly violated important age-appropriate societal rules (truancy, smoking marijuana at school) and the basic rights of others (stealing). This repetitive and pervasive pattern indicates a Conduct Disorder. There is apparently no impairment in her ability to form relations with peers, thus indicating the Socialized subtype. Since her violation of rules and the rights of others has involved primarily nonaggressive acts, the Conduct Disorder is further subtyped as Nonaggressive. (The DSM-III criteria for the Aggressive subtype include fire-setting as an example of aggressive behavior. However, it seems to us that setting one fire in a vacant lot hardly involves sufficient destruction of property to be regarded as "aggressive.")

The immediate diagnostic problem for the doctor on call is how to characterize her "fit." There are several features that suggest it was not a genuine epileptic seizure. During a genuine grand mal seizure, one would expect urinary, and possibly fecal, incontinence. One would also expect a period of postictal (postseizure) confusion during which the patient would not be fully alert and able to protect herself from hitting herself in the face when her hand was dropped.

Since there is a close temporal relationship between her being upset and the "fit," it is reasonable to assume that the fit is related to a

psychological conflict or need. There are three diagnostic possibilities: Conversion Disorder, Factitious Disorder with Physical
Symptoms, and the V code Malingering. Both Malingering and Factitious Disorder assume that the symptom is consciously faked. In this
case, we do not see any evidence to support the notion that the
patient had voluntary control over the fit. Without additional evidence of her conscious production of the fit, we would prefer to give
her the benefit of the doubt, assume that the symptom was not under
voluntary control, and diagnose it as Conversion Disorder. We
would indicate our lack of certainty by qualifying the diagnosis as
Provisional. If she were later to acknowledge that, angry with the
staff, she decided to give them a hard time by faking the fit, we would
change the diagnosis to the V code Malingering. In the unlikely event
that she developed a pattern of exhibiting fake fits for no purpose
other than to be a patient, we would change the diagnosis to Factitious Disforder with Physical Symptoms.

DSM-III Diagnosis:

Axis I: 300.11 Conversion Disorder (Provisional) (p. 247)
            R/O Malingering
            312.21 Conduct Disorder, Socialized, Nonaggressive
            (p. 49)

Gloria

144 The patient is an attractive, well-dressed, 43-year-old
woman who became acutely psychotic about one month
before admission to the hospital. Before that time she had
been working with her husband in a mail order gift business. After
completing the Christmas catalog, under considerable pressure because of printer's deadlines, the patient began to have vague fears that
her husband would hurt her. She felt an "evil presence" in the building
in which they lived and ran away to a friend's house. There she tried to
write a letter to her husband, but felt that the electric typewriter she
was using was "canceling people out" and that she might be the last
person left on earth. On the street she felt that people were not who
they seemed to be, and that they were giving her messages by "clicking" their eyes. Intermittently she heard a voice saying, "Gloria (her
name) is nuts," and telling her not to smoke.

On admission she spoke in a rambling, tangential manner. She was
quite labile — she appeared frightened when she spoke about her

husband, cried frequently, but then brightened and said that she felt something "wonderful" was going to happen.

There had been no changes in her sleep or appetite, although in the last few weeks she had become somewhat preoccupied with the necessity of eating "healthy" food.

The patient first had psychiatric treatment at age nine, after being picked up for shoplifting. She spent her senior year of high school in a "residential community" because of conflicts with her aged grandmother, who had reared her. At 27 she had an acute psychotic episode during which she was confused and self-referential, and was hospitalized for nine months. Shortly after leaving the hospital she married her long-time boyfriend, to whom she is still married. Between the ages of 33 and 43 the patient experienced two brief psychotic episodes, which were treated with Mellaril and outpatient psychotherapy. After each episode she apparently recovered completely, with no residual symptoms. She worked successfully as a secretary, traveled with her husband to select items for their import business, kept the books for the company, and had an active social life.

Discussion of Gloria

If there were no history of previous psychotic episodes in this case, there would be no difficulty in diagnosing the current episode. This apparently began one month ago and was characterized by bizarre delusions (the electric typewriter was "canceling people out"), delusions of reference (people were giving her messages by "clicking their eyes"), and auditory hallucinations (". . . a voice saying, 'Gloria is nuts.' "). In the absence of a known organic factor or an affective syndrome, the diagnosis would be Schizophreniform Disorder rather than Schizophrenia, because the duration of the illness is more than two weeks but less than six months.

The diagnosis becomes less certain when we learn of several previous episodes, apparently also of brief duration, with similar symptoms and with complete recovery. Theoretically, it is possible to have recurrent episodes of Schizophreniform Disorder, but the occurrence of many episodes makes full recovery increasingly unlikely. The first psychotic episode, during which the patient was hospitalized for nine months, causes even more diagnostic confusion. If psychotic or residual signs of the illness persisted for the full nine months, then the diagnosis of that episode would have been Schizophrenia! The apparent period of complete recovery would then become Schizophrenia in Remission. Because the very concept of Schizophrenia in Remission (as distinct from Residual subtype) is dubious, DSM-III offers no guidelines for characterizing the course of a new psychotic episode following Schizophrenia in Remission. On the other hand, there is the possibility that despite a nine-month hospitalization, the psychotic illness may have been much briefer. Perhaps she had largely recovered from the psychotic illness after a few months but remained in the hospital because she was "a good psychotherapy patient" or because it took several months to work out suitable living arrangements in the community. Because of the uncertainty about the nine-month episode and the apparently complete recovery from two other short psychotic episodes, we prefer the less ominous diagnosis of Schizophreniform Disorder. We would not quarrel with a clinician who preferred to make a provisional diagnosis of Atypical Psychosis and delayed making a more definitive diagnosis until after records of her nine-month hospitalization had been obtained.

DSM-III Diagnosis:

Axis I: **295.40 Schizophreniform Disorder (Provisional) (p. 200)
R/O Chronic Schizophrenia with Acute Exacerbation**

Peaceable Man

145 The patient is a 20-year-old male who was brought to the hospital, trussed in ropes, by his four brothers. This is his seventh hospitalization in the last two years, each for similar behavior. One of his brothers reports that he "came home crazy" late one night, threw a chair through a window, tore a gas heater off the wall, and ran into the street. The family called the police, who apprehended him shortly thereafter as he stood, naked, directing traffic at a busy intersection. He assaulted the arresting officers, escaped them, and ran home screaming threats at his family. There his brothers were able to subdue him.

On admission the patient was observed to be agitated, his mood fluctuating between anger and fear. He had slurred speech and staggered when he walked. He remained extremely violent and disorganized for the first several days of his hospitalization, then began having longer and longer lucid intervals, still interspersed with sudden, unpredictable periods in which he displayed great suspiciousness, a fierce expression, slurred speech, and clenched fists.

After calming down, the patient denied ever having been violent or acting in an unusual way ("I'm a peaceable man") and said he could not remember how he got to the hospital. He admitted to using alcohol and marijuana socially, but denied phencyclidine (PCP) use except for once, experimentally, three years previously. Nevertheless, blood and urine tests were positive for phencyclidine, and his brother believes "he gets dusted every day."

According to his family, he was perfectly normal until about three years before. He made above-average grades in school, had a part-time job and a girl friend, and was of a sunny and outgoing disposition. Then, at age 17, he had his first episode of emotional disturbance. This was of very sudden onset, with symptoms similar to the present episode. He quickly recovered entirely from that first episode, went back to school, and graduated from high school. From subsequent episodes, however, his improvement was less and less encouraging.

After three weeks of the current hospitalization he is sullen and watchful, quick to remark sarcastically on the smallest infringement of the respect due him. He is mostly quiet and isolated from others, but is easily provoked to fury. His family reports that "This is as good as he gets now." He lives and eats most of his meals at home, and keeps himself physically clean, but mostly lies around the house, will do no housework, and has not held a job for nearly two years. The family does not know how he gets his spending money, or how he spends his time outside the hospital.

Discussion of Peaceable Man

The hospitalization was occasioned by acute effects of PCP on the central nervous system: violence, bizarre and disorganized behavior, psychomotor agitation, emotional lability, slurred speech, and ataxia. This is a typical picture of Phencyclidine Intoxication.

In addition, there is a history of regular use of PCP, resulting in many similar episodes of disturbed behavior. The regular use of PCP for more than a six-month period associated with impairment in functioning indicates the additional diagnosis of Phencyclidine Abuse, Continuous. Finally, there is evidence of a deterioration in his personality — apart from episodes of PCP Intoxication (lies around house, does no work, is suspicious). It is reasonable to assume that these personality changes are a result of the chronic effects of PCP on the central nervous system — hence the additional diagnosis of a Substance-induced Organic Personality Disorder. Since DSM-III does not list any specific Substance-induced Organic Personality Disorders, the only code available for such a disorder is 292.89 for

Other or Unspecified Substance-induced Personality Disorder. However, in such cases the specific drug is noted in the diagnosis.

DSM-III Diagnosis:

Axis I: **305.90 Phencyclidine (PCP) Intoxication (p. 151)**
305.91 Phencyclidine (PCP) Abuse, Continuous (p. 174)
292.89 Phencyclidine (PCP)-induced Personality Disorder (p. 119)

Masters and Johnson

146 A 33-year-old stockbrocker sought treatment because of "impotence." Five months ago a close male friend died of a coronary occlusion, and within the following week the patient developed anxiety about his own cardiac status. Whenever his heart beat fast because of exertion, he became anxious that he was about to have a heart attack. He had disturbing dreams from which he would awaken anxious and unable to get back to sleep. He stopped playing tennis and running.

He began to avoid sexual intercourse, presumably because of his anxiety about physical exertion. This caused difficulties with his wife, who felt that he was deliberately depriving her of her sexual outlets and was also preventing her from becoming pregnant, which she very much desired. In the last month, although no longer worried about his heart, he had avoided sexual intercourse entirely. He claimed to still have some desire for sex; but when the situation arose, he could not bring himself to do it. He became so upset about his sexual difficulties that he began to have trouble concentrating at work. He felt himself to be a failure both as a husband and as a man.

Before his marriage he had no sexual experience, and he would masturbate by rubbing his penis against the bedclothes, without ever manually touching it. Four years previously, at the age of 29 and after 3 years of marriage, he had presented himself for treatment with the complaint that he had never attempted to have sexual intercourse with his wife. Sexual activity consisted of his obtaining an erection without either his wife or himself touching his penis, and ejaculation occurred by rubbing his penis on his wife's abdomen. He was unable to touch his wife's genitalia with his hands or allow his penis to be placed anywhere near his wife's genitalia.

Treatment had consisted of two weeks of intensive couples-therapy, using the techniques laid down by Masters and Johnson, with dramatic success. Sexual activity became frequent, with vaginal penetration and ejaculation. He began to display flirtatious sexuality toward other females, which led to some embarrassing social situations, but not to promiscuity. His wife's anxiety about her own sexuality and the adoption of a more passive role led her to seek treatment in her own right. After one year of psychotherapy, her anxieties were allayed; and sexual intercourse and interpersonal relationships between the patient and his wife had been at a satisfactory level until the present problem arose.

Discussion of Masters and Johnson

This man's reaction to the death of his friend five months ago involved severe anxiety and restriction in his physical activities because of fear that he might have a heart attack; and had he been evaluated at that time, an appropriate diagnosis would have been Adjustment Disorder with Anxious Mood. His anxiety affected his sexual functioning, and it is the sexual symptoms that have persisted and occasioned this evaluation.

His current sexual problem is a recurrence of the problem that caused him to seek sex therapy many years ago: avoidance of sexual intercourse because of the anxiety associated with it. Although he refers to his problem as "impotence," the diagnosis of Inhibited Sexual Excitement (impotence) is made only when the failure to maintain an erection occurs in the context of "sexual activity that is adequate in focus, intensity, and duration." What this man demonstrates is phobic avoidance of sexual intercourse. This suggests the diagnosis of Simple Phobia, but DSM-III asserts that the diagnosis of Phobia should not be made if the phobic avoidance is limited to sexual activities. The reason for this is that avoidance of sexual activities is a common associated feature of psychosexual dysfunctions, and usually the treatment of the phobic avoidance is part of the treatment of the psychosexual dysfunction. (Some experts in the area of sexual dysfunction believe that this was a mistake and that phobic avoidance of sexual activity should be classified and treated as a subtype of Phobia.)

In this case there is only avoidance, no specific psychosexual dysfunction. Therefore, the only way to indicate that there is a sexual problem is with the diagnosis Psychosexual Disorder Not Elsewhere Classified. If there were a specific psychosexual dysfunction (e.g., if he complained of a total lack of desire or that when he attempted intercourse he lost his erection), then that specific dysfunction would be diagnosed, and it would not be necessary to make an additional diagnosis to account for any phobic avoidance that might be present.

DSM-III Diagnosis:

Axis I: 302.89 Psychosexual Disorder Not Elsewhere Classified (p. 282)

Vodka

147 A 45-year-old, twice-married woman has been drinking a pint of vodka daily for 13 years. Before that she had been a light drinker. During the period of her first divorce she became depressed and found that alcohol made her feel better. While drinking in a bar she met her second husband, also a heavy drinker. They continued to drink at home in the evenings. She increasingly found reasons not to go to work, and was eventually dismissed from her job. She began drinking throughout the day, allowing herself an ounce of vodka per hour, interspersed with occasional beers. She hid bottles and beer cans so her husband would not know she was drinking so much. Her husband, finding her intoxicated on his return home, began complaining and threatened to leave her. She vowed to drink only beer. She kept this up for a month, drinking two or three six-packs a day. Then she became worried about her weight and decided not to drink at all except for "two" drinks before dinner. The two drinks became three, and soon she was drinking a pint of vodka again. She began having memory lapses. Once she burned a hole in the divan and did not remember it. Her husband moved out after a violent argument. Drinking alone, she cried a good deal and thought about suicide. She finally called Alcoholics Anonymous for help.

Discussion of Vodka

This case seems to be fairly straightforward. There is a long history of maladaptive use of alcohol leading to considerable social and occupational impairment. There is also evidence of physiologic tolerance—that is, the need for markedly increased amounts of alcohol in order to achieve the desired effect (drinking an ounce of vodka per hour or two to three six-packs of beer a day). These features indicate Alcohol Dependence.

On the other hand, "alcohologists" take issue with making the diagnosis of Alcohol Dependence when the evidence for dependence is only tolerance and not also withdrawal. They claim that many heavy drinkers of alcohol may develop tolerance, but do not develop withdrawal symptoms on cessation of alcohol use. They thus argue that the diagnosis of Alcohol Dependence should require evidence of withdrawal—not mere tolerance. In this case they would diagnose Alcohol Abuse, since there is no evidence of a history of Alcohol Withdrawal.

DSM-III Diagnosis:

Axis I: 303.91 Alcohol Dependence, Continuous (p. 170)

Wash before Wearing

148 A 41-year-old male was referred to a community mental health center's activities program for help in improving his social skills. He had a lifelong pattern of social isolation, and spent long hours worrying that his angry thoughts about his older brother would cause his brother harm. He had previously worked as a clerk in civil service, but had lost his job because of poor attendance and low productivity.

On interview the patient was distant and somewhat distrustful. He described in elaborate and often irrelevant detail his rather uneventful and routine daily life. He told the interviewer that he had spent an hour and a half in a pet store deciding which of two brands of fish food to buy, and explained their relative merits. For two days he had studied the washing instructions on a new pair of jeans — Did "Wash before wearing" mean that the jeans were to be washed before wearing the first time, or did they need, for some reason, to be washed each time before they were worn? He did not regard concerns such as these as senseless, though he acknowledged that the amount of time spent thinking about them might be excessive. When asked about his finances, he could recite from memory his most recent monthly bank statement, including the amount of every check and the running balance as each check was written. He knew his balance on any particular day, but sometimes got anxious if he considered whether a certain check or deposit had actually cleared. He was very sensitive to questions put by the interviewer, reading in criticism where none was intended.

Discussion of Wash before Wearing

This man's long-standing maladaptive pattern of behavior indicates a Personality Disorder. Prominent symptoms include social isolation, magical thinking (worrying that his angry thoughts would cause his brother harm), inadequate rapport (observed to be "distant" in the interview), odd speech (providing elaborate and often irrelevant details), and hypersensitivity to criticism (reading in criticism where none was intended). These features are characteristic of Schizotypal Personality Disorder.

Although social isolation is also characteristic of Schizoid Personality Disorder, this patient's eccentricities of thought and speech preclude that diagnosis. There are many similarities between Schizotypal Personality Disorder and the symptoms seen in the Residual subtype of Schizophrenia, but the absence of a history of overt psychotic features rules out that diagnosis.

His concerns with choosing the best brand of fish food and understanding the instructions for washing his jeans suggest obsessions, but the ego-syntonic nature of the concerns indicates that they are not true obsessions, but rather examples of indecisiveness and perfectionism. Since these are traits of Compulsive Personality Disorder, we have noted them. (The full criteria for Compulsive Personality *Disorder* are not met.)

DSM-III Diagnosis:

Axis II: **301.22 Schizotypal Personality Disorder (p. 312)**
           Compulsive traits

Foster Mother

149 A 44-year-old mother of three teen-agers is hospitalized for treatment of depression. She gives the following history: One year previously, after a terminal argument with her lover, she became acutely psychotic. She was frightened that people were going to kill her and heard voices of friends and strangers talking about killing her, sometimes talking to each other. She heard her own thoughts broadcast aloud and was afraid that others could also hear what she was thinking. Over a three-week period she stayed in her apartment, had new locks put on the doors, kept the shades down, and avoided everyone but her immediate family. She was unable to sleep at night because the voices kept her awake, and unable to eat because of a constant "lump" in her throat. In retrospect, she cannot say whether she was depressed, denies being elated or overactive, and remembers only that she was terrified of what would happen to her. The family persuaded her to enter a hospital, where, after six weeks of treatment with Thorazine, the voices stopped. She remembers feeling "back to normal" for a week or two, but then she seemed to lose her energy and motivation to do anything. She became increasingly depressed, lost her appetite, and woke at 4:00 or 5:00 every morning and was unable to get back to sleep. She could no longer read a newspaper or watch TV because she couldn't concentrate.

The patient's condition has persisted for nine months. She has done very little except sit in her apartment, staring at the walls. Her children have managed most of the cooking, shopping, bill-paying, etc. She has continued in outpatient treatment, and was maintained on Thorazine until four months before this admission. There has been no recurrence of the psychotic symptoms since the medication was discontinued; but her depression, with all the accompanying symptoms, has persisted.

In discussing her past history, the patient is rather guarded. There is, however, no evidence of a diagnosable illness before last year. She apparently is a shy, emotionally constricted person who "has never broken any rules." She has been separated from her husband for ten years, but in that time has had two enduring relationships with boyfriends. In addition to rearing three apparently healthy and very likable children, she cared for a succession of foster children full time in the four years before her illness. She enjoyed this, and was highly valued by the agency she worked for. She has maintained close relationships with a few girl friends and with her extended family.

Discussion of Foster Mother

During her initial period of illness this patient demonstrated such characteristic schizophrenic symptoms as bizarre delusions (people could hear what she was thinking) accompanied by auditory hallucinations (voices of friends and strangers talking to each other). There was deterioration in functioning to the point that she was unable to take care of her house. With treatment, after about nine weeks, the psychotic symptoms remitted, but she remembers being "back to normal" for only about a week. She then developed the characteristic symptoms of a major depressive episode with depressed mood, poor appetite, insomnia, lack of energy, loss of interest, and poor concentration. The depressive period has lasted for about nine months.

Are the two periods of illness two separate disorders, or a single illness? If they represent two separate disorders, they could be characterized as either (1) Schizophreniform Disorder (because duration is less than six months) followed by Major Depression, or (2) Schizophrenia (the period after the psychotic phase being considered a residual phase of Schizophrenia) with a superimposed Atypical Depression (for the second period of illness). If there is a single disorder, it is hard to know what to call it (Schizophrenia with depressive features?).

This case would seem to be an example of an instance in which it is impossible to make a differential diagnosis with any degree of certainty between an Affective Disorder and Schizophrenia or Schizophreniform Disorder; hence, a diagnosis of Schizoaffective Disorder seems appropriate. This diagnosis conveys the lack of certainty and the prominence of both affective and schizophreniclike features.

DSM-III Diagnosis:

Axis I: 295.70 Schizoaffective Disorder (p. 202)

The Conversion

150 A 22-year-old male was referred for treatment at the insistence of his priest "to change me from a homosexual to a heterosexual." He had had homosexual arousal from the age of 12 and numerous sexual encounters with males. He left home at 17 and entered the homosexual world, appearing in male sex shows and go-go bars. Although he had attempted sexual activity with women on two occasions, he was unable to obtain an erection. His sexual fantasies involved males exclusively. He fully accepted a homosexual life-style.

Six months previously, a boy aged 19 whom the patient claims he had seduced against his will and with whom he had an on-and-off sexual relationship committed suicide with a drug overdose. This tragedy sent the patient back to the Church, and he started to receive counseling from his local priest. He has accepted the priest's interpretation that his friend's death was due to his seduction of him, that his homosexuality is sinful, and that his only chance of salvation is to renounce his homosexual impulses and become heterosexual. He continues to find girls pleasant company but in no way sexually stimulating. Although he is able to abstain from homosexual contacts and masturbation, he wants to be able to be stimulated sexually by females, to fall in love, marry, and become fully heterosexual.

Discussion of The Conversion

As a result of the suicide of his friend and his subsequent counseling experience with a priest, this young man now finds his homosexuality repugnant. This suggests the diagnosis of Ego-dystonic Homosexuality, which is defined as (1) a sustained pattern of overt homosexual arousal that the individual explicitly states has been unwanted and a persistent source of distress, and (2) a desire to acquire or increase heterosexual arousal so that heterosexual relationships can be initiated or maintained. This category is reserved for homosexuals for whom changing sexual orientation is a *persistent* concern; it should not be used in cases in which the distress about being homosexual is brief or temporary. In view of this patient's apparently total satisfaction with his homosexual life-style until very recently, it seems more appropriate at this point to defer making a diagnosis until it is clear that his desire to change is not simply a temporary reaction to the death of his friend and the suggestion of the priest.

DSM-III Diagnosis:

Axis I: **799.90 Diagnosis Deferred on Axis I (p. 335)**
R/O Ego-dystonic Homosexuality

The Basketball Player

151 Ms. G., the mother of an 18-year-old boy, requested help from the Visiting Nurse Association. Her son, a recent high-school graduate with no previous medical history, had suffered a myocardial infarction 16 days previously. After being released from the hospital he was told to remain in bed, with only bathroom privileges, for one week, until his next appointment with the cardiologist. When seen at home by the visiting nurse two days after leaving the hospital, the boy was playing basketball in the back yard. He acknowledged that he had had a "heart attack," but said he now felt "fine" and therefore saw no need to further restrict his activities. He was planning to begin a full-time job in a local factory in two weeks and was unwilling to consider the possible effect of his physical condition on his plans.

The patient had been popular, a high-school football hero, with many friends and a series of steady girl friends. He had gotten average grades and never been in any trouble. His use of alcohol had been moderate, and he had smoked marijuana only a few times. He was not interested in talking about plans beyond the next year, but guessed he would probably go into the army at some point. His relationship with his family was distant but harmonious. The boy's mother had stopped trying to enforce the regimen prescribed by his doctor after her son had reassured her that he would go to bed if he felt any pain.

Discussion of The Basketball Player

By not following standard medical advice, this patient may kill himself. Why does he persist in acting as if he does not have a life-threatening illness? It is certainly not because he has rationally considered the pros and cons of the prescribed treatment, as might be the case, for example, with a patient with breast cancer who has chosen not to undergo postoperative chemotherapy recommended by her surgeon, in view of the controversy surrounding the effectiveness of the treatment. One can only conclude that our patient is now demonstrating massive denial, a lesser degree of which may have served him well up to now. Apparently, it is only in this unusual situation that his denial may cause him serious problems.

Although his noncompliance with medical treatment is maladaptive and represents psychopathology (broadly defined), it may not be sufficient to make the diagnosis of a mental disorder. We therefore would note the V code Noncompliance with Medical Treatment. The V codes are "for conditions not attributable to a mental disorder that are [nevertheless] a focus of attention or treatment." Therefore, using a V code to characterize this problem does not preclude offering treatment.

We would not quarrel with a clinician who, wishing to emphasize the seriousness of the psychological problem, preferred the diagnosis 300.90 Unspecified Mental Disorder (nonpsychotic).

DSM-III Diagnosis:

Axis I:V15.81 Noncompliance with Medical Treatment (p. 333)

The Socialite

152 This 42-year-old socialite has never had any psychiatric problems before. A new performance hall is to be formally opened with the world premiere of a new ballet; and the patient, because of her position on the cultural council, has taken on the responsibility for coordinating that event. However, construction problems, including strikes, have made it uncertain that the finishing details will meet the deadline. The set designer has been volatile, threatening to walk out on the project unless the materials meet his meticulous specifications. The patient has had to attempt to calm this volatile man while attempting to coax disputing groups to negotiate. She has also had increased responsibilities at home since her housekeeper has had to leave to visit a sick relative.

In the midst of these difficulties, the patient's best friend is decapitated in a tragic auto crash. The patient herself is an only child, and her best friend had been very close to her since grade school. People have often commented that the two women were like sisters. Immediately following the funeral, the patient becomes increasingly tense and jittery, and able to sleep only two to three hours a night. Two days later she happens to see a woman driving a car just like the one that her friend had driven. She immediately becomes puzzled, and after a few hours she becomes convinced that her friend is alive, that the accident had been staged, along with the funeral, as part of a plot. Somehow the plot is directed toward deceiving the patient, and she senses that somehow she is in great danger and must solve the mystery to escape alive. She begins to distrust everyone except her husband, and begins to believe that the phone is tapped and the rooms "bugged." She pleads with her husband to help save her life. She begins to hear a high-pitched, undulating sound, which she fears is an ultrasound beam aimed at her. She is in a state of sheer panic, gripping her husband's arm in terror, as he brings her to the emergency room the next morning.

Discussion of The Socialite

Our initial impression was that this was a rather straightforward example of Brief Reactive Psychosis. A severe psychosocial stressor (the death and funeral of her friend) preceded the development of psychotic symptoms (persecutory delusions and, later, auditory hallucinations) in a thus far short-lived illness. On further reflection, however, we realized that the psychotic symptoms did not begin *immediately* after the stressor, as is the case in Brief Reactive Psychosis, but two days later. Moreover, although the patient was tense and jittery, she displayed no evidence of emotional turmoil — that is, rapid shifts from one dysphoric affect to another without the persistence of any one affect.

Since the predominant symptoms are persecutory delusions, Acute Paranoid Disorder needs to be considered; but that diagnosis requires a duration of illness of at least one week. Furthermore, some clinicians would regard the patient's delusion of an ultrasound "beam aimed at her" as bizarre, which would rule out a Paranoid Disorder and suggest Schizophreniform Disorder. We are therefore left with the residual category of Atypical Psychosis. If the illness persists for more than a week or two (but less than six months), the diagnosis can be changed to Acute Paranoid Disorder or Schizophreniform Disorder.

DSM-III Diagnosis:

Axis I: 298.90 Atypical Psychosis (p. 202) (Provisional)
R/O Acute Paranoid Disorder, Schizophreniform Disorder

Boyfriend

153 A 22-year-old male came to the emergency room after having cut his left wrist, superficially, in a suicide gesture. He did this following an argument with his parents about his girl friend. He went into the bathroom and came out showing them the wound and saying "See what you made me do!"

He has always been a very dramatic and emotional person, but this characteristic has become more prominent in the past six months, since he started seeing a girl whom his parents describe as "flashy and unsuitable." He describes himself as a "dramatic person" who likes to make the most of a situation and tells how he got out of a previous relationship by telling the girl he was an epileptic and throwing a "fit" in her company while they were in a line outside a theater, and how he seduced another girl by swallowing a hundred aspirins in her presence because she wouldn't go to bed with him. He is currently a student at fashion design school, but insists on living with his parents, who "are the only people who can understand and support me." Over the past three months he has had serious problems with his current girl friend, who is urging him to move out of his parents' home and live with her. He has had problems sleeping and is worrying about his future at college and his relationship with his girl friend. He has been losing weight because he is worrying so much, and feels "down in the dumps" because no one really cares about him or understands him. He thinks he is becoming a failure at school and in his relationships, and he has been contemplating ending it all. His schoolwork has suffered because he cannot concentrate and no longer enjoys it as much as he used to.

Discussion of Boyfriend

We suspect that many readers will be as unconvinced as we are that this fellow is in the throes of a depressive episode with persistent depressed mood, trouble sleeping and concentrating, loss of weight, and loss of interest and pleasure. The only thing that is certain is that he has made a suicide gesture. We make the diagnosis of Major Depression without Melancholia provisionally (and reluctantly), because we cannot discount what he is telling us. Further exploration might reveal that he does not have persistently depressed mood or pervasive loss of interest or pleasure, but rather an unstable mood that is acutely responsive to environmental events. If this were the case, we would prefer to regard his current problems as either an Adjustment Disorder with Depressed Mood (related to pressure from his girl friend to move out of his parents' house),or merely an exacerbation of his long-standing personality difficulties (in which case we would not make an Axis I diagnosis, despite the dramatic suicide gesture).

His long-term personality functioning is characterized by high drama and manipulation of others to get his own way. These suggest Histrionic Personality Disorder. Based on the limited sample of behavior described in this case, we are reluctant to make this diagnosis. His description of himself as "an emotional person" suggests the affective instability of Borderline Personality Disorder. However, the full criteria for this Personality Disorder are clearly not met. We therefore would diagnose Mixed Personality Disorder and would hope that with further contact, the presence of a more specific Personality Disorder could be determined.

DSM-III Diagnosis:

Axis I: 296.22 Major Depression, without Melancholia, Single Episode (p. 213) (Provisional)

Axis II: 301.89 Mixed Personality Disorder
R/O Borderline and Histrionic Personality Disorders

Triple Divorcée

154 This 37-year-old thrice divorced woman was hospitalized in a private psychiatric facility because of an attempt to end her life by putting her head into the oven and turning on the gas. When the acute effects of central nervous system depression had worn off, she complained of hopelessness and uselessness, inordinate fatigue, guilt about having abandoned her five-year-óld daughter, and total anhedonia; she displayed marked psychomotor retardation and slept 12–14 hours a night.

This was the patient's sixth episode of this kind. The first episode, at the age of 23, had been triggered by marital separation; but the patient could suggest no explanation for subsequent episodes — "I just seem to sink into a gloomy despair." She had received individual psychotherapy and small doses of all kinds of psychotropic drugs except, ironically, tricyclics. During the present episode she was given increasing doses of desipramine; and in ten days, at a daily dosage level of 200 mg, her mood became elated, flirtatious, and over-confident, and she did not sleep more than four to five hours a night. This mood receded in four days with a downward adjustment of her tricyclic dose.

Retrospective anamnesis revealed that the patient had had one previous "high period," which had occurred at the tail end of her second depressive episode, when she was on no medication. It had lasted for two weeks. She recalled "being on Cloud 9," having an overabundance of energy and a decreased need for sleep, keeping the house immaculate, arranging and rearranging the furniture two to three times a day, and kissing the children every time they passed by. She denied having racing thoughts and inflated self-esteem, and there was no evidence of poor judgment.

Discussion of Triple Divorcée

The current episode of illness has all the features of a major depressive episode, with disturbances in mood, sleep, psychomotor activity, and energy level and feelings of hopelessness and guilt. While being treated pharmacologically with a tricyclic antidepressant, the patient developed symptoms suggesting a manic episode; but the disturbance was too mild and too brief to be considered a manic episode in Bipolar Disorder.

Tricyclic-induced hypomanic episodes are not rare. Because there is some evidence that most individuals in whom this occurs have a family history of Bipolar Disorder, it is probably more useful to classify such an episode as a manifestation of an Atypical Bipolar Disorder than as an Organic Affective Syndrome. In this particular case there is a retrospective history of a similar hypomanic episode not associated with pharmacological treatment, which further supports the diagnosis.

DSM-III Diagnosis:

Axis 1:   296.70 Atypical Bipolar Disorder (p. 223)

Hardworking Businessman

155 A 49-year-old businessman reluctantly came for evaluation at the insistence of his wife of 20 years. During the first session, only the following information emerged.

The couple has four children. The wife's complaint is that her husband's behavior is such that the marriage is in danger and she is thinking of leaving him, although she still loves him and does not want to break up the marriage, for her own sake as well as the children's. The husband's viewpoint is that there is nothing wrong that they cannot sort out themselves, and he does not think his behavior is wrong under the circumstances. Over the past ten years the couple has advanced from being poor and hardworking small shopkeepers to affluence and an income in excess of $100,000 annually. Both of them left school at the age of 17. Four years ago, the wife decided to go to college; and reluctantly the husband agreed to her suggestion, although he could see no reason why she would want to do so. After the first year in college, the husband asked her to stop going, but she insisted on continuing to take part-time courses. He then restricted her contacts with her college friends and refused to allow her to bring them to their house or entertain them socially. At the same time, he insisted that she accompany him to many of his business meetings and all his social activities connected with his business. Over the past year there have been increasing arguments about his demands and her wishes to pursue social contacts apart from him; and on each occasion, the argument has led to physical violence on the part of the husband, which has always been restricted to breaking up the furniture.

The referral was precipitated by the husband's arguing with her at a social function in the neighborhood because she was wearing a blouse that was too revealing, and his demanding that she return home to change it. She refused to do so, and he physically lifted her and tried to carry her to their car. This altercation was witnessed by everyone at the party. When they got home, the husband became extremely abusive. The wife threatened to leave, and he locked himself in the bathroom and threatened to shoot himself. This led to the wife's calling his brother. Finally, the husband came out of the bathroom and handed over the gun, the wife having promised not to leave, and he, that he would seek psychiatric help.

Discussion of Hardworking Businessman

Does this man have a mental disorder or only a marital problem? DSM-III recognizes that not all difficulties between spouses are symptoms of a mental disorder. If their difficulties had been limited to conflict over the wife's changing goals, we would see no need to infer the presence of a mental disorder. However, the extent of the husband's narcissism, reflected in his inability to allow his wife to grow as an independent person and culminating in his locking himself in the bathroom and threatening to kill himself, strongly suggests a pervasive maladaptive pattern of relating to other people—that is, a Personality Disorder. It is true that there is no evidence that such behavior has caused him problems in the past. It is conceivable that his narcissistic traits were accommodated by his wife and that the equilibrium was disturbed only when she decided to develop herself. Nevertheless, the diagnosis of a Personality Disorder seems appropriate even in cases in which special environmental circumstances minimize the extent of the underlying pathology.

Since on the basis of the available information the full criteria for Narcissistic Personality are not met, the diagnosis is Atypical Personality Disorder (Provisional), R/O Narcissistic Personality Disorder.

DSM-III Diagnosis:

Axis II: 301.89 Atypical Personality Disorder (Provisional)
         R/O Narcissistic Personality Disorder

The Reporter

156 A 29-year-old newspaper reporter had been a heavy drinker for 10 years. One evening after work, having finished a feature article, he started drinking with friends and continued to drink through the evening. He fell asleep in the early morning hours. Upon awakening he had a strong desire to drink again and decided not to go to work. Food did not appeal to him, and instead he had several Bloody Marys. Later he went to a local tavern and drank beer throughout the afternoon. He met some friends and continued drinking into the evening.

The pattern of drinking throughout the day persisted for the next seven days. On the eighth morning he tried to drink a cup of coffee and found his hands were shaking so violently he could not get the cup to his mouth. He managed to pour some whiskey into a glass and drank as much as he could. His hands became less shaky, but now he was nauseated and began having "dry heaves." He tried repeatedly to drink, but could not keep the alcohol down. He felt ill and intensely anxious and decided to call a doctor friend. The doctor recommended hospitalization.

When evaluated on admission the patient was alert; he had a marked resting and intention tremor of the hands, and his tongue and eyelids were tremulous. He had feelings of "internal" tremulousness. Lying in the hospital bed, he found the noises outside his window unbearably loud and began seeing "visions" of animals and, on one occasion, a dead relative. He was terrified and called a nurse, who gave him a tranquilizer. He became quieter, and his tremor, less pronounced. At all times he realized that the visual phenomena were "imaginary." He always knew where he was and was otherwise oriented. He had no memory impairment. After a few days, the tremor disappeared, and the patient no longer hallucinated. He still had trouble sleeping, but otherwise felt normal. He vowed never to drink again.

When questioned further about his history of drinking, the patient claimed that although during the last ten years he had developed the habit of drinking several Scotches each day, his drinking had never interfered with his work or relations with colleagues or friends. He denied having aftereffects of drinking other than occasional mild hangovers; ever going on binges before this one; and that he had needed to drink every day in order to function adequately. He admitted, however, that he had never tried to reduce or stop drinking.

Discussion of The Reporter

This heavy drinker markedly increases his amount of drinking for a week and then stops drinking as he becomes sick with nausea and vomiting. He then develops visual hallucinations; tremor of the hands, tongue, and eyelids; and anxiety. Significantly, he realizes that the hallucinations are imaginary; and he remains alert, fully oriented, and without memory impairment. These symptoms, associated with the reduction in heavy alcohol use, indicate Alcohol Withdrawal.

Many clinicians might conclude that this was Alcohol Withdrawal Delirium (Delirium Tremens) because of the visual hallucinations. Delirium, however, requires clouding of consciousness, disorientation, and memory impairment, in addition to whatever perceptual disturbances may be present. The visual hallucinations with intact reality testing that this patient experienced are rather common in simple Alcohol Withdrawal.

Does the presence of Alcohol Withdrawal invariably indicate the presence of Alcohol Dependence? This is controversial. In developing the DSM-III criteria for Alcohol Dependence, a decision was made to give the diagnosis only if, in addition to evidence of tolerance or withdrawal, there was either a pathological pattern of use or social or occupational impairment resulting from the alcohol use. This was done because some heavy recreational use of alcohol might result in tolerance or withdrawal without any consequent maladaptive behaviorior. In such cases it was thought not appropriate to make a diagnosis of a mental disorder. In this case the patient denies previous binges, the need for daily use to function, and any interference with his work or social relations. If this is true, he would not have the additional diagnosis of Alcohol Dependence.

On the other hand, some clinicians would take the view that withdrawal always indicates physiological dependence and that the diagnosis of Dependence should be made even in the absence of evidence of maladaptive behavior. Given that the patient admits he has never tried to control his drinking, we would see if he is able to stop, as he has vowed to do. If he is unable to do so, then he will indeed, even by DSM-III criteria, warrant the diagnosis of Alcohol Dependence. Thus, we note the need to rule out this diagnosis.

DSM-III Diagnosis:

Axis I: 291.80 Alcohol Withdrawal (p. 133)
**   R/O Alcohol Dependence**

Cases for Testing

Cases for Testing

This chapter includes 20 adult and 15 child case vignettes that can be used as a test of familiarity with the diagnostic categories and concepts of DSM-III. These relatively brief and straightforward cases can be used for testing in a number of different ways. The most stringent test is to diagnose the cases without any reference materials, such as DSM-III itself, the *Quick Reference to the Diagnostic Criteria from DSM-III*, or even just the DSM-III classification. This tests a knowledge of the exact terminology and the concepts included in the diagnostic criteria. A less stringent test is to have available only the DSM-III classification. Under these conditions the reader needs only to be familiar with the diagnostic concepts to find the correct diagnostic term and code number from the classification. Finally, the cases can be diagnosed with the aid of either DSM-III or the Quick Reference. This requires only that the reader be able to use the manual to assist in making the correct DSM-III diagnoses.

Norms are not yet available for different levels of competence under these various conditions. On the basis of our experience in giving these case vignettes as a test, we have observed the following: Under the most stringent test, only clinicians with a great deal of familiarity with DSM-III can be expected to make the correct diagnoses in 80% to 90% of the cases. With only the DSM-III classification available, a similar score can generally be achieved by clinicians with a good working knowledge of DSM-III. Finally, given sufficient time, any clinician with a good knowledge of psychopathology should be able to use the manual to diagnose correctly nearly all of the cases.

In scoring each case, partial credit can be given if the error is limited to a fourth- or fifth-digit subtype. For example, correctly identifying Major Depression without including the correct subtype might earn a half-credit. When there are two diagnoses for a case, each correct diagnosis earns a half-credit (and a partially correct diagnosis a quarter-credit). A half-credit can be subtracted when an incorrect additional diagnosis is made (for example, adding a Personality Disorder without sufficient evidence). The mind boggles at the possible permutations of ever more precise scoring systems. We suggest that the scoring be kept simple. Therefore, we recommend ignoring disagreements about which of two diagnoses is the principal diagnosis and whether a diagnosis should be given provisionally.

Most clinicians can complete the 20 adult cases easily within an hour, and the 15 child cases, within 45 minutes.

ADULT CASES

Stonemason

157 A 55-year-old stonemason is admitted to a medical service because of loss of appetite and a 23 kg (50 pound) weight loss over the preceding 6 months. His loss of appetite has been accompanied by a burning pain in his chest, back, and abdomen, which he has become convinced indicates a fatal abdominal cancer. He is withdrawn and isolated, unable to work, disinterested in friends and family, and unresponsive to their attempts to make him feel better. He awakes at 4:00 A.M. and is unable to fall back asleep. He claims to feel worst in the mornings and to improve slightly as the day wears on. On mental status examination he is markedly agitated and speaks of feelings of extreme unworthiness. He says that he would be better off dead and that he welcomes his impending demise from cancer. He has no previous history of emotional disturbance. Physical examination and laboratory tests are within normal limits.

Discussion of Stonemason

This patient does not complain of feeling depressed; but he does complain of a pervasive loss of interest and pleasure. This, plus several of the other symptoms of the depressive syndrome (loss of appetite, insomnia, feelings of worthlessness, and recurrent thoughts of death), suggests the presence of a major depressive episode. The normal physical examination and laboratory findings rule out the possibility of an Organic Affective Syndrome. The somatic delusion that he has a fatal cancer is in keeping with an Affective Disorder, and there is no suggestion of any other psychotic disorder.

He also demonstrates the melancholic syndrome: loss of pleasure in all, or almost all, activities, lack of reactivity (unresponsive to family's attempts to make him feel better), diurnal mood variation (depression worse in the morning), early morning awakening, significant weight loss, and marked psychomotor agitation.

According to DSM-III, when psychotic features and the melancholic syndrome are both present, the coding system requires that the clinician code whichever is more clinically significant, noting the other condition in parentheses. In our view, coding either condition would be acceptable in this case; but because the somatic delusion is so understandable in the context of marked weight loss and abdominal pain, our preference would be for coding Melancholia.

DSM-III Diagnosis:

Axis I: 296.23 Major Depression, Single Episode, with Melancholia (with Mood-congruent Psychotic Features) (p. 213)

Running

158 A 24-year-old, single, female, copy editor was presented at a case conference two weeks after her first psychiatric hospitalization. Her admission followed an accident in which she had wrecked her car while driving at high speed late at night when she was feeling "energetic" and that "sleep was a waste of time." The episode began while she was on vacation, when she felt "high" and on the verge of a "great romance." She apparently took off all her clothes and ran naked through the woods. On the day of admission she reported hearing voices telling her that her father and the emergency-room staff were emissaries of the devil, out to "get" her for no reason that she could understand.

At the case conference she was calm and cooperative and talked of the voices she had heard in the past, which she now acknowledged had not been real. She realized she had an illness, but was still somewhat irritated at being hospitalized. She was on lithium, 2100 mg/day, with a blood level of 1.0 mEq/1.

Discussion of Running

The characteristic features of a manic episode are present: elevated mood (feeling "high"), increased energy, decreased need for sleep, and involvement in activities with a high potential for painful consequences (reckless driving). The reference to being on the verge of a "great romance" also suggests the presence of grandiosity. In DSM-III the presence of a manic episode, even without a history of a depressive episode, is sufficient to make a diagnosis of Bipolar Disorder, Manic, since the familial history, course, and treatment response of "unipolar mania" are apparently the same as in illnesses with both manic and major depressive episodes.

The presence of the persecutory hallucinations is noted in the fifth-digit as with Psychotic Features. Since the content has no apparent connection with themes of either inflated worth, power, knowledge, identity, or a special relationship to a deity or famous person, the hallucinations are mood-incongruent. This can be indicated in parentheses.

If the diagnosis referred to her condition at the time of the case conference, the fifth-digit coding would be changed to 6—in Remission.

DSM-III Diagnosis:

Axis I: **296.44 Bipolar Disorder, Manic, with Psychotic Features (Mood-incongruent) (p. 217)**

Farm Worker

159 Three months after its initial contact with the patient, a 26-year-old male migratory farm worker, a community mental health team was contacted by the city police. The patient, who had been maintained in an outpatient clinic for the past few months, had suddenly appeared in a judge's chamber and demanded to be put to death because he felt he was responsible for the production of evil and violence in the world. When team members reached the jail, they found the patient agitated, easily angered, suspicious, and guarded. His speech was disorganized and often incoherent. He stated that he could not eat meat or terrible violence and evil would be unleashed on the world. He also described a plot by the California Mafia to keep him from working, and he spoke of voices that told him what to do and that "must be obeyed."

Past history included similar episodes over the previous five years, resulting in several year-long periods of inpatient hospitalization. At no time did he exhibit a full manic or depressive syndrome. Between hospitalizations the patient lived in hobo jungles, flophouses, and gospel missions; rode freight trains from town to town; and worked, picking fruit, for only a few days at a time. Since adolescence he has lived the life of a drifting loner.

Discussion of Farm Worker

The bizarre delusions, incoherence, and chronic course with marked impairment in functioning, in the absence of an affective syndrome, leave little doubt as to the diagnosis of Schizophrenia. The delusion of guilt, although often associated with Major Depression with Psychotic Features, is not sufficient, in the absence of other symptoms of a major depressive episode, to seriously raise the question of a Major Affective Disorder.

The subtype is classified as Paranoid because of the prominent persecutory delusions. The course is coded as chronic because the illness has lasted longer than two years. The fifth digit is used to record both the chronic course and the current flare-up (acute exacerbation).

DSM-III Diagnosis:

Axis I: 295.34 Schizophrenia, Paranoid Type, Chronic with Acute Exacerbation (p. 191)

Cough Medicine

160 A 42-year-old executive in a public relations firm was referred for psychiatric consultation by his surgeon, who discovered him sneaking large quantities of a codeine-containing cough medicine into the hospital. The patient had been a heavy cigarette smoker for 20 years and had a chronic, hacking cough. He had come into the hospital for a hernia repair, and found the pain from the incision unbearable when he coughed.

An operation on his back five years previously had led his doctor to prescribe codeine to help relieve the incisional pain at that time. Over the intervening five years, however, he had continued to use codeine-containing tablets and had increased his intake to 60–90 5-mg tablets daily. He stated that he often "just took them by the handful—not to feel good, you understand, just to get by." He had tried several times to stop using codeine, but had failed. During this period he lost two jobs because of lax work habits and was divorced by his wife of 11 years.

Discussion of Cough Medicine

The presence of tolerance to codeine, that is, markedly increased amounts are needed to achieve the desired effect (his taking 60–90 tablets a day), indicates Substance Dependence. The diagnosis is coded as Opioid Dependence, because codeine is classified as an opioid. However, the name of the specific substance, codeine, rather than the class of substance, opioid, is recorded. The course is classified as Continuous since there has been more or less regular maladaptive use for over six months.

Although the criteria for Substance Abuse are also met in this case (a pathological pattern of use with social and occupational impairment), the diagnosis of Substance Dependence takes precedence because abuse is generally a prerequisite of the development of physiological tolerance or withdrawal (dependence).

DSM-III Diagnosis:

Axis I: 304.01 Codeine Dependence, Continuous (p. 172)

The Musician

161 A 31-year-old musician was referred for psychotherapy by her boyfriend's therapist. She complained of feeling angry a good part of her life and of being in "conflict" with the man with whom she was now involved. He was "an alcoholic" who was possessive, demanding, and physically and verbally abusive. Initially she had hoped to be "the woman he had never had," but more recently she felt in a rage and was provocative and abusive herself.

The patient had been married in her early twenties, but was divorced after three years of bitter fighting. There followed a succession of boyfriends with whom she fell in love but eventually ridiculed and "hated." She was rarely not involved with some man. She said she "panicked" at the thought of being alone. On several occasions when she had been dropped by a boyfriend she made a suicide attempt by an overdose of Valium and alcohol, which she admitted she occasionally took to excess, but she was never admitted to hospital. Although somewhat accomplished in her art, she freqently felt bored, empty, and as if she had chosen the wrong field. She claimed that she did not know who she really was and said, "I always act the way people expect me to act." She had had two brief contacts with psychotherapy before, but both times she dropped out after several sessions that "weren't getting me anywhere" and were "too far to travel to."

Discussion of The Musician

Borderline Personality Disorder is indicated by the long-standing maladaptive pattern of behavior that includes: affective instability (". . . feeling angry a good part of her life . . ."), inappropriate displays of anger (". . . felt in a rage and was provocative and abusive herself"), intense and unstable interpersonal relationships with idealization and devaluation (". . . she fell in love but eventually ridiculed and 'hated' " her boyfriends), intolerance of being alone (". . . she 'panicked' at the thought . . ."), identity disturbance (". . . she did not know who she really was . . ."), and chronic feelings of emptiness and boredom. In addition, there is evidence of physically self-damaging acts (several suicide attempts).

The reference to several overdoses involving Valium and occasionally taking it "to excess" suggests the possible additional diagnosis of Valium Abuse, Episodic. In the absence of clear evidence of social or occupational impairment from the use of Valium, the diagnosis is qualified as provisional.

Although she had made several suicide attempts, there is no evidence of a sustained dysphoric mood that would suggest Dysthymic Disorder or Major Depression superimposed on the Borderline Personality Disorder.

DSM-III Diagnosis:

Axis I: 305.42 Valium Abuse, Episodic (Provisional) (p. 171)
Axis II: 301.83 Borderline Personality Disorder (Principal Diagnosis) (p. 322)

Silent Student

162 A 21-year-old pre-law student was called in by her advisor for a discussion of her performance. Although she did very well on tests, she was totally unable to participate in classroom discussions. She had managed with a succession of excuses to avoid all formal presentations well into her junior year, but her avoidance was finally catching up with her, as professors began to lower her grades. She admitted with great embarrassment that she was terrified of speaking before others and had on more than one occasion left her classroom in a state of panic, fearful that she would be called upon to speak. At such times she was short of breath, sweaty, was conscious of her heart racing, and felt faint.

She explained to her advisor that she felt that she had an unpleasant accent and was not as articulate as her fellow students. She was convinced that they would find her "dumb" and think she was a "fool" for trying to become a lawyer.

Discussion of Silent Student

This patient's avoidance of speaking in the classroom is due to an excessive fear of humiliation, a common example of a Social Phobia. Since her panic attacks apparently occur only when she is exposed to the phobic stimulus, the additional diagnosis of Panic Disorder is not made; and since there is no evidence of avoidance of interpersonal relationships in general, the diagnosis of Avoidant Personality Disorder is not appropriate.

DSM-III Diagnosis:

Axis I: 300.23 Social Phobia (p. 228)

Carbon Monoxide

163 The patient is a 25-year-old female graduate student in physical chemistry who was brought to the emergency room by her roommates, who found her sitting in her car with the motor running and the garage door closed. The patient had entered psychotherapy two years previously, complaining of long-standing unhappiness, feelings of inadequacy, low self-esteem, chronic tiredness, and a generally pessimistic outlook on life. While in treatment, as before, periods of well-being were limited to a few weeks at a time. During the two months before her emergency-room visit she became increasingly depressed, developed difficulty falling asleep and trouble concentrating, and had lost ten pounds. The onset of these symptoms coincided with a rebuff she received from a chemistry laboratory instructor to whom she had become attracted.

Discussion of Carbon Monoxide

The recent development of a sustained and more severe depressed mood, insomnia, trouble concentrating, and weight loss, plus the suicide attempt, indicate a major depressive episode. There is no history of a previous *episode,* and there are no symptoms suggesting the melancholic syndrome, such as pervasive loss of interest or pleasure and lack of reactivity. Thus the diagnosis of Major Depression, Single Episode, without Melancholia is made.

In addition there is a history of long-standing mild depressive symptoms (pessimism, feelings of inadequacy, and low energy level) that are insufficient to meet the criteria for a major depressive episode. This warrants the additional diagnosis of Dysthymic Disorder. Episodes of Major Depression are often superimposed, as in this case, on Dysthymic Disorder. Examination of the criteria for a major depressive episode and for Dysthymic Disorder suggests that their differentiation is largely a matter of the number of symptoms. In practice, what is more helpful in differentiating the two disorders is that in a major depressive episode all of the symptoms are present nearly every day, whereas in Dysthymic Disorder the various symptoms are likely to wax and wane from day to day. In addition, in a major depressive episode typically the onset of the disturbance is a distinct change from usual functioning, whereas Dysthymic Disorder often represents the individual's usual pattern of functioning.

Since the suicide attempt, a symptom of the major depressive episode, occasioned the emergency-room visit, Major Depression is listed first.

DSM-III Diagnosis:

**Axis I: 296.22 Major Depression, Single Episode, without Melancholia (p. 213)
300.40 Dysthymic Disorder (p. 222)**

Blackout

164 A perplexed internist asked for a psychiatric consultation on a 50-year-old divorced and unemployed secretary. When first encountered the patient was lying in bed in a contorted position, with occasional jerking movements of her arms, one every few seconds. Within ten minutes she was sitting up and explaining that she had been having "a seizure" that was "still there, in my spine. At any minute it can break out and overwhelm me again." Her present difficulties began two-and-a-half months previously with nausea, abdominal cramps, and pain in the extremities that kept her bedridden for several days.

The patient reported having abdominal pain since age 17, necessitating exploratory surgery that yielded no specific diagnosis. She had several pregnancies, each with severe nausea, vomiting, and abdominal pain; she ultimately had a hysterectomy for a "tipped uterus." Since age 40 she had experienced dizziness and "blackouts," which she eventually was told might be multiple sclerosis or a brain tumor. She continued to be bedridden for extended periods of time, with weakness, blurred vision, and difficulty urinating. At age 43 she was worked up for a hiatal hernia because of complaints of bloating and intolerance of a variety of foods. She also had additional hospitalizations for neurological, hypertensive, and renal workups, all of which failed to reveal a definitive diagnosis.

She has been divorced since age 32 and has worked very sporadically. She lives with her only child, an adult son. They lead a rather vagabond life, settling for a few months at a time in a residential hotel, then moving on to another city. They have no significant relationships other than with each other. She avoids heterosexual encounters, explaining that "sex has never turned me on."

Discussion of Blackout

This is a chronic, polysymptomatic disorder of physically unexplainable symptoms involving multiple organ systems. There are gastrointestinal symptoms (nausea, abdominal cramps, vomiting, bloating, food intolerance), conversion or pseudoneurological symptoms (seizure, blurred vision, and blackouts), female reproductive symptoms (nausea and vomiting during pregnancy), psychosexual symptoms (sexual indifference), pain (extremity, abdominal), and cardiopulmonary symptoms (dizziness). These symptoms have led to numerous medical workups and hospitalizations. This clinical picture, far more common in women than in men, in the past referred to as Hysteria or Briquet's syndrome, is now called Somatization Disorder.

Although conversion symptoms are present (e.g., seizure), the diagnosis of Conversion Disorder is not made since the full clinical picture of Somatization Disorder is present. In this case there is no evidence of voluntary production of the symptoms, which would suggest Factitious Disorder with Physical Symptoms. Frequently, although not invariably, Somatization Disorder is associated with Histrionic Personality Disorder. In this case there is no evidence to justify that additional diagnosis.

DSM-III Diagnosis:

Axis I: 300.81 Somatization Disorder (p. 243)

Happy Ending

165 A 24-year-old, single, female nursery-school teacher terminated brief psychotherapy after ten sessions. She had entered treatment two weeks after she discovered that the man she had been involved with for four months was married and wanted to stop seeing her. She reacted with bouts of sadness and crying, felt she was falling apart, took a week's sick leave from her job, and had vague thoughts that the future was so bleak that life might not be worth the effort. She felt that she must be in some essential way "flawed"; otherwise she would not have gotten so involved with someone who had no intentions of maintaining a long-term relationship. She felt that others "would have seen it," that only she was "so stupid" as to have been deceived. There were no other signs of a depressive syndrome, such as loss of interest or appetite or trouble concentrating. She responded to mixed supportive-insight psychotherapy and, toward the end of treatment, began dating a law student whom she met at a local cafe.

Discussion of Happy Ending

Depressive symptoms (sadness and crying, thoughts that the future was bleak) raise the possibility of a major depressive episode. In this case, however, there are no other signs of the depressive syndrome, so a diagnosis of a Major Depression is ruled out. The maladaptive nature of her reaction to the psychosocial stressor (the man she was seeing wanted to stop seeing her) indicates a diagnosis in the residual category of Adjustment Disorder with Depressed Mood.

A V code diagnosis of Other Interpersonal Problem is not appropriate since her feeling as if she were falling apart and her taking a week's sick leave are clearly in excess of a normal or expected reaction to the stressor.

This is an example of a case with a happy ending!

DSM-III Diagnosis:

Axis I: 309.00 Adjustment Disorder with Depressed Mood (p. 300)

Edgy Electrician

166 A 27-year-old, married electrician complains of dizziness, sweating palms, heart palpitations, and ringing of the ears of more than eighteen months' duration. He has also experienced dry throat, periods of uncontrollable shaking, and a constant "edgy" and watchful feeling that often interfered with his ability to concentrate. These feelings have been present most of the time over the previous two years; they have not been limited to discrete periods.

Because of these symptoms he had seen a family practitioner, a neurologist, a neurosurgeon, a chiropractor, and an ENT specialist. He had been placed on a hypoglycemic diet, received physiotherapy for a pinched nerve, and told he might have "an inner ear problem."

For the past two years he has had few social contacts because of his nervous symptoms. Although he has sometimes had to leave work when the symptoms became intolerable, he continues to work for the same company for which he has worked since his apprenticeship following high-school graduation. He tends to hide his symptoms from his wife and children, to whom he wants to appear "perfect," and reports few problems with them as a result of his nervousness.

Discussion of Edgy Electrician

Symptoms of motor tension (uncontrollable shaking), autonomic hyperactivity (dizziness, sweating palms, heart palpitations), and vigilance and scanning ("a constant 'edgy' and watchful feeling") suggest an Anxiety Disorder. Since the symptoms are not limited to discrete periods, as in Panic Disorder, and are not focused on a discrete stimulus, as in a Phobic Disorder, the diagnosis is Generalized Anxiety Disorder.

Although the patient has consulted numerous physicians for his symptoms, the absence of preoccupation with fears of having a specific physical disease precludes a diagnosis of Hypochondriasis.

DSM-III Diagnosis:

Axis I: 300.02 Generalized Anxiety Disorder (p. 233)

Construction Worker

167 A 37-year-old construction worker was admitted to the medical service because he was vomiting blood. On the second hospital day the patient began to complain vociferously about the tests and procedures and was noted by the intern to be tremulous and sweaty, with a pulse of 120. The patient admitted to the intern that he was a heavy drinker, and the intern prescribed an injection of 25 mg of Librium just after the evening meal. At 2:00 A.M. he was called to see the patient, whom he found "out of touch," thrashing about in the bed, and screaming incoherently. History revealed that a similar episide of gastric bleeding had occurred a year ago, at which time the patient was advised to stop drinking.

Discussion of Construction Worker

When noted by the intern on the second hospital day to be tremulous and sweaty and to have tachycardia, the patient, with a history of heavy alcohol use, was apparently experiencing Alcohol Withdrawal. However, at 2:00 A.M. the next morning, because of the inadequate treatment, he developed a delirium characterized by clouding of consciousness ("out of touch"), increased psychomotor activity (thrashing about in the bed), and incoherence. (If able to be tested, he probably would have demonstrated disorientation and memory impairment.) The more pervasive disturbance, Alcohol Withdrawal Delirium, takes precedence over the diagnosis of the less serious Alcohol Withdrawal.

The additional diagnosis of Alcohol Dependence, Continuous, is justified by evidence of physiological dependence (withdrawal syndrome) and a pattern of pathological use of over six months' duration (continuation of drinking despite a serious physical disorder — gastritis — that the individual knows is exacerbated by alcohol).

DSM-III Diagnosis:

Axis I: **291.00 Alcohol Withdrawal Delirium (p. 135)**
           303.91 Alcohol Dependence, Continuous (p. 170)

The Apathetic Accountant

168 A 57-year-old accountant complained to his internist that for the last month he had been increasingly tired, apathetic, disinterested in almost everything, and pessimistic about the future. In addition, he had trouble sleeping and had sustained a 4.5 kg (10 pound) weight loss. Physical findings were negative as was his medical history, with the exception that six months previously he had been noted to have blood pressure of 150/110 and had started taking antihypertensive medication.

Discussion of The Apathetic Accountant

The temporal association between the development of the depressive syndrome and the initiation of antihypertensive therapy suggests the possibility of an Organic Affective Disorder, that is, a predominant disturbance of mood that is due to a known specific organic factor. "Provisional" is used to indicate lack of certainty regarding the etiological role of the medication, since there is no way to be sure that the patient might not have developed an affective disorder coincidentally. If the depression lifted when the medication was discontinued, the diagnosis of Organic Affective Disorder would be supported; but if the symptoms persisted, the clinician should change the diagnosis to Major Depression. (Note that for Substance-induced Organic Mental Disorders the name of the specific substance is indicated.)

DSM-III Diagnosis:

Axis I: 292.84 **Alphamethyldopa-induced Affective Disorder (Provisional) (p. 118)**
R/O Major Depression

Coquette

169 A 30-year-old cocktail waitress sought treatment after breaking up her relationship with her 50-year-old boyfriend. Although initially she was tearful and suicidal, she brightened up within the first session and became animated and coquettish with the male interviewer. During the intake evaluation interviews she was always attractively and seductively dressed, wore carefully applied facial makeup, and crossed her legs in a revealing fashion. She related her story with dramatic inflections and seemed very concerned with the impression she was making on the interviewer. Although she often cried during sessions, her grief appeared to be without depth and mainly for effect. Several times she asked that the next appointment be changed to accommodate her plans; and when this was not possible, she became furious and talked of how "doctors have no concern for their patients."

The patient's history reveals that she is frequently the life of the party and has no problem making friends, although she seems to lose them just as easily and feels lonely most of the time. People apparently accuse her of being selfish, immature, and unreliable. She is often late for appointments; borrows money, which she rarely returns; and breaks dates on impulse or if someone more attractive turns up. She is competitive with and jealous of other women, believes that they are catty and untrustworthy, and is known for being particularly seductive with her friends' boyfriends.

Discussion of Coquette

The patient's seductive behavior both in the interview situation and with her friends' boyfriends and her "performances" at parties are evidence of incessant attention-seeking. This, combined with her dramatic storytelling (self-dramatization) and irrational anger at not being able to reschedule her appointments, is presumably characteristic of her personality style. Her frequent crying for effect in the interviews is indicative of shallowness, and there is ample evidence of her self-indulgent lack of consideration for others, such as not returning borrowed money and often breaking dates. All of these personality traits, which clearly cause severe problems for this woman, add up to a prototypical description of Histrionic Personality Disorder.

Although there are narcissistic traits (e.g., her constantly seeking attention and admiration and sense of entitlement and exploitiveness in interpersonal relationships), the absence of grandiosity or a sense of uniqueness precludes the diagnosis of the Narcissistic Personality Disorder. There are also borderline personality traits, such as inappropriate anger, but no evidence of several of the other characteristics of Borderline Personality Disorder, such as instability in mood and self-image and impulsivity.

Adjustment Disorder with Depressed Mood is not appropriate as an Axis I diagnosis since the affective symptoms (fearfulness, suicidal ideation) were fleeting and apparently part of a pattern of overreaction that is characteristic of Histrionic Personality Disorder.

DSM-III Diagnosis:

Axis II: 301.50 Histrionic Personality Disorder (p. 315)

Axe Killing

170 A 44-year-old sanitation worker was seen in jail following his brutal killing of a fellow worker. He had gone to work that morning as usual. During a coffee break he precipitously knocked the other worker to the ground, grabbed his shovel, and began to strike him on the head and chest for several minutes. He then took an axe and continued to beat him. Observers who saw this related that he had struck the deceased at least fifteen or twenty times with the axe. A number of people tried to stop him but he held them at bay. After several minutes he stopped, whereupon the police apprehended him.

When seen in jail, he showed no evidence of psychosis or other florid psychopathology. He recalled most details of the murder, but could not explain the reason for his behavior other than to allege that the deceased had "bothered him" by making racial inferences and by grabbing his arm and holding it behind his back. The latter incident was not corroborated by witnesses. The patient and the deceased had worked together for 15 years and seemed to relate well to one another, and witnesses had not observed any tension between the two.

In a review of the patient's history, it was noted that he had received a diagnosis of "inadequate personality" while in military service; but there was no history of any previous aggressive outbursts or any psychiatric hospitalizations.

Discussion of Axe Killing

Loss of impulse control that results in violence may be symptomatic of many disorders, such as Schizophrenia, Antisocial Personality Disorder, or an Organic Mental Disorder. In this case the violent act, which was clearly out of proportion to any possible precipitating stressor, appears to have been an isolated act, not a symptom of a more pervasive mental disorder. Thus, the diagnosis of Isolated Explosive Disorder is made.

The diagnosis the patient had received in military service raises the question of a coexisting Personality Disorder, but this vignette does not provide enough information to make such a DSM-III diagnosis. Even if there were a clear diagnosis of a coexisting Personality Disorder (other than Antisocial Personality Disorder), however, the diagnosis Isolated Explosive Disorder would still be made (on Axis I).

DSM-III Diagnosis:

Axis I: 312.35 Isolated Explosive Disorder (p. 298)

Alice

171 Alice is a 20-year-old single white female, junior in a southern college, who came to a student health clinic with complaints of "turbulence" in her life, which she experienced as vague feelings of anxiety, depression, and worries about the uncertainty of her future. She felt confused and directionless, and these feelings often interfered with her ability to concentrate on her schoolwork.

Alice had looked forward to coming to college in her freshman year, and when she arrived, was excited by the diversity of people she met. Sometimes she enjoyed being with her "arty, more way-out and kind of radical" friends, and at other times she felt more comfortable with her "traditional, more moderate preppie" friends. In the past year, however, she had increasingly had the feeling that she did not fit into any one group of friends, and was confused about who she "really was." She experienced this not only with regard to her friends but in her academic studies as well: a second-semester junior, she still did not have a clear idea of what she really wanted to study or, in a larger sense, what she wanted to do with her life after finishing college. At the end of her sophomore year she had decided on chemistry, but then had changed to sociology at the beginning of her junior year, and more recently had changed to art history; yet she was not completely happy with her choice—"It's as if I want to do everything and yet I don't really want to do anything in particular."

Discussion of Alice

Many adolescents or young adults are troubled about the choices they must make regarding careers, life styles, group loyalties, and other issues relating to a sense of identity. In this case the patient's uncertainty about issues related to identity (choice of career, choice of friends, not knowing who she "really was") is sufficiently severe to cause not only subjective distress but impairment in academic functioning. Since this disturbance has been apparent for more than three months and is not due to another mental disorder, such as an Affective Disorder or a psychotic disorder, the diagnosis of Identity Disorder is made.

Because the patient is over 18, the diagnosis of Borderline Personality Disorder might be considered; but there is no evidence of this more pervasive disorder, such as affective instability, impulsivity, and intense and unstable interpersonal relationships.

DSM-III Diagnosis:

Axis I: 313.82 Identity Disorder (p. 67).

The Housewife

172 A 28-year-old housewife presented with the complaint that she was afraid she would no longer be able to care for her three young children. Over the past year she has had recurrent episodes of "nervousness," light-headedness, rapid breathing, trembling, and dizziness, during which things around her suddenly feel strange and unreal.

Formerly active and outgoing, over the past six months the patient has become afraid to leave home unless in the company of her husband or mother. She now avoids supermarkets and department stores and states that any crowded place makes her uneasy. When unable to avoid such situations, she tries to get near the doorways and always checks for windows and exits. Last summer the family did not go on their usual country vacation because the patient told her husband, "I wouldn't feel safe so far away; it would make me a nervous wreck." Neither she nor her family can understand what is happening to her. Recently she has wanted her mother to stay with her when the children are at home as she worries about what would happen if an accident occurred and she, immobilized by one of her nervous episodes, were unable to help them.

Discussion of The Housewife

Clearly this woman has had recurrent panic attacks, characterized by light-headedness, rapid breathing, trembling, dizziness, and derealization (things around her feel unreal). If she had been seen six months ago, the diagnosis of Panic Disorder might have been made. Now, however, she has developed a common complication of Panic Disorder: because she associates her panic attacks with various places where they might have occurred, she now has a fear of leaving her home and avoids being in public places (supermarkets and department stores) from which escape might be difficult or help not available in case of sudden incapacitation (she tries to get near the doorways and always checks for windows and exits). The increasing constriction of her activities and the domination of her life by these fears indicate the diagnosis of Agoraphobia. Since, as is usually the case with Agoraphobia, there is a history of panic attacks, the full diagnosis is Agoraphobia with Panic Attacks.

DSM-III Diagnosis:

Axis I: 300.21 Agoraphobia with Panic Attacks (p. 227)

Harassed

173 An 18-year-old student sought treatment at the student health center at the request of his dormitory counselor. A shy and rather "straight" young man who had never been involved in any drug use, he had been well until approximately ten days previously. At that time he started college and moved into the dormitory. Shortly after moving in, he became uncomfortable and unhappy because of the noise and lack of privacy. He began to have difficulty sleeping and became increasingly suspicious that people were watching him. One week after entering college, he complained to the counselor that he was being "harassed" and that the FBI and CIA, which suspected him of being the leader of a drug ring, were attempting to entrap him. Thereafter he became increasingly agitated and restless, sometimes angrily accusing other students of being involved in this plot. He was brought to the student health center after such an outburst, in which he also physically attacked another student who he believed had been "watching him too closely."

Discussion of Harassed

Persecutory delusions similar to those in this case are seen in many disorders, e.g., Organic Delusional Disorder, Schizophrenia, Affective Disorder, and Paranoid Disorder. The negative drug history rules out a Substance-induced Organic Delusional Disorder, such as, for example, one due to amphetamine. The absence of bizarre delusions (i.e., delusions that are patently absurd, with no possible basis in fact), prominent hallucinations, and incoherence or loosening of associations excludes a diagnosis of Schizophrenia or Schizophreniform Disorder. There is no pervasive disturbance of mood, as would be expected in an Affective Disorder.

The presence of persecutory delusions for more than one week, in the absence of features suggesting any of the previously mentioned disorders, indicates a Paranoid Disorder, in this case Acute Paranoid Disorder, because the illness has been present for less than six months.

Brief Reactive Psychosis is not an appropriate diagnosis for two reasons. First, the stressor is not sufficiently severe: beginning college is stressful for most people, but it certainly does not cause significant symptoms in almost anyone, as is the case with a death in the family or combat experience. Second, in Brief Reactive Psychosis the psychotic symptoms develop almost immediately following the stressor, whereas in this case they developed over a period of ten days.

DSM-III Diagnosis:

Axis I: 298.30 Acute Paranoid Disorder (p. 197)

Burned

174 A psychiatrist was called to see a 28-year-old woman one week after she had been admitted to the Burn Unit. She had incurred a 28% burn injury in a house fire in which her children, aged three and five, had also been injured and her husband killed. The circumstances of the injury had been quite traumatic in that she was trapped, found it difficult to escape, and risked her own life in attempting to save her children.

On examination the patient was alert and oriented, but quite fearful and anxious. She was noted by the nurses to awaken repeatedly during the night, and she reported recurrent nightmares in which she relived the experience of escaping from her home. During the day she was emotionally labile, at times seeming inappropriately cheerful, given her recent experiences, and at other times responding fearfully to slight noises, such as traffic. The consultation was requested because the nursing staff had become concerned that she seemed almost "numb" to her husband's death and did not appear to be working through her grief appropriately.

Discussion of Burned

In response to an overwhelming stress, this woman is having recurrent dreams of the trauma, symptoms of anxiety (hyperalertness and sleep disturbance), and a numbing of responsiveness to the environment (not experiencing grief about her husband's death). This constitutes the well-recognized syndrome of Post-traumatic Stress Disorder. The subclassification Acute indicates an onset of the symptoms within six months of the stressor and a duration of less than six months at the time of the evaluation.

> This diagnosis takes precedence over Adjustment Disorder, which is a residual category for disturbances that are not severe enough to meet the criteria for a more serious disorder.
>
> **DSM-III Diagnosis:**
>
> **Axis I: 308.30 Post-traumatic Stress Disorder, Acute (p. 238)**

The Boards

175 A 29-year-old married woman was presented as the neurology patient of a Psychiatric Specialty Board examination. Three months previously she had been riding in a car driven by her husband that was involved in a minor traffic accident. She was thrown forward, but was kept from hitting the window or dashboard by her seat belt. Three days later she began to complain of a stiff neck and sharp, radiating pains down both arms, her spine to the small of her back, and both legs. Because an orthopedic consultation failed to uncover the cause of the pain, she was referred to the neurology clinic.

The patient was an attractive, statuesque woman in obvious distress who described her injury and her symptoms in vivid detail, tracing the course of her pains down her arms and legs with her hands. She smiled frequently at the young psychiatrist and at the two examiners who were observing him. She performed each test of neurologic function with precision and appeared to relish the attention. The neurologic examination findings were totally normal.

The psychiatrist inquired into the patient's past history and present life. There was no previous history of emotional disturbance. The patient currently worked as a computer programmer. She had been married for four years and had no children. Until recently her marriage had been smooth, except that her husband sometimes complained that they were "mismatched" sexually, in that he seemed considerably more interested in frequent and "imaginative" sex, while she seemed satisfied with weekly intercourse without variation or much foreplay.

Two weeks before the accident the patient had discovered a woman's phone number in her husband's wallet. When she confronted him with it, he admitted that he had seen several women over the preceding year, mainly for "sexual release." The patient was bitterly hurt and disappointed for several days, then began to get angry and attacked him for his "hang-ups." At the time of the accident, they had been arguing in the car on the way to a friend's house for dinner. After the accident they decided to try harder to please each other in their marriage, including sexually; but because of the pains that the patient was experiencing, they had not been able to have any sexual contact.

The young psychiatrist passed the exam.

Discussion of The Boards

The absence of physical findings and the apparent genuineness of the symptoms rule out physical disorder, Malingering, and a Factitious Disorder. This leaves us with the pain as an undiagnosed physical symptom or Psychogenic Pain Disorder. The issue then revolves around positive evidence for the role of psychological factors in initiating the disorder.

It is difficult to escape the conclusion that this woman's pain serves the function of enabling her to avoid an activity that is noxious to her: having to deal with both her husband's increasing sexual demands and their apparent sexual incompatibility. Further positive evidence of the role of psychological factors is the temporal relationship between the onset of the symptoms and the discovery of and argument about the husband's extramarital sexual activity.

In the past this might have been referred to as Hysterical Pain or Hysterical Neurosis, Conversion Type. In DSM-III, Psychogenic Pain Disorder is used when "conversion" symptoms are limited to pain.

DSM-III Diagnosis:

Axis I: 307.80 Psychogenic Pain Disorder (p. 249)

The Hiker

176 At the age of 61, a high-school science department head, an experienced and enthusiastic camper and hiker, became extremely fearful while on a trek in the mountains. Gradually over the next few months he lost interest in his usual hobbies. Formerly a voracious reader, he stopped reading. He had difficulty doing computations and made gross errors in home financial management. On several occasions he became lost while driving in areas that were formerly familiar to him. He began to write notes to himself so that he would not forget to do errands. Very abruptly, and in uncharacteristic fashion, he decided to retire from work, without discussing his plans with his wife. Intellectual deterioration gradually progressed. He spent most of the day piling miscellaneous objects in one place and then transporting them to another place in the house. He became stubborn and querulous. Eventually he required assistance in shaving and dressing.

When examined six years after the first symptoms had developed, the patient was alert and cooperative. He was disoriented with respect to place and time. He could not recall the names of four of five objects after a five-minute interval of distraction. He could not remember the names of his college and graduate school or the subject in which he had majored. He could describe his job by title only. He thought that Kennedy was President of the United States (1978). He did not know Stalin's nationality. His speech was fluent and well articulated, but he had considerable difficulty finding words and used many long, essentially meaningless, phrases. He called a "cup" a "vase" and identified the rims of glasses as "the holders." He did simple calculations poorly. He could not copy a cube or draw a house. His interpretation of proverbs was concrete, and he had no insight into the nature of his disturbance.

An elementary neurologic examination revealed nothing abnormal, and routine laboratory tests were also negative. A computerized tomography (CT) scan, however, showed marked cortical atrophy.

Discussion of the Hiker

Although the life circumstances of this patient are quite different from those of case number 34, the diagnostic considerations are similar. This patient also has a loss of intellectual abilities (difficulties doing computations and making gross errors in home financial management), memory impairment, impairment in abstract thinking (concrete response to proverbs), other disturbances in higher cortical functioning (aphasia), and personality changes (becoming stubborn and querulous). These signs of global cognitive impairment, in the absence of clouding of consciousness, indicate a Dementia. As in case 34 there are an insidious onset, uniformly progressive deteriorating course, and an absence of focal neurological signs. Thus, the diagnosis is Primary Degenerative Dementia, Presenile Onset, because the age at onset was before 65.

DSM-III Diagnosis:

Axis I: 290.10 Primary Degenerative Dementia, Presenile Onset (p. 126)

CHILD CASES

Musical Bill

177 Bill, age five, was brought by his mother for evaluation because she felt that he was not progressing and developing like other children. She says he speaks only in simple phrases, does not use the pronoun "I" to refer to himself, and does not say "yes" or "no": to indicate agreement, he repeats what he has been told. Upon inquiry, it turns out that the only communication Bill has with others is repeating what he has heard (echolalia). Bill does speak to himself at times, but in a disjointed, disconnected, rambling manner.

Though these were the only spontaneous complaints of the mother, questioning her revealed that Bill does not relate to other children and is totally uninterested in other youngsters. Although he seems to recognize his parents, he is not affectionate or responsive to them. His eye contact is very poor, and he is described as "looking through people." When approached affectionately, he shrinks away and screams.

Bill is described as being extremely interested in music and very good at remembering songs and tunes. He spends a great deal of time listening to records while he rocks back and forth or from foot to foot. At other times, however, he grinds his teeth and stares at his hands while making motions with his fingers.

His mother reports that he was fine until he was about three, when he began to change. Within a few months he began to act in company as though no one were around, and he did not seem to recognize people who were familiar to him. He started spending long periods of time staring into space, looking self-absorbed, as if he were deaf. Since then he has been remote and inaccessible.

Discussion of Musical Bill

This child has severe impairment in social relationships (does not relate to other children, shrinks away and screams when approached), constricted affect ("remote and inaccessible," "looking through people"), oddities of motor movement ("rocks back and forth," makes "motions with his fingers" as he stares at his hands), and abnormalities of speech (echolalia).

This syndrome, developing after 30 months of age and before 12 years of age, in the absence of delusions, hallucinations, incoherence, or marked loosening of associations, indicates Childhood Onset Pervasive Developmental Disorder. The current presence of the full syndrome is coded in the fifth digit.

DSM-III Diagnosis:

Axis I: **299.90 Childhood Onset Pervasive Developmental Disorder, Full Syndrome Present (p. 91)**

Tiny Tina

178 Tina is a small, sweet-faced, freckled, ten-year-old who has been referred by a pediatrician who was unsuccessful in treating her for refusing to go to school. Her difficulties began on the first day of school one year ago when she cried and hid in the basement. She agreed to go to school only when her mother promised to go with her and stay to have lunch with her at school. For the next three months, on school days Tina had a variety of somatic complaints, such as headaches and "tummyaches," and each day would go to school only reluctantly, after much cajoling by her parents. Soon thereafter she could be gotten to school only if her parents lifted her out of bed, dressed and fed her, and drove her to school. Often she would leave school during the day and return home. Finally, in the spring the school social-worker consulted Tina's pediatrician, who instituted a behavior-shaping program with the help of her parents. Because this program was of only limited help, the pediatrician had referred Tina now, at the beginning of the school year.

According to her mother, despite Tina's many absences from school last year, she performed well. During this time she also happily participated in all other activities, including Girl Scout meetings, sleepovers with several friends (usually also with her sister), and family outings. Her mother wonders if her taking a part-time bookkeeping job two years ago, and the sudden death of a maternal grandfather to whom Tina was particularly close, might have been responsible for the child's difficulties.

When Tina was interviewed, she at first minimized any problems about school, insisting that "everything is okay," and that she got good grades and liked all the teachers. When this subject was pursued, she became angry and gave a lot of "I don't know" responses as to why, then, she often refused to go to school. Eventually she said that kids teased her about her size, calling her "Shrimp" and "Shorty"; but she gave the impression, as well as actually stated, that she liked school and her teachers. She finally admitted that what bothered her was leaving home. She could not specify why, but hinted that she was afraid something would happen, though to whom or to what she did not say; but she confessed that she felt uncomfortable when all of her family was out of sight.

On the Rorschach there was evidence of obsessive rumination about catastrophic events involving injury to members of her family and themes concerning family disruption.

Discussion of Tiny Tina

All of Tina's problems involve a fear of going to school. The question is: Is it school that she is really afraid of, or is it separating herself from her parents? The evidence that she is really afraid of school is her claim that the other children tease her and her willing participation in other activities away from home, such as sleepovers and Girl Scout meetings. But Tina herself concludes that it is really her fear that something bad will happen when her family is out of her sight that is behind her refusal to go to school. We are inclined to accept this explanation. An enforced six hours away from her family every day is apparently more troubling to her than an occasional hour at a Girl Scout meeting or a sleepover, usually with her sister.

In the absence of any more pervasive disorder, the excessive anxiety concerning separation from the family and unrealistic worry about harm befalling them, reluctance to go to school, and complaints of physical symptoms on school days, over a period of more than two weeks, all indicate Separation Anxiety Disorder. We would not quarrel with a clinician who wished to make this diagnosis provisional pending further clarification of Tina's distress about being teased. If she is excessively fearful of the possibility of being humiliated or embarrassed in public, then the diagnosis of Social Phobia should be considered as an alternative or as an additional diagnosis.

DSM-III Diagnosis:

Axis I: 309.21 Separation Anxiety Disorder (p. 53)

Helen

179

Helen is a little girl, 6 years, 10 months of age, who presented with an essentially unremarkable early history that included walking at 11 months, standing at 9 months, first words at 12 months, toilet training at 24 months, and self-dressing at 36 months. The mother reported that problems started when the girl began first grade, at which time Helen started soiling and wetting, both in class and at night in bed, and talking less. These problems continued throughout the first grade and into the second grade, despite a change of schools and numerous consultations with a pediatrician, who reported that the only medical problem was epilepsy, for which phenobarbital was prescribed. Recently, Helen had started making remarks such as "I'm dumb" and "I can't do things." She cried easily and had no close friends. The schoolteacher reported that, according to test results, the girl had a full-scale intelligence of 90 and at the beginning of second grade was reading at fourth-grade level and doing spelling and arithmetic at early third-grade level.

During the mental state examination Helen sat quietly, looking unhappy. She did not admit to being sad, but did state that she had "scary nightmares" and that she didn't have any friends at school because she got teased.

Discussion of Helen

Helen has a variety of problems: urinary and fecal soiling, low self-esteem, "scary nightmares," no close friends at school, and epilepsy. With the information available, the only diagnosable mental disorders are Functional Enuresis and Functional Encopresis, because of the repeated involuntary soiling beyond the time when continence is usually expected (five to six years old for urine, and four years old for feces). Although she has a seizure disorder, it is probably not the cause of the incontinence, since there is no mention that the incontinence occurs only during seizures. Nonetheless, the seizure disorder, because of its importance in management of this child, would be noted on Axis III.

Her problems with self-esteem and social isolation might well be related to the Functional Enuresis and Encopresis.

DSM-III Diagnosis:

Axis I: **307.60 Functional Enuresis (p. 80)**
               307.70 Functional Encopresis (p. 82)
Axis III: **Epilepsy**

George

180 George, five years old, was referred by his pediatrician for evaluation of global developmental delays and bizarre behavior. The parents' chief complaint is that George has been "unable to learn."

George was bottle-fed, and within the first several months demonstrated a resistance to being held, screaming and becoming rigid. He was soon noted by his parents to be "different" from his two older siblings in that he seemed to be oblivious to both people and objects in his environment. In addition, he spent what appeared to be an excessive amount of time sleeping. At about six months he developed a recurrent pattern of screaming for several hours that was unresponsive to any intervention.

Developmental milestones were delayed. He sat at 9 months with assistance, and without assistance at 21 months. He did not begin walking until almost two and a half. Toilet training has not been accomplished even now. He has never used words with meaning, although he started babbling at 15 months and continues to do so.

His parents have sought help at this time because George is unable to continue to attend a specialized residential school program because of the following behaviors, which have recently intensified: He bites other children and teachers indiscriminately and without any clear-cut precipitants. He sometimes bites or scratches himself, particularly when some ritualistic behavior that he is engaging in is interrupted, such as standing on his toes for hours at a time, slapping himself, wandering around the room, or standing for long periods of time in front of a radiator. He often seems to be unaware of his environment and bumps into people or objects. He has no communicative speech and does not seem to comprehend speech. He shows no particular interest in toys or other play objects, and when offered something either puts the object in his mouth or drops it.

George was a planned-for and desired child. Labor and delivery were all normal. Two years ago he had a grand mal seizure, and since that time has been on anticonvulsant medication. Since then he has had a total of five seizures. His medical history is otherwise unremarkable. Formal psychological testing could not be performed.

Discussion of George

Almost from birth it was apparent that George was seriously disturbed in the way he was relating to his environment. He was unresponsive to "people and objects in his environment." There was

279

virtually no language development (he never used words with meaning, although he started babbling at 15 months and continues to do
so). His responses to the environment were frequently bizarre
(screaming and becoming rigid when held, standing on his toes for
hours at a time, standing for long periods of time in front of a radiator).
All of these features beginning before the age of 30 months indicate
the Pervasive Developmental Disorder Infantile Autism. This is
further subclassified as Full Syndrome Present to differentiate it from
a residual state.

Some children with Infantile Autism may be normally or even
exceptionally intelligent. In George's case, however, the developmental milestones that do not involve language development, such
as standing, walking, and toilet training, have all been delayed. This
indicates the additional diagnosis of Mental Retardation—a feature
that makes the prognosis for the Infantile Autism extremely poor.
Since testing is not possible, the subtype (level of severity) of the
Mental Retardation is Unspecified.

DSM-III Diagnosis:

Axis I: **299.00 Infantile Autism, Full Syndrome Present (p. 89)**
          319.00 Unspecified Mental Retardation (p. 40)
Axis III: Seizure Disorder

Evelyn

181 The parents of 13½-year-old Evelyn were very concerned that she was not doing well in seventh grade. She
had failed one grade in the past and, although anxious to
achieve and hardworking, she was not doing well again. Her mother,
who was a teacher, spent many hours in the evenings tutoring her
daughter, and the girl had been to the school psychologist for a battery
of tests, which indicated above-average intelligence. The mother reported that the girl was good in sports and in good health, although
she had allergies and wore glasses.

Examination revealed a pleasant, well-dressed, left-handed girl who
expressed considerable fears and worries centered around school and
tests. She was given the Wide-Range Achievement Test and scored at
grade levels 9.4 for arithmetic, 5.5 for spelling, and 4.8 for reading.
When asked to read a passage aloud, she made many substitutions of
words, generally choosing words with appropriate meanings that did
not resemble the correct word visually or phonetically. For example,
she read "officers" for "police" and "point" for "spot." Occasionally

she reversed the order of the words she read, but her comprehension was good.

Discussion of Evelyn

The difficulties here are apparently limited to reading and spelling. Evelyn has above-average intelligence and normal scores on achievement tests of arithmetic, but markedly low scores for spelling and reading. When examined, she displays difficulties in recognizing words and in reversing their order, but is able to compensate owing to good comprehension. Although she wears glasses, presumably reduced visual acuity is not responsible for her reading difficulties. Thus, the diagnosis is Developmental Reading Disorder, noted on Axis II.

DSM-III Diagnosis:

Axis II: 315.00 Developmental Reading Disorder (p. 94)

Abducted

182 Amy, a three year-old girl, was referred by the pediatric clinic because her mother reported that her daughter has had a variety of problems for the last five months, ever since she had been abducted for one month by her father, who lives out of state. According to her mother, although Amy had been successfully toilet trained, she wet her bed constantly during the abduction. Since that time she "chews the skin off her fingers below the nails and twists her hands. She is scared of the dark and wakes up seeing things or thinks someone is after her or coming into her room." She describes scary dreams of "monsters" and has trouble sleeping.

Her parents were unhappy during the two years they were together and quarreled frequently. Her father came from a financially poor family and did not complete high school. He always talked as if he had lots of money; but after they had separated, the mother discovered that he had a long police record, involving rape and assault and battery. He was involved in using illegal credit cards, doing contract work without a license, and not paying state and federal income taxes. There was a warrant out for his arrest in their state.

When interviewed, Amy had her hair attractively styled with pigtails, and had small red earrings and colorful play clothes. She was cooperative and left her mother with only slight hesitation. She quickly showed the interviewer that she could tie her own shoelaces with ease. She easily became engaged in play, but her play involved many frightening themes: a father puppet repeatedly scared a baby puppet, a tiger choked a mouse, and a cow was eaten up by a frog.

Discussion of Abducted

Amy's difficulties apparently began when she was abducted by her father five months previously. Since that time she has had various symptoms of anxiety (chewing the skin off her fingers, fears of the dark and nightmares). A transient reaction to the abduction might be expected, but the persistence of the symptoms for five months is in excess of a normal and expected reaction.

The absence of the multiplicity of symptoms that would suggest a generalized and persistent anxiety state rules out the diagnosis of Overanxious Disorder. There is no evidence of any of the other anxiety disorders, such as Separation Anxiety Disorder or a Phobic Disorder.

When anxiety symptoms not severe enough to meet the criteria for a specific mental disorder are precipitated by a psychosocial stressor and are in excess of an expected reaction, the diagnosis Adjustment Disorder with Anxious Mood is made.

Amy was incontinent during the one-month abduction by her father, but since this did not persist, it would seem to be not significant enough to warrant a separate diagnosis of Functional Enuresis.

DSM-III Diagnosis:

Axis I: 309.24 Adjustment Disorder with Anxious Mood (p. 300)

Compulsions

183 Alan, a ten-year-old boy, is brought for a consultation by his mother because of "severe compulsions." The mother reports that the child at various times has to run and clear his throat, touch the doorknob twice before entering any door, tilt his head from side to side, rapidly blink his eyes, and touch the ground with his hands all of a sudden by flexing his whole body. These "compulsions" began two years ago. The first was the eye-blinking, and then the others followed, with a waxing and waning course. The movements occur more frequently when the patient is anxious or under stress. The last symptom to appear was the repetitive touching of the doorknobs. The consultation was scheduled after the child began to make the middle finger sign while saying "fuck."

When examined, Alan reported that he did not know most of the time when the movements were going to occur except for the touching of the doorknob. Upon questioning he said that before he felt he had to touch the doorknob, he got the thought of doing it and tried to push it out of his head, but he couldn't because it kept coming back until he touched the doorknob several times. Then he felt better. When asked what would happen if someone did not let him touch the doorknob, he said he would just get mad, and that his father had tried to stop him and he had had a temper tantrum. During the interview the child grunted, cleared his throat, turned his head, and rapidly blinked his eyes several times. At other times he tried to make it appear as if he had voluntarily been trying to perform these movements.

Past history and physical and neurological examination were totally unremarkable except for the abnormal movements and sounds. The mother reported that her youngest uncle had had similar symptoms when he was an adolescent, but she could not elaborate any further. She stated that she and her husband had always been "very compulsive," by which she meant only that they were quite well organized and stuck to routines.

Discussion of Compulsions

The mother describes Alan's difficulties as "compulsions," because she realizes that he is compelled to perform senseless acts. In a true compulsions, however, there are also mounting anxiety and the sense that the compulsion will ward off an undesirable future event or situation. For example, in a hand-washing or counting compulsion the patient may have the feeling that something terrible will happen unless the compulsion is acted upon. In this case there is only mounting frustration until the act is performed, and then a sense of relief. Hence, these are not compulsions, but a variety of motor and verbal tics that often look purposeful but in fact serve no purpose. In an effort to avoid embarrassment, the patient sometimes tries to disguise them as voluntary, purposeful movements.

The combination of motor and verbal tics with a duration of over one year establishes the diagnosis of Tourette's Disorder.

DSM-III Diagnosis:

Axis I: 307.23 Tourette's Disorder (p. 77)

What's Happening?

184 The parents of nine-year-old Benjamin consulted a pediatrician after he had awakened many nights, very frightened by what they assumed to be bad dreams. Beginning several months earlier, and several times a week thereafter, Benjamin would come downstairs, after having been asleep for only a short time, looking dazed and terrified, breathing rapidly, with widely dilated pupils and "goose pimples." At such times he kept asking, "What's happening?" It usually took 15 or 20 minutes to calm him down enough so that he could return to bed. He was never able to remember any bad dreams, but said that he just woke up feeling very strange and frightened that something terrible would happen.

The event that prompted the consultation occurred when Ben was home from school recovering from an ear infection. His mother had left the house to do some shopping, and he apparently fell asleep on the couch, awoke in a state of terror, and ran out of the house, in winter, in his bare feet, and hitched a ride to a neighbor's house, where his frantic mother finally found him.

Discussion of What's Happening?

Benjamin's sleep disturbance is characterized by abrupt awakening after being asleep for only a short time, signs of extreme anxiety (rapid breathing, dilated pupils, piloerection), and relative unresponsiveness to the efforts of others to comfort him. Rapid eye movement (REM) sleep nightmares are ruled out by the occurrence of the episodes shortly after falling asleep (during non-REM sleep) and by Benjamin's inability to recall distinct and vivid dreams. Epileptic seizures during sleep with postictal confusion may present a similar clinical picture, but this diagnosis is unlikely as there is no mention of seizures occurring during the day. Sleepwalking Disorder is suggested by Benjamin's running out of the house; but if there is any anxiety in Sleepwalking Disorder, it is mild and occurs only *after* the sleepwalking.

In fact, Benjamin's mother was happy to hear from her pediatrician that Benjamin suffered from Pavor Nocturnus, a relatively innocuous disorder that usually disappears in adolescence. In DSM-III it is called simply Sleep Terror Disorder.

DSM-III Diagnosis:

Axis I: 307.46 Sleep Terror Disorder (p. 86)

Sad Sandy

185 Sandy, a bright nine-year-old boy was taken to the pediatric emergency room after his mother found him in the bathroom pressing a knife to his stomach. Examination revealed no more than a minor scratch. Upon questioning, the child told the psychiatric resident that he wanted to die because he didn't want to continue to live the way he did. When specifically questioned, he reported that he was feeling sad, bad, and angry most of the time, that he wasn't having any fun anymore, and that he felt very tired all the time. He had no difficulty falling asleep, but regularly woke up at about 3:00 A.M. and then again at 5:30 A.M. and couldn't fall asleep again. He also reported that he had heard a single voice talking to him, telling him to kill himself with a knife to his belly. He identified the voice as that of his grandfather, who had died four years previously from a stroke. He had been hearing such a voice for the last month.

Sandy's mother corroborated his report from her observations and added that the onset was about six months ago and that he had gotten progressively worse. Four months ago he began to steal from her and became quite disobedient and had temper tantrums. During the last two weeks he had resisted going to school and cried all the way there. She also reported that he had been very preoccupied with the separation of his parents two years earlier, and felt it was all his fault. His teacher had reported to her that his attention span was rapidly decreasing and that he had withdrawn from friends and appeared quite sluggish.

Discussion of Sad Sandy

This case illustrates that a major depressive episode, identical with that seen in adults, can occur in a prepubertal child. There is the persistent depressed mood (feeling sad and bad), loss of pleasure, and such associated depressive symptoms as suicidal ideation and impulses, loss of energy, hypoactivity (appeared quite sluggish), sleep disturbance, inappropriate guilt, and diminished concentration. The fifth-digit subclassification of with Psychotic Features is made because of the presence of auditory hallucinations, although it is not clear whether the child recognizes that the voice is a product of his imagination, which would indicate intact reality testing and, therefore, strictly speaking, no psychotic features.

Although in this case there is also a disturbance of conduct (stealing and disobedience) and school refusal, these are considered age-specific associated features of the depressive episode and do not indicate the need for an additional diagnosis, such as a Conduct Disorder.

DSM-III Diagnosis:

Axis I: **296.24 Major Depression, Single Episode, with Psychotic Features (p. 213)**

It's Time to Go

186 Otto, 3 years, 9 months, old, was referred by a pediatrician for "poor speech development." The pediatrician also noted a history of chronic ear infections with intermittent hearing loss. His mother reported that the child was "fine," having only a few minor problems with sleep, eating, shyness, and tantrums.

Otto was not currently attending any school, but his mother had taken him for six months to a preschool. For the first four months he had cried almost constantly and had had no contact with peers or teachers, but for the last two months he had had some limited interactions with the other children. He never spoke directly to the teacher, but toward the end of the six months in school he had become otherwise cooperative.

Testing by a psychometrist revealed a performance intelligence of 100. No verbal intelligence score was obtained because of Otto's refusal to take part in verbal tasks. The psychometrist reported that he cried throughout most of the evaluation and made no spontaneous remarks at all, although he did echo one or two of her sentences.

During the mental status examination Otto was completely silent. He showed a great deal of misery at separating from his mother, but finally was able to stay alone with the examiner and not cry. He was very guarded and took part in only limited play with the examiner. His affect was somewhat apathetic. Upon leaving he was heard to say to his mother, "It's time to go now."

Discussion of It's Time to Go

This unhappy child apparently has a variety of problems, such as shyness, tantrums, and problems with sleeping and eating, in addition to refusing to talk. Many of these problems are not described in sufficient detail to make even provisional diagnoses—for example, the shyness suggests the possibility of Avoidant Disorder of Childhood or Adolescence, and the constricted affect and impairment in social relations suggest the possibility of a Pervasive Developmental Disorder. However, the refusal to speak to the schoolteacher, the psychometrist, and the interviewer would seem to warrant a provisional diagnosis of Elective Mutism. If, with more information, it appeared that Otto had a mental disorder other than Elective Mutism, then one would have to consider to what extent the refusal to speak was merely a symptom of that other mental disorder. If such were the case, Elective Mutism would not be given as an additional diagnosis.

Since the chronic ear infections with intermittent hearing loss may have some relationship to the refusal to speak, they should be recorded on Axis III as potentially relevant to the Axis I mental disorder.

DSM-III Diagnosis:

Axis I: **313.23 Elective Mutism (Provisional) (p. 63)**
Axis III: Chronic ear infections with intermittent hearing loss

Baby Susan

187 Susan was admitted to the hospital at six months of age, by an aunt, for evaluation of failure to gain weight. She had been born into an impoverished family after an unplanned, uncomplicated pregnancy. During the first four months of her life, she gained weight steadily. Regurgitation was noted during the fifth month and increased in severity to the point where she was regurgitating after every feeding. After each feeding, Susan would engage in one of two behaviors: *(a)* she would open her mouth, elevate her tongue, and rapidly thrust it back and forward, after which milk would appear at the back of her mouth and slowly trickle out; or *(b)* she would vigorously suck her thumb and place fingers in her mouth, following which milk would slowly flow out of the corner of her mouth.

In the past two months Susan had been cared for by a number of people, including her aunt and paternal grandmother. Her parents were making a marginal marital adjustment.

Discussion of Baby Susan

Failure to gain weight or weight loss in an infant, once organic illnesses such as congenital anomalies have been ruled out, suggests either an Eating Disorder (Rumination Disorder of Infancy) or failure to thrive because of grossly inadequate care (Reactive Attachment Disorder of Infancy). It is clear that in this case the child is not gaining weight because of the regurgitation after each feeding. This, plus the history of a normal period of eating and weight gain, is characteristic of Rumination Disorder.

DSM-III Diagnosis:

Axis I: 307.53 Rumination Disorder of Infancy (p. 73)

Creative Misfit

188 Rachel, a 16-year-old suburban high-school junior, agreed to see a social worker at the urging of her mother, who was very upset when she found drugs in Rachel's room. The patient is an attractive, fairly articulate girl who says that she has been smoking marijuana almost daily since age 14. She has also "tripped" on LSD five or six times. Although she admits to intermittent feelings of depression and loneliness, she claims she smokes only because it intensifies her perceptions. She is a talented painter, and has been "hanging around the art room" with a group of creative misfits since her freshman year. She is fairly productive in her artwork, but her academic average has declined from A in the 8th grade to her current C. She usually smokes in the morning before school, has a "joint" for lunch, and gets "high" with her friends after school. Her friendships with both sexes are close and relatively stable. There have been no serious problems at home until the incident that prompted this visit.

Discussion of Creative Misfit

Although she claims to use marijuana merely to heighten her sensitivity, this young lady shows signs of impaired functioning (her academic average has declined) that, it is reasonable to assume, are related to drug use. This, in conjunction with a pathological pattern of use (daily use during school hours), justifies the diagnosis of

Cannabis Abuse. The course is coded as Continuous since she has been maladaptively using the drug for over six months.

She has also used LSD five or six times; but there is no additional information, such as frequent "bad trips," that would justify the additional diagnosis of Hallucinogen Abuse.

An associated Personality Disorder is likely, but there is inadequate information in this area.

DSM-III Diagnosis:

Axis I: 305.21 Cannabis Abuse, Continuous (p. 176)

Thin Tim

189 Eight-year-old Tim was referred by a pediatrician who asked for an emergency evaluation because of a serious weight loss during the past year. Tim is extremely concerned about his weight and weighs himself daily. He complains that he is too fat, and if he does not lose weight, he cuts back on food. He has lost ten pounds in the past year and feels that he is too fat, though it is clear that he is underweight. In desperation his parents have removed the scales from the house; and, as a result, Tim is keeping a record of the calories that he eats daily. He spends a lot of time on this, checking and rechecking that he has done it just right.

In addition, he is described as being obsessed with cleanliness and neatness. Currently he has no friends because he refuses to visit them, feeling that their houses are "dirty"; he gets upset when another child touches him. He is always checking whether he is doing things the way they "should" be done. He becomes very agitated and anxious about this. He has to get up at least two hours before leaving for school each day in order to give himself time to get ready. Recently, he woke up at 1:30 in the morning to prepare for school.

Discussion of Thin Tim

The emergency evaluation is because of Tim's recent weight loss. He has lost ten pounds in the last year, during which time a boy of his age might have been expected to gain about that amount. This means he has actually lost 20 pounds, which undoubtedly equals the weight loss of 25% that is required for a diagnosis of Anorexia Nervosa.

Although it is unusual to see this disorder in a male and in one so young, Tim also has the other characteristic features: fear of becoming fat, feeling fat even when obviously underweight, and refusal to maintain his weight in the normal range.

Although not the focus of attention, Tim's preoccupation with various recurrent thoughts concerning dirtiness causes him considerable distress. Moreover, he has to check whether he is doing things the way they "should" be done, and such activities apparently interfere with his normal functioning (he has to get up several hours before school in order to get ready). Although he does not describe these recurrent thoughts and repetitive acts as senseless, it is reasonable to assume that they do intrude into his consciousness and are beyond his control, and hence represent true obsessions and compulsions. Thus, an additional diagnosis of Obsessive Compulsive Disorder is made and is listed second, since the initial focus of attention is the eating problem.

There is phobic avoidance (he won't visit friends' houses because they might be dirty), but the additional diagnosis of a Simple Phobia is not made because phobic avoidance is a commonly associated feature of Obsessive Compulsive Disorder.

DSM-III Diagnosis:

Axis I: **307.10 Anorexia Nervosa (p. 69)**
300.30 Obsessive Compulsive Disorder (p. 235)

Hard to Handle

190 Eight-year-old Fred was referred to a school counselor because his teacher "could not handle" his behavior. The boy was reported to be inattentive, often not listening or being easily distracted. He was inappropriately active in the classroom, often fidgeting in his seat and needing to get up to sharpen his pencil or go to the bathroom. His teachers complained that he frequently yelled out answers to questions in class without waiting to hear them to their conclusion. He had difficulty concentrating and organizing his schoolwork and needed constant supervision to get his homework done.

Discussion of Hard to Handle

This child shows signs of developmentally inappropriate inattention (often not listening, easily distracted, difficulty concentrating on schoolwork), impulsivity (calling out in class, difficulty organizing schoolwork, needing constant supervision), and hyperactivity (constant fidgeting and difficulty staying seated). When the disturbances are not due to a more serious disorder, such as Schizophrenia or Severe or Profound Mental Retardation, these are the hallmarks of Attention Deficit Disorder with Hyperactivity.

DSM-III Diagnosis:

Axis I: 314.01 Attention Deficit Disorder with Hyperactivity (p. 43)

Carnival Con

191 Dennis, a 15-year-old boy, was referred to a child guidance clinic after being caught with 9 others, stealing tickets from a carnival. He was well known to the police and was considered skilled in the art of petty larceny. A community worker was able to arrange for him to go to a summer camp for eight weeks, where he became leader of a clique in his cabin. At camp he showed no respect for the ownership of articles he wanted to use. He displayed a strong, personal loyalty to his buddies, refusing to implicate them in any way, but great hostility to the police. He expressed no guilt about stealing.

Discussion of Carnival Con

The V code Childhood or Adolescent Antisocial Behavior is not appropriate because there is a *pattern* of antisocial behavior, rather than one or two isolated episodes.

The repeated stealing and use of other children's belongings without respect for their ownership indicate a pattern of conduct in which the basic rights of others are violated. When this pattern has been present for at least six months, a diagnosis of Conduct Disorder is made. The subtype of the Conduct Disorder is Socialized because of the boy's adequate peer relations (became leader of a clique and showed loyalty to buddies) and Nonaggressive because the antisocial behavior does not involve physical violence against persons or robbery outside the home involving confrontation with a victim.

DSM-III Diagnosis:

Axis I: 312.21 Conduct Disorder, Socialized, Nonaggressive (p. 49)

Special Dinners

192 At their wits' end, the parents of Jordan, a six-year-old boy, brought him to a child psychiatrist for evaluation. Their already shaky marrige was being severely tested by conflict over their son's behavior at home and at school. The mother complained bitterly that the father, frequently away from home on business, "overindulged" their son. In point of fact, the son would argue and throw temper tantrums and insist on continuing games, books, etc., whenever his father put him to bed, so that a 7:30 P.M. bedtime was delayed until 10:30, 11:00, or even 11:30 at night. Similarly, the father had been known to cook four or five different meals for his son's dinner if the son stubbornly insisted that he would not eat what had been prepared. At school several teachers had complained that he was stubborn, often spoke out of turn, and refused to comply with classroom rules.

On questioning by the psychiatrist, the parents denied that their son had ever been destructive of property, lied excessively, or stole. When interviewed, the child was observed to be cheerful and able to sit quietly in his chair, listening attentively to the questions that were asked him. His answers, however, were brief, and he tended to minimize the extent of the problems he was having with his parents and teachers.

Discussion of Special Dinners

Although disturbances in the functioning of this family unit may well have contributed to this child's difficulties, the child now shows a pervasive pattern of maladaptive behavior that is not limited to his interaction with his parents. Temper tantrums, breaking school rules, argumentativeness, provocative behavior, and stubbornness are all part of a persistent pattern of disobedience, negativism, and provocative opposition to authority figures. Since this does not involve the violation of the basic rights of others or of major age-appropriate societal norms or rules (such as physical aggression or truancy), this is not a Conduct Disorder. Since there is no evidence of a more serious disorder, such as Schizophrenia or a Pervasive Developmental Disorder, the diagnosis of Oppositional Disorder is made.

The specification of the V code for Parent–Child Problem is not made because the disturbance is not limited to interaction between the child and his parents; the disturbed behavior is also seen at school. Parent–Child Problem is not given in *addition* to Oppositional Disorder because the disturbed parent–child interaction is symptomatic of the child's mental disorder.

DSM-III Diagnosis:

Axis I: 313.81 Oppositional Disorder (p. 64)

Historical Cases

Historical Cases

Emil Kraepelin (1856–1926)

Kraepelin, a professor of psychiatry in Germany, provided the basis for modern classification of mental disorders. He used the natural history of the illness—its onset, course, and outcome—and its clinical picture as the basis for classification. Thus, he differentiated Maniacal-Depressive Insanity from Dementia Praecox (later renamed Schizophrenia by Bleuler). He subdivided Dementia Praecox into three types: catatonic, hebephrenic, and paranoid.

His major textbook was first published in 1883, and went into nine editions. The following cases are taken verbatim from his *Lectures in Clinical Psychiatry,** first published in 1904. They provided generations of clinicians with detailed illustrations of his diagnostic concepts.

Music Student

193 You see here before you a student of music, aged nineteen, who has been ill for about a year. The highly-gifted patient, without any tangible cause, while studying music, became depressed, felt ill at ease and lonely, made all manner of plans, which he always gave up, for changing his place of residence and his profession, for he could come to no fixed resolutions. During a visit to Munich, he felt as if people in the street had something to say to him, and as if he were talked about everywhere. He heard an offensive remark at an inn at the next table, which he answered rudely. Next day he was seized with the apprehension that his remark might be taken as *lèse majesté*. He heard that students asked for him at the door, and he

---

*Kraepelin E: *Lectures on Clinical Psychiatry.* Translated by Thomas P. Johnstone, New York, Hafner Publishing Co., 1968. "Music Student," p. 74; "Schoolmaster," p. 262; "Wicked Young Lady," p. 265; "Innkeeper," p. 97; "Stately Gentleman," p. 140; "Widow," p. 157; "Farmer," p. 4; "Oberrealschul Student," p. 77; "Suffering Lady," p. 252; "Onanistic Student," p. 21; "Factory Girl," p. 83.

left Munich post-haste with every precautionary measure, because he thought himself accompanied and followed on the way. Since then he overheard people in the street who threatened to shoot him, and to set fire to his house, and on that account he burned no light in his room. In the streets voices pointed out the way he ought to go so as to avoid being shot. Behind doors, windows, hedges, pursuers seemed everywhere to lurk. He also heard long conversations of not very flattering purport as to his person. In consequence of this, he withdrew altogether from society, but yet behaved in such an ordinary way that his relatives, whom he visited, did not notice his delusions. At last the many mocking calls which he heard at every turn provoked the thought of shooting himself.

After about six months he felt more free, "comfortable, enterprising, and cheerful," began to talk a lot, to compose, criticised everything, concocted great schemes, and was insubordinate to his teacher. The voices still continued, and he recognised in them the whisperings of master spirits. Hallucinations of sight now became very marked. The patient saw Beethoven's image radiant with joy at his genius; saw Goethe, whom he had abused, in a threatening attitude; masked old men and ideal female forms floated through his room. He saw lightning and glorious brilliancy of colours, which he interpreted partly as the flowing out of his great genius, partly as attestations of applause from the dead.

He regarded himself as the Messiah, preached openly against prostitution, wished to enter into an ideal connection with a female student of music, whom he sought for in strange houses, composed the "Great Song of Love," and on account of this priceless work was brought to the hospital by those who envied him, as he said.

The patient is quite collected, and gives connected information as to his personal circumstances. He is clear as to time and place, but betrays himself by judging his position falsely, inasmuch as he takes us for hypnotizers, who wish to try experiments with him. He does not look upon himself as ill; at the most as somewhat nervously overexcited. Through diplomatic questions we learn that all people know his thoughts; if he writes, the words are repeated before the door. In the creaking of boards, in the whistle of the train, he hears calls, exhortations, orders, threats. Christ appears to him in the night, or a golden figure as the spirit of his father; coloured signs of special meaning are given through the window. In prolonged conversation the patient very quickly loses the thread, and produces finally a succession of fine phrases, which wind up unexpectedly with some facetious question. His mood is arrogant, conceited, generally condescending, occasionally transitorily irritated or apprehensive. The patient speaks much and willingly, talks aloud to himself, and marches boisterously up and down the ward, interests himself more than is desirable in his fellow-patients, seeking to cheer them and to manage them. He is very busy, too, with letter-writing and composing, but only produces fugitive, carelessly jotted down written work, with numerous marginal notes.

Kraepelin's Diagnosis: Manical-Depressive Insanity

Discussion of Music Student

There are two phases of this illness. The first appears to be a severe major depressive episode, with psychotic features, although the only other affective features mentioned in addition to depressed mood are indecisiveness (". . . he could come to no fixed resolutions.") and suicidal ideas (". . . the thought of shooting himself"). The psychotic features during this period consisted of mood-incongruent persecutory delusions and hallucinations, since they apparently had no relation to typical depressive themes such as deserved punishment, personal inadequacy, or guilt. There were persecutory delusions ("Behind doors, windows, hedges, pursuers seemed everywhere to lurk.") and hallucinations (". . . long conversations of not very flattering purport as to his person"). There were ideas of reference (". . . he felt as if people in the street had something to say to him, . . . as if he were talked about everywhere") and delusions of reference ("He heard that students asked for him at the door, and he left Munich post-haste with every precautionary measure, because he thought himself accompanied and followed on the way.").

Currently the patient is clearly in a manic episode. There is an elevated mood with grandiosity ("He regarded himself as the Messiah . . ."), hyperactivity (". . . marches boisterously up and down the ward . . ."), overtalkativeness, and poor judgment (". . . interests himself more than is desirable in his fellow-patients, seeking to cheer them and to manage them"). There is a suggestion of loose associations and possibly flight of ideas ("In prolonged conversation the patient very quickly loses the thread, and produces finally a succession of fine phrases, which wind up unexpectedly with some facetious question."). Most of the other psychotic features are mood-congruent in that they are associated with themes of inflated worth, knowledge, and identity. Hallucinations ("The patient saw Beethoven's image radiant with joy at his genius . . .") and delusions (". . . composed the 'Great Song of Love,' and on account of this priceless work was brought to the hospital by those who envied him . . .") are present. In addition, there were illusions ("In the creaking of boards, in the whistle of the train, he hears calls, exhortations, orders, threats.").

It is interesting to note the presence of certain psychotic symptoms such as possible thought broadcasting (". . . all people know his thoughts; if he writes, the words are repeated before the door"). Even though many clinicians have regarded such symptoms as indicative of Schizophrenia, both Kraepelin and DSM-III do not regard these as incompatible with an Affective Disorder. In this case there are both a manic and a major depressive episode, but the presence of a manic episode alone is sufficient for a diagnosis of Bipolar Disorder.

DSM-III Diagnosis:

Axis I: **296.44 Bipolar Disorder, Manic, with Psychotic Features (Mood-congruent) (p. 217)**

The Schoolmaster

194 First you see a schoolmaster, aged thirty-one, who came to the hospital of his own accord four weeks ago in order to be treated here. The patient was, in fact, violently agitated when he had to come here, sank down on his bed, and said that the discussion in the hospital would cost him his life. He begged to be allowed to sit in the hall before the lecture began, so that he could see the audience come in gradually, as he could not face a number of people so suddenly.

The patient is quite collected, clear, and well-ordered in his statements. He says that one of his sisters suffers in the same way as himself. He traces the beginning of his illness back to about eleven years ago. Being a very clever lad, he became a schoolmaster, and had to do a great deal of mental work to qualify. Gradually he began to fear that he had a serious disease, and was going to die of heart apoplexy. All the assurances and examinations of his doctor could not convince him. For this reason he suddenly left his appointment and went home one day, seven years ago, being afraid that he would die shortly. After this he consulted every possible doctor, and took long holidays repeatedly, always recovering a little, but invariably finding that his fears returned speedily. These were gradually reinforced by the fear of gatherings of people. He was also unable to cross large squares or go through wide streets by himself. He avoided using the railway for fear of collisions and derailments, and he would not travel in a boat lest it might capsize. He was seized with apprehension on bridges and when skating, and at last the apprehension of apprehension itself caused palpitations and oppression on all sorts of occasions. He did not improve after his marriage three years ago. He was domesticated, good-natured, and manageable, only "too soft." On the way here, when he had finally made up his mind to place himself in our hands, he trembled with deadly fear.

The patient describes himself as a chicken-hearted fellow, who, in spite of good mental ability, has always been afraid of all sorts of diseases—consumption, heart apoplexy, and the like. He knows that these anxieties are morbid, yet cannot free himself from them. This apprehensiveness came out in a very marked way while he was under observation in the hospital. He worried about every remedy, whether it was baths, packs, or medicine, being afraid it would be too strong for him, and have a weakening effect. He always wished to have a warder within call in case he got agitated. The sight of other patients disturbed him greatly, and when he went for a walk in the garden with the door shut he was tormented by the fear of not being able to get out of it in case anything happened. At last he would hardly venture in front of the house, and always had to have the door open behind him so that he could take refuge indoors in case of necessity. He begged to have a little bottle of "blue electricity" that he had brought with him to give him confidence. Sometimes he was seized with violent palpitation of the heart while he was sitting down. Some little acne spots gave him so much alarm that he could neither go for a walk nor sleep. It struck him that his look had got very gloomy, and he thought it was the beginning of a mental disturbance which would certainly seize upon him while he was here.

Kraepelin's Diagnosis: Insanity of Irrepressible Ideas

Discussion of The Schoolmaster

The patient demonstrates three significant diagnostic features. First of all, there is a morbid preoccupation with a fear of having a serious physical disease (". . . he began to fear that he had a serious disease, and was going to die of heart apoplexy. All the assurances and examinations of his doctor could not convince him."). This, along with his impairment in occupational functioning, justifies the diagnosis of Hypochondriasis. Secondly, there is the irrational avoidance of being in public places from which escape might be difficult or help unavailable in case of sudden incapacitation ("He was also unable to cross large squares or go through wide streets by himself. . . . He was seized with apprehension on bridges . . ."), justifying the diagnosis of Agoraphobia. Finally, there is a strong suggestion of recurrent panic attacks ("Sometimes he was seized with violent palpitation of the heart while he was sitting down. . . .

He trembled with deadly fear."). Perhaps because Kraepelin did not recognize recurrent panic attacks as a distinct clinical syndrome, there is no mention of other characteristic symptoms such as shortness of breath, dizziness, sweating. If panic attacks are present in this case, it is likely that they played a role in the development of the Agoraphobia — hence the diagnosis of Agoraphobia with Panic Attacks.

Some clinicians might wish to make the additional diagnosis of a Simple Phobia to account for the fear and avoidance of trains and boats, because the patient attributes his anxiety to concern that an accident might occur rather than to the possibility that he might be incapacitated while alone.

DSM-III Diagnosis:

Axis I: **300.21 Agoraphobia with Panic Attacks (p. 226)**
300.70 Hypochondriasis (p. 249)

Wicked Young Lady

195 A young lady, aged twenty-six . . . The slightly-built, ill-nourished, sickly-looking girl has an expression of pain and trouble. Her hands and fingers are always in slight movement, reflecting her mental restlessness. She is quite collected and clear, but only gives monosyllabic answers. . . . She was constitutionally healthy herself, lively, and cheerful, but fell ill ten years ago of chronic inflammation of the tarsal joint, which brought her under medical treatment for a year. Even now walking is made difficult and slightly painful by the stiffness of the joint. In answer to our questions, the patient says that she is not insane, but only a wicked person who would be sent to the devil if people knew how continually she sins. She does not deserve to be well treated, and she cannot bear that people should look on her as an invalid, when in reality she is only pretending. It is impossible to get any details from her, as she evades every attempt to extract information. We can only learn that she has been to confession unworthily, and so could find no rest, even if she went to the end of the world. She must go away, anywhere, only not to her home, where she has lied and deceived. She cannot stay here either, as people are far too good to her.

So far as we know, this state of depression has developed quite gradually in the last year or two. It struck the patient's relations that her mood changed quickly and abruptly. She occasionally expressed religious doubts, on account of which she was sent to the priest, and also to a place of pilgrimage. But this only produced an aggravation of her condition each time. The restlessness increased, and the patient's sleep and appetite became worse and worse, her strength gradually becoming very much reduced in consequence. She felt burdened with grievous sins, of which she could not properly repent, and so was fallen into the power of the devil. She had neither wishes nor will; everything had become indifferent to her. Her whole previous life, with all her transgressions, stood out clearly before her, so that she was surprised at her own memory. She could not help brooding and having unclean thoughts, which broke her heart. Hence she worked feverishly, just to avoid thinking, although everything was very difficult for her.

After great reluctance, she has informed me of the purport of her tormenting thoughts. She was almost continually haunted by ideas associated with the reproductive organs of the opposite sex, which need not be detailed here. Thoughts of this kind, concerned in different ways with the same object, persecute her unceasingly without her being able to ignore them. Hence she says that she must really wish to have such thoughts; she must find pleasure in them, or they would not come. It is very difficult to divert the patient's mind from her painful self-torture; she always returns to it. She is quite unable to read, or to occupy herself mentally in any other way, as these sexual ideas attach themselves, by the most remarkable connections, to her course of thought, however remote it may be. In her general thinking the patient is clumsy and slow. She has always to overcome great disinclination, even when she has to write a simple letter. She generally obeys the doctor's orders, but has a number of peculiarities. The baths give her pains; meat is not good for her; she must follow certain paths in her whole way of life if she is not to grow worse. No physical disturbances have appeared except stiffness, swelling, and pain in the left instep, and a tendency to constipation, which has existed for many years. She sleeps badly.

Kraepelin's Diagnosis: Maniacal-Depressive Insanity

Discussion of Wicked Young Lady

What apparently disturbs this patient the most are the sexual ideas that force themselves into her awareness against her will. As Kraepelin notes in his discussion of the case, even though she says that she must really "wish" to have such ideas, ". . . it is clear that she has a strong desire to be freed from her tormenting thoughts, but cannot refrain from them." These thoughts have all the characteristrics of obsessions, or what Kraepelin referred to as "irrepressible ideas."

These obsessions occur in the context of an episode of illness that meets the criteria for Major Depression. In addition to the depressed mood there are guilt, disturbed sleep, decreased appetite and energy (". . . sleep and appetite became worse and worse, her strength gradually becoming very much reduced . . ."), loss of interest ("She had neither wishes nor will; everything had become indifferent to her"), difficulty concentrating, and, possibly, psychomotor agitation ("restlessness").

Her guilt is of psychotic proportions—she believes that she has "fallen into the power of the devil." This delusion is mood–congruent in that it involves the theme of guilt and deserved punishment.

Do the prominent obsessions justify a separate diagnosis in addition to the diagnosis of Major Depression? As Kraepelin notes ". . . a single symptom, however characteristic it may be, never justifies a definite diagnosis by itself, and that only the whole picture can ever be decisive of the clinical hypothesis."

The obsessions were present only during the episode of depression, and are therefore best understood as an associated feature of the Major Depression rather than as a manifestation of Obsessive Compulsive Disorder. If this were actually the case, one would expect that when the depression remitted, the obsessions would also disappear. In fact, Kraepelin provides follow-up information in a footnote: "When it had lasted between three and four years, the patient's illness ended in a complete cure, which still continues, five years later."

DSM-III Diagnosis:

Axis I: 296.24 Major Depression, Single Episode, with Psychotic Features (Mood-congruent) (p. 218)

The Innkeeper

196 The innkeeper, aged thirty-four, whom I am bringing before you to-day was admitted to the hospital only an hour ago. He understands the questions put to him, but cannot quite hear some of them, and gives a rather absentminded impression. He states his name and age correctly . . . Yet he does not know the doctors, calls them by the names of his acquaintances, and thinks he has been here for two or three days. It must be the Crown Hotel, or, rather, the "mad hospital." He does not know the date exactly.

. . . He moves about in his chair, looks round him a great deal, starts slightly several times, and keeps on playing with his hands. Suddenly he gets up, and begs to be allowed to play on the piano for a little at once. He sits down again immediately, on persuasion, but then wants to go away "to tell them something else that he has forgotten." He gradually gets more and more excited, saying that his fate is sealed; he must leave the world now; they might telegraph to his wife that her husband is lying at the point of death. We learn, by questioning him, that he is going to be executed by electricity, and also that he will be shot. "The picture is not clearly painted," he says; "every moment someone stands now here, now there, waiting for me with a revolver. When I open my eyes, they vanish." He says that a stinking fluid has been injected into his head and both his toes, which causes the pictures one takes for reality; that is the work of an international society, which makes away with those "who fell into misfortune innocently through false steps." With this he looks eagerly at the window, where he sees houses and trees vanishing and reappearing. With slight pressure on his eyes, he sees first sparks, then a hare, a picture, a head, a washstand-set, a half-moon, and a human head, first dully and then in colours. If you show him a speck on the floor, he tries to pick it up, saying that it is a piece of money. If you shut his hand and ask him what you have given him, he keeps his fingers carefully closed, and guesses that it is a lead-pencil or a piece of indiarubber. The patient's mood is half apprehensive and half amused. His head is much flushed, and his pulse is small, weak, and rather hurried. His face is bloated and his eyes are watery. His breath smells strongly of alcohol and acetone. His tongue is thickly furred, and trembles when he puts it out, and his outspread fingers show strong, jerky tremors. The knee-reflexes are somewhat exaggerated.

. . . Our patient has drunk hard since he was thirteen years old. . . . At last, by his own account, he drank 6 or 7 litres of wine a day and five or six stomachic bitters, while he took hardly any food but soup. Some weeks ago he had occasional hallucinations of sight — mice, rats, beetles, and rabbits. He mistook people at times, and came into his inn in his shirt. His condition has grown worse during the last few days.

Kraepelin's Diagnosis: Delirium Tremens

Discussion of The Innkeeper

This is a classic case of Delirium Tremens, which in DSM-III is called Alcohol Withdrawal Delirium to differentiate it from Delirium caused by withdrawal from other drugs, such as barbiturates. The

Delirium is evidenced by clouding of consciousness ("He understands the questions put to him, but cannot quite hear some of them,
and gives a rather absentminded impression."); perceptual disturbance (". . . he looks eagerly at the window, where he sees houses
and trees vanishing and reappearing [hallucination]. . . . If you show
him a speck on the floor, he tries to pick it up, saying that it is a piece
of money" [illusion]); increased psychomotor activity ("He moves
about in his chair . . . and keeps on playing with his hands"); and
disorientation (". . . he does not know the doctors . . . [nor] the
date").

In addition, he shows the autonomic hyperactivity that characteristically accompanies a Delirium due to Alcohol Withdrawal ("His
head is much flushed, and his pulse is small, weak, and rather
hurried.") He also demonstrates persecutory delusions (". . . he is
going to be executed by electricity"), which are also often present.

Although the case description makes no mention of a recent reduction in alcohol ingestion, it is reasonable to assume that the Delirium
resulted from alcohol withdrawal in a person who has been dependent on alcohol.

DSM-III Diagnosis:

Axis I: **291.00 Alcohol Withdrawal Delirium (p. 134)**
           303.91 Alcohol Dependence, Continuous (p. 169)

Stately Gentleman

197 The stately gentleman, aged sixty-two, who presents
himself before us with a certain courtly dignity, with his
carefully-tended moustaches, his eye-glasses, and his
well-fitting if perhaps somewhat shabby attire, gives quite the impression of a man of the world. He is somewhat testy at first because he has
to allow himself to be questioned before the young gentlemen, but
soon enters into a long, connected conversation in a quiet and positive
manner. We learn from him that as a young man he went to America,
and there went through many vicissitudes, finally settling in Quito,
where as a merchant he made a small fortune. With this he returned
home twenty-one years ago, but on the dissolving of his business
connections he was done out of considerable sums. At home he lived at
first on his money, spending his time in amusements, reading the
newspaper, playing billiards, going for walks, and sitting about in
cafes. At the same time he occupied himself with all sorts of schemes
from which he hoped for recognition and profit. Thus, he submitted to

the leading Minister the plan (with a map) whereby Germany could lay claim to a lot of still unpossessed land . . . A short time after that same Minister travelled to Berlin, and now began the German Colonial Policy, without . . . due thanks falling to the lot of the real originator . . . Then our patient drew up a plan for the cultivation of cinchona and cacao in our colonies; he also made several inventions for the better connection of railway-metals, by which the jolting, an important cause of derailment, would be done away with. Finally, he applied for a number of situations which seemed suited to him, including that of the consulship at Quito, but had always only failures to record.

. . . He was enticed into a district asylum, under the false pretext that he would be given a post, and there he assisted in the management till it became evident to him that they had no intention of paying him for his services. When, on that account, he tried hard for other situations, they sent him, also under false pretences, to the hospital, where he is now illegally detained. That, he concluded with bitterness, was the thanks which the Fatherland bestowed upon him for his services.

. . . [He] then relates, little by little, that a woman whom he calls by the nickname of Bulldog, and who was the daughter of the English Consul at Quito, had persecuted him for twenty-three or twenty-four years with her plans of marriage, and sought in every way to cross his steps in order to reduce him to submission. Even in America things ultimately never went as he wished, and a hundred stuffed birds had, out of spite, been stolen from him by means of a skeleton key; everywhere he noticed the frauds of the Bulldog and her accomplices. "If people do everything differently from what I should have wished, there must be something more than meets the eye." The half-crazy American also travelled home after him, had insinuated herself into this neighbourhood, had the impudence to dress herself up in man's clothes, and to force marriage by preventing him from finding a post, and by these means brought him to want. This artful person had approached him under various names, though he had always told her that one did not win a man's love through such chicanery. He would perhaps be one of the richest men in California if the Bulldog had not prevented it. She was also to blame for his being brought to the asylum. "Who else, then, could it possibly be?" Both at home and abroad he was eternally meeting her. . . . All objections that one raises to these ideas are received by the patient in a superior, incredulous manner, and glance off from his steadfast conviction without leaving the slightest impression.

Kraepelin's Diagnosis: Paranoia

Discussion of Stately Gentleman

This is a classic example of the traditional notion of paranoia. The patient demonstrates an elaborate system of persecutory delusions: his contributions to German foreign policy are not acknowledged; he is employed by the district asylum—without pay; he is pursued by the "Bulldog," who dresses in men's clothes and prevents him from obtaining employment. As is frequently the case in patients with Paranoid Disorders, there is associated grandiosity. For example, his ideas were incorporated in to German colonial policy; he would ". . . perhaps be one of the richest men in California if the Bulldog had not prevented it."

This condition is distinguished from Paranoid Schizophrenia by the absence of such characteristic symptoms as delusions that are patently absurd, prominent hallucinations, marked loosening of associations, or incoherence. Furthermore, whereas in Schizophrenia continued deterioration in social functioning is common, in Paranoid Disorders it is generally absent, as in this case. In the traditional concept of Paranoia, the illness has an insidious onset and a chronic course of many years, as is true in this patient. All such cases fall within the more inclusive DSM-III category of Paranoia, which does not require an insidious onset and requires a duration of only two years.

DSM-III Diagnosis:

Axis I: 297.10 Paranoia (p. 197)

The Widow

198 The widow, aged thirty-five, whom I will now bring before you . . . gives full information about her life in answer to our questions, knows where she is, can tell the date and the year, and gives proof of satisfactory school knowledge. It is noteworthy that she does not look at her questioner, and speaks in a low and peculiar, sugary, affected tone. When you touch on her illness, she is reserved at first, and says that she is quite well, but she soon begins to express a number of remarkable *ideas of persecution*. For many years she has heard voices, which insult her and cast suspicion on her chastity. They mention a number of names she knows, and tell her she will be stripped and abused. The voices are very distinct, and, in her opinion, they must be carried by a telescope or a machine from her home. Her thoughts are dictated to her; she is obliged to think them, and hears them repeated after her. She is interrupted in her work, and has all kinds of uncomfortable sensations in her body, to which something is "done." In particular, her "mother parts" are turned inside out, and people send a pain through her back, lay ice-water on her heart, squeeze her neck, injure her spine, and violate her. There are also hallucinations of sight — black figures and the altered appearance of people — but these are far less frequent. She cannot exactly say who carries on all the influencing, or for what object it is done. Sometimes it is the people from her home, and sometimes the doctors of an asylum where she was before who have taken something out of her body.

The patient makes these extraordinary complaints without showing much emotion. She cries a little, but then describes her morbid experiences again with secret satisfaction and even with an erotic bias. She demands her discharge, but is easily consoled, and does not trouble at all about her position and her future. Her use of numerous strained and hardly intelligible phrases is very striking. She is ill-treated "flail-wise," "utterance-wise," "terror-wise"; she is "a picture of misery in angel's form," and "a defrauded mamma and housewife of sense of order." They have "altered her form of emotion." She is "persecuted by a secret insect from the District Office. . . ." Her former history shows that she has been ill for nearly ten years. The disease developed gradually. About a year after the death of her husband, by whom she has two children, she became apprehensive, slept badly, heard loud talking in her room at night, and thought that she was being robbed of her means and persecuted by people from Frankfort, where she had formerly lived. Four years ago she spent a year in an asylum. She thought she found the "Frankforters" there, noticed poison in the food, heard voices, and felt influences. After her discharge she brought accusations against the doctors of having mutilated her while she was there. She now thought them to be her persecutors, and openly abused the public authorities for failing to protect her, so she had to be admitted to this hospital two months ago. Here she made the same complaints day after day, without showing much excitement, and wrote long-winded letters full of senseless and unvarying abuse about the persecution from which she suffered, to her relations, the asylum doctors, and the authorities. She did not occupy herself in any way, held no intercourse with her fellow-patients, and avoided every attempt to influence her.

Kraepelin's Diagnosis: Dementia Praecox, Paranoid

Discussion of The Widow

This patient demonstrates numerous characteristic symptoms of Schizophrenia. The most conspicuous are bizarre persecutory delusions (". . . voices . . . must be carried by a telescope or a machine from her home. Her thoughts are dictated to her; she is obliged to think them . . ."; ". . . persecuted by a secret insect from the District Office."), some of which are also somatic (". . . her 'mother parts' are turned inside out . . ."). She also has persecutory hallucinations (". . . she has heard voices, which insult her and cast suspicion on her chastity."). Her speech is at times incoherent (". . . she is . . . a defrauded mamma and housewife of sense of order."), with neologisms ("flail-wise, utterance-wise, terror-wise"). Her affect is both flat ("The patient makes these extraordinary complaints without showing much emotion.") and inappropriate ("She . . . describes her morbid experiences again with secret satisfaction and even with an erotic bias.").

In addition, common associated features of Schizophrenia are described: apathy (". . . does not trouble at all about her position and her future"); lack of insight (". . . says that she is quite well . . ."); and social withdrawal (". . . held no intercourse with her fellow-patients . . .").

These characteristic symptoms, the deterioration from a previous level of functioning, onset before age 45, and the ten-year duration of the illness, in the absence of a significant mood disturbance, justify the diagnosis of Chronic Schizophrenia. The predominance of persecutory delusions and hallucinations warrants the Paranoid Subtype (p. 191).

DSM-III Diagnosis:

Axis I: 295.32 Schizophrenia, Paranoid Type, Chronic (p. 188)

The Farmer

199 I will first place before you a farmer, aged fifty-nine, who was admitted to the hospital a year ago. The patient looks much older than he really is, principally owing to the loss of the teeth from his upper jaw. He not only understands our questions without any difficulty, but answers them relevantly and correctly; can tell where he is, and how long he has been here; knows the doctors, and can give the date and the day of the week. His expression is dejected. The corners of his mouth are rather drawn down, and his eyebrows drawn together. . . . On being questioned about his illness, he breaks into lamentations, saying that he did not tell the whole truth on his admission, but concealed the fact that he had fallen into sin in his youth and practised uncleanness with himself; everything he did was wrong. "I am so apprehensive, so wretched; I cannot lie still for anxiety. O God, if I had only not transgressed so grievously!" He has been ill for over a year . . . It began with stomach-ache and head troubles, and he could not work any longer. "There was no impulse left." He can get no rest now, and fancies silly things, as if someone were in the room. Once it seemed to him that he had seen the Evil One: perhaps he would be carried off. . . . As a boy, he had taken apples and nuts. "Conscience has said that that is not right; conscience has only awakened just now in my illness." He had also played with a cow, and by himself. "I reproach myself for that now." It seemed to him that he had fallen away from God . . . His appetite is bad, and he has no stools. He cannot sleep. "If the mind does not sleep, all sorts of thoughts come. . . ." He fastened his neckerchief to strangle himself, but he was not really in earnest. Three sisters and a brother were ill too. The sisters were not so bad; they soon recovered. "A brother has made away with himself through apprehension."

The patient tells us this in broken sentences, interrupted by wailing and groaning. In all other respects, he behaves naturally, does whatever he is told, and only begs us not to let him be dragged away — "There is dreadful apprehension in my heart." Except for a little trembling of the outspread fingers and slightly arrhythmic action of the heart, we find no striking disturbances at the physical examination. As for the patient's former history, he is married, and has four healthy children, while three are dead. The illness began gradually seven or eight months before his admission, without any assignable cause. Loss of appetite and dyspepsia appeared first, and then ideas of sin. . . .

Kraepelin's Diagnosis: Melancholia

Discussion of The Farmer

This patient is clearly suffering from a major depressive episode. There is a pervasive depressed mood ('I am so apprehensive, so wretched'; "His expression is dejected."). In addition there are the typical associated features: loss of interest ('There was no impulse left.'), self-reproach for earlier sexual activities ("He had also played with a cow, and by himself."), insomnia, poor appetite, weight loss, and thoughts of suicide. This is a severe depression that almost certainly would meet the criteria for the subtype Melancholia. The loss of interest would appear to be pervasive. It seems likely that his severely depressed mood is unresponsive to environmental events. In addition, there are several other characteristic features of Melancholia: psychomotor agitation ('. . . I cannot lie still for anxiety.'), anorexia, weight loss, and excessive guilt. There is a suggestion of a hallucination ("Once it seemed to him that he had seen the Evil One . . ."); however, in the context of his culture, this may not have great pathological significance. Similarly, his guilt, although excessive, does not seem to be of delusional severity when viewed in the context of his culture.

When both psychotic features and Melancholia are present, DSM-III requires that the clinician record the single most clinically significant characteristic — in this case, clearly the Melancholia.

DSM-III Diagnosis:

Axis I: 296.23 Major Depression, Single Episode, with Melancholia (p. 218)

Oberrealschul Student

200 The patient I will show you to-day has almost to be carried into the room, as he walks in a straddling fashion on the outside of his feet. On the coming in, he throws off his slippers, sings a hymn loudly, and then cries twice (in English), "My father, my real father!" He is eighteen years old, and a pupil of the Oberrealschul [high school], tall, and rather strongly built, but with a pale complexion, on which there is very often a transient flush. The patient sits with his eyes shut, and pays no attention to his surroundings. He does not look up even when he is spoken to, but he answers, beginning in a low voice, and gradually screaming louder and louder. When asked where he is, he says, "You want to know that too; I tell you who is being measured and is measured and shall be measured. I know all that, and could tell you, but I do not want to." When asked his name, he screams, "What is your name? What does he shut? He shuts his eyes. What does he hear? He does not understand; he understands not. How? Who? Where? When? What does he mean? When I tell him to look, he does not look properly. You there, just look! What is it? What is the matter? Attend; he attends not. I say, what is it, then? Why do you give me no answer? Are you getting impudent again? How can you be so impudent? I'm coming! I'll show you! You don't turn whore for me. You mustn't be smart either; you're an impudent, lousy fellow, an impudent, lousy fellow as stupid as a hog. Such an impudent, shameless, miserable, lousy fellow I've never met with. Is he beginning again? You understand nothing at all—nothing at all; nothing at all does he understand. If you follow now, he won't follow, will not follow. Are you getting still more impudent? Are you getting impudent still more? How they attend, they do attend," and so on. At the end he scolds in quite inarticulate sounds.

The patient understands perfectly, and has introduced many phrases he has heard before into his speech, without once looking up. He speaks in an affected way, now babbling like a child, now lisping and stammering, sings suddenly in the middle of what he is saying, and grimaces. He carries out orders in an extraordinary fashion, gives his hand with the fist clenched, goes to the blackboard when he is asked, but, instead of writing his name, suddenly knocks down a lamp, and throws the chalk among the audience. He makes all kinds of senseless movements, pushes the table away, crosses his arms, and turns round on his axis, chair and all, or sits balancing, with his legs crossed and his hands on his head. Catalepsy can also be made out. When he is to go away, he will not get up, has to be pushed, and calls out loudly, "Good-morning, gentlemen; it has not pleased me."

. . . The patient himself was always quiet and very industrious, but of moderate mental endowment. Seven months ago, during the holidays, he suddenly began to learn in a quite senseless way, and then became confused, thought he was laughed at for being dirty, and washed himself all day long, was afraid his effects would be taken, broke the windows, seemed to hear voices, attacked his mother without any cause, became wet and dirty in his habits, and would not speak a word. In the hospital he was almost dumb, was cataleptic, gave his hand stiffly and jerkily, and almost entirely refused to eat. His expression was generally indifferent, though sometimes cheerful, and visits from his relations made no impression at all on him.

The patient understood quite well what was taking place around him, but as a rule he did not obey orders; indeed, he sometimes did the exact opposite of what was wanted. Thus, he shut his eyes when his pupils were mentioned, covered his face with his handkerchief if you wished to see it, and drew his hand back when he ought to have stretched it out. He was often dirty, and also smeared faeces about, and rolled them into little balls — a sign diagnostic of great emotional dullness. After refusing food for a long time, he suddenly asked for Swiss cheese and then for chocolate, and devoured them both greedily. From this we can plainly see the senseless and impulsive nature of his refusal of food. Once he laid his outstretched leg on the next bed, and remained in that position when the bed was moved away. In the seventh month of the illness the patient began to be excited, after having sung occasionally during the period of dumbness. In the middle of the night he threw away his bedding, rocked rhythmically up and down on the bedstead, and screamed incessantly, "Now, I want to know where my brother is." Since then he has been in a continual state of excitement, is destructive and abusive, and talks in a confused way. He briefly informed his relations, from whom he takes the eatables they bring when they come to see him, without talking to them much, that he was going to travel by Gibraltar to the Cameroons and by Constantinople to Bucharest.

Kraepelin's Diagnosis: Katatonic Excitement

Discussion of Oberrealschul Student

In the absence of any known organic factor, the combination of marked incoherence and grossly disorganized behavior clearly suggests the diagnosis of Schizophrenia. The diagnosis is further confirmed by the history of onset of symptoms seven months previously and a clear deterioration in functioning. Although the hyperactivity, confused speech, and irritability might suggest a manic episode, there is no description of a period with a persistent and predominant elevated, expansive, or irritable mood. Although he often is irritable and even violent, his mood seems to fluctuate unpredictably. When irritability is seen in mania, it usually is a response to frustration of grandiosity or hyperactivity.

Although delusions and hallucinations have been present, the most prominent and persistent features are the disorganization of speech and behavior. His illness does meet the DSM-III criteria for Disorganized Type because of the frequent incoherence, absence of systematized delusions, and blunted, inappropriate, and silly affect. However, there are numerous prominent examples of classic catatonic behavior: he exhibits negativism (refuses to do what is asked of him or does the opposite), catatonic excitement (senseless movements while ignoring his surroundings), and posturing (kept his leg in an awkward position). Since according to the history the illness began suddenly seven months before the examination, the course should be noted as Subchronic. The patient demonstrates, over the course of his relatively brief illness, alternation between catatonic stupor (became wet and dirty in his habits, and would not speak a word) and his current catatonic excitement.

The DSM-III criteria do not indicate, as perhaps they should, that the Disorganized Subtype should be recorded only in the absence of prominent catatonic symptoms, which represent more specific forms of disorganized behavior.

DSM-III Diagnosis:

Axis I: **295.21 Schizophrenia, Catatonic Type, Subchronic (p. 190)**

The Suffering Lady

201 The young lady, aged thirty, carefully dressed in black, who comes into the hall with short, shuffling steps, leaning on the nurse, and sinks into a chair as if exhausted, gives you the impression that she is ill. She is of slender build, her features are pale and rather painfully drawn, and her eyes are cast down. Her small, manicured fingers play nervously with a handkerchief. The patient answers the questions addressed to her in a low, tired voice, without looking up, and we find that she is quite clear about time, place, and her surroundings. After a few minutes, her eyes suddenly become convulsively shut, her head sinks forward, and she seems to have fallen into a deep sleep. Her arms have grown quite limp, and fall down as if palsied when you try to lift them. She has ceased to answer, and if you try to raise her eyelids, her eyes suddenly rotate upwards. Needlepricks only produce a slight shudder. But sprinkling with cold water is followed by a deep sigh; the patient starts up, opens her eyes, looks round her with surprise, and gradually comes to herself. She says that she has just had one of her sleeping attacks, from which she has suffered for seven years. They come on quite irregularly, often many in one day, and last from a few minutes to half an hour.

Concerning the history of her life, the patient tells us that . . . she was educated in convent schools, and passed the examination for teachers. As a young girl, she inhaled a great deal of chloroform, which she was able to get secretly, for toothache. She also suffered from headaches, until they were relieved by the removal of growths from the nose. She very readily became delirious in feverish illnesses. Thirteen years ago she took a place as governess in Holland, but soon began to be ill, and has passed the last seven years in different hospitals, except for a short interval when she was in a situation in Moravia.

It would appear from the statements of her relations and doctors that the patient has suffered from the most varied ailments, and been through the most remarkable courses of treatment. For violent abdominal pains and disturbances of menstruation, ascribed to stenosis of the cervical canal and retroflection of the uterus, recourse was had five

315

years ago to the excision of the wedge supposed to cause the obstruction, and the introduction of a pessary. At a later period loss of voice and a contraction of the right forearm and the left thigh set in, and were treated with massage, electricity, bandaging, and stretching under an anaesthetic. Heart oppression and spasmodic breathing also appeared, with quickly passing disablements of various sets of muscles, disturbances of urination, diarrhoea, and unpleasant sensations, now in one and now in another part of the body, but particularly headaches. Extraordinarily strong and sudden changes of mood were observed at the same time, with introspection and complaints of want of consideration in those about her and in her relations, although the latter had made the greatest sacrifices. Brine baths, Russian baths, pine-needle baths, electricity, country air, summer resorts, and, finally, residence on the Riviera—everything was tried, generally with only a brief improvement or with none at all.

The immediate cause of the patient being brought to the hospital was the increase in the "sleeping attacks" two years ago. They came on at last even when the patient was standing, and might continue for an hour. The patient did not fall down, but simply leaned against something. The attacks continued in the hospital, and spasmodic breathing was also observed, which could be influenced by suggestion.

After spending eight months here, the patient went away at first to her sister's. But after a few months she had to be taken to another asylum, where she stayed about a year, and then, after a short time spent with her family, came back to us.

During her present residence here, so-called "great attacks" have appeared, in addition to her previous troubles. We will try to produce such an attack by pressure on the very sensitive left ovarian region. After one or two minutes of moderately strong pressure, during which the patient shows sharp pain, her expression alters. She throws herself to and fro with her eyes shut, and screams to us loudly, generally in French, not to touch her. "You must not do anything to me, you hound, cochon, cochon!" She cries for help, pushes with her hands, and twists herself as if she were trying to escape from a sexual assault. Whenever she is touched, the excitement increases. Her whole body is strongly bent backwards. Suddenly the picture changes, and the patient begs piteously not to be cursed, and laments and sobs aloud. This condition, too, is very soon put an end to by sprinkling with cold water. The patient shudders, wakes with a deep sigh, and looks fixedly round, only making a tired, senseless impression. She cannot explain what has happened.

The physical examination of the patient shows no particular disturbances at present, except the abnormalities already mentioned. There is only a well-marked weakness, in consequence of which she often keeps her bed or lies about. All her movements are limp and feeble, but there is no actual disablement anywhere. She often sleeps very badly. At times she wanders about in the night, wakes the nurses, and sends for the doctor. Her appetite is very poor, but she has a habit of nibbling between her meals at all kinds of cakes, fruit, and jam, which are sent to her, at her urgent request, by her relations.

With her growing expertness in illness, the emotional sympathies of the patient are more and more confined to the selfish furthering of her own wishes. She tries ruthlessly to extort the most careful attention from those around her, obliges the doctor to occupy himself with her by day or by night on the slightest occasion, is extremely sensitive to any supposed neglect, is jealous if preference is shown to other patients, and tries to make the attendants give in to her by complaints, accusations, and outbursts of temper. The sacrifices made by others, more especially by her family, are regarded quite as a matter of course, and her occasional prodigality of thanks only serves to pave the way for new demands. To secure the sympathy of those around her, she has recourse to more and more forcible descriptions of her physical and mental torments, histrionic exaggeration of her attacks, and the effective elucidation of her personal character. She calls herself the abandoned, the outcast, and in mysterious hints makes confession of horrible, delightful experiences and failings, which she will only confide to the discreet bosom of her very best friend, the doctor.

Kraepelin's Diagnosis: Hysterical Insanity

Discussion of The Suffering Lady

Although Somatization Disorder is a new diagnostic category in DSM-III, this nineteenth-century case is a classic example of the disorder. First of all, there is a history of physical symptoms, not adequately explained by a physical disorder or injury, that go back to the patient's adolescence. The DSM-III criteria for the disorder require fourteen symptoms for women (twelve for men) from seven groups of symptoms. We count thirteen in this case history: sickly for most of her life, loss of voice, loss of consciousness, memory loss, seizures, trouble walking, muscle weakness, urinary problems, abdominal pain, diarrhea, menstrual problems, shortness of breath, and chest pain. There is no mention of her psychosexual functioning; it seems likely that on inquiry she would acknowledge symptoms in that area, such as sexual indifference or pain during intercourse.

As is commonly the case, genuine physical problems coexist, but are hardly adequate to explain the myriad physical complaints.

Although the "sleeping attacks" represent periods of dissociation — that is, temporary, nonorganic alterations of consciousness — in this case they are better thought of as pseudoneurological symptoms of Somatization Disorder. Thus, the additional diagnosis of an Atypical Dissociative Disorder is not made.

Although Kraepelin's description of the way in which this woman relates to others is based on his observations of her current condition, it is reasonable to assume that it is characteristic of her long-term functioning. The vivid portrayal of the patient as self-dramatizing, incessantly drawing attention to herself, given to angry outbursts, self-indulgent, and demanding is sufficient evidence for a diagnosis of Histrionic Personality Disorder. Certain features of Narcissistic Personality Disorder are also present: a sense of the uniqueness of her problems, the need for constant attention, entitlement, and interpersonal exploitation; but there is no evidence of a central feature of the disorder: preoccupation with fantasies of unlimited success, power, brilliance, beauty, or ideal love. Nevertheless, we would have no quarrel with a provisional diagnosis of Narcissistic Personality Disorder based on the suspicion that the patient might well have fantasies of ideal love with "her very best friend, the doctor."

DSM-III Diagnosis:

Axis I: 300.81 Somatization Disorder (p. 241)
Axis II: 301.50 Histrionic Personality Disorder (p. 313)

Onanistic Student

202 You have before you to-day a strongly-built and well-nourished man, aged twenty-one, who entered the hospital a few weeks ago. He sits quietly looking in front of him, and does not raise his eyes when he is spoken to, but evidently understands all our questions very well, for he answers quite relevantly, though slowly and often only after repeated questioning. From his brief remarks, made in a low tone, we gather that he thinks he is ill, without getting any more precise information about the nature of the illness and its symptoms. The patient attributes his malady to the onanism he has practised since he was ten years old. He thinks that he has thus incurred the guilt of a sin against the sixth commandment, has very much reduced his power of working, has made himself feel languid and miserable, and has become a hypochondriac. Thus, as the result of reading certain books, he imagined that he had a rupture and suffered from wasting of the spinal cord, neither of which was the case. He would not associate with his comrades any longer, because he thought they saw the results of his vice and made fun of him. The patient makes all these statements in an indifferent tone, without looking up or troubling about his surroundings. His expression betrays no emotion; he only laughs for a moment now and then. There is occasional wrinkling of the forehead or facial spasm. Round the mouth and nose a fine, changing twitching is constantly observed.

The patient gives us a correct account of his past experiences. His knowledge speaks for the high degree of his education; indeed, he was ready to enter the University a year ago. He also knows where he is and how long he has been here, but he is only very imperfectly acquainted with the names of the people round him, and says that he has never asked about them. He can only give a very meagre account of the general events of the last year. In answer to our questions, he declares that he is ready to remain in the hospital for the present. He would certainly prefer it if he could enter a profession, but he cannot say what he would like to take up. . . . The patient makes his statements slowly and in monosyllables, not because his wish to answer meets with overpowering hindrances, but because he feels no desire to speak at all. He certainly hears and understands what is said to him very well, but he does not take the trouble to attend to it. He pays no heed, and answers whatever occurs to him without thinking. No visible effort of the will is to be noticed. All his movements are languid and expressionless, but are made without hindrance or trouble. There is no sign of emotional dejection, such as one would expect from the nature of his talk, and the patient remains quite dull throughout, experiencing neither fear nor hope nor desires. He is not at all deeply affected by what goes on before him, although he understands it without actual difficulty. It is all the same to him who appears or disappears where he is, or who talks to him and takes care of him, and he does not even once ask their names.

. . . He broods, staring in front of him with expressionless features, over which a vacant smile occasionally plays, or at the best turns over the leaves of a book for a moment, apparently speechless, and not troubling about anything. Even when he has visitors, he sits without showing any interest, does not ask about what is happening at home, hardly even greets his parents, and goes back indifferently to the ward. He can hardly be induced to write a letter, and says that he has nothing to write about. But he occasionally composes a letter to the doctor, expressing all kinds of distorted, half-formed ideas, with a peculiar and silly play on words, in very fair style, but with little connection. He begs for "a little more allegro in the treatment," and "liberationary movement with a view to the widening of the horizon," will "ergo extort some wit in lectures," and "nota bene for God's sake only does not wish to be combined with the club of the harmless." "Professional work is the balm of life."

The development of the illness has been quite gradual. Our patient . . . did not go to school till he was seven years old, as he was a delicate child and spoke badly, but when he did he learned quite well. He was considered to be a reserved and stubborn child. Having practised onanism at a very early age, he became more and more solitary in the last few years, and thought that he was laughed at by his brothers and sisters, and shut out from society because of his ugliness. For this reason he could not bear a looking-glass in his room. After passing the written examination on leaving school, a year ago, he gave up the viva voce, because he could not work any longer. He cried a great deal, masturbated much, ran about aimlessly, played in a senseless way on the piano, and began to write observations " 'On the Nerve-play of Life,' which he cannot get on with." He was incapable of any kind of work, even physical, felt "done for," asked for a revolver, ate Swedish matches to destroy himself, and lost all affection for his family. From time to time he became excited and troublesome, and shouted out of the window at night. In the hospital, too, a state of excitement lasting for several days was observed, in which he chattered in a confused way, made faces, ran about at full speed, wrote disconnected scraps of composition, and crossed and recrossed them with flourishes and unmeaning combinations of letters. After this a state of tranquillity ensued, in which he could give absolutely no account of his extraordinary behaviour.

Kraepelin's Diagnosis: Dementia Praecox (Insanity of Adolescence)

Discussion of Onanistic Student

The most prominent features of the illness are delusions of guilt (his onanism has caused his illness), persecutory delusions ("he thought [his comrades] saw the results of his vice and made fun of him"), incoherence, and flat and inappropriate affect ("His expression betrays no emotion; he only laughs for a moment now and then.") These features, plus the chronic nature of the illness, establish the diagnosis of Schizophrenia.

The DSM-III subtypes of Schizophrenia are based on the predominant clinical picture that occasioned the evaluation or admission to clinical care. If this patient were seen at the time that he "chattered in a confused way, made faces, ran about at full speed," the appropriate subtype might be Catatonic or Disorganized. At the point at which he was presented by Kraepelin, he was neither frequently incoherent nor excited; the appropriate subtype is therefore Undifferentiated.

The initial description of the patient might lead some clinicians to consider the possibility of a major depressive episode: psychomotor retardation, delusions of guilt, and hypochondriacal preoccupation are present. However, as Kraepelin later notes, "There is no sign of emotional dejection, such as one would expect from the nature of his talk."

DSM-III Diagnosis:

Axis I: 295.92 Schizophrenia, Undifferentiated Type, Chronic (p. 191)

Factory Girl

203 The factory girl, aged thirty-two, who now comes into the room with an awkward and very deep curtsey, presents an entirely different aspect from the last patient. She declines to sit down to talk to us, thanks us for the "honour," goes up and down with affected, waddling steps, and begins to declaim and recite verses, and to interpolate witty remarks in our discussion of her condition. Her name is what the parson christened her, and she is as old as her little finger. She knows her position, the date, where she is, and the people around her, and can give the most exact information about her past experiences. She does not consider herself insane. She often interweaves her disconnected talk with scraps of bad French and senselessly altered quotations, such as, "Ingratitude is the world's praise," "Many hands, many minds." She rides single phrases to death in uninterrupted repetition — "Devil's dung on the soul's foot, the soul's foot in devil's dung." She often uses very strange and almost incomprehensible compound words and phrases.

Her mood is silly, cheerful, sometimes erotic, and then again irritable. She takes pleasure in the most indecent sexual allusions, and occasionally in outbursts of the wildest abuse. She does not obey orders, and refuses to give her hand on the ground that they are *her* hands. She will not write, and pertly refuses to do anything she is asked. She chatters continually, and will not let anyone get in a word. Her speech is extremely laboured. She cuts the separate syllables sharply asunder, accentuates the final syllables sharply, pronounces *g* like *k*, and *d* like *t*, talks like a child, in imperfectly formed sentences, distorts words, inserts senseless expletives and strangely-formed words, and constantly changes the subject. All her movements and gestures are clumsy, angular, and stiff, and are very lavishly employed, but monotonous; she hops about, bends down, claps her hands, and makes faces. She has ornamented her clothes in an extraordinary way with embroidery and crochet-work of staringly bright wool. From her talk it appears that she looks on herself as the mistress of the house; she pays the nurses and appoints them, and will get herself better doctors. Moreover, she complains of being exposed to sexual assaults, and says that her lungs, heart, and liver have been taken out. She says she is engaged to a doctor in the asylum where she was before. She tells her name with the prefix "von." She also seems to have heard voices, but will only make evasive statements about them.

 . . . The patient . . . was considered very selfish and obstinate . . . from her youth up. She was first a servant girl and then a factory hand, had two illegitimate children, and then aborted once. About six months later, two years ago now, she saw gray men and women's heads, and heard knocking and voices which called abusive words to her. Later on she wrote a love-letter to the proprietor of her factory, and was dismissed and picked up helpless on the street. When taken to an asylum, she was quiet and collected at first, but soon had brief attacks of the most violent excitement, during which she undressed herself completely, hit out round her in a senseless way, and bit. Later on she showed a repellent, discontented disposition and a tendency to stereotypism and impulsive actions. When she was brought here a year and a quarter ago she presented the same picture as now in all essential features. It should perhaps be added that she showed echopraxis, followed the same track — a figure of eight, for instance — for hours in the garden, and was very refractory. For a long time she had to be kept quite alone in the garden and in her room, because, though quite collected and free from great emotional excitement, she was very dangerous to the other patients.

Kraepelin's Diagnosis: Katatonic Excitement

Discussion of Factory Girl

There are many features that suggest the manic syndrome. The mood is described as alternately silly, cheerful, and irritable. There is pressure of speech ("She chatters continually, and will not let anyone get in a word.") and hyperactivity ("she hops about, bends down, claps her hands . . ."). She is also grandiose (". . . she looks on herself as the mistress of the house; she pays the nurses and appoints them. . .") and sexually provocative. However, the onset of the illness was characterized by persecutory hallucinations, apparently not accompanied by any disturbance in mood. According to the DSM-III criteria, a manic episode should not be diagnosed when mood-incongruent psychotic features dominate the clinical picture either before the affective syndrome begins (as in this case) or after it has remitted. Many clinicians might even question the presence of the manic syndrome at any time, considering the mood described more shallow and silly than elevated or expansive.

The clear presence of incoherence, grossly disorganized behavior, hallucinations, and inappropriate affect in an illness that has lasted more than two years, and that represents a distinct change from the patient's usual level of functioning, all indicate Chronic Schizophrenia.

Kraepelin notes the primary disturbance as one of behavior rather than mood. He emphasizes the negativism ("She does not obey orders . . . and pertly refuses to do anything she is asked."), stereotypism ("she . . . followed the same track—a figure of eight, for instance — for hours in the garden"), and mannerisms ("All her movements and gestures are clumsy, angular, and stiff, and are very lavishly employed"). These features, plus the "attacks of the most violent excitement," disorganized speech, and lack of any deep emotion led him to make a diagnosis of Katatonic Excitement.

We believe that an equally good case can be made for Schizophrenia, Disorganized Type, rather than Catatonic, on the basis of the prominence of the disorganization of speech, the absence of systematized delusions, and the silly and inappropriate affect. Furthermore, the symptoms suggesting catatonic excitement do not seem to be as persistent as the signs of disorganization.

We would not, however, quarrel with clinicians who, impressed with the manic features, might want to make a diagnosis of Schizoaffective Disorder and even try a course of lithium therapy!

DSM-III Diagnosis:

Axis I: 295.12 Schizophrenia, Disorganized Type, Chronic (p. 190)

Eugen Bleuler (1857–1939)

Bleuler, a Swiss psychiatrist, coined the term *Schizophrenia* to describe what he considered to be the fundamental disturbance—a splitting of the psychic functions that, in extreme cases, leads to disorganization of the personality. Whereas Kraepelin by and large limited himself to describing the clinical picture and course of the illness, Bleuler attempted to understand the underlying psychopathological process as well. He differed from Kraepelin in maintaining that deterioration was not characteristic of the illness. He added a nonpsychotic subtype, Simple, which he believed occurred as frequently as the other subtypes, although it was rarely seen in hospitals.

The following case is taken verbatim from a translation of his major work, *Dementia Praecox or the Group of Schizophrenias,* * first published in 1911.

Domestic Tyrant

204 A normal, intelligent girl marries at twenty and lives happily for more than five years. Very gradually she becomes irritable, gesticulates while talking, her peculiarities continue to increase; she cannot keep a servant anymore; she is constantly quarrelling with her neighbors. Within her own family group, she has developed into an unbearable domestic tyrant who knows no duties, only rights. She is unable to manage the household or do the housework any more because she makes all kinds of silly, stupid, and useless purchases and is proving herself utterly impractical. During the many years in which she is in the hospital, she exhibits the same behavior only in increasing measure, so that it is only possible to keep her either in her own room or outdoors where there are very few people. However, after some ten years of hospitalization, she can be released although she still causes trouble by her gossiping and disagreeableness. She complains continually of some vague nervous troubles because, as she says, she was not properly treated in the hospital. Yet she is entirely indifferent to important things such as her relations to her family, etc. She has no love for her children. She is incapable of pulling herself together although she knows quite well that she could have a very decent life if she were less of a nag and a scold. There were no traces of paranoid or catatonic symptoms.

Bleuler's Diagnosis: Simple Schizophrenia

---

*Bleuler E: *Dementia Praecox or the Group of Schizophrenias*. Translated by Joseph Zinkin. New York, International Universities Press, 1950, p. 238.

Discussion of Domestic Tyrant

According to the information available, this woman functioned well until she was 25. She then developed a progressively incapacitating illness characterized by poor judgment, irritability, and indifference to others. No psychotic symptoms, disorder of mood, or symptoms suggesting an Organic Mental Disorder are described. This peculiar picture corresponds to no DSM-III Axis I disorder! Many of the features of her illness suggest a severe Personality Disorder, but Bleuler's description of her as living "happily" until her illness began at age 25 suggests a distinct change in functioning. This is inconsistent with the concept of a Personality Disorder, since manifestations of a Personality Disorder are generally recognizable by adolescence or earlier. We are therefore left with the rather unsatisfying but accurate diagnosis of Unspecified Mental Disorder (nonpsychotic).

Bleuler was able to diagnose this patient as having Schizophrenia because he emphasized the "primary symptoms" (disturbances of association and affect, ambivalence and autism) and did not require, as does DSM-III, the presence of psychotic symptoms, such as delusions or hallucinations. We suspect that a clinician interviewing this patient today would uncover either evidence of some period with psychotic symptoms, suggesting Schizophrenia, or an earlier onset, suggesting a severe Personality Disorder, or perhaps both.

DSM-III Diagnosis:

Axis I: 300.90 Unspecified Mental Disorder (nonpsychotic) (p. 335)

Alois Alzheimer (1864–1915)

Alzheimer was a German neuropathologist who investigated the relationship between anatomical changes in the brain and mental disorder. In 1907 he described a deceased patient of the insane asylum in Frankfurt-am-Main whose nervous system had been given to him for investigation because the patient presented with an unusual clinical picture that could not be categorized under any of the known diseases.*

Perplexed Woman

205 A woman, 51 years old, showed jealousy toward her husband as the first noticeable sign of the disease. Soon a rapidly increasing loss of memory could be noticed. She could not find her way around in her own apartment. She carried objects back and forth and hid them. At times she would think that someone wanted to kill her and would begin shrieking loudly.

In the institution her entire behavior bore the stamp of utter perplexity. She was totally disoriented to time and place. Occasionally she stated that she could not understand and did not know her way around. At times she greeted the doctor like a visitor, and excused herself for not having finished her work; at times she shrieked loudly that he wanted to cut her, or she repulsed him with indignation, saying that she feared from him something against her chastity. Periodically she was totally delirious, dragged her bedding around, called her husband and her daughter, and seemed to have auditory hallucinations. Frequently, she shrieked with a dreadful voice for many hours.

Because of her inability to comprehend the situation, she always cried out loudly as soon as someone tried to examine her. Only through repeated attempts was it possible finally to ascertain anything.

Her ability to remember was severely disturbed. If one pointed to objects, she named most of them correctly, but immediately afterwards she would forget everything again. When reading, she went from one line into another, reading the letters or reading with a senseless emphasis. When writing, she repeated individual syllables several times, left out others, and quickly became stranded. When talking, she frequently used perplexing phrases and some paraphrastic expressions (milk-pourer instead of cup). Sometimes one noticed her getting stuck. Some questions she obviously did not comprehend. She seemed no longer to understand the use of some objects. Her gait was not impaired. She could use both hands equally well. Her patellar reflexes

*Wilkins, RH, Brody, IA: "Alzheimer's disease." *Archives of Neurology*, July 1969, 21:109-110, American Medical Association, Chicago, 1969.

were present. Her pupils reacted. Somewhat rigid radial arteries; no enlargement of cardiac dullness; no albumin.

During her subsequent course, the phenomena that were interpreted as focal symptoms were at times more noticeable and at times less noticeable. But always they were only slight. The generalized dementia progressed however. After 4½ years of the disease, death occurred. At the end, the patient was completely stuporous; she lay in her bed with her legs drawn up under her, and in spite of all precautions she acquired decubitus ulcers.

Alzheimer's Diagnosis: A Peculiar Disease of the Cerebral Cortex

Discussion of Perplexed Woman

The first sign of the illness was apparently delusional jealousy. Persecutory delusions, and possibly auditory hallucinations, developed later. However, the more significant disturbance is the gradual development of a progressive Dementia. The patient is disoriented to time and place, has marked impairment in immediate and recent memory, and shows many signs of disturbed higher cortical functioning. For example, her use of "paraphrastic expressions (milk-pourer instead of cup)" indicates aphasia, and her inability to understand the use of some objects indicates agnosia.

Although Alzheimer refers to her as periodically being "totally delirious," he may have been referring more to periods of agitation and excitement than to clouding of consciousness (reduced clarity of awareness of the environment), a requirement for the DSM-III concept of Delirium. In any case, her usual state is not characterized by clouding of consciousness.

The evidence of a Dementia with insidious onset and a uniformly progressive deteriorating course, plus the exclusion of all other specific causes of the Dementia, indicate Primary Degenerative Dementia. Because the illness began before the patient was 65, the onset is presenile. The presence of delusions is indicated in the fifth digit.

The historical significance of this case is that it was the first one in which microscopic examination of the brain revealed the characteristic histopathological changes of what has become known as Alzheimer's disease: senile plaques, neurofibrillary tangles, and granulovacuolar degeneration of neurons.

DSM-III Diagnosis:

Axis I: **290.12 Primary Degenerative Dementia, Presenile Onset, with Delusions (p. 126)**

Josef Breuer (1842–1925)

Breuer was a Viennese physician who collaborated with Freud in using hypnosis to treat patients with hysteria. The case of "Anna O." was abstracted from Breuer and Freud's *Studies in Hysteria*,* published in 1895. Anna O. was treated and her case reported by Breuer. It was the case that suggested to Freud the possibility of a "talking cure"—later known as psychoanalysis.

Anna O.

206 Anna O. was the only daughter of a wealthy Viennese Jewish family. She became ill when she was 21, in 1880.

Up to the onset of the disease, the patient showed no sign of nervousness, not even during pubescence. She had a keen, intuitive intellect, a craving for psychic fodder, which she did not, however, receive after she left school. She was endowed with a sensitiveness for poetry and fantasy, which was, however, controlled by a very strong and critical mind . . . . Her will was energetic, impenetrable and persevering, sometimes mounting to selfishness; it relinquished its aim only out of kindness and for the sake of others. . . . Her moods always showed a slight tendency to an excess of merriment or sadness, which made her more or less temperamental. . . . With her puritanically-minded family, this girl of overflowing mental vitality led a most monotonous existence.

She spent hours daydreaming, making up fanciful plots in what she called her "private theatre." She was at times so engrossed in fantasy that she did not hear when people spoke to her.

In July, 1880, her father, whom she admired and "loved passionately," developed tuberculosis. From July through November Anna was his night nurse, sitting up with him every night, observing his pain and deterioration, with the knowledge that he would not recover.

Her own health eventually began to decline:

. . . she became very weak, anemic, and evinced a disgust for nourishment, so that despite her marked reluctance, it was found necessary to take her away from the sick man. The main reason for this step was a very intensive cough about which I [Breuer] was first consulted. I found that she had a typical nervous cough. Soon, there also developed a striking need for rest, distinctly noticeable in the afternoon hours, which merged in the evening into a sleep-like state, followed by strong excitement. . . . From the eleventh of December until the first of April the patient remained bedridden.

---

*Breuer J, Freud S: *Studies in Hysteria*. Translated by AA Brill. Boston, Beacon Press, 1937, p. 14.

In rapid succession there seemingly developed a series of new and severe disturbances.

Left-sided occipital pain; convergent strabismus (diplopia), which was markedly aggravated through excitement. She complained that the wall was falling over (obliquus affection). Profound analyzable visual disturbances, paresis of the anterior muscles of the throat, to the extent that the head could finally be moved only if the patient pressed it backward between her raised shoulders and then moved her whole back. Contractures and anesthesia of the right upper extremity, and somewhat later of the right lower extremity. . . .

It was in this condition that I took the patient under treatment, and I soon became convinced that we were confronted with a severe psychic alteration. There were two entirely separate states of consciousness, which alternated very frequently and spontaneously, moving further apart during the course of the disease. In one of them she knew her environment, was sad and anxious, but relatively normal; in the other, she hallucinated, was "naughty"—i.e., she scolded, threw the pillows at people whenever and to what extent her contractures enabled her to, and tore with her movable fingers the buttons from the covers and underwear, etc. If anything had been changed in the room during this phase, if someone entered, or went out, she then complained that she was lacking in time, and observed the gap in the lapse of her conscious ideas. . . . In very clear moments she complained of the deep darkness in her head, that she could not think, that she was going blind and deaf, and that she had two egos, her real and an evil one, which forced her to evil things, etc. . . . there appeared a deep, functional disorganization of her speech. At first, it was noticed that she missed words; gradually, when this increased her language was devoid of all grammar, all syntax, to the extent that the whole conjugation of verbs was wrong. . . . In the further course of this development she missed words almost continuously, and searched for them laboriously in four or five languages, so that one could hardly understand her. . . . She spoke only English and understood nothing that was told her in German. The people about her were forced to speak English. . . There then followed two weeks of complete mutism. Continuous effort to speak elicited no sound.

About ten days after her father died, a consultant was called in whom she ignored as completely as all strangers, while I demonstrated to him her peculiarities. . . . It was a real "negative hallucination," which has so often been reproduced experimentally since then. He finally succeeded in attracting her attention by blowing smoke into her face. She then suddenly saw a stranger, rushed to the door, grabbed the key, but fell to the floor unconscious. This was followed by a short outburst of anger, and then by a severe attack of anxiety, which I could calm only with a great deal of effort.

The family was afraid Anna would jump from the window, so she was removed from her third-floor apartment to a country house where, for three days ". . . she remained sleepless, took no nourishment, and was full of suicidal ideas. . . She also broke windows, etc., and evinced hallucinations [of black snakes, death's heads, etc.] without absences [dissociated periods].

Breuer treated Anna by asking her, under hypnosis, to talk about her symptoms, a technique she referred to as "chimney sweeping." As the treatment proceeded, she had longer periods of lucidity and began to lose her symptoms. After 18 months of treatment, as Anna prepared to spend the summer in her country home, Breuer pronounced her well and said he would no longer be seeing her. That evening he was called back to the house, where he found Anna thrashing around in her bed, going through an imaginary childbirth. She insisted that the baby was Breuer's. He managed to calm her by hypnotizing her. According to Ernest Jones, Breuer then "fled the house in a cold sweat" and never saw her again.

Anna remained ill intermittently over the next six years, spending considerable time in a sanatorium, where she apparently became addicted to morphine. She was often fairly well in the daytime, but still suffered from hallucinatory states toward evening.

By 30 she had apparently completely recovered, and moved to Frankfort with her mother. There she became a feminist leader and social worker. She established an institution for "wayward girls" and spoke out against the devaluation of women that she believed was inherent in orthodox Judaism.

Anna never married, but was said to be an attractive and passionate woman who gathered admirers wherever she went. She had no recurrences of her illness and never spoke about it — in fact, apparently asked her relatives not to speak of it to anyone. In her later years her attitude toward psychoanalysis was clearly negative, and she became quite angry at the suggestion that one of her "girls" be psychoanalyzed.

Anna died at 77, of abdominal cancer.

Breuer's Diagnosis: Hysteria

Discussion of Anna O.

Anna O. presents a clinical picture that was apparently seen with some frequency in consulting rooms in the Victorian period. We doubt that many clinicians at the present time see patients quite like Anna O. For this reason, DSM-III does not have a single category that would encompass the variety of symptoms and the often chronic course that correspond to the traditional concept of Hysteria. Anna O. is therefore a diagnostic enigma for today's clinician.

There is little doubt that Anna O. had a straightforward major depressive episode. She is described as despondent over her father's death—"she remained sleepless, took no nourishment, and was full of suicidal ideas." Hence, the diagnosis Major Depression, Single Episode, Unspecified ("unspecified" because of the difficulty determining whether she in fact had genuine psychotic symptoms) is warranted.

The most striking feature, however, and the reason for Breuer's being called in on the case, was the numerous physical symptoms: cough, left-sided occipital pain, convergent strabismus, visual disturbance, weakness of throat muscles, contractures, and anesthesia of the extremities. If we assume that Breuer had correctly ruled out an organic etiology for these symptoms, they indicate a Conversion Disorder.

Her "sleep-like state[s]," going through an imaginary childbirth, and alternating states of consciousness all indicate a Dissociative Disorder; but since the description does not correspond to any of the specific DSM-III Dissociative Disorders, the diagnosis must be Atypical Dissociative Disorder.

Anna had many other symptoms that suggest a psychotic disorder—incoherence ("her language was devoid of all grammar, all syntax, to the extent that the whole conjugation of verbs was wrong"), hallucinations of black snakes and death's heads, and possible delusions ("she complained . . . that she had two egos, her real and an evil one, which forced her to evil things").

Because of these seemingly psychotic symptoms, rigid use of the DSM-III criteria might lead to a diagnosis of either Major Depression with Psychotic Features or Schizophrenia. However, these diagnoses fail to capture the essence of Anna O.'s illness. The problem is that DSM-III does not recognize "hysterical" psychotic symptoms, with the exception of Factitious Disorder with Psychological Symptoms. Did Anna O. have voluntary control over her symptoms, as in a Factitious Disorder? Certainly Breuer and Freud did not think so. We also doubt that Anna O. "decided" to produce her various symptoms.

If forced to give a DSM-III diagnosis that would account for these "psychotic" symptoms, we would add Atypical Psychosis, thereby indicating the unusual nature of her psychotic disorder. Admittedly, the approach taken here fragments Anna O.'s illness into several different diagnoses, each of which describes a different phase.

DSM-III Diagnosis:

Axis I: 300.11 Conversion Disorder (p. 244)
296.20 Major Depression, Single Episode, Unspecified (p. 218)
298.90 Atypical Psychosis (p. 202)
300.15 Atypical Dissociative Disorder (p. 260)

Sigmund Freud (1856–1939)

Sigmund Freud, the originator of psychoanalysis, attempted to explain the mechanisms by which unconscious conflicts result in the clinical manifestations of psychopathology. The cases that follow have been edited to focus on the descriptive features rather than on the psychodynamic explanations of the symptoms. These cases, first published between 1909 and 1911, were abstracted from Volume III of Freud's *Collected Papers.* *

Little Hans

207 Little Hans's parents were friends and early followers of Freud who had agreed to bring up their first child with ". . . no more coercion than might be absolutely necessary for maintaining good behavior. And, as the child developed into a cheerful, good-natured, and lively little boy, the experiment of letting him grow up and express himself without being intimidated went on satisfactorily."

Freud asked Hans's father to collect observations on the sexual life of his child, and received frequent letters reporting on Hans, beginning just before his third birthday. All went well until Hans was nearly five, at which time Fred received the following letter from his father:

> My dear Professor, I am sending you a little more about Hans — but this time, I am sorry to say, material for a case history. As you will see, during the last few days he has developed a nervous disorder, which has made my wife and me most uneasy, because we have not been able to find any means of dissipating it. . . . No doubt the ground was prepared by sexual over-excitation due to his mother's tenderness; but I am not able to specify the actual exciting cause. He is afraid *that a horse will bite him in the street,* and this fear seems somehow to be connected with his having been frightened by a large penis. . . . I cannot see what to make of it. Has he seen an exhibitionist somewhere? Or is the whole thing simply connected with his mother? It is not very pleasant for us that he should begin setting us problems so early. Apart from his being afraid of going into the street and from his being depressed in the evening, he is in other respects the same Hans, as bright and cheerful as ever.

It was some months later that Hans remembered an incident which had, in fact, occurred just before his symptoms began. He had been

*From *The Collected Papers of Sigmund Freud,* ed. by Ernest Jones, M.D., authorized translation by Alix and James Strachey. Published in the U.S.A. by arrangement with The Hogarth Press, Ltd. and the Institute for Psychoanalysis, London. New York, Basic Books, Inc. 1959. "Little Hans," p. 149; "The Rat Man," p. 296; "Dr. Schreber," p. 390.

walking with his mother and had been frightened when a large horse pulling a bus had fallen down and kicked its feet around violently.

The first evidence of the disturbance was noticed in the first few days of January (1908): "Hans woke up one morning in tears. Asked why he was crying, he said to his mother: 'When I was asleep I thought you were gone and I had no Mummy to coax* with.' " Several days later, on January 7:

> . . . he went to the Stadtpark with his nursemaid as usual. In the street he began to cry and asked to be taken home, saying that he wanted to "coax" with his Mummy. At home he was asked why he had refused to go any further and had cried, but he would not say. Till the evening he was cheerful, as usual. But in the evening he grew visibly frightened; he cried and could not be separated from his mother, and wanted to "coax" with her again. Then he grew cheerful again and slept well.
>
> On January 8 my wife decided to go out with him herself, so as to see what was wrong with him. They went to Schonbrunn, where he always likes going. Again he began to cry, did not want to start, and was frightened. In the end he did go, but was visibly frightened in the street. On the way back from Schonbrunn he said to his mother, after much internal struggling: "I was afraid a horse would bite me." (He had, in fact, become uneasy at Schonbrunn when he saw a horse.) In the evening he seemed to have had another attack similar to that of the previous evening, and to have wanted to be "coaxed" with. He was calmed down. He said, crying: "I know I shall have to go for a walk again tomorrow." And later: "The horse'll come into the room."

On Freud's instructions, Hans's father had some discussion with the little boy about his desire to be taken into his mother's bed and his excessive interest in "widdlers"† — his own and everyone else's.

There ensued a fairly quiet period during which Hans could be persuaded to walk in the park, but felt compelled to look at the horses: "I have to look at horses, and then I'm frightened."

After two weeks in bed with influenza, and then a tonsillectomy, his phobia became much worse. "He goes out on to the balcony, it is true, but not for a walk. As soon as he gets to the street door he hurriedly turns round."

In late March, with some persuasion, he consented to go to the zoo with his father. There he was afraid of the large animals but not the small ones, and would not even look at the elephant or the giraffe. "During the next few days it seemed as though his fears had again somewhat increased. He hardly ventured out of the front door, to which he was taken after luncheon."

It was during this period that there was much discussion between father and son about Hans's masturbation, about the nature of the

---

*Cuddle.

†Penises.

female sexual apparatus, and about Hans's desire to get into bed and "coax" with his mother.

Freud had one session with Hans, during which he made a connection between the white horses that Hans was particularly afraid of and Hans's father, and explained to Hans that he was afraid of his father ". . . precisely because he was so fond of his mother."

In subsequent weeks Hans alluded to his fear that his mother and father would go away and leave him.

Over a period of some months, Hans's symptoms disappeared, and he became closer to his father. Freud saw Hans only once again, when he was "a strapping youth of nineteen" who "suffered from no troubles or inhibitions." He had no memory of the anxiety, the phobia, or the analysis.

Freud's Diagnosis: Phobia

Discussion of Little Hans

There can be little doubt that Hans has a Phobia. He has an irrational fear of and compelling desire to avoid horses. Since the dreaded object does not involve a fear of being alone, in public places from which escape is impossible, or in social situations with the possibility of public embarrassment, this is a Simple Phobia.

There are other important features. Hans has nightmares about being separated from his mother ("When I was asleep I thought you [his mother] were gone and I had no Mummy to coax with.") In the evenings, when anticipating going to bed, he is extremely distressed, perhaps to the point of panic, and cannot be separated from his mother. Finally, he has an unrealistic fear that his parents will "go away and leave him." These are all expressions of excessive anxiety concerning separation from his parents, and together support the additional diagnosis of Separation Anxiety Disorder.

DSM-III Diagnosis:

Axis I: 300.29 Simple Phobia (p. 228)
         309.21 Separation Anxiety Disorder (p. 50)

The Rat Man

208 A youngish man of university education introduced himself to [Freud] with the statement that he had suffered from obsessions ever since his childhood, but with particular intensity for the last four years. The chief features of his disorder were *fears* that something might happen to two people of whom he was very fond — his father and a lady whom he admired. Besides this he was aware of *compulsive impulses* — such as an impulse, for instance, to cut his throat with a razor; and further he produced *prohibitions*, sometimes in connection with quite unimportant things. He had wasted years, he told me, in fighting against these ideas of his, and in this way had lost much ground in the course of his life. He had tried various treatments, but none had been of any use to him. . . .

The experience that precipitated this patient's first visit to Freud occurred when he was on maneuvers with a military unit. An officer had described to him a form of torture in which the prisoner was tied up, a pot of rats was turned upside down on his buttocks, and the rats bored their way into his anus. He reported: "At that moment the idea flashed through my mind *that this was happening to a person very dear to me*" [in fact, to the lady he loved, and to his father, who had actually died nine years before]. When the officer had spoken of this ghastly punishment, and the obsessions had come into his head, he had warded them off by employing a particular "formula." He said to himself, "But," accompanied by a gesture of repudiation, and then "Whatever are you thinking of?"

> That evening, he continued, the same Captain had handed him a packet that had arrived by the post and had said: "Lt. A. has paid the charges for you. You must pay him back." . . . At that instant, however, a "sanction" had taken shape in his mind, namely *that he was not to pay back the money* or it would happen — (that is, the phantasy about the rats would come true as regards his father and the lady). And immediately, in accordance with a type of procedure with which he was familiar [to make sure the fantasy would not come true], there had arisen a command in the shape of a vow: *"You must pay back the 3.8 crowns to Lt. A."* He had said these words to himself almost half aloud.

The necessity of obeying his vow sent him on a complicated journey during which he went in search of Lt. A. He discovered that Lt. A. was not, in fact, the one who had paid the charges. He therefore devised numerous complicated schemes in order to follow the exact wording of his vow (that is, pay back the 3.8 crowns to Lt. A.) even though it was now clear that he did not owe the money to Lt. A.

The first instances of obsessive thoughts had occurred when the patient was six or seven. As he grew older, they waxed and waned, but they had now persisted since his father's death. Freud describes the "exciting cause" of his incapacitation as follows. After his father's death the patient's mother proposed that he marry a wealthy cousin, thus ensuring

> . . . a business connection with the firm [which] would offer him a brilliant opening in his profession. This family plan stirred up in him a conflict as to whether he should remain faithful to the lady he loved in spite of her poverty, or whether he should follow in his father's footsteps and marry the lovely, rich, and well-connected girl who had been assigned to him. And he resolved his conflict, which was in fact one between his love and the persisting influence of his father's wishes, by falling ill; or, to put it more correctly, by falling ill he avoided the task of resolving it in real life. . . . the chief result of his illness was an obstinate incapacity for work, which allowed him to postpone the completion of his education for years. . . .

Freud relates numerous examples of his patient's obsessions and compulsions in relation to his "lady":

> . . . as they were sitting together during a thunderstorm, he was obsessed, he could not tell why, with the necessity for *counting* up to forty or fifty between each flash of lightning and its accompanying thunder-clap. On the day of [the lady's] departure he knocked his foot against a stone lying in the road, and was *obliged* to put it out of the way by the side of the road, because the idea struck him that her carriage would be driving along the same road in a few hours time and might come to grief against this stone. But a few minutes later it occurred to him that this was absurd, and he was *obliged* to go back and replace the stone in its original position in the middle of the road. After her departure he became a prey to an *obsession for understanding*, which made him a curse to all his companions. He forced himself to understand the precise meaning of every syllable that was addressed to him, as though he might otherwise be missing some priceless treasure. Accordingly he kept asking: "What was it you said just then?" And after it had been repeated to him he could not help thinking it had sounded different the first time, so he remained dissatisfied.

Freud's analysis focused on the patient's ambivalence toward his father and his lady, originating in his precocious and intense sexuality and early feelings of rage against his father—both of which had been severely repressed. The rat symbol led Freud and his patient through a series of associations that included anal eroticism, the patient's having been beaten by his father at age four for biting someone, the father's early problems with gambling [in German a gambler is a *"Spielratte"* — or "play-rat"], the infantile notion of anal birth, and the patient's own real childhood experience of having worms. After a year of analysis, the patient was cured of his symptoms and, in Freud's words, "the rat delirium disappeared."

Freud's Diagnosis: Obsessive Compulsive Neurosis

Discussion of The Rat Man

The Rat Man is plagued by both obsessions and compulsions. The obsessions are recurrent persistent ideas (e.g., that something terrible will happen to his sweetheart), impulses (e.g., to cut his throat), and images (e.g., that a rat is boring into the anus of his father). He experiences them as alien and senseless (ego-dystonic) and evolves complicated formulas in an effort to ward them off (e.g., He said to himself: "But," accompanied by a gesture of repudiation, and then, "Whatever are you thinking of?").

The compulsions are repetitive and seemingly purposeful behaviors that are performed according to certain rules and are designed to prevent some future event (e.g., he had to remove a stone from the road and replace it so that his sweetheart's carriage would not "come to grief against this stone"). As with the obsessions, he recognizes that the behavior is senseless and derives no pleasure from carrying it out, other than the release of tension.

Minor obsessions and compulsions that do not cause significant distress or interfere with social or role functioning do not warrant a diagnosis. However, the Rat Man has "wasted years . . . in fighting against these ideas." In the absence of any other disorder that could account for these symptoms, such as Schizophrenia, a diagnosis of Obsessive Compulsive Disorder is indicated. Although Obsessive Compulsive Disorder is often seen in individuals with Compulsive Personality Disorder, in this case there is no description of the patient's personality functioning, apart from the symptoms of his Obsessive Compulsive Disorder.

DSM-III Diagnosis:

Axis I: 300.30 Obsessive Compulsive Disorder (p. 234)

Dr. Schreber

209 In 1903 a German judge, Dr. Daniel Paul Schreber, published his own case history, translated as *Memoirs of a Neurotic*. Freud made his analytic interpretations of the connection between unconscious homosexuality and paranoia on the basis of this document and a report prepared by Dr. Schreber's physician for a mental competency hearing. Freud quotes at length from both.

All we know about Dr. Schreber's first illness, in 1884, is that it was diagnosed as "an attack of severe hypochondria," from which he recovered completely after six months, and returned to his wife and his judicial position. It is unclear how old he was at this time; but since he was already married and had some status in his profession, he cannot have been very young. Subsequent to this illness he was elected to a high judicial position.

The second illness, in 1893, began with the idea that he was to be transformed into a woman. In Dr. Schreber's words:

> . . . a conspiracy against me was brought to a head. . . Its object was to contrive that, when once my nervous complaint had been recognized as incurable or assumed to be so, I should be handed over to a certain person in a particular manner. Thus my soul was to be delivered up to him, but my body . . . was to be transformed into a female body, and as such surrendered to the person in question with a view to sexual abuse, and was then simply to be "left where it was" — that is to say, no doubt, abandoned to corruption.

Dr. Weber, the director of the Sonnenstein Sanatorium in which Schreber was a patient, described his condition as follows:

> . . . he was chiefly troubled by hypochondriacal ideas, complained that he had softening of the brain, that he would soon be dead, etc. But ideas of persecution were already finding their way into the clinical picture, based upon sensorial illusions which, however, seemed only to appear sporadically at first, while simultaneously a high degree of hyperaesthesia was observable — great sensitiveness to light and noise. Later, the visual and auditory illusions became much more frequent. . .
> He believed that he was dead and decomposing, that he was suffering from the plague; he asserted that his body was being handled in all kinds of revolting ways; and, as he himself declares, to this day, he went through worse horrors than any one could have imagined, and all on behalf of a sacred cause. The patient was so much occupied with these pathological phenomena that he was inaccessible to any other impression and would sit perfectly rigid and motionless for hours. . . On the other hand, they tortured him to such a degree that he longed for death. He made repeated attempts at drowning himself in his bath, and asked to be given the cyanide of potassium that was intended for him. His delusional ideas gradually assumed a mystical and religious character; he was in direct communication with God, he was the plaything of devils, he saw "miraculous apparitions," he heard "holy music," and in the end he even came to believe that he was living in another world.

It may be added that there were certain people by whom he thought he was being persecuted and injured, and upon whom he poured abuse. The most prominent of these was his former physician, Flechsig, whom he called a "soul-murderer." The voices he heard during this period mocked him and jeered at him.

Over the next few years there was a gradual change in Dr. Schreber's condition, as his distress about being transformed into a "strumpet" developed into a conviction that it was all part of a divine plan, and that he had a mission to redeem the world. In Schreber's words: "Now, however, I became clearly aware that the order of things imperatively demanded my emasculation, whether I personally liked it or no, and that no *reasonable* course lay open to me but to reconcile myself to the thought of being transformed into a woman. The further consequence of my emasculation could, of course, only be my impregnation . . . by divine rays to the end that a new race of men might be created." And, Schreber elaborates:

> The *only thing* which could appear unreasonable in the eyes of other people is the fact, already touched upon in the expert's report, that I am sometimes to be found, standing before the mirror or elsewhere, with the upper portion of my body partly bared, and wearing sundry feminine adornments, such as ribbons, trumpery necklaces and the like. This only occurs, I may add, when I am by myself, and never, at least so far as I am able to avoid it, in the presence of other people.

Dr. Weber, in a report dated 1900, described Schreber's changed condition as follows:

> Since for the last nine months Herr President Schreber has taken his meals daily at my family board, I have had the most ample opportunities of conversing with him on every imaginable topic. Whatever the subject was that came up for discussion (apart, of course, from his delusional ideas), whether it concerned events in the field of administration and law, or of politics, or of art, or of literature, or of social life — in short, whatever the topic, Dr. Schreber gave evidence of a lively interest, a well-informed mind, a good memory and sound judgment; his ethical outlook, moreover, was one which it was impossible not to endorse. So, too, in his lighter talk with the ladies of the party, he was both courteous and affable, and if he touched upon matters in a more humorous vein he invariably displayed tact and decorum. Never once, during these innocent talks round the dining-table, did he introduce subjects which should more properly have been raised at a medical consultation.

Dr. Schreber made numerous appeals to regain his liberty. In Freud's words:

> . . . he did not in the least disavow his delusion or make any secret of his intention of publishing [his memoirs]. On the contrary, he dwelt upon the importance of his ideas to religious thought, and upon their invulnerability to the attacks of modern science; but at the same time he laid stress upon the absolute harmlessness of the actions which, as he was aware, his delusions obliged him to perform. Such, indeed, were his acumen and the cogency of his logic that finally, and in spite of his being an acknowledged paranoiac, his efforts were crowned with success. In July 1902 Dr. Schreber's civil rights were restored. . .

Freud's Diagnosis: Dementia Paranoides

Discussion of Dr. Schreber

Dr. Schreber's illness is characterized by bizarre (patently absurd) delusions, which begin as persecutory (that he will be transformed into a woman, with a view to sexual abuse) and later become somatic (softening of the brain), nihilistic (he was dead and decomposing), religious (he was in direct communication with God), and, finally, grandiose (he had a mission to redeem the world). What Dr. Weber refers to as "hypochondriacal ideas" are, in fact, somatic delusions. This leads one to suspect that the original illness, diagnosed as "attack of severe hypochondria," also involved somatic delusions. The delusions were accompanied by auditory hallucinations (holy music), visual hallucinations (seeing miraculous apparitions), and probably tactile hallucinations as well (his body being handled in all kinds of revolting ways). His sitting "rigid and motionless for hours" suggests catatonic stupor, that is, marked decrease in reactivity to the environment and reduction in spontaneous movements and activity. The same behavior might suggest depressive stupor; but, apart from the suicidal ideas, there is no other reference to characteristic depressive symptomatology.

All of these features, with a deterioration from a previous level of functioning, suggest a diagnosis of Schizophrenia. This diagnosis is given only if the first signs of the illness appear before age 45. In Dr. Schreber's case, this seems likely.

The subtype of Schizophrenia is Paranoid, because the clinical picture is dominated by first persecutory, and then grandiose, delusions. The course is considered chronic because the disturbance lasted for more than two years.

Although the predominant psychotic symptoms are paranoid delusions, the diagnosis of a Paranoid Disorder is not made because of the hallucinations and the bizarre nature of the delusions.

DSM-III Diagnosis:

Axis I: **295.32 Schizophrenia, Paranoid Type, Chronic (p. 188)**

Jacob S. Kasanin (1897–1946)

Kasanin provided a bridge between Schizophrenia and Affective Disorder by first proposing, in 1933, the term *Schizoaffective*. According to Kasanin, this disorder occurs in "fairly young individuals, quite well integrated socially, who suddenly blow up in a dramatic psychosis and present a clinical picture which may be called either schizophrenic or affective, and in whom the differential diagnosis is extremely difficult." The following cases have been extracted from his article "The Acute Schizoaffective Psychoses."*

Suspicious Wife

210 S.R., female, white, married, age 25, admitted to the hospital February 25, 1927. . . Diagnosis: dementia praecox. Chief Complaint. . . . The patient was sent to a psychiatric hospital from the [city] hospital where she was restless, excited and showed a "schizophrenic reaction type."

Personal History. . . . The patient was always an active, energetic, industrious person. She was ambitious, full of life, was very much interested in her house and held several positions after marriage. She was extremely affectionate, demonstrative and romantic. . . . The patient has one child, a boy of 6 years, to whom she was extremely devoted. . . .

Present illness. . . . [Six months before admission] when the little boy began to attend school, the patient felt that she ought to escort him to school. Her husband [a policeman] ridiculed her anxiety about the boy. She became upset and told the husband that if anything ever happened to the boy she would be through with him. [A month before admission] a policeman in their neighborhood committed suicide. The husband came home, told his wife about the incident and said that such work would drive anybody to suicide. This seemed to have affected the patient and she became depressed afterward. When the husband asked the patient about the cause of her depression she told him that somebody was coming between them and complained about the interference of his parents. . . . The patient cried a good deal and [a week later] she said that her heart was bad and that she was going to die. [A few days] later she became very upset, said something was going to happen in the house, said the pedlar who came to the door was going to hurt her and had a feeling that the chimney was going to fall down and kill her. She said that her house was a house of ill

*Kasanin J: "The Acute Schizoaffective Psychoses," American Journal Of Psychiatry, 13:97-126, 1933, American Psychiatric Association, Washington, D.C., 1933

omen. . . . [Five days before admission] the patient suddenly got up in the middle of the night, dressed, packed her suitcase and said that she was going to her parents. The husband helped his wife to do it. Immediately on her arrival at her father's home the patient commenced to accuse her father and mother of being in league to influence her husband against her. She stayed there that day and the next night the sleeplessness was repeated. She got up and went into her brother's room. She accused him of intending to poison her husband and that he was trying to come between them. Suddenly she left the house, called up the police and asked them to come to her parents' house and rescue her, as something dreadful was going to happen. The husband succeeded in preventing the police from coming, and took her over to the city hospital.

When the husband came to see the patient at the city hospital she accused him of trying to wean the boy away from her and complained of all kinds of peculiar noises in the hospital. She felt that the other patients in the ward were discussing her affairs, swore at her, said that her husband was unfaithful to her and that he was going to steal the boy away from her. The other patients also said that her husband was "four in one," intimating that he was of mixed blood and part Negro. She thought that these voices were "rayed" from someone who was in a trance in one of the other rooms. When her husband visited her at the hospital he appeared "funny" — his eyes were glassy and had a peculiar staring expression in them.

[She was then transferred to a psychiatric hospital.] She said that she felt sad, unhappy and depressed. The intellectual functions were intact. She expressed a large number of ideas, revolving around her relationship to her husband. She complained that there was a good deal of interference in their home life. She also felt that she was going to be harmed, thought that her husband was going to shoot her rather than shoot himself. She said that when she was at the city hospital she heard her name being called out over the loud speaker. She denied any hallucinations in the psychiatric hospital. She also said that while at the city hospital she smelled many and various odors. [Two weeks after admission] she was transferred to a state hospital. There she was sullen, morose and made very little attempt to get interested in the ward. She was mildly depressed and was quite embarrassed when asked about her illness. She spoke freely about her illness and said that while she was in the psychopathic hospital she saw "studies" of her husband from childhood to manhood. She saw him as a boy, a sailor, and a police officer. She said that she had had many somatic sensations before she came to the hospital and had "funny impressions which seem to spell danger." She could not help but feel that something dreadful was going to happen to her child, and that her husband would blame her if anything happened to him. She had the suspicion that her husband was unfaithful to her, and that he had begun to take "dope," as he seemed very dull and stupid. She intimated that her gastric symptoms may have been due to poison. Within a few weeks the patient changed a great deal. She began to laugh, appeared happy, talked very freely and spoke a great deal about "radio hypnotism," to which she attributed all her troubles.

[She was discharged after two months, and at a six-month follow-up] . . . appeared perfectly well, resumed her care of the house and got a job in a department store during the Christmas rush. [Two years later] She, herself, analyzed the whole situation and described the conditions which led to her breakdown. . . . The patient [had] moved into a new house which she bought with her own savings. She had a great deal of work to do putting the house in order, as it was an old house. . . . She was troubled by the fact that the furnace was not working properly and she could smell gas in the house. She lost her appetite, could not sleep and felt very badly. . . . Things did not go very well with her personal life. Her husband loved and adored her, but he was under the influence of his mother who disliked the patient. One night while she was in bed she saw three bright stars from her window. She could not fall asleep. The stars were bright red in color. She did close her eyes, but when she opened them again the stars would still be there. She felt that something terrible was going to happen.

A review of the family situation brought out the fact that there was a real foundation for some of the patient's beliefs. Both her family and her husband's family were doing everything possible to estrange the patient and her husband. . . . The patient said that the psychosis was a good thing as somehow it has helped to straighten out the various tangles in her life, and gave her courage, confidence in herself. The patient is doing very well now and handles unusually well the affairs which are just as complicated as they were before.

Kasanin's Diagnosis: Schizoaffective Schizophrenia

Discussion of Suspicious Wife

Less than four months elapsed from the onset of the first definite symptoms (after the suicide of her husband's friend) until this patient apparently completely recovered. The illness is characterized by depressed mood and a variety of changing persecutory delusions, some of which are bizarre. In addition, there are auditory hallucinations (or at least illusions) with a persecutory content, and problems with appetite and sleep and thoughts of her own death.

Although the patient is frequently described as depressed and unhappy, the persistence of a prominent depressed mood is not established. In fact, within a few weeks "She began to laugh, appeared happy, talked very freely and spoke a great deal about 'radio hypnotism,' to which she attributed all her troubles." This indicates that even if there were a sustained depressed mood and the associated symptoms of the depressive syndrome, the psychotic symptoms apparently were present when she was no longer depressed. For this reason the diagnosis of a major depressive episode cannot be made, and the differential diagnosis is thus between Schizoaffective Disorder and Schizophreniform Disorder. Because there is not specific evidence of the full depressive syndrome, we prefer the diagnosis of Schizophreniform Disorder. However, we would not quarrel with the diagnosis of Schizoaffective Disorder.

DSM-III Diagnosis:

Axis I: **295.40 Schizophreniform Disorder (p. 199)**

Magnet Man

211 E.F., male, age 20, single laborer, white, [was] admitted to the hospital March 15, 1929. . . Diagnosis: dementia praecox.

Chief Complaint. . . . The patient was sent to the hospital by his family because about two weeks before admission he became overactive, exhibited queer behavior and spoke a great deal about his theories of life. Finally he became so excited that he was taken to the out-patient department from which he was referred to the hospital.

Personal History. . . . The patient did well in the various positions in which he was employed. . . . He was a model employee, but very quiet and shy. . . . As far as his personality is concerned he was quite an average young man. . . . His outside interests were mostly athletic. He took part in several sports and played baseball with amateur groups. . . . Several months prior to admission he fell in love with a girl who worked in the same factory where he worked and told his family about it. He wanted to bring the girl to the house but his mother told him he was too young to go out with girls. Although the patient spoke about having dates with the girl, she told her foreman that their acquaintance was very casual.

Present illness. . . . Two weeks before admission the co-workers in the factory noticed that the patient began to talk a great deal and that he began to sing very loudly. Quite suddenly he declared that he was going on the stage or else would join a professional baseball team. The same behavior was observed at home. He sent a telegram to a Boston baseball team which was at that time playing in the South, asking the manager for a position. He told his family that he was going to make a great deal of money and they should finance him for the trip. He slept very poorly and was very restless at night. A week before admission he went to one of the Harvard physicians and offered him his body for scientific purposes. The latter referred him to the hospital. He was quite excited for several days and spoke a great deal about scientific experiments on his brain and the cure of insanity. Finally he was brought to the out-patient clinic. . . .

For several days the patient was quite active and restless, but responded very well to continuous baths. He was very cooperative and talked freely to the physician. He took a fair amount of interest in the ward routine and was friendly with other patients. His speech was relevant but at times incoherent and he spoke about a great many things. The patient spoke a great deal about his philosophy of life giving several variants of his theory of personal magnetism. For some time the patient has had a conflict over auto-erotism which he has practiced since childhood. He also had sex relations with a nine-year-old girl when he was of the same age and it disturbed him. The conflict was intensified by the fact that he was quite religious. He met a girl a year ago and fell in love with her, but it took him a long time before he was introduced to her. Finally he asked her for a date, about four months ago. She refused. He felt badly but he asked again three months ago, and she told him she was going to the beach with her parents. He finally got a date about a week prior to his admission to the hospital, they went to her house after the movies, and they "got to loving on the sofa." He felt magnetism go over him when he kissed her, and when he passed his hand over her hair he "felt the flow of magnetism just like in a wet dream."

He began speculating about causes of this and thought he had made a new discovery. The patient said that he was able to solve all his conflicts by this discovery. He found that the brain controlled the fluid which traveled throughout the whole body and could be drawn from mouth, teeth, roof of the mouth, lips and nose, if touched. This fluid would travel throughout the whole body producing a magnetic feeling passing over him, the same as a sexual act. . . . Not only did he get this magnetic feeling when he touched an animate object but an inanimate object as well. When in church he felt that the holy images might be alive and that God was in communication with him. He stated that when he expectorated, the saliva was equivalent to spermatic fluid. . . . [He felt this power came to him from God.] The patient said that he could see God if he closed his eyes. He could see God moving about, saw Him moving His fingers and saw His features. He saw God sitting on the throne pointing His fingers and controlling the movement of the world. God never talked to him. At one time he saw God mold clay and blow the breath of life into it.

Clinical Course. . . . Within a few days the patient became quiet, cooperative but still insisted on elaborating his ideas. Commitment to a state institution was recommended but nine days after the patient entered the hospital he was taken home by his family. Within a few weeks he joined one of the branches of the governmental service and has been doing very well in his field of service.

Kasanin's Diagnosis: Schizoaffective Schizophrenia

Discussion of Magnet Man

This brief illness is characterized by elevated and expansive mood, pressure of speech, grandiosity, and hyperactivity. The patient is described as sleeping "very poorly" and being "very restless at night." We assume that this represents the characteristic decreased need for sleep seen in a manic episode. In addition, there are many delusions, all of them involving grandiose themes, and hallucinations of God. Thus, his psychotic symptoms are all congruent with his elevated mood.

Kasanin undoubtedly made a diagnosis of Schizoaffective Schizophrenia because he believed that the prominent bizarre delusions were incompatible with a diagnosis of mania; but in recent years, in this country, the concept of mania has broadened. Hence, in DSM-III even the most bizarre delusions do not necessarily exclude a diagnosis of mania. Because of the rather clear evidence of the full manic syndrome and no evidence that the psychotic symptoms were present at a time when there was no affective disturbance, the diagnosis in this case is Bipolar Disorder, Manic, with Psychotic Features.

DSM-III Diagnosis:

Axis I: 296.44 Bipolar Disorder, Manic, with Psychotic Features (p. 217)

Paul Hoch (1902–1964) and Philip Polatin (1905–1980)

Drs. Hoch and Polatin, from the New York State Psychiatric Institute, proposed in 1949 the concept of Pseudoneurotic Schizophrenia. According to them, this diagnosis applies to patients who have "the basic mechanisms of schizophrenia" yet, because of their "subtle" manifestations, "there is no way to demonstrate it clinically." Many of the patients in question had been analyzed "for a considerable period of time; and the suspicion [had] never been raised that they were not psychoneurotic." The following case is abstracted from their article "Pseudoneurotic Forms of Schizophrenia."*

Fearful Girl

212 S.S. is a 21-year-old girl who was hospitalized because she had not improved after a year of outpatient psychotherapy.

On admission, she stated, "I have fears of food; I have fears of something happening to my family; I cannot sleep; I get depressed; I become tense, anxious and agitated."

She was cooperative and pleasant, gave a coherent and reasonably complete history, and denied delusions or hallucinations (although she had sometimes been afraid that she might someday have hallucinations). Her affect was labile, with a shallow quality.

At times she speaks of feeling very hopeless and of feeling that suicide is the only answer in the end; but usually she does not appear to feel this way, and more often seems rather to enjoy the uniqueness which she feels her illness possesses. Occasionally a really depressing thought will strike her; at such times she will appear truly depressed, with ready tears and a more convincing attitude of despair. Ideas suggesting irreparable organic damage or deficits in the field of emotional experience seem most capable of provoking these markedly depressed moods which are usually short-lived.

S.S. dates the beginning of her illness to a night in her 15th year when she overheard her parents having intercourse. She became sexually aroused and describes

. . . feeling there was something wrong with me, like I was going up in an elevator, and I thought it would never go away; I thought maybe I couldn't experience any sexual feeling. Soon afterward, the word "fuck" was popping in my mind and kept going over and over, and not for a minute could I get it out of my thoughts. A couple of months later it was

*Hoch P, Polatin P: "Pseudoneurotic Forms of Schizophrenia," *Psychiatric Quarterly* 23:248-76, 1949. Human Sciences Press, New York, 1949.

still going over in my mind, and then I told myself, "Why should you think such a word like that, that you cannot tell to anyone, if they asked you what is wrong", so I changed it to "worry." . . . I don't know how I ever got through school. Ever since I was 15, "worry" kept rotating in my mind continually. I got so I couldn't swallow; I couldn't eat. Food did not agree with me because I was worried. The word "fuck" made me feel nauseated; I couldn't sleep. I would lie there with agitation, with the idea of the word going over and over.

Since that time, she has had a number of similar preoccupations — the fear that she would some day be so concerned about the cleanliness of food that she would be able to eat only kosher food; the fear that she would come to believe in Christ and thus upset her orthodox Jewish family; the worry that she might upset her sisters so much that they would become insane. She also had some compulsions, such as having to turn off the light six times each night and having to leave her shoes in a parallel line when she went to bed; but these were not elaborate or time consuming.

She has had many crushes on boys, but no sexual relationships. She has stated, in an amytal interview, that she does not know whether she is male or female, that she fears she cannot lead a normal life or be happy. She appears to have had no close girl friends, but to have been intensely and ambivalently involved with her extended family.

She finished high school and a one-year business course and was able to work as a clerk until a year ago, when she came home from work with a dazed appearance and refused to talk to anyone, saying "You wouldn't understand." It was at that time that she was referred for outpatient treatment. She spent the year at home, doing very little except trying to "understand" her illness.

On the ward she is described as careless and listless, staying in bed all day, with no initiative. "She manifests a belief in thought magic and also shows a fluctuating appraisal of reality and, at times, depersonalization."

Hoch and Polatin's Diagnosis: Pseudoneurotic Schizophrenia

Discussion of Fearful Girl

This woman suffers from a variety of symptoms: morbid fears of possible future events, labile but "shallow" affect, obsessions (thinking about the words "fuck" and "worry"), compulsions (turning off the light and lining up her shoes), identity disturbance (that she might be male or become a Christian), difficulties in interpersonal relations (no close girl friends), magical thinking, depersonalization, and markedly impaired functioning (spending the last year at home thinking about her illness). Undoubtedly, this plethora of chronically disabling symptoms was a major factor in Hoch and Polatin's diagnosis of Schizophrenia. However, the absence of delusions, hallucinations, flat affect, and loosening of associations or incoherence rules out a DSM-III diagnosis of Schizophrenia.

An Axis I diagnosis of Obsessive Compulsive Disorder is justified by the prominence of the obsessions and compulsions and the degree of distress and interference in functioning they cause the patient. She probably does not recognize the morbid fears as senseless, and they are therefore ego-syntonic, not true obsessions. However, they are best understood as an associated feature of the Obsessive Compulsive Disorder.

The Axis I diagnosis does not account for the patient's chronic maladaptive pattern of relating to and thinking about her environment and herself. Some of her symptoms are characteristic of Borderline Personality Disorder: identity disturbance and affective instability. Others are characteristic of Schizotypal Personality Disorder: magical thinking, social isolation, and depersonalization. It is likely that other features of these disorders were present, although not noted. In the absence of positive evidence that the criteria for these specific personality disorders are met, a diagnosis of Mixed Personality Disorder is appropriate.

DSM-III Diagnosis:

Axis I: 300.30 Obsessive Compulsive Disorder (p. 235)
Axis II: 301.89 Mixed Personality Disorder (with Borderline and Schizotypal features) (p. 329)

Albert Hofmann (1906 —   )

Dr. Hofmann, a chemist working in a large Swiss pharmaceutical company, had been studying the synthesis of various natural ergot alkaloids. In April 1943 he described the following experiences.*

Dr. Hofmann

213 Last Friday, April 16, 1943, I was forced to stop my work in the laboratory in the middle of the afternoon and to go home, as I was seized by a peculiar restlessness associated with a sensation of mild dizziness. On arriving home, I lay down and sank into a kind of drunkenness which was not unpleasant and which was characterized by extreme activity of imagination. As I lay in a dazed condition with my eyes closed (I experienced daylight as disagreeably bright) there surged upon me an uninterrupted stream of fantastic images of extraordinary plasticity and vividness and accompanied by an intense, kaleidoscope-like play of colors. This condition gradually passed off after about two hours.

[Dr. Hofmann suspected that his strange experiences were the result of accidentally ingesting the drug that he had been working on. Three days later he conducted an experiment on himself by taking the smallest dose of the substance that he believed could be expected to have any effect. After 40 minutes, in his laboratory notes he reported "slight dizziness, unrest, difficulty in concentration, visual disturbances, marked desire to laugh. . . ." At this point, his laboratory notes are discontinued. Later he describes what happened.]

I asked my laboratory assistant to accompany me home as I believed that I should have a repetition of the disturbance of the previous Friday. While we were cycling home, however, it became clear that the symptoms were much stronger than the first time. I had great difficulty in speaking coherently, my field of vision swayed before me, and objects appeared distorted like images in curved mirrors. I had the impression of being unable to move from the spot, although my assistant told me afterwards that we had cycled at a good pace. . . . Once I was at home the physician was called.

By the time the doctor arrived, the peak of the crisis had already passed. As far as I remember, the following were the most outstanding symptoms: vertigo; visual disturbances; the faces of those around me

---

*Ayd FJ, Blackwell B: *Discoveries in Biological Psychiatry.* Philadelphia, JB Lippincott Co., 1970, p. 91.

appeared as grotesque, colored masks; marked motoric unrest, alternating with paralysis; an intermittent heavy feeling in the head, limbs and the entire body, as if they were filled with lead; dry, constricted sensation in the throat; feeling of choking; clear recognition of my condition, in which state I sometimes observed, in the manner of an independent, neutral observer, that I shouted half insanely or babbled incoherent words. Occasionally I felt as if I were out of my body.

The doctor found a rather weak pulse but an otherwise normal circulation. . . . Six hours after ingestion of the [drug] my condition had already improved considerably. Only the visual disturbances were still pronounced. Everything seemed to sway and the proportions were distorted like the reflections in the surface of moving water. Moreover, all objects appeared in unpleasant, constantly changing colors, the predominant shades being sickly green and blue. When I closed my eyes, an unending series of colorful, very realistic and fantastic images surged in upon me. A remarkable feature was the manner in which all acoustic perceptions (e.g., the noise of a passing car) were transformed into optical effects, every sound evoking a corresponding colored hallucination constantly changing in shape and color like pictures in a kaleidoscope. At about one o'clock I fell asleep and awoke next morning feeling perfectly well.

Dr. Hofmann's Diagnosis: an "Extraordinary Disturbance" caused by the ingestion of a hallucinogen

Discussion of Dr. Hofmann

The many symptoms, predominantly perceptual changes, clearly are related to the ingestion of a drug. In fact, the drug that Dr. Hofmann was working with was lysergic acid diethylamide, better known now as LSD. His description of his own reaction illustrates the characteristic features of a Hallucinogen Hallucinosis: illusions (faces appeared grotesque), depersonalization (". . . I felt as if I were out of my body."), hallucinations (". . . colored hallucination constantly changing in shape and color . . ."), and synesthesias (". . . acoustic perceptions . . . were transformed into optical effects. . ."). He also describes another characteristic feature: all of the symptoms occur during a state of full wakefulness and alertness and with full recognition that the symptoms are the effect of the drug (". . . clear recognition of my condition, in which state I sometimes observed, in the manner of an independent, neutral observer . . .").

The DSM-III criteria for a Hallucinogen Hallucinosis also require certain physical symptoms, such as pupillary dilation, tachycardia, tremors, and incoordination. Although these are not reported by Dr. Hofmann, we would assume that some of them were present. Needless to say, the inability of Dr. Hofmann to continue working while experiencing the effect of the drug is evidence of maladaptive behavioral effects, also required to make the diagnosis.

DSM-III Diagnosis:

Axis I: 305.30 Hallucinogen Hallucinosis (p. 154)

Hervey Cleckley (1905–   )

In *The Mask of Sanity*,* published in 1955, Cleckley attempted to clarify the confusing and paradoxical nature of Psychopathic Personality. According to him, individuals with the disorder are "outwardly intact, showing excellent peripheral function, but centrally deficient or disabled in such a way that abilities . . . cannot be utilized consistently for sane purposes or prevented from regularly working toward self-destructive and other seriously pathologic results." The following case is extracted from his book.

Tom

214 This young man, twenty-one years of age, does not look at all like a criminal type or a shifty delinquent. . . . Tom looks and is in robust physical health. His manner and appearance are pleasing. . . . There is nothing to suggest that he is putting on a bold front or trying to adopt any attitude or manner that will be misleading. Though he knows the examiner has evidence of his almost incredible career, he gives such an impression that it seems for the moment likely he will be able to explain it all away. In his own attitude he has evidently brushed aside so satisfactorily such matters as those to be mentioned that others, also, caught up in the magic of his equanimity, almost share his invulnerable disregard.

. . . This poised young man's immediate problem was serious but not monumental. His family and legal authorities were in hope that if some psychiatric disorder could be discovered in him he might escape a jail sentence for stealing.

. . . Evidence of his maladjustment became distinct in childhood. He appeared to be a reliable and manly fellow but could never be counted upon to keep at any task or to give a straight account of any situation. He was frequently truant from school. . . . Though he was generously provided for, he stole some of his father's chickens from time to time, selling them at stores downtown. Pieces of table silver would be missed. These were sometimes recovered from those to whom he had sold them for a pittance or swapped them for odds and ends which seemed to hold no particular interest or value for him.

. . . Often when truant from high school classes Tom wandered more or less aimlessly, sometimes shooting at . . . chickens, setting fire to a rural privy around the outskirts of town, or perhaps loitering about a cigar store or a pool room, reading the comics, throwing rocks at

*Cleckley H: *The Mask of Sanity*, 5th ed. St. Louis, C.V. Mosby, 1976, p. 64.

squirrels in a park, perpetrating small thefts or swindles. He often charged things in stores to his father, stole cigarettes, candy, cigars, etc. . . . He lied so plausibly and with such utter equanimity, devised such ingenious alibis or simply denied all responsibility with such convincing appearances of candor that for many years his real career was poorly estimated. . . . Though he often fell in with groups or small gangs, he never for long identified himself with others in a common cause.

. . . At fourteen or fifteen, having learned to drive, Tom began to steal automobiles with some regularity. . . . After he had tried to sell a stolen car his father consulted advisers and, on the theory that he might have some specific craving for automobiles, bought one for him as a therapeutic measure. On one occasion while out driving he deliberately parked his own car and, leaving it, stole an inferior model which he left slightly damaged on the outskirts of a village some miles away. . . . Meanwhile Tom continued to forge his father's name to small checks and steal change, pocketknives, textbooks, etc., at school. Occasionally, on the pretext of ownership he would sell a dog or a calf belonging to some member of the community.

. . . Tom was sent to a federal institution in a distant state, where a well-organized program of rehabilitation and guidance was available. He soon impressed authorities at this place with his attitude and in the way he discussed his past mistakes and plans for a different future.

. . . He found employment in a drydock at a nearby port and talked modestly but convincingly of the course he would now follow, expressing aims and plans few could greatly improve. . . . His employers found him at first energetic, bright, and apparently enthusiastic about the work. Soon evidence of inexplicable irresponsibility emerged and accumulated. Sometimes he missed several days and brought simple but convincing excuses of illness. As the occasions multiplied, explanations so detailed and elaborate were made that it seemed only facts could have produced them. Later he sometimes left the job, stayed away for hours, and gave no account of his behavior except to say that he did not feel like working at the time.

. . .Reliable information indicates that he has been arrested and imprisoned approximately fifty or sixty times. It is estimated that he would have been put in jails or police barracks for short or long periods of detention on approximately 150 other occasions if his family had not made good his small thefts, damages, etc., and paid fines for him.

Sometimes he was arrested for fomenting brawls in low resorts, provoking fights, or for such high-handed and disturbing behavior as to constitute public nuisance. Though not a very regular drinker or one who characteristically drank to sodden confusion or stupefaction, he exhibited unsociable and unprepossessing manners and conduct after taking even a few beers or highballs. In one juke-joint imbroglio he is credited with having struck a fellow reveler on the head with a piece of iron.

. . .Tom's mother had over years suffered special anxiety and distress through his unannounced absences. After kissing her goodbye, saying he was going downtown for a Coca-Cola or to a movie, he might not appear for several days or even for a couple of weeks! . . . This young man has, apparently, never formed any substantial attachment for another person. Sexually he has been desultorily promiscuous under a wide variety of circumstances. A year or two earlier he married a girl who had achieved considerable local recognition as a prostitute and as one whose fee was moderate. He had previously shared her offerings during an evening (on a commercial basis) with friends or with brief acquaintances among whom he found himself. He soon left the bride and never showed signs of shame or chagrin about the character of the woman he had espoused or any responsibility toward her.

Cleckley's Diagnosis: Psychopathic Personality

Discussion of Tom

Tom illustrates all of the features required for a DSM-III diagnosis of Antisocial Personality Disorder: current age over 18 (to distinguish it from Conduct Disorder), onset of antisocial behavior before age 15 (truancy, stealing, lying, vandalism, delinquency, chronic violations of rules at home), and since age 18, pervasive manifestations of the disorder (failure to hold a job, multiple arrests, fights, and abandonment of his wife).

One of the controversies regarding the DSM-III criteria for Antisocial Personality Disorder is that they do not require evidence of a lack of socialization, that is, absence of guilt feelings, loyalty to others, and empathy. Tom certainly demonstrates these characteristics, which Cleckley also believed were central to the concept of Psychopathic Personality. These features were not included in the DSM-III criteria for Antisocial Personality Disorder for two reasons. First of all, they require more inferential judgments than do the largely behavioral symptoms listed in the criteria. Second, it seemed likely that, for the most part, individuals who met the behavioral criteria for Antisocial Personality Disorder in DSM-III would, like Tom, be undersocialized.

DSM-III Diagnosis:

Axis II: 301.70 Antisocial Personality Disorder (p. 320)

Appendices

Decision Trees for Differential Diagnosis*

The purpose of these decision trees is to aid the clinician in understanding the organization and hierarchical structure of the classification. Each decision tree starts with a set of clinical features. When one of these features is a prominent part of the presenting clinical picture, the clinician can follow the series of questions to rule in or out various diagnostic categories. The questions are only approximations of the actual diagnostic criteria. The decision trees are not meant to replace the specific diagnostic criteria.

*Prepared by Robert L. Spitzer, M.D. and Janet B.W. Williams, M.S.W., and included in Appendix A in DSM-III. To more closely reflect the logic of the DSM-III classification, the decision tree for "psychotic features" has been revised for the *DSM-III Case Book* with the help of Lyman Wynne, M.D., Ph.D.

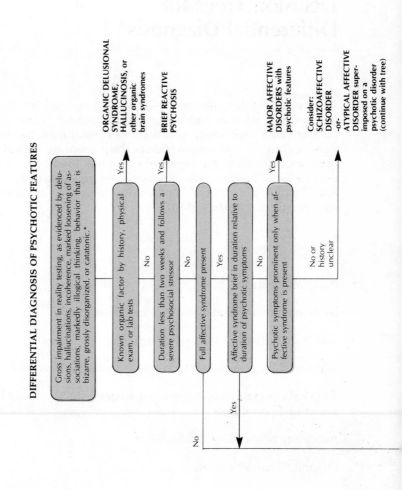

DIFFERENTIAL DIAGNOSIS OF PSYCHOTIC FEATURES

Gross impairment in reality testing, as evidenced by delusions, hallucinations, incoherence, marked loosening of associations, markedly illogical thinking, behavior that is bizarre, grossly disorganized, or catatonic.*

Known organic factor by history, physical exam, or lab tests — Yes → ORGANIC DELUSIONAL SYNDROME, HALLUCINOSIS, or other organic brain syndromes

No

Duration less than two weeks and follows a severe psychosocial stressor — Yes → BRIEF REACTIVE PSYCHOSIS

No

Full affective syndrome present — Yes

Affective syndrome brief in duration relative to duration of psychotic symptoms — Yes

No

Psychotic symptoms prominent only when affective syndrome is present — Yes → MAJOR AFFECTIVE DISORDERS with psychotic features

No or history unclear → Consider: SCHIZOAFFECTIVE DISORDER -or- ATYPICAL AFFECTIVE DISORDER superimposed on a psychotic disorder (continue with tree)

No

Yes

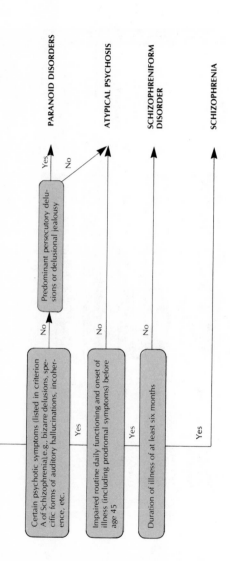

PARANOID DISORDERS

ATYPICAL PSYCHOSIS

SCHIZOPHRENIFORM DISORDER

SCHIZOPHRENIA

Yes

No

Predominant persecutory delusions or delusional jealousy

No

Certain psychotic symptoms (listed in criterion A of Schizophrenia),e.g., bizarre delusions, specific forms of auditory hallucinations, incoherence, etc.

Yes

No

Impaired routine daily functioning and onset of illness (including prodromal symptoms) before age 45

Yes

No

Duration of illness of at least six months

Yes

*Other disorders that may suggest psychotic features need to be ruled out, such as Factitious Disorders, Malingering, Somatization Disorder, certain Dissociative Disorders, and Schizotypal, Borderline, and Paranoid Personality Disorders. If onset of distortions in the development of *multiple* basic psychological functions occurs before age 12, consider Pervasive Developmental Disorders.

DIFFERENTIAL DIAGNOSIS OF IRRATIONAL ANXIETY AND AVOIDANCE BEHAVIOR

Irrational anxiety or avoidance behavior* is the predominant clinical feature

Known organic etiology
- Yes → **ORGANIC MENTAL DISORDER** (e.g., Organic Affective Syndrome, Substance Intoxication)
- No ↓

Psychotic features
- Yes → **See psychotic decision tree**
- No ↓

Onset in childhood or adolescence
- No →
- Yes ↓

Excessive anxiety concerning separation from those to whom the individual is attached
- Yes → **SEPARATION ANXIETY DISORDER**
- No ↓

Persistent shrinking from familiarity or contact with strangers
- Yes → **AVOIDANT DISORDER OF CHILDHOOD OR ADOLESCENCE**
- No ↓

Generalized and persistent anxiety or worry
- Yes → **OVERANXIOUS DISORDER**
- No → **ATYPICAL ANXIETY DISORDER**

Irrational avoidance of objects or situations
- Yes →
- No →

Irrational avoidance of leaving the home
- Yes →
- No →

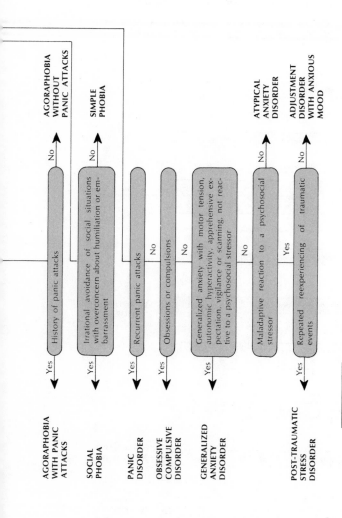

AGORAPHOBIA WITH PANIC ATTACKS

History of panic attacks — Yes ↓ / No → AGORAPHOBIA WITHOUT PANIC ATTACKS

SOCIAL PHOBIA

Irrational avoidance of social situations with overconcern about humiliation or embarrassment — Yes ↓ / No → SIMPLE PHOBIA

PANIC DISORDER

Recurrent panic attacks — Yes ↓ / No

OBSESSIVE COMPULSIVE DISORDER

Obsessions or compulsions — Yes ↓ / No

GENERALIZED ANXIETY DISORDER

Generalized anxiety with motor tension, autonomic hyperactivity, apprehensive expectation, vigilance or scanning, not reactive to a psychosocial stressor — Yes ↓ / No

Maladaptive reaction to a psychosocial stressor — No → ATYPICAL ANXIETY DISORDER

Yes

Repeated reexperiencing of traumatic events — Yes ↓ / No → ADJUSTMENT DISORDER WITH ANXIOUS MOOD

POST-TRAUMATIC STRESS DISORDER

* Also consider Personality Disorders (Axis II), such as Avoidant, Borderline, Compulsive, and Schizotypal Personality Disorders.

DIFFERENTIAL DIAGNOSIS OF MOOD DISTURBANCE

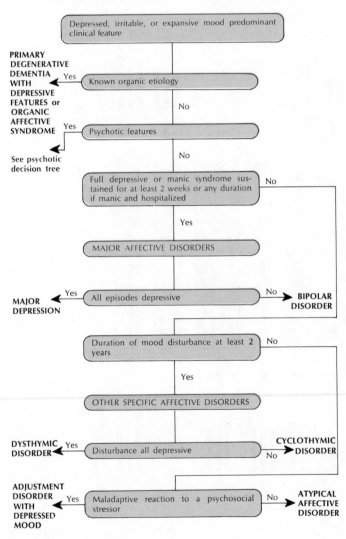

DIFFERENTIAL DIAGNOSIS OF ANTISOCIAL, AGGRESSIVE, DEFIANT, OR OPPOSITIONAL BEHAVIOR

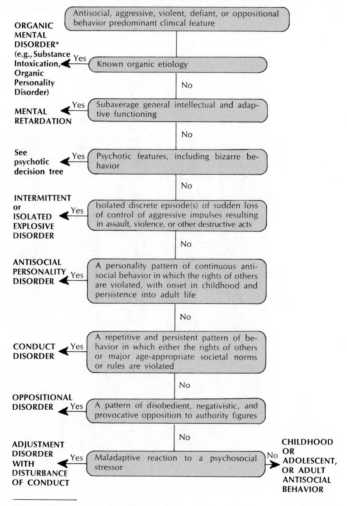

*Also consider Intermittent Explosive Disorder, which can be diagnosed when symptomatic of an Organic Mental Disorder.

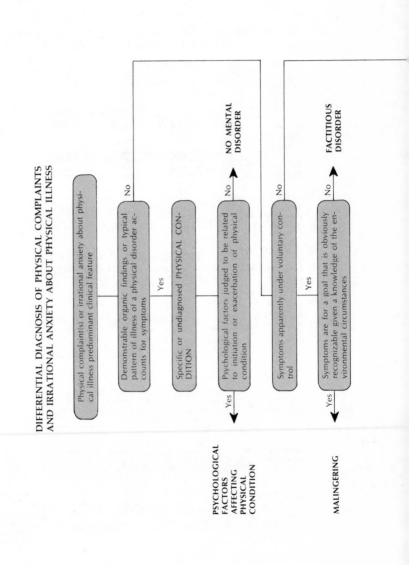

DIFFERENTIAL DIAGNOSIS OF PHYSICAL COMPLAINTS
AND IRRATIONAL ANXIETY ABOUT PHYSICAL ILLNESS

Physical complaint(s) or irrational anxiety about physical illness predominant clinical feature

Demonstrable organic findings or typical pattern of illness of a physical disorder accounts for symptoms

No

Specific or undiagnosed PHYSICAL CONDITION

Yes

Psychological factors judged to be related to initiation or exacerbation of physical condition

No → **NO MENTAL DISORDER**

Yes → PSYCHOLOGICAL FACTORS AFFECTING PHYSICAL CONDITION

Symptoms apparently under voluntary control

No

Symptoms are for a goal that is obviously recognizable given a knowledge of the environmental circumstances

No → **FACTITIOUS DISORDER**

Yes → MALINGERING

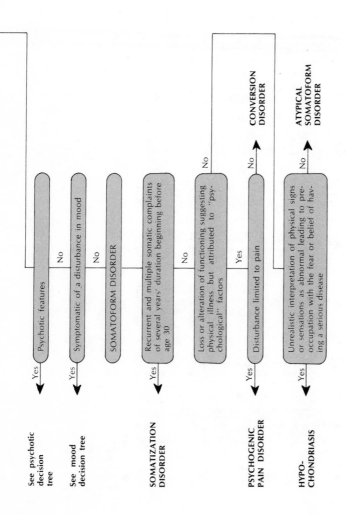

See psychotic
decision
tree

Yes — Psychotic features — No

See mood
decision tree

Yes — Symptomatic of a disturbance in mood — No

SOMATOFORM DISORDER

SOMATIZATION
DISORDER

Yes — Recurrent and multiple somatic complaints of several years' duration beginning before age 30 — No

Loss or alteration of functioning suggesting physical illness but attributed to "psychological" factors — No — CONVERSION DISORDER

Yes

PSYCHOGENIC
PAIN DISORDER

Yes — Disturbance limited to pain — No — ATYPICAL SOMATOFORM DISORDER

HYPO-
CHONDRIASIS

Yes — Unrealistic interpretation of physical signs or sensations as abnormal leading to preoccupation with the fear or belief of having a serious disease — No

DIFFERENTIAL DIAGNOSIS OF ACADEMIC OR LEARNING DIFFICULTIES

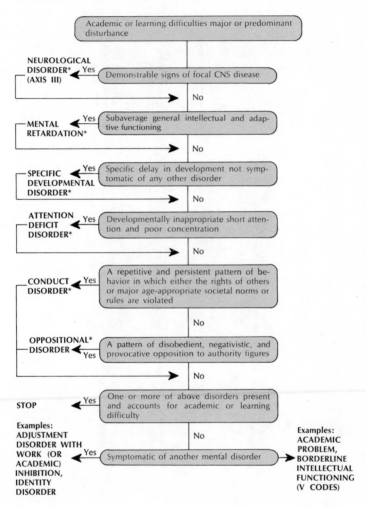

Academic or learning difficulties major or predominant disturbance

NEUROLOGICAL DISORDER* (AXIS III) ◄ Yes — Demonstrable signs of focal CNS disease

No

MENTAL RETARDATION* ◄ Yes — Subaverage general intellectual and adaptive functioning

No

SPECIFIC DEVELOPMENTAL DISORDER* ◄ Yes — Specific delay in development not symptomatic of any other disorder

No

ATTENTION DEFICIT DISORDER* ◄ Yes — Developmentally inappropriate short attention and poor concentration

No

CONDUCT DISORDER* ◄ Yes — A repetitive and persistent pattern of behavior in which either the rights of others or major age-appropriate societal norms or rules are violated

No

OPPOSITIONAL* DISORDER ◄ Yes — A pattern of disobedient, negativistic, and provocative opposition to authority figures

No

STOP ◄ Yes — One or more of above disorders present and accounts for academic or learning difficulty

No

Examples: ADJUSTMENT DISORDER WITH WORK (OR ACADEMIC) INHIBITION, IDENTITY DISORDER ◄ Yes — Symptomatic of another mental disorder ► **Examples: ACADEMIC PROBLEM, BORDERLINE INTELLECTUAL FUNCTIONING (V CODES)**

* The arrows returning to the trunk of the tree indicate the possibility of multiple diagnoses.

DIFFERENTIAL DIAGNOSIS OF ORGANIC BRAIN SYNDROMES

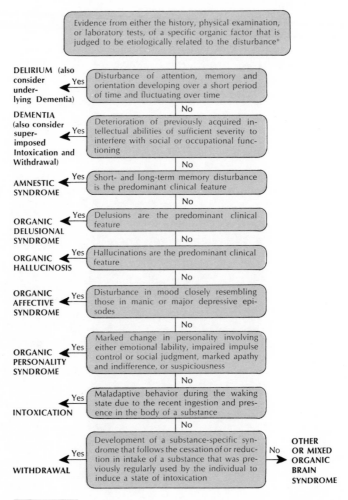

Evidence from either the history, physical examination, or laboratory tests, of a specific organic factor that is judged to be etiologically related to the disturbance*

DELIRIUM (also consider underlying Dementia) ← Yes — Disturbance of attention, memory and orientation developing over a short period of time and fluctuating over time

No

DEMENTIA (also consider superimposed Intoxication and Withdrawal) ← Yes — Deterioration of previously acquired intellectual abilities of sufficient severity to interfere with social or occupational functioning

No

AMNESTIC SYNDROME ← Yes — Short- and long-term memory disturbance is the predominant clinical feature

No

ORGANIC DELUSIONAL SYNDROME ← Yes — Delusions are the predominant clinical feature

No

ORGANIC HALLUCINOSIS ← Yes — Hallucinations are the predominant clinical feature

No

ORGANIC AFFECTIVE SYNDROME ← Yes — Disturbance in mood closely resembling those in manic or major depressive episodes

No

ORGANIC PERSONALITY SYNDROME ← Yes — Marked change in personality involving either emotional lability, impaired impulse control or social judgment, marked apathy and indifference, or suspiciousness

No

INTOXICATION ← Yes — Maladaptive behavior during the waking state due to the recent ingestion and presence in the body of a substance

No

WITHDRAWAL ← Yes — Development of a substance-specific syndrome that follows the cessation of or reduction in intake of a substance that was previously regularly used by the individual to induce a state of intoxication — No → **OTHER OR MIXED ORGANIC BRAIN SYNDROME**

---

* In the absence of such evidence, an organic factor can be presumed if conditions outside of the Organic Mental Disorders category have been reasonably excluded and if the disturbance meets the symptomatic criteria for Dementia.

The DSM-III Classification

Axes I and II Categories and Codes

All official DSM-III codes and terms are included in ICD-9-CM. However, in order to differentiate those DSM-III categories that use the same ICD-9-CM codes, unofficial non-ICD-9-CM codes are provided in parentheses for use when greater specificity is necessary.

The long dashes indicate the need for a fifth-digit subtype or other qualifying term.

DISORDERS USUALLY FIRST EVIDENT IN INFANCY, CHILDHOOD OR ADOLESCENCE

Mental retardation

(Code in fifth digit: 1 = with other behavioral symptoms [requiring attention or treatment and that are not part of another disorder], 0 = without other behavioral symptoms.)

317.0(x) Mild mental retardation, _____
318.0(x) Moderate mental retardation, _____
318.1(x) Severe mental retardation, _____
318.2(x) Profound mental retardation, _____
319.0(x) Unspecified mental retardation, _____

Attention deficit disorder

314.01 with hyperactivity
314.00 without hyperactivity
314.80 residual type

Conduct disorder

312.00 undersocialized, aggressive
312.10 undersocialized, nonaggressive
312.23 socialized, aggressive
312.21 socialized, nonaggressive
312.90 atypical

Anxiety disorders of childhood or adolescence

309.21 Separation anxiety disorder
313.21 Avoidant disorder of childhood or adolescence
313.00 Overanxious disorder

Other disorders of infancy, childhood or adolescence

313.89 Reactive attachment disorder of infancy
313.22 Schizoid disorder of childhood or adolescence
313.23 Elective mutism
313.81 Oppositional disorder
313.82 Identity disorder

Eating disorders

307.10 Anorexia nervosa
307.51 Bulimia
307.52 Pica
307.53 Rumination disorder of infancy
307.50 Atypical eating disorder

Stereotyped movement disorders

307.21 Transient tic disorder
307.22 Chronic motor tic disorder
307.23 Tourette's disorder
307.20 Atypical tic disorder
307.30 Atypical stereotyped movement disorder

Other disorders with physical manifestations

307.00 Stuttering
307.60 Functional enuresis
307.70 Functional encopresis
307.46 Sleepwalking disorder
307.46 Sleep terror disorder (307.49)

Specific developmental disorders
Note: These are coded on Axis II.

315.00 Developmental reading disorder
315.10 Developmental arithmetic disorder
315.31 Developmental language disorder
315.39 Developmental articulation disorder
315.50 Mixed specific developmental disorder
315.90 Atypical specific developmental disorder

Pervasive developmental disorders

Code in fifth digit: 0 = full syndrome present, 1 = residual state.

299.0x Infantile autism, _____
299.9x Childhood onset pervasive developmental disorder, _____
299.8x Atypical, _____

ORGANIC MENTAL DISORDERS

Section 1. Organic mental disorders whose etiology or pathophysiological process is listed below (taken from the mental disorders section of ICD-9-CM).

Dementias arising in the senium and presenium

Primary degenerative dementia, senile onset,

290.30 with delirium
290.20 with delusions
290.21 with depression
290.00 uncomplicated

Code in fifth digit: 1 = with delirium, 2 = with delusions, 3 = with depression, 0 = uncomplicated.

290.1x Primary degenerative dementia, presenile onset, _____
290.4x Multi-infarct dementia, _____

Substance-induced

Alcohol
303.00 intoxication
291.40 idiosyncratic intoxication
291.80 withdrawal
291.00 withdrawal delirium
291.30 hallucinosis
291.10 amnestic disorder

Code severity of dementia in fifth digit: 1 = mild, 2 = moderate, 3 = severe, 0 = unspecified.
291.2x Dementia associated with alcoholism, _____

Barbiturate or similarly acting sedative or hypnotic
305.40 intoxication (327.00)
292.00 withdrawal (327.01)
292.00 withdrawal delirium (327.02)
292.83 amnestic disorder (327.04)

Opioid
305.50 intoxication (327.10)
292.00 withdrawal (327.11)

Cocaine
305.60 intoxication (327.20)

Amphetamine or similarly acting sympathomimetic
305.70 intoxication (327.30)
292.81 delirium (327.32)
292.11 delusional disorder (327.35)
292.00 withdrawal (327.31)

Phencyclidine (PCP) or similarly acting arylcyclohexylamine
305.90 intoxication (327.40)
292.81 delirium (327.42)
292.90 mixed organic mental disorder (327.49)

Hallucinogen
305.30 hallucinosis (327.56)
292.11 delusional disorder (327.55)
292.84 affective disorder (327.57)

Cannabis
305.20 intoxication (327.60)
292.11 delusional disorder (327.65)

Tobacco
292.00 withdrawal (327.71)

Caffeine
305.90 intoxication (327.80)

Other or unspecified substance
305.90 intoxication (327.90)
292.00 withdrawal (327.91)
292.81 delirium (327.92)
292.82 dementia (327.93)
292.83 amnestic disorder (327.94)
292.11 delusional disorder (327.95)
292.12 hallucinosis (327.96)
292.84 affective disorder (327.97)
292.89 personality disorder (327.98)
292.90 atypical or mixed organic mental disorder (327.99)

Section 2. Organic brain syndromes whose etiology or pathophysiological process is either noted as an additional diagnosis from outside the mental disorders section of ICD-9-CM or is unknown.

293.00 Delirium
294.10 Dementia
294.00 Amnestic syndrome
293.81 Organic delusional syndrome
293.82 Organic hallucinosis
293.83 Organic affective syndrome
310.10 Organic personality syndrome
294.80 Atypical or mixed organic brain syndrome

SUBSTANCE USE DISORDERS

Code in fifth digit: 1 = continuous, 2 = episodic, 3 = in remission, 0 = unspecified.

305.0x Alcohol abuse, _____
303.9x Alcohol dependence (Alcoholism), _____
305.4x Barbiturate or similarly acting sedative or hypnotic abuse, _____
304.1x Barbiturate or similarly acting sedative or hypnotic dependence, _____
305.5x Opioid abuse, _____
304.0x Opioid dependence, _____
305.6x Cocaine abuse, _____
305.7x Amphetamine or similarly acting sympathomimetic abuse, _____
304.4x Amphetamine or similarly acting sympathomimetic dependence, _____
305.9x Phencyclidine (PCP) or similarly acting arylcyclohexylamine abuse, _____ (328.4x)
305.3x Hallucinogen abuse, _____
305.2x Cannabis abuse, _____
304.3x Cannabis dependence, _____
305.1x Tobacco dependence, _____
305.9x Other, mixed or unspecified substance abuse, _____
304.6x Other specified substance dependence, _____
304.9x Unspecified substance dependence, _____
304.7x Dependence on combination of opioid and other nonalcoholic substance, _____

304.8x Dependence on combination of substances, excluding opioids and alcohol, _____

SCHIZOPHRENIC DISORDERS

Code in fifth digit: 1 = subchronic, 2 = chronic, 3 = subchronic with acute exacerbation, 4 = chronic with acute exacerbation, 5 = in remission, 0 = unspecified.

Schizophrenia,
295.1x disorganized, _____
295.2x catatonic, _____
295.3x paranoid, _____
295.9x undifferentiated, _____
295.6x residual, _____

PARANOID DISORDERS

297.10 Paranoia
297.30 Shared paranoid disorder
298.30 Acute paranoid disorder
297.90 Atypical paranoid disorder

PSYCHOTIC DISORDERS NOT ELSEWHERE CLASSIFIED

295.40 Schizophreniform disorder
298.80 Brief reactive psychosis
295.70 Schizoaffective disorder
298.90 Atypical psychosis

NEUROTIC DISORDERS: These are included in Affective, Anxiety, Somatoform, Dissociative, and Psychosexual Disorders. In order to facilitate the identification of the categories that in DSM-II were grouped together in the class of Neuroses, the DSM-II terms are included separately in parentheses after the corresponding categories. These DSM-II terms are included in ICD-9-CM and therefore are acceptable as alternatives to the recommended DSM-III terms that precede them.

AFFECTIVE DISORDERS

Major affective disorders

Code major depressive episode in fifth digit: 6 = in remission, 4 = with psychotic features (the unofficial non-ICD-9-CM fifth digit 7 may be used instead to indicate that the psychotic features are mood-incongruent), 3 = with melancholia, 2 = without melancholia, 0 = unspecified.

Code manic or mixed episode in fifth digit: 6 = in remission, 4 = with psychotic features (the unofficial non-ICD-9-CM fifth digit 7 may be used instead to indicate that the psychotic features are mood-incongruent), 2 = without psychotic features, 0 = unspecified.

Bipolar disorder,
296.6x mixed, _____
296.4x manic, _____
296.5x depressed, _____

Major depression,
296.2x single episode, _____
296.3x recurrent, _____

Other specific affective disorders

301.13 Cyclothymic disorder
300.40 Dysthymic disorder (or Depressive neurosis)

Atypical affective disorders

296.70 Atypical bipolar disorder
296.82 Atypical depression

ANXIETY DISORDERS

Phobic disorders (or Phobic neuroses)
300.21 Agoraphobia with panic attacks
300.22 Agoraphobia without panic attacks
300.23 Social phobia
300.29 Simple phobia

Anxiety states (or Anxiety neuroses)
300.01 Panic disorder
300.02 Generalized anxiety disorder
300.30 Obsessive compulsive disorder (or Obsessive compulsive neurosis)

Post-traumatic stress disorder
308.30 acute
309.81 chronic or delayed
300.00 Atypical anxiety disorder

SOMATOFORM DISORDERS

300.81 Somatization disorder
300.11 Conversion disorder (or Hysterical neurosis, conversion type)
307.80 Psychogenic pain disorder
300.70 Hypochondriasis (or Hypochondriacal neurosis)
300.70 Atypical somatoform disorder (300.71)

DISSOCIATIVE DISORDERS (OR HYSTERICAL NEUROSES, DISSOCIATIVE TYPE)

300.12 Psychogenic amnesia
300.13 Psychogenic fugue
300.14 Multiple personality
300.60 Depersonalization disorder (or Depersonalization neurosis)
300.15 Atypical dissociative disorder

PSYCHOSEXUAL DISORDERS

Gender identity disorders

Indicate sexual history in the fifth digit of Transsexualism code: 1 = asexual, 2 = homosexual, 3 = heterosexual, 0 = unspecified.

302.5x Transsexualism, _____
302.60 Gender identity disorder of childhood
302.85 Atypical gender identity disorder

Paraphilias

302.81 Fetishism
302.30 Transvestism
302.10 Zoophilia
302.20 Pedophilia
302.40 Exhibitionism
302.82 Voyeurism
302.83 Sexual masochism
302.84 Sexual sadism
302.90 Atypical paraphilia

Psychosexual dysfunctions

302.71 Inhibited sexual desire
302.72 Inhibited sexual excitement
302.73 Inhibited female orgasm
302.74 Inhibited male orgasm
302.75 Premature ejaculation
302.76 Functional dyspareunia
306.51 Functional vaginismus
302.70 Atypical psychosexual dysfunction

Other psychosexual disorders

302.00 Ego-dystonic homosexuality
302.89 Psychosexual disorder not elsewhere classified

FACTITIOUS DISORDERS

300.16 Factitious disorder with psychological symptoms
301.51 Chronic factitious disorder with physical symptoms
300.19 Atypical factitious disorder with physical symptoms

DISORDERS OF IMPULSE CONTROL NOT ELSEWHERE CLASSIFIED

312.31 Pathological gambling
312.32 Kleptomania
312.33 Pyromania
312.34 Intermittent explosive disorder
312.35 Isolated explosive disorder
312.39 Atypical impulse control disorder

ADJUSTMENT DISORDER

309.00 with depressed mood
309.24 with anxious mood
309.28 with mixed emotional features
309.30 with disturbance of conduct
309.40 with mixed disturbance of emotions and conduct
309.23 with work (or academic) inhibition
309.83 with withdrawal
309.90 with atypical features

PSYCHOLOGICAL FACTORS AFFECTING PHYSICAL CONDITION

Specify physical condition on Axis III.

316.00 Psychological factors affecting physical condition

PERSONALITY DISORDERS

Note: These are coded on Axis II.

301.00 Paranoid
301.20 Schizoid
301.22 Schizotypal
301.50 Histrionic
301.81 Narcissistic
301.70 Antisocial
301.83 Borderline
301.82 Avoidant
301.60 Dependent
301.40 Compulsive
301.84 Passive-Aggressive
301.89 Atypical, mixed or other personality disorder

V CODES FOR CONDITIONS NOT ATTRIBUTABLE TO A MENTAL DISORDER THAT ARE A FOCUS OF ATTENTION OR TREATMENT

V65.20 Malingering
V62.89 Borderline intellectual functioning (V62.88)
V71.01 Adult antisocial behavior
V71.02 Childhood or adolescent antisocial behavior
V62.30 Academic problem
V62.20 Occupational problem

V62.82 Uncomplicated bereavement
V15.81 Noncompliance with medical treatment
V62.89 Phase of life problem or other life circumstance problem
V61.10 Marital problem
V61.20 Parent-child problem
V61.80 Other specified family circumstances
V62.81 Other interpersonal problem

ADDITIONAL CODES

300.90 Unspecified mental disorder (nonpsychotic)
V71.09 No diagnosis or condition on Axis I
799.90 Diagnosis or condition deferred on Axis I

V71.09 No diagnosis on Axis II
799.90 Diagnosis deferred on Axis II

Index of Diagnoses, Case Names and Technical Terms

This Index includes the DSM-III diagnostic categories represented by cases in this book. Case names are listed under the appropriate diagnostic categories. Also included, in italics, are terms from the DSM-III Glossary of Technical Terms that refer to signs or symptoms illustrated in the cases.

The case numbers are shown in bold face, followed by the page number.

dependence
  Construction Worker **167** 263
  Disabled Vet **84** 114
  Housepainter **29** 41
  Runaway **56** 74
  Sickly **125** 184
  The Innkeeper **196** 304
  Threatening Voices **15** 27
  Thunderbird **78** 104
  Vodka **147** 233
Amphetamine or similarly acting
  sympathomimetic abuse
  Bridge Boy **24** 36
  Narcolepsy **123** 181
Barbiturate or similarly acting
  sedative or hypnotic abuse
  The Musician **161** 256
dependence
  Sleeping Pills **54** 72
Cannabis abuse
  Creative misfit **188** 288
Opioid dependence
  Cough Medicine **160** 255

Other, mixed or unspecified
  substance abuse
  Shoelaces **90** 129
Phencyclidine (PCP) or similarly
  acting arylcyclohexylamine
  abuse
  Peaceable Man **145** 229
Tobacco dependence
  Emphysema **38** 53
  Math Teacher **26** 38

Tic disorder, Atypical
  Blinker **132** 206
  See also Tourette's disorder.
Tobacco dependence
  Emphysema **38** 53
  Math Teacher **26** 38
Tobacco, organic mental disorder
  Withdrawal
  Math Teacher **26** 38
Tourette's disorder
  Compulsions **183** 282
  Embarrassed **81** 110
Transsexualism
  Charles **47** 63

Transvestism
  The Fashion Plate **86** 119

Undersocialized conduct disorder,
  Aggressive type
  Killer **105** 153
Undifferentiated type,
  Schizophrenic disorder
  Onanistic Student **202** 318
  Star Wars **141** 220
Unspecified mental disorder
  (nonpsychotic)
  Domestic Tyrant **204** 324
  Minister's Daughter **139** 218

V codes for conditions not
  attributable to a mental disorder
  that are a focus of attention or
  treatment
  Adult antisocial behavior
  Supply Sergeant **128** 195
Malingering
  Sam Schaefer **2** 7
Marital problem
  Equal Rights **11** 22
  Mr. and Ms. A. **80** 108
  The Heiress **61** 80
  Trapped **27** 39
Noncompliance with medical
  treatment
  The Basketball Player **151** 238
Voyeurism
  Binoculars **31** 44

Withdrawal, alcohol
  The Reporter **156** 245
Barbiturate
  Sleeping Pills **54** 72
Tobacco
  Math Teacher **26** 38
Withdrawal delirium, Alcohol
  Construction Worker **167** 263
  The Innkeeper **196** 304
  Thunderbird **78** 104
Work (or academic) inhibition,
  Adjustment disorder with
  Writer's Block **41** 57

Zoophilia
  Beasts **87** 121

Index of
Case Names

Each case name is followed by the case number in bold face.